LANGST ES

US

LANGSTON HUGHES
BLACK GENIUS
A Critical Evaluation

Edited by Therman B. O'Daniel

For the College Language Association

William Morrow & Company, Inc., New York, 1971

Grateful acknowledgment is made to:

Alfred A. Knopf, Inc., for permission to include excerpts and poems from *The Weary Blues* by Langston Hughes (copyright © 1926); *Selected Poems of Langston Hughes* (copyright © 1959); *Ask Your Mama: 12 Moods for Jazz* by Langston Hughes (copyright © 1961); *The Panther and the Lash: Poems of Our Times* by Langston Hughes (copyright © 1967);

Harold Ober Associates Inc. for permission to include fragments and entire poems from *One-Way Ticket* by Langston Hughes (copyright © 1948 by Alfred A. Knopf, Inc.); *Gypsy Ballads* by Federico García Lorca, translated by Langston Hughes (copyright © 1951 by Langston Hughes); *Cuba Libre,* Poems by Nicolás Guillén, translated from the Spanish by Langston Hughes and Ben Frederic Carruthers (copyright © 1948 by Langston Hughes and Ben Frederic Carruthers); *Selected Poems of Langston Hughes* (copyright © 1951 by Langston Hughes); *Troubled Island,* a three-act tragedy by Langston Hughes and William Grant Still (copyright © 1945 by Langston Hughes);

The Indiana University Press for permission to reprint from *Selected Poems of Gabriela Mistral,* translated by Langston Hughes (copyright © 1957);

New Directions for permission to reprint the poem "A Pact" from *Selected Poems of Ezra Pound* (copyright © 1957);

Freedomways (Spring, 1968) for permission to reprint the essay, "The Short Fiction of Langston Hughes" by James A. Emanuel.

To my wife, Lillian

PREFACE

This book, *Langston Hughes: Black Genius*, is the result of a cooperative effort on the part of twelve persons, eleven of whom are members of the College Language Association, and all interested in some aspects of Langston Hughes's work. Six of the essays included were first presented in the June 1968 issue of the *CLA Journal* dedicated to the memory of the famous author, and published a little over a year after his death. In addition to these essays—including one which has been revised and considerably expanded—eight new pieces have been added.

In these essays, we see Langston Hughes as poet, novelist, playwright, and translator; we are made aware of his great love for the common man—the little fellow, and of his extensive use of folklore; we get several illuminating views of one of the most remarkable of his creations, the character Jesse B. Semple; we see the Harlem poet compared and contrasted with Walt Whitman; and our attention is drawn to a wide variety of literary experiments which he carried out with considerable success. All in all, these essays should increase the readers' respect and appreciation for the scope, quality, and versatility of Langston Hughes's art and literary genius.

As editor, I thank the College Language Association and

all contributing authors for granting permission to use the copyrighted material presented.

Individually, I thank Professors Arthur P. Davis, Darwin T. Turner, Blyden Jackson, John F. Matheus, and James A. Emanuel, whose essays first appeared in the Special Langston Hughes Number of the *CLA Journal* (June 1968) and are here reprinted by their kind permission. Also, I thank Professors Nancy B. McGhee, Donald B. Gibson, William Edward Farrison, Eugenia W. Collier, Harry L. Jones, and George E. Kent, whose essays are here printed for the first time by their kind permission.

For his double contribution to this volume, I thank Professor James A. Emanuel a second time. In this case, I thank him for permitting his essay, "The Short Fiction of Langston Hughes," to be reprinted from the Spring, 1968 edition of *Freedomways* magazine.

An additional expression of appreciation is extended to Professor William Edward Farrison for the helpful suggestions which he offered for improving the manuscript; to the library staff of Morgan State College for prompt and courteous assistance in locating needed books and periodicals; and to Phil W. Petrie, Senior Editor, William Morrow and Company, who suggested the possibility of such a volume and offered expert guidance from the planning stage to its completion.

Finally, thanks to my wife, Lillian, for living with this book in progress, and remaining sincerely interested in it until the end.

Therman B. O'Daniel

CONTENTS

LANGSTON HUGHES

By Therman B. O'Daniel

James Mercer Langston Hughes, who stopped using his first two names early in life, was one of the most talented and prolific American writers of the twentieth century. Internationally known and famous as a poet, he also produced a wide variety of prose. It is this mastery of a multiplicity of literary forms that makes him one of the most versatile authors of his generation. He was a poet, short-story writer, novelist, author of a two-volume autobiography, ten children's books in both verse and prose, a playwright, a translator of literary works written in Spanish and French, an editor of literary anthologies of American and African writers, the author of operatic librettos, of a Christmas cantata, and of lyrics for dramatic musicals. He also wrote numerous radio and television scripts, and is the lyricist for a long list of songs—some of which have been sung by leading concert artists, while others have been used on radio programs and in motion pictures. He frequently wrote articles and essays on various subjects for many magazines, newspapers and journals; and, during an extraordinarily active professional career spanning more than forty years, served as a newspaper columnist for the Chicago *Defender* and the New York *Post*, and as a correspondent in Spain, during the Spanish Civil War, for the Baltimore *Afro-American*.

Beginning with *The Weary Blues*, in 1926, Langston Hughes published fifteen books of verse, including such full-length, major volumes as *Fine Clothes to the Jew, The Dream Keeper and Other Poems, Shakespeare in Harlem, Fields of Wonder, One-Way Ticket, Montage of a Dream Deferred, Ask Your Mama*, and *The Panther and the Lash: Poems of Our Times*, which had been completed and was on press at the time of his death.

In collaboration with his friend of many years, Arna Bontemps, Hughes wrote *Popo and Fifina*, a children's book set in Haiti. Also with Bontemps, he edited two comprehensive anthologies, *The Poetry of the Negro, 1746–1949*, and *The Book of Negro Folklore*.

In collaboration with Mercer Cook, he translated, from the French, the Haitian novel, *Gouverneurs de la Rosée* (*Masters of the Dew*); and with Ben F. Carruthers, he translated, from the Spanish, *Cuba Libre*, a book of poems by Nicolás Guillén.

Langston Hughes was also the translator of the *Gypsy Ballads* of Federico García Lorca; of the *Selected Poems of Gabriela Mistral* (Lucila Godoy Alcayaga, who was awarded the Nobel Prize for Literature in 1945); and a number of separate poems, written in French and Spanish, by Jacques Roumain, David Diop, Jean-Joseph Rabéarivelo, Léon Damas, and Regino Pedroso. He independently collected and edited *The Best Short Stories of Negro Writers, The Book of Negro Humor, An African Treasury, Poems from Black Africa*, and *New Negro Poets: U. S. A.*

His historical works include: *A Pictorial History of the Negro in America* and *Black Magic: A Pictorial History of the Negro in American Entertainment*, both written with Milton Meltzer; *Fight For Freedom: The Story of the NAACP*; two series of juvenile works—the *Famous Negro*

Series and *The First Book* Series; and two autobiographies, *The Big Sea* and *I Wonder as I Wander.*

When one adds to this list, *Not Without Laughter* (1930), his first novel, and the five that followed; three volumes of short stories—*The Ways of White Folks* (1934) being the first; the full-length plays, including *Mulatto* (1935), which played for a year on Broadway and eight months on the road, and *Simply Heavenly* (1957) and *Tambourines to Glory* (1963) which also had Broadway runs; the many one-act plays, including *Don't You Want to Be Free*, which, in the thirties, set a record of 135 performances at the Hughes-founded Suitcase Theatre; the popular gospel song-plays of recent years; collections, such as *The Langston Hughes Reader* (1958), *Selected Poems of Langston Hughes* (1959), and *The Best of Simple* (1961); and his voluminous body of miscellaneous writings; an extensive exhibition of a truly prolific talent emerges.

And yet, even the length and the tremendous variety of this list did not exhaust the versatility and creativity of this amazing man of letters. For indeed, Langston Hughes was also a world traveler, a successful lecturer of long experience, and a superb reader of poetry—especially his own. At home, he made ten cross-country lecture tours reading his poetry in hundreds of schools, colleges and universities throughout the nation. On numerous trips abroad, he attracted large audiences in the West Indies, and in South America, Europe, Africa, and Asia.

In addition to these activities, Langston Hughes taught English in Mexico, served as Visiting Professor of Creative Writing at Atlanta University, and served also as Poet-in-Residence at the Laboratory School of the University of Chicago.

His book, *The Sweet Flypaper of Life*, a photographic

essay done in collaboration with Roy DeCarava, appeared in 1955. In it, the memorable urban folk character, Sister Mary Bradley, was created. One year later, a foreign version of this work was published in Germany under the title *The Harlem Story*, with parallel texts in English and German.

In 1961 he was chosen as a member of the National Academy of Arts and Letters and during the fall of 1962—the year that *Fight for Freedom: The Story of the NAACP* was published—he was one of a select group of distinguished American poets invited to read their poems and to participate in the National Poetry Festival held at the Library of Congress.

In addition to his usual contributions of verse, prose, fiction, and non-fictional prose to newspapers, magazines and journals, the following works appeared in book form in 1963: a volume of short stories entitled *Something in Common and Other Stories; Poems from Black Africa*, an anthology of African verse, which he edited for the University of Indiana Press; *Five Plays by Langston Hughes*, edited by Webster Smalley, also published by the Indiana University Press; and a new edition of *The Big Sea*, the first volume of his autobiography.

While these books were coming off press, his song play, *Black Nativity*, the outstanding event at Gian Carlo Menotti's "Festival of Two Worlds" in Spoleto, Italy, in July of 1962, opened its American tour. And a new play based on his novel, *Tambourines to Glory*, had its Broadway premiere.

What was the background of this remarkable contemporary author? The question is answered in Hughes's own terms in *The Big Sea*, the first volume of his autobiography. Born in Joplin, Missouri, in 1902, he lived in many places—Buffalo, Cleveland; Lawrence, Kansas City, and Topeka, Kansas; Mexico City and Toluca, in Mexico; Colorado Springs; Lincoln, Illinois, where he finished grammar school; and Cleve-

land again, where he was graduated from Central High
School. Years later, from these experiences, he wrote an
amusing essay entitled "Ten Thousand Beds." The excerpt
below found in *The Langston Hughes Reader* (pp. 489-490)
tells what he had to say:

> Often I hear a person say, "I can't sleep in [a] strange bed."
> Such a person I regard with wonder and amazement,
> slightly tinged with envy. Wonder and amazement that such
> a small change as a strange bed would keep a person from
> sleeping, and envy that there are people who stay put so
> well that any bed other than their own upsets them. At a
> most conservative estimate, I figure I have slept in at least
> ten thousand strange beds.
>
> As a child I was often boarded out, sent to stay with rela-
> tives, foster-relatives, or friends of the family. And my
> family itself was always moving, so quite early in life I got
> used to a variety of beds from the deep feather beds of the
> country to the studio couches of the town, from camp cots
> to my uncle's barber chair in Kansas City elongated to
> accommodate me. If strange beds had been given to up-
> setting me, I would have lost many a good night's sleep in
> my life. And there is nothing I like better than to sleep.

His mother, father, and maternal grandmother were educated people. Again, from *The Big Sea* (p. 13), we learn
that his grandmother was a proud woman who "would never
beg or borrow anything from anybody." Her first husband,
Sheridan Leary, believed that all people should be free and
died for his noble principle with John Brown at Harpers
Ferry. Later, she married Charles Langston, a man with the
same beliefs as Leary, who was the poet's grandfather.

After his parents separated, his father went to Mexico
where he prospered. His mother was not so successful, and
was continually on the move looking for a better job. So it was
that Hughes spent most of his early years with Grandma

Langston in Lawrence. Once, however, while living with his mother in Topeka, he was refused admission to the Harrison Street School until his mother, "who was always ready to do battle for the rights of a free people," went directly to the school board and succeeded in getting him admitted (*The Big Sea*, p. 14).

While he was living with his mother in Topeka, she took him to see plays that came to town, and once they even attended the opera, hearing *Faust*. These boyhood experiences in what he must have considered the glamorous theater made a profound impression upon Langston Hughes—an impression which lasted throughout his life. Fascinated by the theater from early youth, he continued to write plays. To solve the problem of a commercial stage uninterested in Negro drama, he founded his own theatrical groups in three major cities: the Suitcase Theater in Harlem, the Negro Art (or New Negro) Theater in Los Angeles; and the Skyloft Players in Chicago.

When still a child, he went to live with his grandmother, who read the Bible and the *Crisis* magazine to him and told him "long, beautiful stories about people who wanted to make the Negroes free." In these stories, nobody ever cried, he wrote. "They worked, or schemed, or fought," but there was no crying. "When my grandmother died," he continues in *The Big Sea*, "I didn't cry either. Something about my grandmother's stories (without her ever having said so) taught me the uselessness of crying about anything" (p. 17).

Years later when he had become a writer, he entitled his first novel, *Not Without Laughter*, and his second volume of short stories, *Laughing to Keep From Crying*.

It was while he lived with his grandmother that he first discovered books. Being an only child, he was sometimes lonely until he began to read the books that came his way. Of this period in his life, he has written: "I began to believe

in nothing but books, and the wonderful world in books—
where if people suffered, they suffered in beautiful language,
not in monosyllables, as we did in Kansas. And where almost always the mortgage got paid off, the good knights won,
and the Alger boy triumphed" (*The Big Sea*, p. 16).

After his grandmother's death, he lived for a time with
the Reeds, who were her friends. The wife was very religious
and always went to church; the husband never went. "But
both of them were very good and kind," wrote the poet in
his autobiography, "the one who went to church and the one
who didn't. And no doubt from them I learned to like both
Christians and sinners equally well" (p. 18).

He rejoined his mother, this time in Lincoln, Illinois, where
he completed grammar school and began to write poetry. He
tells us that he had never thought of writing poetry until
classmates elected him class poet. Some time later, after carefully observing "the ways of white folks," he looked back
upon his youthful experience in his characteristically humorous and mildly satirical way, and commented that he was
elected class poet while in grammar school because, as he put
it, "Everybody knows—except us—that all Negroes have
rhythm."

From Lincoln, Illinois, he moved to Cleveland, Ohio, where
later he was graduated from Central High School in the Class
of 1920. While there, he "held many class and club offices
. . . because often when there was a religious deadlock, a
Negro student would win the election. They would compromise on a Negro, feeling, I suppose, that a Negro was
neither Jew nor Gentile!" He "was on the track team (as
runner on the championship relay team and as high jumper),
. . . was a lieutenant in the military training corps," and,
in his senior year, "edited the Year Book" (*The Big Sea*,
p. 30).

He had some very good teachers there, including the

daughter of the famous black writer, Charles W. Chesnutt, and an English teacher who introduced him and his classmates to some of the new, experimental American poets: Carl Sandburg, Amy Lowell, Vachel Lindsay, and Edgar Lee Masters. Then it was that he began to write poetry like Carl Sandburg. Before that time, although he had read and liked the stories of many authors, the only poet he had liked was Paul Laurence Dunbar. Thus it was that he wrote many poems—some in imitation of Dunbar, and some "without rhyme like Sandburg's." He has called these "the first real poems" that he tried to write. He wrote "about love, about the steel mills where [his] stepfather worked, the slums where [he] lived, and the brown girls from the South, prancing up and down Central Avenue on a spring day," and he published these verses in the high school magazine called the *Belfry Owl*.

After his graduation, he reluctantly went again to visit his father in Mexico, but only because his father had promised to send him to college, and because he had a strong feeling that his formal education would end if he did not go. Hughes disliked his father who "had a great contempt for all poor people" because "he thought it was their own fault that they were poor." Returning to Mexico, therefore, was anything but a pleasant prospect for him, yet it was on this trip that he composed one of his best-known poems. He reveals this in *The Big Sea* (p. 54).

> My mother let me go to the station alone, and I felt pretty bad when I got on the train. I felt bad for the next three or four years, to tell the truth, and those were the years when I wrote most of my poetry. (For my best poems were all written when I felt the worst. When I was happy, I didn't write anything.)
>
> The poem that has perhaps been most often reprinted in anthologies was written on the train during this trip to Mexico when I was feeling very bad. It's called "The Negro

Speaks of Rivers" and was written just outside of St. Louis, as the train rolled toward Texas.

The elder Hughes was in excellent financial circumstances and kept his promise about sending his son to college. As a matter of fact, since no investment was considered to be bad by the businessman father as long as it had prospects of paying high dividends later, he really wanted to send his son to Switzerland and Germany for his professional training. Having very strong objections to this plan, the son managed to get his father to compromise on Columbia University, which the poet suggested, "mainly because," even at that early period, he "wanted to see Harlem." For his son's major, the father picked mining engineering because he saw that such technical training was much in demand in Mexico. Langston Hughes never had the slightest interest in engineering, so he finished the first year at Columbia and quit. When he did this, he severed forever the relationship between his father and himself.

Between this time and the time when he entered Lincoln University, Hughes had a variety of experiences that were excellent, no doubt, for his later career as a professional writer, but, at that time, they certainly did not appear attractive at all. His most serious problem was the great difficulty he had in finding employment. He went everywhere looking for a job, but when he answered the advertisements in the newspapers, he discovered that no one wanted a Negro worker. Finally, he found a job on a truck-garden farm on Staten Island, and when the season ended there, he worked as a delivery boy for a florist until, following an argument about the working hours, he quit.

At twenty-one, Langston Hughes went to sea as mess boy to the petty officers aboard the S. S. *Malone*, a trading freighter bound for Africa. After stops, along the way, at the Azores and the Canary Islands, the *Malone* steamed into the port of Dakar and he was thrilled by seeing for the first time and by touching the soil of the great Africa of his dreams. Leaving Dakar, the ship moved down the coast of West Africa, stopping and trading at other ports—some thirty-two in all—before making the return trip to New York. He would make many more trips to Africa, Europe, Asia, and other distant parts of the world in later years, but this was his first, and a memorable one it was!

With jobs still hard to find, when he returned to New York, the poet's recent experience on the S. S. *Malone* caused him to seek other employment aboard a ship bound for foreign ports. Even this was very difficult and unpromising at first. Eventually, however, he was hired as a mess boy on a ship "bound for Constantinople and Odessa," but was discharged, before sailing, when a new steward refused to work with a Negro crew. This proved very lucky for Hughes because some thirty days later this ill-fated boat struck a mine and sank in the Black Sea, losing more than half of its crew. The next job was also of short duration. It was on a vessel whose run was from Hoboken to the West Indies, but when a vicious cook outlined an endless list of duties that he was required to perform—many of them having nothing to do with being a mess boy—he quit. Finally, he obtained work "on a big, clean-looking freighter" which ran regularly between Rotterdam and New York. He made one round trip on this boat, and signed for a second, but when the ship arrived in Rotterdam, he drew his money and took the night train for Paris, arriving there on a snowy February morning.

He knew not a soul in the French metropolis, had only a few dollars in his pocket and no prospects at all for a job, but being in Paris was another dream come true, and he was determined to spend the winter there. He found a job as doorman at a small nightclub in Montmartre at five francs per night and dinner. Later, Rayford Logan, who had read

his poems in the *Crisis,* helped him find a job as second
cook (dishwasher) at the Grand Duc which paid him fifteen
francs a night and breakfast. At the Grand Duc Hughes
heard some of the greatest Negro musicians, singers and
entertainers of that day in Paris, who, though not working
there, met there after hours and performed without pay for
the sheer joy of it.

When the Grand Duc closed for the summer, he accepted
the invitation of two Italian workers at the club, Luigi the
barman, and Romeo the lone waiter, to accompany them
to their home in Italy. He did.

Before Hughes left Paris, Alain Locke had talked with
him about using some of his poems in a special Negro number
of the *Survey Graphic* which he was editing. Locke also
arranged for the poet to meet Albert C. Barnes, the Merion,
Pennsylvania, art collector. While in Italy, Locke wrote
that he would give the poet a guided tour of Venice if
Hughes would meet him there. Thus it was that Hughes
went to Venice, a city that he had always wished to see.
When this visit was over, he headed back to Paris, having
planned one stop along the way to meet Claude McKay in
Toulon on the Riviera. On the train, that night, he was
robbed of his passport and all the money he had. He never
reached the Riviera or Paris, on this trip, but had to leave
the train in Genoa where he was stranded for some weeks as
a beachcomber.

Finally, after what seemed an interminable time of trying
to eke out the barest living in Genoa, he found a captain
who was willing to sign him on as a workaway member of
his crew, without pay, for the trip back to New York. He
had been away ten months and had visited France, Italy,
and Spain, and returning, had enjoyed a Grand Tour of the
Mediterranean. When he arrived in Paris he had seven dollars; when he returned to New York, he had twenty-five

cents, "so [his] first European trip [had] cost [him] exactly six dollars and seventy-five cents!" (*The Big Sea*, p. 201)

On the afternoon of the day of his return to New York, Langston Hughes took some of his new poems to show to Countee Cullen, and Cullen informed him of a benefit cabaret party which the NAACP was giving that night. Hughes attended and met Walter White, Mary White Ovington, James Weldon Johnson, and Carl Van Vechten. Besides having a fine time, he also learned that the *Crisis* office had cabled him twenty dollars to Genoa which had been returned. The next day he collected the money, and, later in the week, set out for Washington, D. C., where his mother was now living with what he called the "high-class branch" of his family, "being direct descendants of Congressman John M. Langston."

In Washington he became a keen observer of Negro society, which disturbed him, and about which he later wrote an article in *Opportunity*, V (August, 1927) called "Our Wonderful Society: Washington"; spent much time on Seventh Street among "the ordinary Negroes," whom he thoroughly enjoyed; tried to find "a dignified job" without success; and, desiring to return to college, talked with Dean Kelly Miller and Alain Locke about a scholarship at Howard, also without success. He ended his futile search for one of the "good" jobs by working in a wet wash laundry. Later, when an old school friend of his mother's interceded, Dr. Carter G. Woodson gave him a job as his assistant in the office of the Association for the Study of Negro Life and History. He was a great admirer of Dr. Woodson and the great work he was doing, but Hughes did not like the tedious duties that he had to perform, so he gave up what he called "*a position*" and found himself another *job*.

This decision proved to be a very fortunate one for the

young and struggling poet, for this new job, <u>that of a busboy</u> <u>at the Wardman Park Hotel, led to his meeting Vachel Lind-</u> <u>say and being introduced to the American public as a poet by</u> <u>that well-established and famous contemporary autho</u>r.

Diplomats and cabinet members in the dining room [he later wrote in *The Big Sea*, p. 212] did not excite me much, but I was thrilled the day Vachel Lindsay came. I knew him, because I'd seen his picture in the papers that morning. He was to give a reading of his poems in the little theater of the hotel that night. I wanted very much to hear him read his poems, but I knew they did not admit colored people to the auditorium.

That afternoon I wrote out three of my poems, "Jazz-onia," "Negro Dancers," and "The Weary Blues," on some pieces of paper and put them in the pocket of my white busboy's coat. In the evening when Mr. Lindsay came down to dinner, quickly I laid them beside his plate and went away, afraid to say anything to so famous a poet, except to tell him I liked his poems and that these were poems of mine. I looked back once and saw Mr. Lindsay reading the poems, as I picked up a tray of dirty dishes from a side table and started for the dumbwaiter.

The next morning on the way to work, as usual I bought a paper—and there I read that Vachel Lindsay had discovered a Negro busboy poet! At the hotel the reporters were already waiting for me. They interviewed me. And they took my picture holding up a tray of dirty dishes in the middle of the dining room. The picture, copyrighted by Underwood, appeared in lots of newspapers throughout the country. It was my first publicity break.

From that time on, Langston Hughes's rise in the literary world was steady, although his economic condition showed no comparable improvement. As a matter of fact, for a time things worsened in the latter regard, for he became such a showpiece in the dining room and was always being exhibited, by the head waiter, "before some table whose curious guests wished to see what a Negro busboy poet looked like," that the constant embarrassment forced him to quit his job.

Otherwise, there was a general brightening of his fortunes. In 1925 he won first prize in the *Opportunity* magazine's Poetry Contest with his poem, "The Weary Blues." He also won a literary prize in the *Crisis*-sponsored contest. In 1926, with Carl Van Vechten's assistance, he published his first volume of poetry, using as its title, *The Weary Blues*, and it was in that same year, the second semester of the 1925–1926 school year, that he received a scholarship and entered Lincoln University, in Pennsylvania, to complete his college education. During this period he began to sell some individual poems to *Vanity Fair*, *New Republic*, and *The Bookman*.

As a student at Lincoln, he won the Witter Bynner Undergraduate Poetry Award; published his second volume of verse; and wrote his first novel, *Not Without Laughter*. After that time, as previously indicated, almost every type of poetic and prose literature poured from his prolific pen.

In the nineteen-twenties and early thirties, Langston Hughes was a prominent member—in fact, one of the young leaders—of that memorable Harlem group of talented and productive artists whom Alain Locke described as *New* Negroes, and who ushered in that great artistic period known popularly as "The Negro Renaissance."

The Negro poets, painters, sculptors, novelists, essayists, and musicians of that period openly and defiantly proclaimed their pride in race and color; in Negro-ness and in blackness. As a matter of fact, Langston Hughes was one of the most vocal of the literary spokesmen.

In his very first volume of verse, *The Weary Blues*, beginning with the "Proem," or introductory poem, Hughes was faithful to his proclaimed creed of pride in race and in color. He wrote—

> I am a Negro:
>   Black as the night is black,
>   Black like the depth of my Africa.

And down through his more than forty years of professional writing, he never wrote anything that betrayed his early convictions.

In 1950 he published the first of his *Simple* books, and introduced to American readers one of the most original characters in American literature. He first created Jesse B. Semple (better known as Simple) in a series which he wrote in his column in the Chicago *Defender*, and called the first published book *Simple Speaks His Mind*, which was followed —at intervals of three, four, and eight years—by *Simple Takes a Wife, Simple Stakes a Claim*, and *Simple's Uncle Sam*.

Simple, often referred to as the poet's "mouthpiece," was described by Saul Maloff in *Newsweek* (June 5, 1967) as "the wry, ironic, crafty, folkloristic, garrulous, beer-swilling, homegrown barfly philosopher . . . a man who once he got his hands on your lapels, never let go, a hilarious black Socrates of the neighborhood saloons who would at the drop of his hat discourse on anything from marital relations to international relations, lynching to lexicography, the foibles of mankind and the follies of womankind. Whatever it was, Simple had the shrewd and loony answer."

Unfortunately and paradoxically for Hughes, who all of his life had been a true "race" man, "it was," Maloff continues, "precisely the mellow, low-keyed amiability of Simple (this wonderful, original creation) that stuck in the craw of a younger, fiercer generation of Negro writers and that made his creator seem, in the last years of his life, old-fashioned and outmoded, a relic of another, less turbulent and explosive time."

Some years ago, when Langston Hughes had published his twenty-first—not counting translations, anthologies, and paper-bound booklets of various sorts—book (he published a good many more than that before he died), he wrote a piece in the Chicago *Defender* (1955) which was titled, "An Author With 21 Books Must Be Coming Of Age." In the last paragraph of that discussion of his "literary coming of age," he asked and answered a few questions about his writing career:

> How have I written so many books—and one so long as is my latest manuscript? By not doing anything else much in my life. Is writing fun? Sure! Is it lucrative? Yes, if you are Frank Yerby or Ernest Hemingway. As for me, when young writers ask me if it is possible to make a living from writing, I usually answer, "Yes—but not necessarily a good living. I haven't got a Cadillac. I don't own a house. I haven't got a wife, or a television set. Not even a dog. All I've got is a lot of books—with another book on the way."

It is true that Langston Hughes never had a *real big* best seller—but it is also true that Langston Hughes never wrote in any other way but as he sincerely and honestly wanted to write. He never compromised his beliefs or his principles in order to produce a best seller. Just like his character, Jesse B. Semple, Langston Hughes always spoke his mind.

Nevertheless, he had some *good* sellers, and almost all of his books have been *steady* sellers. Of all of the books that he wrote, only a few are out of print. The others have been reissued regularly and have been available in one edition or another down through the years.

In December 1967, seven months after his death, a student organization at Columbia University, The Forum, sponsored an impressive "Langston Hughes Memorial Evening." In addition to the speakers and artists who participated, the program opened and closed with the taped voice of Langston Hughes himself.

An anonymous reporter for the *New Yorker* magazine (December 30, 1967) gives us this description of the conclusion of that memorial service:

> The memorial to Langston Hughes ended as it had begun, with Langston Hughes' low, bemused voice—this time telling about how he came from the Midwest to Columbia to go to school, and caused great consternation when he presented himself at Hartley Hall. That was in 1921, and no one of African descent, he says, had ever lived in a dormitory at Columbia. "There are many barriers people try to break down," he told an audience (which had also been a Columbia audience) when the tape was made in 1964, "I try to do it with poetry."

This frank statement in the taped voice of the poet was characteristic of fearless, amiable, and honest Langston Hughes, who made it a lifelong practice, not only in his poetry, but in his prose as well, always to speak his mind and to tell things as they were.

LANGSTON HUGHES: COOL POET

By Arthur P. Davis

In 1965, Langston Hughes published the following lines:

> I play it cool
> And dig all jive
> That's the reason
> I stay alive.
>
> *My motto,*
> As I live and learn,
>   is:
> *Dig and Be Dug*
> *In Return.*

This catchy little poem, entitled "Motto," like so many of Mr. Hughes's works "begins in delight and ends in wisdom." It makes us smile, but we soon discover beneath the surface humor an important statement. In these playful verses, Hughes has actually characterized his own life as man and artist; in short he has written his credo.

In "hip" speech, the word *cool* is often used to describe a person who, without becoming too much involved, knows and can, therefore, control a given situation. To lose one's cool is to lose along with one's objectivity the mastery which the cool posture gives. It is in this sense that I speak of Langston

Hughes as a cool poet. Throughout his life he remained the objective observer and appraiser of human actions, particularly those which grew out of the racial situation in America. Of course, he had convictions and took sides, but he never became a fanatical supporter of any one cause. The *Simple* series is perhaps Mr. Hughes's most characteristic and revealing work because it shows best this quality of coolness. Insofar as an author may be his own creations, Langston Hughes is the earthy, prejudiced, and race-conscious Simple as well as the urbane, tolerant, and sophisticated "straight man" in the sketches. The two characters are the opposite sides of the same coin, and from their observations and insights, interacting one upon the other, we get the twofold vision found in much of Mr. Hughes's best work, whether prose or poetry.

This ambivalent attitude showed itself early in Langston Hughes's career. In the *Nation* for June 23, 1926, he wrote the following manifesto:

> We younger Negro artists who create now intend to express our individual dark-skinned selves without fear or shame. If the white folks seem pleased, we are glad. If they are not, it doesn't matter. We know we are beautiful. Ugly too. The tom-tom cries and the tom-tom laughs. If colored people are pleased, we are glad. If they are not, their displeasure doesn't matter either. We build our temples for tomorrow, strong as we know them, and we stand on top of the mountain, free within ourselves.

Note the last phrase, "free within ourselves." Mr. Hughes was, I believe, the most independent person I have known. His independence stemmed, like his coolness, from a strong belief in himself and in his work. He was not arrogant, but he possessed to a great degree the kind of creative egotism that every successful artist must have.

In the early pages of his autobiography, *The Big Sea*, Hughes describes an interesting and revealing incident.

Having quit Columbia College, he had secured a job on the S. S. *Malone*. Leaning over the rail of this ship as it sailed out of New York, the young Hughes took all of his books—those he had used at Columbia and those he had recently bought to read on the trip—took all of them and threw them in the sea. This gesture symbolized his emancipation from the derivative world of book domination. A second act of emancipation came later when he severed all financial ties with a rich Park Avenue patroness who wanted him to stress the "primitive" in his writing.

These two incidents tell us a great deal about Langston Hughes. From the very beginning of his literary career, he was determined to forge his art, not of the secondhand material which came from books, not of fads dictated by a demanding patron, but out of the stuff of human experience as he saw it. He remained faithful to this decision. His vision was, of course, not flawless, but it was usually clear-eyed and always his. A keen and tolerant observer, he possessed deep insights and a profound knowledge of human nature. And above all else, he had the gift of simplicity.

Langston Hughes wrote poetry for over forty years, and in this long span, he touched on many subjects and experimented with various techniques. Though he often went afield, he always returned to certain forms and certain themes. The great bulk of Mr. Hughes's poetry, therefore, tends to fall into the following categories: poems on and about Harlem; poems concerning the American Negro's African background; poems of protest and social commentary; poems based on or influenced by folk material; and miscellaneous poems. There is, of course, a considerable amount of overlapping among these categories.

Harlem is the predominating theme in the poetry of Mr. Hughes. Either stated or implied, used as subject or background or protagonist, and on occasion even as a symbol for Negroes everywhere, Harlem has been a constantly recurring theme in Langston Hughes's poetry. Fascinated by the Black Metropolis and its colorful inhabitants, he never tired of delineating the endlessly changing moods of that ghetto. Speaking of the people of Harlem, Hughes once wrote: "I love the color of their language; and, being a Harlemite myself, their problems and interests are my problems and interests." On another occasion, the author, speaking through a character in *Simple*, has this to say: "I didn't come here to Harlem to get away from my people. I came here because there's more of 'em. . . . I love my people." In every major poetical publication except one, from *The Weary Blues*, published in 1926, down to *The Panther and the Lash*, published in 1967, there are references to Harlem—many and diverse references to the Black Ghetto.

It is intriguing to note how the picture of Harlem changes over the years. In 1926, the Harlem of *The Weary Blues* is generally the swinging, joyous Harlem of the New Negro Renaissance. A nighttime Harlem, it is "Jazzonia," an exciting never-never land in which "sleek black boys" blow their hearts out on silver trumpets while "shameless gals" "strut and wiggle" in a "whirling cabaret." But even in this first publication one finds Hughes's customary twofold vision. The joyousness of "Jazzonia" is not unmixed. "The rhythm of life/Is a jazz rhythm" for this cabaret world, but it brings eventually "The broken heart of love/The weary, weary heart of pain." Even as a young man living in the excitement of the New Negro Renaissance, Langston Hughes saw that Harlem in spite of surface appearance was a sad and not a gay place.

In subsequent pictures of Harlem, the moods become darker. By the time of *One Way Ticket* (1949) Harlem has gone through the Depression, has had its riot, and now a thoroughly disillusioned city, it has become the "edge of hell"; and yet characteristically it could still be, as it is in "Negro Servant," a refuge for the black folks who worked downtown and had to bow and scrape to white folks all day. Hughes was always aware that there are many Harlems, not just one.

Moreover, he was always quick to discover the humor even in so-called serious incidents. For example, his reaction to a certain near-riot in Harlem is given in the "Ballad of Margie Polite," who

> Kept the Mayor
> And Walter White
> And everybody
> Up all night.
> When the PD car
> Taken Margie away
> It wasn't Mother's
> Nor Father's—
>   It were
> Margie Day.

The fullest and most penetrating treatment of this many-sided black city appears in *Montage of a Dream Deferred* (1951). Actually one long poem of seventy-five pages, this work employs a "jam session" technique that allows the poet to make use of a host of varied, blending and contrasting vignettes to paint a full picture of Harlem's frustrations. The whole work asks one all-powerful question about Harlem and its people:

> What happens to a dream deferred?
>
> Does it dry up
> like a raisin in the sun?
> Or fester like a sore—

And then run?
Does it stink like rotten meat?
Or crust and sugar over—
like a syrupy sweet?

Maybe it just sags
like a heavy load.

Or does it explode?

Very few cities have received the in-depth analysis that
Harlem receives in this volume. Many critics believe that
Montage of a Dream Deferred is Hughes's best work. If so, it
is most fitting that his finest production should be on the
Harlem theme. In a real sense, Hughes is the poet laureate of
Harlem.

Hughes's treatment of the African theme, like that of
Harlem, changed and matured over the years. Like other
New Negro poets, he features in his early works the alien-
and-exile theme. Made famous by Countee Cullen's "Heri-
tage," this attitude was an effort on the part of American
Negro writers to make Africa a literary homeland for the
creative artist. In all probability, it was influenced by the
Garvey Movement of the period. As it appeared in New
Negro poetry, the alien-and-exile tradition portrayed the
American Negro as an alien, perpetually estranged, and
deeply nostalgic over the loss of his beautiful sundrenched
home.

In Hughes, the theme was never important, but it did color
his early poems. He stated or implied the superiority of black
beauty and black wisdom to the pale, washed-out looks and
the foolishness of the whites. He also, from time to time,
spoke of "jungle joys," and he imagines that the "night-dark
girl of the swaying hips," who dances in a cabaret has slept

beneath jungle trees bathed in the splendor of a tropical "star-white moon." In the "Lament for Dark Peoples," the speaker protests his being taken from the African motherland and "caged in the circus of civilization." In another poem called "Afraid," the speaker moans:

> We cry among the skyscrapers
> As our ancestors
> Cried among the palms in Africa
> Because we are alone . . .

At its best, the alien-and-exile movement was an attempt on the part of New Negro poets to find productive traditional roots. At its worst, it was a phony and unconvincing kind of literary black nationalism—phony and unconvincing because it dealt, not with the real Africa but an Africa of fantasy. The African poems in Hughes's first publication appear almost childish when compared with those in his last work. In one, he is writing about a world that never existed on land or sea; in the other, he writes about the world of Lumumba and Kenyatta, the real world of an emerging embittered Africa for whom

> The past has been a mint
> Of blood and sorrow.
> That must not be
> True of tomorrow.

This concern with Africa brings to mind Mr. Hughes's connection with *negritude*—a word as popular now and as indefinable as that other popular and indefinable term, *black power*. In recent years, Leopold Senghor, the high priest of *negritude*, and other African and West Indian writers, have insisted that Langston Hughes is one of the fathers of the Negritude Movement. During a visit to Washington in the fall of 1966, Senghor had a talk with a few friends which was

taped and subsequently printed in the May, 1967, issue of
Negro Digest (now called *Black World*).

Senghor was asked the question: "In which poems of our,
American, literature [do] you find evidence of Negritude?"
His reply was:

> "Ah, in Langston Hughes; Langston Hughes is the most
> spontaneous as a poet and the blackest in expression. For
> me, it is Langston Hughes and also the popular poems of
> Sterling Brown. You see? It appears to me that Langston
> Hughes and Sterling Brown are the most Negro. I do not
> say that theirs are the best poems on an artistic level. Take
> for instance, Countee Cullen. . . . He has beauty, but the
> songs of Langston Hughes are pure, spontaneous and
> simple."

I am not sure I know what *negritude* is. The term obviously
has a wide range of meaning and no two critics I have read
agree on a definition. I am convinced, however, that for the
West African poets, the word has mystical and philosophical
connotations which may not be applicable to our Afro-American *negritude*. And I am also convinced that Langston
Hughes, characteristically, had more than one attitude toward
negritude. In an article entitled, "The Twenties: Harlem and
Its Negritude" (*African Forum*, Spring, 1966), he tends to
use the term very loosely. "To us," he wrote, "negritude was
an unknown word, but certainly pride of heritage and consciousness of race was ingrained in us." At the Dakar Festival,
however, he was much more specific. As reported by the
New York Times (April 24, 1966), he states, "As I understand it, . . . negritude has its roots deep in the beauty of the
black people—in what younger American writers and musicians call *soul*." Mr. Hughes then defined *soul* as "the essence
of Negro folk art redistilled—particularly the old music and
its flavor, the ancient basic beat out of Africa, the folk rhymes
and Ashanti stories—all expressed in contemporary ways so

emotionally colored with the old that it gives a distinctly
Negro flavor to today's music, painting or writing." In short,
he is saying "soul is contemporary Harlem's negritude."

Hughes, as one would expect, had more than one type of
negritude poem. For example, in "Note on Commercial
Theatre," he has what I would call *negritude*, Afro-American
style—the kind which simply shows a consciousness *of*, and a
pride *in*, the American Negro's unique contribution to world
culture. It also urges the Negro to make greater artistic use of
his gifts.

> You've taken my blues and gone—
> You sing 'em on Broadway . . .
> And you fixed 'em
> So they don't sound like me.
> Yep, you done taken my blues and gone.
> You also took my spirituals and gone. . . .
>
> But someday somebody'll
> Stand up and talk about me,
> And write about me—
> Black and beautiful—
> And sing about me,
> And put on plays about me!
> I reckon it'll be
> Me myself!
> Yes, it'll be me.

But one finds another kind of *negritude* in the following
lines, one whose tone is closer to that mystical emphasis on
blackness which the West Africans have in their poetry:

> Body out of Africa
> Strong and black
> As iron

> First smelted in
> Africa
> Song
> Out of Africa
> Deep and mellow song
> Rich as the black earth
> Strong as black iron . . .
> My song
> From the dark lips
> Of Africa.

The protest-and-social commentary theme like the Harlem theme runs through the whole body of Mr. Hughes's poetry, but in his early works the stream is just a trickle. In *The Weary Blues* and *Fine Clothes to the Jew*, there are few poems of this type, but by the time of *One Way Ticket* in 1949 the stream is flowing fully. Like other New Negro poets, he used lynching as the major symbol of American injustice to the Negro, and in *One Way Ticket* Hughes devotes a whole section of the work ("Silhouette") to lynching poems. From this work on down to his last, protest and social commentary became increasingly important in the publications of Mr. Hughes. He never stopped needling America. He wrote or commented on particular incidents such as "Roland Hayes Beaten" or "Restrictive Covenants"; he also commented on our general failures as a "Democracy."

It is interesting to compare Hughes's attitude toward protest poetry with that of Countee Cullen. During his later years, Cullen used to agonize over being a *Negro poet*. "To make a poet black and bid him sing," Cullen thought a peculiar kind of malevolence on the part of God. Hughes, on the other hand, seemed to accept and to glory in his mission as a Negro writer. The word *mission* may be too strong, but I sincerely believe Langston Hughes looked upon his protest poetry as a weapon in the arsenal of American democracy.

Moreover, he evidently had his own ideas about the need for his kind of poetry. During the 1950's, many Negro poets, influenced by the new climate in America which the Integration Movement brought, either stopped writing protest poetry or drastically changed their approach to such poetry. Langston Hughes did neither. He still wrote and reprinted pre-1950 type poems. In his last publication, he includes along with an obviously recent poem like "Stokely Malcolm Me," such old-fashioned protest poems as "Jim Crow Car" and "Christ in Alabama."

Hughes's protest poems ran the gamut from the lynching poems of his early years down to pointed and informed comment on the problems of the 1960's. During his middle period, he wrote a considerable number of leftist poems. Typical of these is "Good Morning, Stalingrad":

> Good morning, Stalingrad
> Where I live down in Dixie
> Things is bad—
> But they're not so bad
> I still can't say,
> Good morning, Stalingrad!
> And I'm not so dumb
> I still don't know
> That as long as your red star
> Lights the sky
> We won't die.

Langston Hughes was never a fanatic or impassioned leftist. Like other young men of the thirties and early forties, he saw hope for the oppressed in the Marxist position. One of his best *and* best-known poems, "Let America Be America Again," was written during this period:

O, Let America be America again—
The land that never has been yet—
And yet must be—the land where every man is free. . . .

O, yes,
I say it plain,
America never was America to me,
And yet I swear this oath—
America will be!

In his social commentary poems, Hughes seldom lost his twofold vision. Though it has been fashionable in recent years to damn the Negro middle class and to play up the black masses, Langston Hughes has reported objectively on both groups in companion poems. In "Low To High," the speaker complains:

How can you forget me?
But you do!
You said you was gonna take me
Up with you
Now that you've got your Cadillac
You done forgot that you are black . . .

In the second, "High To Low":

God knows/We have our troubles too—
One trouble is you:
You talk too loud,
cuss too loud
Look too black,
don't get anywhere . . ./And sometimes it seems
you don't even care.

We note that there is no weighting the evidence on either side. The poet obviously understands and sympathizes with both positions.

To take another example of this objectivity, note the first two stanzas of "Cross":

> My old man's a white old man
> And my old mother's black
> If ever I cursed my white old man
> I takes my curses back.

> If ever I cursed my black old mother
> And wished she were in hell,
> I am sorry for that evil wish
> And now I wish her well.

Here again is a damning of both sides—at first anger at both and then forgiveness, equal forgiveness, growing presumably out of deeper understanding of the human factors involved.

In his last publication, *The Panther and the Lash* (1967), with the sub-title, *Poems of Our Times*, Hughes has left us a kind of testament on his social stand. He brought together in this volume, not only his most recent efforts but also a good number of poems from earlier works—poems which he believed reflected his views on "our times." In this collection, he comes as near to bitterness as he has ever come. Note his scathing indictment of "Elderly Leaders":

> The old, the cautious, the over-wise—
> Wisdom reduced to the personal equation:
> Life is a system of half-truths and lies,
> Opportunistic, convenient evasion.
> > Elderly,
> > Famous
> > Very well paid,
> They clutch at the egg
> > Their master's goose
> > Laid: $$$$.

He also takes a swing at the "Northern Liberal," who "above the struggle" is "well-fed, degreed,/not beat—elite,/up North." And characteristic of him, he shows some sympathy though ironic for the white man when he confesses:

> I am the American heartbreak—
> The rock on which Freedom
> Stumped its toe—
> The great mistake
> That Jamestown made
> Long ago.

And we have his ambivalent vision once more, in "Impasse," when he cleverly and succinctly characterizes the attitudes of both parties in the racial dilemma:

> I could tell you,
> If I wanted to,
> What makes me
> What I am.
>
> But I don't
> Really want to—
> And you don't
> Give a damn!

If one were to arrange Langston Hughes's poetical works in chronological order one would have an excellent, penetrating, topical commentary on the American race issue since 1926— a commentary far more perceptive and meaningful than a library of sociological works. Often ironic but seldom bitter, he seemed to be surprised by White America's stupidity on the Problem or saddened by its blindness.

Although Dunbar and Chesnutt had tapped the reservoir of Negro folk material during the late nineteenth century, the

New Negro writers were the first to make broad use of this impressive body of folk song and literature. They were the first to see in the blues, in the spirituals, in the work and dance songs, in the sermons, and in other types, new forms for contemporary expression. The most important and the most dedicated experimenter with these forms was Langston Hughes. Again, from *The Weary Blues* down to *The Panther and The Lash*, he has adopted, transformed, paraphrased, imitated—in short, he has experimented more fully with folk material than any other writer I know.

In his first works, he emphasized the blues form, a form which because of its spirit was congenial to Hughes:

> I'm gonna walk to de graveyard
> 'Hind ma friend, Miss Cora Lee.
> Gonna walk to de graveyard
> 'Hind ma dear friend Cora Lee
> Cause when I'm dead some
> Body'll have to walk behind me.

In *Fine Clothes to the Jew*, there are seventeen poems written in the blues form. But he also made liberal use of the ballad form and dance rhythms as in:

> Me and ma baby's
> Got two mo'ways,
> Two mo'ways to do de Charleston!
>   Da, da,
>   Da da, da!
> Two mo'ways to do de Charleston.

The experimentation with folk forms and rhythms reached its most brilliant peak in two later works: *Montage of a Dream Deferred* and *Ask Your Mama: 12 Moods for Jazz.* In the first work, the poet tries to capture, as he stated it, "the conflicting changes, sudden nuances, sharp and impudent interjections, broken rhythms, and passages sometimes in the manner of the jam session, sometimes the popular song, . . ." In short, he blends light and shadow, serious and comic, important and trivial, harmony and dissonance into one impressive, unified picture of Harlem. *Montage of a Dream Deferred* technically is a subtle and highly successful experiment in the poetic use of jazz rhythm. One example will suffice to show how effectively Hughes handles the boogie rhythm:

> Good evening daddy!
> I know you have heard
> The boogie-woogie rumble
> Of a dream deferred—
> Trilling the treble
> And twining the bass
> Into midnight ruffles
> Of catgut lace.

Ask Your Mama is a different kind of experiment and almost, though not quite, as brilliant as *Montage of a Dream Deferred.* For this second jazz work, the poet tells us, "The traditional folk melody of 'The Hesitation Blues' is the leitmotif. . . . In and around it, along with the other recognizable melodies employed, there is room for spontaneous jazz improvisation. . . ." Printed in the margin beside each of the poems one finds elaborate directions for the musical accompaniment. Hughes, it must be remembered, is a pioneer in (according to some critics, the father of) the poetry-to-jazz movement. Langston Hughes has always been keenly sensitive to the cadence and timing of folk music and speech. His long years of experimentation in this area paid off brilliantly in *Ask Your Mama.*

> I moved out to Long Island
> Even farther than St. Albans

(which lately is stone nowhere)
I moved out even farther, further, farther
On the sound way off the Turnpike
And I'm the only colored.

Got there! Yes, I made it!
Name in the papers every day. . . .

Yet they asked me out on my patio
Where did I get my money!
I said, From Your Mama!

Beyond poems dealing with Harlem, Africa, Injustice, and Negro folk material a fifth group, "Miscellaneous Poems," is obviously a catchall. This group contains many pieces which have nothing to do with race. It includes poems of inspiration, nature poems, love poems (not many, of course), travel poems, and children's verses, the best of which come from the volume entitled *The Dream Keeper and Other Poems* (1932). In this group are also poems dealing with cabaret and night life in places other than Harlem. Although one doesn't expect to find them, there are many religious poems in Hughes's works. In reading these poems, we must not equate the author with the speaker of the poem. Hughes appreciated all types of conviction and belief and could therefore write the highly controversial "Goodbye to Christ" as well as "The Ballad of Mary's Son," which has an orthodox Christian theme. Of all his religious poems, the one entitled "Litany" represents best for me Mr. Hughes's characteristic concern for the troubled and lowly:

Gather up
In the arms of your pity
The sick, the depraved,
The desperate, the tired,
All the scum

Of our weary city
Gather up
In the arms of your pity.
Gather up
In the arms of your love—
Those who expect
No love from above.

Perhaps the greatest number of these miscellaneous poems
deal with vignettes of life, sometimes tragic, sometimes comic.
Among the best of the latter type is that series, "Madam to
You" or "The Life and Times of Alberta K. Johnson" (*One
Way Ticket*). Madam is almost as great a creation as Simple,
whom she resembles in some respects. Like Simple, she shows
Mr. Hughes's humorous yet profound understanding of the
Negro urban character. "Madam's Past History" gives us
the background of this tough, intelligent, and realistic lady:

My name is Johnson—
Madam Alberta K.
The Madam stands for business.
I'm smart that way.

I had a
HAIR DRESSING PARLOR
Before
The depression put
The prices lower.

Then I had a
BARBECUE STAND
Till I got mixed up
With a no-good man.

Cause I had a insurance
The WPA

Said, We can't use you
Wealthy that way.

I said,
DON'T WORRY 'BOUT ME!
Just like the song,
You WPA folks take care of yourself—
And I'll get along.

I do cooking,
Day's work, too!
Alberta K. Johnson—
MADAM to you.

The poetry of Langston Hughes tends to be the poetry of statement rather than of symbol. He wrote as though the "new critics" never existed, showing little or no interest in the neo-metaphysical school of writing which has flourished since the thirties. Of course, like other New Negro poets, he was influenced by Sandburg, Lindsay, Masters and other poets of the New Poetry Movement of the twenties, but he never became a follower of any one writer. Moreover, unlike M. B. Tolson and, to a lesser extent, Gwendolyn Brooks, he made no drastic changes in his techniques. The jazz experiments of his later works, though they strike us as being very new and very "contemporary," are actually continuations and flowerings of earlier workings in the field. I am not saying that the techniques and diction and forms of 1967 are exactly the same as those used in 1926. There were minor changes.

For example, in his later works, he tended to use more often than formerly catalogs of suggestive names.

Send for Lenin! (Don't you dare! He can't come here!)
Send for Trotsky! (What? Don't confuse the issue please!)
Send for Uncle Tom on his mighty knees. . . .

> Send for Marcus Garvey (What?) Sufi (Who?) Father
>   Divine (Where?)
> Du Bois (When?) Malcolm (Oh!) Send for Stokely
>   (No?) Then
> Send for Adam Powell on a non-subpoena day.
> Send for the Pied Piper to pipe our rats away.

He also made greater use of free-association, occasionally approaching a kind of obscurity which, it seems to me, is alien to his genius:

> For Niagara Falls is frozen
> As is custom below zero.
> Mama's fruitcake sent from Georgia
> Crumbles as it's nibbled
> To a disc by Dinah
> In the run that wafts Maracas
> From another distant quarter
> To this quarter of the Negroes. . . .

In spite of these minor innovations of his last years, Langston Hughes's poetry remained basically and deceptively simple. I say *deceptively*, because he usually requires the second look. When we think he has written a surface commonplace, we are often brought up sharp with a second level of meaning. Moreover, to complicate matters he has a light touch; or to be more exact, he possessed a very rich and subtle sense of humor. Unfortunately, most readers are reluctant to associate "high seriousness" with humor, whereas Hughes often laughs us into an awareness of a serious problem or situation. For example, note the following poem (ironically entitled "Hope"):

> He rose up on his dying bed
> and asked for fish
> His wife looked it up in the dream book
> and played it.

We smile at the idea of a wife so caught up in the policy habit that she could play her dying husband's dream number; and then it dawns upon us that Langston Hughes suggests something in these four lines far more serious than humor and the superstitions of the numbers game. In his way, he is suggesting obliquely that a community which forces a wife to resort to such desperate expedience is not a healthy community. And this is his characteristic approach.

Langston Hughes wanted always to be understood, to "Dig and Be Dug / In Return." He, therefore, counted on the light touch and gambled on the enduring quality of the people's speech and rhythms. And above all else, he remained *cool*; he never lost his objective vision. He saw clearly, he saw with understanding and sympathy, and he wrote down what he saw in the simple speech patterns of the man in the street.

It is probably far too soon to attempt an evaluation of Langston Hughes's place as a poet, although the temptation to do so is too great to be resisted. We must remember that a considerable portion of his work is topical, and like topical verse in any age will become dated. But Mr. Hughes was a very prolific poet—and along with his many poems of passing interest there are many others which will endure because they have crystallized into art, an emotion or an experience of abiding and universal interest. Langston Hughes is an uneven poet; he occasionally fails to observe the line which separates simplicity from triviality. His instincts, however, are usually right; his good ear, his sense of rhythm, and his dependence on the folk reservoir have not failed him too often. A recent critic has called him the "one sure Negro classic." I think of him in broader terms: Langston Hughes is an *American* classic and will outlast his century.

LANGSTON HUGHES: POET
IN THE FOLK MANNER

By Nancy B. McGhee

I got de weary blues
And I can't be satisfied
Got de weary blues
And I can't be satisfied.
I ain't happy no mo'
And I wish I had died.

The mood, the words, the rhythm of this poem have come to be identified with the poetry of a man who is sometimes characterized as "Poet Laureate of the Negro People." Devoting a lifetime to the art of writing, Langston Hughes adapted, explored and experimented with numerous significant literary forms or motifs in an effort to give vivid portrayal to the plight of the black man in America. From the juvenilia of his high school days when the steel mills provided inspiration, to the finest expression of his mature years, the artistic endeavors of Hughes found their roots in his avowed concern for the human condition, and particularly for the Afro-American condition. Although his writings embraced every major literary genre and extended to numerous related art forms, the basic underlying and unifying element reflected his insistent championship of the "common people." Deliberately, he turned to the rich heritage of black people—their loves and hates, their joys and sorrows, their folk life.

The professional discussions of folklore, and specifically the contribution to and effect of Negro folklore upon American culture, are extensive, complex, and sometimes tedious. The history of collecting the folktales, superstitions, customs, and the accounts of the search for relationship and provenience provide materials and stimuli for research and study. Critics and scientists have devoted and continue to devote long years to these studies and, similarly, the poet, Langston Hughes, found in them a compelling force and inspiration. There is little doubt that Hughes recognized the full implication of what Richard Dorson has expressed with respect to the place of Negro folklore in American culture:

> With the publication of the *Slave Songs* [1867] and the Uncle Remus stories, Negro folklore assumed a conspicuous place in American culture. On three different fronts it commanded attention: in the fields of creative literature and music, which found inspiration in Negro folk sources; in the world of popular entertainment and performance; and in scholarly collections and studies which raged over the question of African versus white origins. [*American Folklore*, p. 174]

Some lay readers will agree with Francis Lee Utley when he expressed in *Our Living Traditions* (edited by Tristram P. Coffin, 1968) that everybody thinks he knows what folklore is, even if he merely accepts the simple operational definition that it is "literature orally transmitted." This concept, however, permits anthropologists to restrict folklore mainly to "folk literature." Those critics who find this definition too limited and wish to extend the concept to include the "enrichment of folklore" through the "physical conditions which actually surround it" have come to perceive this entity as "folklife." Considering the word as one "relatively new in

English language," Don Yoder points out (also in *Our Living Traditions*, pp. 47–48) that it is an adaptation by scholars of the Swedish *folkliv*, which in turn seems to have been patterned on the German *Volksleben*. Yoder believes that

> . . . the term "folklore" is intended to include the total range of folk-cultural phenomena, material as well as oral and spiritual. It is consciously intended to be a broader range than the older English word "folklore" . . . The folklife movement is the twentieth-century rediscovery of the total range of the folk culture.

If the consideration of the poems written by Langston Hughes embraces this broad view of literature of the "folk," there may well be discernible evidence of the concept as a unifying and universal theme which undergirded this poet's view of his art, and at the same time supported the thesis which he expounded throughout his writing. In this context the penetrating comment of James Emanuel in his book, *Langston Hughes* (p. 140), suggests the significance of Hughes for the modern scholar, when he points out that through such poetry

> . . . Negro experience in and out of slavery has been transfused into folk art. Scholarship is uncovering the necessity, in the interdisciplinary examination of American culture, of a thorough study of the Negro folk tradition: spirituals, plantation, chain-gang, and levee songs; blues and jazz—to mention only some songs. Hughes's innovations in the poetry of blues and jazz will be more perceptively judged as this folk art and literature become widely understood.

The last sentence of the statement of Emanuel is noteworthy in the whole matter involving perception and delineation of black folklore as it is characterized in the twentieth century. Studies and investigations of the origin or sources of folk tales told by aunties and mammies on the plantation, or accounts of folk sermons chanted by plantation exhorters, self-appointed old-time preachers, may serve as fundamental examples suggesting the literary use of multifarious "folk-things."

Writing and interpreting a tradition as he wrote, Langston Hughes developed his unique poetic form and proposed his own mode of expression as he explored subjects and scenes depicting prostitutes, laborers and drunks, at a time when, says Donald C. Dickinson in *A Bio-Bibliography of Langston Hughes* (p. 43), "conservative white writers peopled their poems with doctors, social workers and dancers." As if he was stating the manifesto of young Black Revolutionaries today, Hughes castigated the "smug, contented respectable folk" of the Negro middle class, and he turned to the common people—those who "live on Seventh Street in Washington or State Street in Chicago." He defended in *Nation* magazine (June 23, 1926) such people as those who "do not particularly care whether they are like white folks or anybody else. Their joy runs, bang! into ecstasy. Their religion soars to a shout."

From these "common people" who lived close to the soil and close to the streets of sprawling cities, Hughes extracted the essence of poetry of the folk, the black heritage of which he was so poignantly conscious. Therefore he was continuously and constantly on the trail of folk art and folk scenes that depict black folklife. Wherever he visited or traveled in his early days he was crowding his inquisitive mind with images, storing his imagination with portraits of people and places, forming a veritable mine of real-life folk materials from which he drew in later years, making poems that revealed a show-case of dramatic moments and interesting people.

Even as this poet absorbed the surging folklife in the haunts of habitués of Beale Street or at the fish fry on

Rampart Street, the active and somewhat restless creative imagination of this unusual man was busy with highlights of the Great Migration to Harlem. Living and laughing with these hordes who thronged Pennsylvania Station he hailed them in *Fine Clothes to the Jew* (p. 77) as

> Dream singers,
> Story tellers,
> Dancers,
> Loud Laughers in the hands of Fate—
> 　　　　My People,
> Dish–washers,
> Elevator–boys,
> Ladies' maids,
> Crap shooters
> 　　　. . .

These "Dream singers" became the "Blues People" whose portraits Hughes etched in bold strokes as he brought them to life to the rhythm of the blues. It is to the folklife of such people that he directed his talents in an effort to express with words what the blues express in melody, tone and rhythm. An achievement of this kind is quite properly assessed by Margaret Walker in a comment upon the pattern of these strange poems in *Phylon*, XI (1950):

> . . . Langston Hughes introduced the pattern of the "blues" into poetry. He made no pretense of being the poet's poet, of writing intellectual poetry. The pattern of the "blues" was, nevertheless, *the first new Negro idiom introduced into American poetry since the time of Paul Laurence Dunbar.* . . . [Italics are mine.]

Preceding the poems in his second volume, *Fine Clothes to the Jew*, Hughes had introduced his own concept of the prosody which had guided his rendition of the "Blues" in poetry by stating:

> The first eight and the last nine poems in this book are
> written after the manner of the Negro folk-songs known
> as *Blues*. The *Blues*, unlike the *Spirituals*, have a strict poetic
> pattern: one long line repeated and a third line to rhyme
> with the first two. Sometimes, but very seldom, it is omitted.
> The mood of the *Blues* is almost always despondency, but
> when they are sung, people laugh.

He might have added that the problems which induce this
despondency include the separation or misfortunes of lovers,
personal sorrow involving death or economic disaster, loneliness and alienation, or other grief. In two or perhaps three
stanzas, developed in the pattern which Hughes described,
reminiscent of an abbreviated dramatic monologue written in
dialect, the blues poem reveals the source of the speaker's
sorrow. Similar in this respect to the folk ballad, the *Blues*
offer few details, and the verse, a type of autobiographical
sketch, emerges through a vivid metaphor or simile. A simple,
crucial experience comes to life through a stark dramatic
picture appealing to the imagination of reader or listener.
Music and rhythm combine to convey the mournful mood.

Hughes had been attracted to this poetry in the writing
of his earliest poems, for he included in the poem, "The
Weary Blues," as he stated it in *The Big Sea* (p. 215), "the
first blues verse I'd heard way back in Lawrence, Kansas,
when I was a kid." Holding in his mind these images of his
early experiences, he drew upon this source of inspiration
for writing throughout his career. For the artist the difficult
task was that of transferring *Blues* from musical statement
into verbal expression. In doing this Hughes employed
dramatic irony, tragic mood, homely images and improvisa-
tions to express emotion just as the popular blues singer
might render in a cabaret, the point of view moving directly
into the heart of the singer or speaker.

In the *Blues* as well as in other folk forms the subject may

range from "A Southern Mammy" to a "Young Gal" or
"Po' gal" who is "Down and Out." The Southern Mammy
has worked hard and long, and from her point of view the
world is in a bad way because white people "ain't got no
heart."

> Miss Gardner's in her garden
> Miss Yardman's in her yard.
> Miss Michaelmas is at de mass
> And I am gettin' tired!
>   Lawd!
> I am gettin' tired!
>
> The nations they is fightin'
> And the nations they done fit.
> Sometimes I think that white folks
> Ain't worth a little bit.
>   No, m'am!
> Ain't worth a little bit.
>
> Last week they lynched a colored boy.
> They hung him to a tree.
> That colored boy ain't said a thing
> But we all should be free.
>   Yes, m'am!
> We all should be free.
>
> Not meanin' to be sassy
> And not meanin' to be smart—
> But sometimes I think that white folks
> Just ain't got no heart.
>   No, m'am!
> Just ain't got no heart.

Unlike certain other blues, each of these four stanzas focuses
on problems beyond the woman's personal suffering. In the
first stanza, upper-class rich white women, unconcerned with

poor mammies, pursue their pleasures; in the second, warring nations led by white people continue fighting; in the third, a black boy has been lynched because he talked of freedom; in the final stanza the speaker holds white people responsible for this state of affairs.

A more personally depicted sorrow is seen in the "Young Gal" who has the blues because of the death of her friend, Miss Cora Lee, who has died, evidently in her youth. Aunt Clew has lived long, but poverty has sent her to the "po'" house. Considering these two unhappy alternatives for resolving the problems of her life, a youthful speaker concludes:

> The po' house is lonely
> An' the grave is cold.
> O, the po' house is lonely,
> The graveyard grave is cold.
> But I'd rather be dead than
> To be ugly an' old.

A third speaker, a "po' gal," is "down and out" because of her economic problems.

> The credit man's done took ma clothes
> And rent time's nearly here.
> I'd like to buy a straightenin' comb,
> An' I need a dime fo' beer.
>
> I need a dime fo' beer.

The "Down and Out" blues displays variations in form and rhythm different from the two preceding blues poems mentioned. While there is the customary repetition in the first stanza, the second stanza quoted above has no rhyme or repetition.

On the other hand, the poem "Hard Daddy" follows more closely the rhythmic blues pattern, including repetition and rhyme. This time the woman speaker is unhappy because of her unresponsive lover and the poem builds to a climax with an unexpectedly sardonic twist at the end of the third stanza:

> I'd fly on ma man an'
> I'd scratch out both his eyes.

The resounding blast in the last line of the "Hard Daddy" blues poem is to be contrasted sharply with that of the woman speaker in "Misery." The latter falls among those which Hughes noted in his anthology of folk literature as "after the manner of Negro folk-songs known as *Blues*." However, he does not follow the pattern he had earlier described in terms of length of line, or rhyme, or number of lines in a stanza. Nevertheless, by repetition and adept arrangement the poem succeeds in creating the sorrow the speaker felt because "A good woman's cryin' for a no-good man." Here the music of the blues serves as anodyne for pain:

> Play de blues for me.
> Play de blues for me.
> No other music
> 'Ll ease my misery.
>
> . . .
>
> Black gal like me,
> Black gal like me
> 'S got to hear a blues
> For her misery.

This is the *Blues* whose scenes portray that state of mind in which the masses of black folk performed the hard, unpleasant labor on the plantation, easing their sorrow and frustrations as well as their small, temporary tragedies by singing "a soothin' song" set to the rhythm of the pick, the shovel, the washboard. The second generation of slave grannies, aunties, and uncles needed often to "ease" their loads, and thereby created almost instinctively their work songs, ballads and blues as accompaniment to daily tasks.

These emotions expressed through blues songs conveyed the music of the *Blues* wherever black folk sang and came together.

The thousands of fugitive slaves fleeing the overseer's lash, hunted by bloodhounds, whisked at night by means of the Underground Railroad to safety in the "free" North, inspired artist and abolitionist alike to engage actively in literary portraiture. Slave narratives, slave fiction and slave poetry give literary permanence to their adventures. Grandchildren of these slaves, witness to a second mass movement of migration to the "free" North, contributed similarly to literary representations and scenes of black folk in search of freedom from want, freedom from fear, freedom from injustices. Bearing in their memories and in their spirits the tales and stories of folklife in Georgia and Alabama, these masses of the common people so dear to Hughes's artistic talent became living exemplars of the mingling folk traditions, fusing the urban and rural folk scene with the peculiar wisdom, humor, and vigor of black folk culture.

Little wonder, then, that Langston Hughes was motivated to reflect these significant trends in two of his best blues poems. In "Bound No'th Blues," the burdened speaker, poor and lonely, trudging from Mississippi, disheartened by the long journey ahead, conveys his woefulness as he tramps to the rhythm of the second stanza:

> Road's in front o' me,
> Nothin' to do but walk.
> Road's in front o' me,
> Walk . . . an' walk . . . an' walk.
> I'd like to meet a good friend
> To come along an' talk.

His fruitless search for a friend has led him to conclude that:

> . . . ever' friend you finds seems
> Like they try to do you bad.

The last stanza marks the rhythm of his feet with the word
road like chords on the piano thumping the blues rhythm
measure:

> Road, road, road, O!
> Road, road . . . road . . . road, road!
> Road, road, road, O!
> On the no'thern road.
> These Mississippi towns ain't
> Fit fer a hoppin' toad.

As this sad, lonely figure fades into the distance, bent
under his "load," an image which his last two lines suggest
in two dimensions persists as he leaves the bystander—the
reader—still spellbound by "rhythm and blues."

Here the blues poem and the blues song converge imagi-
natively into a single basic image in which the central figure
is created as much by the rhythm of the blues on the road
as by the simple words of the song. Like the song of
Wordsworth's "The Solitary Reaper," this "plaintive" tune
lingers long after the dim figure disappears.

Northward-bound black folk finally arrived only to face
a life of perplexities and complexities undreamed of before
they left Mississippi or Georgia. "Evenin' Air Blues," another
of Hughes's successful blues poems depicting black folklife,
reflects the mood of the black who has been "up North"
six months. Working within the restrictions and compression
of the blues form Hughes vividly reveals the biography of a
"blue" person at the same time that he draws a silhouette of
the unhappy black Southerner in Harlem.

> Folks, I came up North
> 'Cause they told me de North was fine.

> I came up North
> 'Cause they told me de North was fine.
> Been up here six months—
> I'm about to lose my mind.

This state of mind is clarified in the next stanza as the speaker, continuing his blues song, reveals that he is simply hungry—for breakfast he "chawed the mornin' air" but for supper he has "evenin' air to spare."

In an article in the *Nation*, the "manifesto" asserting his strong belief that the common people will give to the world its truly great Negro artist, the one who is not afraid to be himself, Langston Hughes also spoke of his own poems:

> Most of my own poems are racial in theme and treatment, derived from the life I know. In many of them I try to grasp and hold some of the meanings and rhythms of jazz.

Pursuing his thoughts on jazz in the same discussion, the poet of the common man hails jazz in these words:

> Let the blare of Negro Jazz bands and the bellowing voice of Bessie Smith singing Blues penetrate the closed ears of near-intellectuals until they listen and perhaps understand . . . We younger Negro artists who create now intend to express our individual dark-skinned selves without fear or shame . . . We know we are beautiful. And ugly too. The tom-tom cries and the tom-tom laughs.

True to his special bent and to his expressed conviction, Hughes also endeavored to create the poems in the more demanding idiom of jazz. He sought to convert jazz musical rhythms into verbal or poetic rhythms. Experimenting and developing new techniques, breaking traditions of conventional poetry, stretching his imagination to the limits, delving into the deepest repositories of folk experience, he emerged with a variety of poems of which "Jazzonia" (1923), written

early in his career, is representative. As time went on he re-
tained this special feeling for jazz and he explored many folk
rhythms, publishing, along with other literary excursions,
Montage of a Dream Deferred (1951) and *Ask Your Mama*
(1961).

Among the successful poems which Hughes entered in
the *Opportunity* Spingarn prizes for literature was a poem
reflecting his excitement over jazz during his working days
in Paris, namely, "To a Negro Jazz Band in a Parisian
Cabaret"; and those that were presented in his first collection
of poems, *The Weary Blues.*

In "Jazzonia" Hughes presages many of the characteristics
of his more mature poetry at the same time that he reflects
the stylistic kinship with the title poem of the collection. It
is quite apparent, even to the casual reader, that he is experimenting with a rhythm and style quite different from "Po'
Boy Blues" or "Bound No'th Blues." For example, the diction
is that of the conventional poet using standard English of
middle-class society. On the other hand, in several respects
there is an obvious congeniality with the poem, "The Weary
Blues." "Jazzonia" is written from a similar point of view in
that the blues poem and the jazz poem at several points
express the speaker's warm enthusiasm for the topic, as for
instance in the lines in which the speaker cries:

> O Blues!
> Swaying to and fro on his rickety stool . . .
> Sweet Blues!
> Coming from a black man's soul
> O Blues!

Compare the first lines of "Jazzonia":

> Oh, silver tree!
> Oh, shining rivers of the soul!

> Oh, singing tree!
> Oh, shining rivers of the soul!

The inspiration of the poet in both poems is a cabaret scene in Harlem. In the blues poem, the "down on Lenox Avenue" scene, the piano player on his "rickety stool" "played that sad rag time like a musical fool." The jazz poem portrays "a Harlem cabaret" where:

> Six long-head jazzers play.
> A dancing girl whose eyes are bold
> Lifts high a dress of silken gold . . .

The brilliance of the images in the latter poem reflect gold and silver in an emotional intensity that produces an effective blend of physical and fanciful qualities of the speaker by allusions to Eve and Cleopatra—sensuous visions reflecting the bold-eyed dancing girl. The refrain repeats the silver in the tree, the shining gold of the dresses. The poem moves to a crescendo of sound projected from the grotesque six long-headed jazzers "who wet the jazz tempo of the whirling cabaret." Impressionistic, glittering, and exciting as one finds these pictures of the Harlem Renaissance poets, the significance of "Jazzonia" for the poetry of Hughes is the expression of an important period in his poetic development and its foreshadowing a long period of preoccupation with jazz rhythms depicting Harlem folklife.

True to his concept of his poetic goals, "to grasp and hold some of the meanings and rhythms of jazz," Hughes employs the rhythmic cabaret scene in a closeup of the Harlem dancer. Blending the "unheard" melody of the music with images of the dance, rhythm and colorful delineation of the imagination, he turns often to a dark girl. He manages to convey rhythmic movement as well as the atmosphere of the "whirling" cabaret. This time in "Song for a Banjo Dance," the dancer is a "brown girl" whose movements are

so vital that the speaker, similar to the caller for square
dances, is moved to cry out directions:

> Shake your brown feet, honey
> Shake your brown feet, chile
> Shake your brown feet, honey
> Shake 'em swift and wil'
> > Get way back, honey
> > Do that low-down step
> > Walk on over, darling
> > > Now come out
> > > With your left

Communication through jazz is frequently direct and beyond
the limits of language, for the rhythm teases the imagination
so poignantly that tingling emotions respond, and the involved onlooker urges the musicians in the poem, "A Negro
Jazz Band in a Parisian Cabaret,"

> Jazz band!
> You know that tune
> That laughs and cries at the same time . . .
> You've got seven languages to speak in

The gaiety and excitement transmitted by jazz into the
cabaret scene focus on performer and participating audience
alike, as jazz rhythm establishes the tempo for the throaty
melody of saxophone, for the finger-snapping tune of "Every-
body/ Loves My Baby/ But My Baby/ Don't Love Nobody/
But Me."

The poem of Hughes at this point throws the spotlight
on the stage and the audience rocks in response, as much a
part of the antiphonal sound as the exhortations of the folk
sermonizer demanding the "Amen" shouts of his hearers.
Likewise, in the hot little room the musical ecstasy generated
by the fever of the *Saxophone Player* was a phenomenon

of the time which characterized the folklife of Harlem Negroes. Not unlike Jesse B. Semple in the story "Jazz, Jive and Jam" (*Simple Stakes A Claim*, p. 190), they danced at the Alhambra or Savoy in competitions, and believed that "jazz makes people get into action." In such a poem as "Negro Dancers" Hughes conveys the keen enjoyment of the dancing couple through the movement, rhythm and refrain:

> Me an' ma baby's
> Got two mo' ways
> Two mo' ways to do de buck!
>
> *Da, da*
> *Da, da da!*
>
> Two mo' ways to do de buck!
>
> Soft light on the tables,
> Music gay,
> Brown-skin steppers,
> In a cabaret . . .

The beat of the music, the contrast between the dark dancing couple, the vigorous movement of the Charleston (or "de buck") and the white onlookers in the cabaret are capsuled dramatically in the flashing scenes of the poem. In vivid contrast to the blues, or perhaps as "an antidote to the blues," as Dickinson suggests, this early poem of Hughes establishes an idiom and style into which the poet probed and with which his readers became familiar for years to come. As if it were the stroke of a painter's brush, this poem sketched the night life and suggested the folklife of a whole era. Downtown on 52nd Street it was different. Here the "soul" music was indeed penetrating, but the spotlight picked up the jazz trumpet player as a feature of entertainment that had become extremely popular. "The excitement and passions of jazz" reads a caption on an advertisement in the *New York Herald Tribune* (Nov. 20, 1961) announcing a new book of soliloquies and dialogues on jazz by George Simon with drawings by Tracy Sugarman. The book pursues "the feelings and lives of the men who play it, sell it and write about it" and could well serve as illustration of Hughes's poem, "Trumpet Player," where in a similar manner the poet views the musician. In spite of "dark moons of weariness under his eyes" the trumpeter soars:

> The music
> From the trumpet at his lips
> Is honey
> Mixed with liquid fire.
> The rhythm
> From the trumpet at his lips
> Is ecstasy
> Distilled from old desire—

Response to this fusing of music and poetry in the setting of the dance hall and cabaret was sometimes sharply critical. Exercising his insights into literary productions by Negro writers of the Renaissance, and in spite of his active encouragement of many young Negro artists of this period, Alain Locke in *Opportunity* wrote that these writers "got jazz-mad and cabaret-crazy instead of folk-wise and sociologically sober."

He warned against the superficiality of relationships between the patrons of Harlem at night and the performers in darktown. That he and Hughes were viewing the same scenes with different lenses was not a new discovery of the dissimilar manner in which these men looked at life and interpreted its values. It had been noted at an earlier time when young Hughes and the older Locke were in Europe and the scholarly professor offered to guide the youthful poet "through the museums of Venice and show [him] the Titians and the Tintorettos," to explain all the old buildings and point out "the place where Wagner had died." Hughes wanted *also* to see the slums and poor people of Venice. From that early time to the publication of his latest innovative and experimental works such as *The Sweet Flypaper of Life, Ask Your Mama* and the numerous plays, poems, gospel songplays and recordings, Hughes was the poet of the people. Just as he wandered about the slums of Venice to meet the poor people there, so did he seek to know the ways of black people on Rampart Street, or on Seventh Street, living, loving, absorbing and recording their moods and manners, their music and movements in dance or in church.

Implementing the role of jazz in the life of the folk he knew, Hughes labeled *Ask Your Mama* as "12 Moods for Jazz" and dedicated the work to Louis Armstrong, "the greatest horn blower of them all." In what would be the foreword of a conventional publication, Hughes prints the melody of the "Hesitation Blues" and offers the following explanation:

> The traditional folk melody of the "Hesitation Blues" is the leitmotif for this poem. In and around it, along with the other recognizable melodies employed, there is room for spontaneous jazz improvisation, particularly between verses, where the voice pauses. The musical figurine indicated after each "Ask your mama" line may incorporate the impudent little melody of the old break, "Shave and a haircut, fifteen cents."

In his review of this "gaily designed book" (*New York Herald Tribune*, November 20, 1961) Rudi Blesh, jazz and art critic, suggests that "though jazz is 'good-time' music, within it has always been something else, something dark yet shining,

harsh yet gentle, bitter yet jubilant—a Freedom Song sung in
our midst unrecognized all these years." He suggests that
within the twelve "moods" of jazz, the poet has established
a theme asserting the freedom which all people must share
or none can have. Hence, the folk-game retort to the
smug, selfish and cruel—"go ask your Mama." The poem
expands the title, the game of mild invective commonly
called "playing the dozens." Thus, the style astounded some
readers and excited others as the refrain, "In the quarter of
the Negroes," binds together the complicated inferences and
references to personalities and incidents:

> Filibuster versus veto
> Like a snapping turtle—
> Won't let it go until it thunders
> Tears the body from the shadow
> Won't let go until it thunders
> In the quarter of the Negroes
> And they asked me right at Christmas
> If my blackness would it rub off?
> I said, Ask your Mama . . .

Reversing the Southern "way of life" the poem pictures
"dreams and nightmares" when all the Dixiecrats have been
voted out of power and the Governor of Georgia is Martin
Luther King. The running marginal notes suggest that this
scene "figure impishly into Dixie ending in high shrill flute
call":

> White sharecroppers work the black plantations
> And colored children have white mammies:
> > Mammy Faubus
> > Mammy Eastland
> > Mammy Patterson
> Dear, dear darling old white mammies

> Sometimes even buried with our family!
> > Dear old
> > Mammy Faubus
> Culture, they say, is a two-way street

The climactic statement above, according to linear notes, is accompanied by "When the Saints Go Marching In" and "joyously for two full choruses." However, the poem is quite complete without the linear notations or *Linear Notes*, "For the Poetically Unhep." The thematic unity emphasized the refrain, the interwoven melodies, allusions, aphorisms, pithy commentary—all enclosed in any of the "twelve moods" with appropriately vivid imagery and suggestive symbols in "Gospel Cha Cha":

> Up that Steep Hill
> The Virgin
> With a Cross
> Lord knows I climbed
> But when I got
> John Jasper Jesus
> When I got to Calvary
> Up there on that hill
> Already there were three
> And one, yes one
> Was Black As Me
>
> Cha-Cha . . . Cha-Cha
> Cha

Ten years before *Ask Your Mama* was published, *Montage of a Dream Deferred* appeared. Saunders Redding in reviewing the book for the *New York Herald Tribune* (March 11, 1915) had described Hughes as "the provocative folk singer who enchanted and sometimes distressed readers of *The Weary Blues, Fine Clothes to the Jew* and *Fields of Wonder*."

He commends Hughes for apparently returning to the "spiritually rewarding" themes expressing "the heritage that was distinctly his in the days of the Negro Renaissance." The mature Hughes continued to illuminate and to highlight the materials of the black folk heritage through the poems collected in *Montage of a Dream Deferred*.

Throughout these poems, as in the earlier works, he delineated some sharp outline or figure which portrays the poverty, injustice and inequities of black folklife in the streets, bars, and shops of Harlem. To communicate his concern for social reform, Hughes devises and creates a new style, the uneven, and according to Redding, "the jarring dissonances and broken rhythms of be-bop." Certainly the movement of this "experimental jazz," as James Emanuel described it in his book *Langston Hughes* (p. 145), was as well known and significant in the world of popular music as the earlier jazz or "Charleston" rhythms. With his peculiarly distinctive ability to verbalize the syncopation and tempo of the songs and dances of Harlem or Chicago's South Side, Hughes accepted the risk of dating himself, as Redding warned, in order to bring forth little vignettes of folklife activated by appropriate musical accompaniment. Enlivening the setting and playing variations on the theme of his famous "Dream Deferred," Hughes pounds out the "Boogie-Woogie" rhythm in the "Dream Boogie":

> Good morning, daddy!
> Ain't you heard
> The boogie-woogie rumble
> Of a dream deferred?
>
> Listen closely:
> You'll hear their feet
> Beating out and beating out a—

> *You think*
> *It's a happy beat?*
>
> Listen to it closely:
> Ain't you heard
> Something underneath
> Like a—
>
> *What did I say?*
>
> Sure,
> I'm happy!
> Take it away!
>
> *Hey, pop!*
> *Re-bop!*
> *Mop!*
>
> *Y-e-a-h !*

Extending the variegated images evoked in the title, the poems in the *Montage* present provocative pictures, vibrant multiplicity of sensory impressions, and a throbbing rhythm as in "Dream Boogie: Variations":

> Tinkling treble
> Rolling bass,
> High noon teeth
> In a midnight face,
> Great long fingers
> On great big hands,
> Screaming pedals
> Where his twelve-shoe lands,
> Looks like his eyes
> Are teasing pain,
> A few minutes late
> For the Freedom Train.

The scenes of the "Montage" travel throughout the folklife

of the Harlem streets. There are the two thousand children,
the "little varmints" who played "Children Rhymes";

>   By what sends
>   the white kids
>   I ain't sent:
>   I know I can't
>   be President.

There are the "Seven ladies and Seventeen gentlemen"
who were planning the typical Harlem parade:

>   Grand Marshal in his white suit
>   Will lead it . . .
>
>   Motorcycle cops,
>   white,
>   will speed it
>   out of sight
>   if they can:
>   Solid black
>   Can't be right.

There are other vivid pictures superimposed in montage
style portraying black folklife, poems whose individual form
is jagged, rhythms odd and syncopated, where the general
contour reaches beyond conventional standards or critics'
acceptance. In the framework of the "montage," however,
they present a totality of folk culture, scenes appealing to the
imagination and the senses. Sometimes through aggregation
the sounds and sights are unified into a rhythmic love poem:

>   I could take the Harlem night
>   and wrap around you,
>   Take the neon lights and make a crown,
>   Take the Lenox Avenue busses,
>   Taxis, subways,
>   And for your love song tone their rumble down.

Take Harlem's heartbeat,
Make a drumbeat,
Put it on a record, let it whirl,
And while we listen to it play,
Dance with you till day—
Dance with you, my sweet brown Harlem girl.

Because the materials of the black folk heritage became the acknowledged milieu which Hughes found most congenial to his artistic tastes, his creativity led him into bizarre experiments in verse forms and styles. Eventually, his simpler, earlier "blues" and "jazz" could be regarded as successful preliminaries to the more complex and unconventional verse, laying the poet open to criticism for seeming to seek extremes of experiments for the sake of the new. Yet within these "shockers" the poet continued to reflect his basic concerns and his first love as evidenced by his constant returning to folk diction and folk people and folk images—the black folklife of America.

In the year when the *Saturday Review* carried a picture of Louis Armstrong on the cover to dedicate a symposium of writing to him at his seventieth birthday, the poet, who also eleven years ago dedicated his longest and perhaps strangest poem to the same jazz artist, seems to be vindicated by the verdict of the years. With the mood of young Americans in 1971 echoing to some extent the mood of young black American artists of the twenties in the revival of interest in folk music and folk art, and in the rediscovery of the "black-is-beautiful" doctrine which Hughes preached, the poetry of Langston Hughes appears "relevant" today even to Americans "past thirty."

Poet Langston Hughes successfully communicated on the level of the folk idiom, particularly the idiom of the Harlem street corners and bars. Many readers agree that Hughes is quite adept in translating the wisdom and humanity of the masses of people into the urban folk idiom. He is a master in employing fanciful rhythms, experimental techniques and in manipulating the folk diction to create a mood and tone that bring the reader into the world of the poem, in full empathy with the humor or irony of the scene. For example, conversational language becomes a diction matched artfully to the character:

> I said, Madam,
> Can it be
> You trying to make a
> Pack-horse out of me?

An innovator in poetry, Hughes was also the creator of numerous characters "in the folk manner": Jesse B. Semple and the speaker of the preceding quotation, Madam Alberta K. Johnson. It is not surprising that such a poet could also bring to life with appropriate photographs their close kin, Sister Mary Bradley, who "done got [her] feet caught in the sweet flypaper of life," who had "no intentions of signing no messages from St. Peter" telling her to "come home."

The conscious artistry of a creative mind, the Langston Hughes inventive genius, shaping and molding the new folk expression of the black man in America, articulates the changing image of the Negro in this country. The poet whose writing is devoted to "racial themes," as Hughes described his efforts, finds himself inevitably drawn to the richness of folk speech, folk music and the whole gamut of folklife. His happy appeal to his readers attests the universality of his materials. If he successfully translates this universality of the folk by projecting the pithy, terse language, the economy of phrase, the homely metaphor, the humor and exaggeration, he thus vitalizes his scenes with a life that perpetuates his creations. He bridges the gap between then and now.

Such was the basic contribution of Langston Hughes to

American poetry. In the preoccupation with the *Blues*, for example, he sensitizes the reader to what Ralph Ellison has called "the special condition of Negroes in the United States." And he accomplishes this goal without frenzy and bitterness. In *Shadow and Act* (pp. 78-79) Ralph Ellison puts it thus in describing *Blues*:

> The blues is an impulse to keep the painful details and episodes of a brutal experience alive in one's aching consciousness, to finger its jagged grain, and to transcend it, not by the consolation of philosophy but by squeezing from it a near-tragic, near-comic lyricism. As a form, the blues is an autobiographical chronicle of personal tragedy expressed lyrically.

From the experience conveyed by the dramatic lyric, the poet using the folk scene writing in the folk manner reaches out to all men. From the tall tales and crude jokes of the plantation to the sidewalks of New York, the Blues People as symbol of the folk element in the lives of all people offer their comment on life. For black folklife Ellison suggests that:

> Their attraction lives in this, that they at once express both the agony of life and the possibility of conquering it through sheer toughness of spirit. They fall short of tragedy only in that they provide no solution, offer no scapegoat but the self.

The prolific production of Langston Hughes may be characterized, perhaps, by this view of the *Blues* to which he was intensively committed, because to all of his writing the language, the thought and the concept of folklife bear a seminal relationship. Indeed this quality which the literature of the folk provided, a quality moving far beyond his poetry "in the folk manner," may be conceived as the quality which earned for him a unique place in the literature of America.

THE GOOD BLACK POET AND THE GOOD GRAY POET: THE POETRY OF HUGHES AND WHITMAN

By Donald B. Gibson

A direct link between Langston Hughes and Walt Whitman is established by Hughes himself in a tribute to the poet called "Old Walt."

> Old Walt Whitman
> Went finding and seeking,
> Finding less than sought
> Seeking more than found,
> Every detail minding
> Of the seeking or the finding.
>
> Pleasured equally
> In seeking as in finding
> Each detail minding,
> Old Walt went seeking
> And finding.

If we were to substitute "Old Lang" for "Old Walt" throughout, we would have a poem as applicable to the one poet as to the other. The easiness of such a substitution is a clue to the relation between the two poets. The meaning of Hughes's poem is in its tone, its spirit rather than its correctness and specificity. It conveys an attitude rather than precise meaning. The relation between the two consists in their sharing common attitudes, certain feelings about what is worthwhile and valuable. Hughes, then, is not a direct descendant of Whitman; he was probably more directly influenced by Carl Sandburg and Vachel Lindsay and hence in regard to influence is at one remove. And Hughes is in some very important ways unlike Whitman—the comparison I am making should not obscure this fact. Yet, had Whitman not written, Hughes could not have been the same poet.

Both reveal in their poems certain rather obvious similarities. Hughes and Whitman are firm believers in the possibilities of realization of the American ideal; both see the American nation as in process of becoming. Both are more cheerful than not. Both approached the writing of their poems in generally non-traditional fashion, though Hughes uses rhyme and traditional metrics more than Whitman. Both are free in their choice of subject, writing about matters (especially sexual matters) traditionally considered unsuitable for poetry. Both adopt personae, preferring to speak in voices other than their own. They are social poets in the sense that they rarely write about private, subjective matters, about the workings of the inner recesses of their own minds. (Hughes thought of himself as a social poet. One of his essays is titled "My Adventures as a Social Poet," *Phylon*, VIII— Third Quarter, 1947—pp. 205-212.) And both have a remarkably similar notion of the nature and function of poetry. Let us now examine these likenesses in greater detail.

Whitman and Hughes are democrats to the bone. Whitman's firm commitment to democracy and to the United States is well enough known. Whitman is most commonly known as the poet of American democracy and his most widely known poems have been such poems as "I Hear America Singing," "For You O Democracy," "O Captain! My Captain!" and others which reflect in various ways his commitment to democracy. Convinced of the essential unity of mankind, Whitman found democracy so appealing because of its promise to do away with social distinctions. Democracy was compatible with Whitman's philosophical notions about the ultimate unity of all things. Indeed the thrust of a good deal of his poetry is toward the doing away with distinctions between things.

Hughes also wanted to break down distinctions. His desire to break down the kinds of distinctions which make racism possible is not unrelated to a yearning to break down distinctions of all kinds. His "I, Too," "Low To High," and "High To Low," "In Explanation of Our Times," "Freedom's Plow," and "Democracy" all express Hughes's desire to see unity among people, social equality, economic equality, and cultural equality among the people not only of America, but of the world. The forms of many of his poems indicate his desire to break down, as did Whitman, the traditionally rigid distinctions between poetry and prose; though he did not go as far as Whitman in his desire to see all things as related, his tendencies were in that direction. He valued flexibility and abhorred rigidity. His temperament was such that he was much more inclined to see the unity of experience than its disparateness. Hence the title of one of his books of short stories, *Something in Common*.

Rather than relating to any developed (or at least publicly stated) philosophical perspective, as Whitman's desire to do away with distinctions does, Hughes's proclivities in this direction seem to be most easily explained by reference to personality. *The Big Sea* and *I Wonder as I Wander* reveal a man of large sympathies, at ease in the world, broad in outlook, and fantastically regardful of other people. One would expect that he would be as strongly anti-fascist as he is and indifferent to puritanical moral values even if his autobiographical writings and poetry did not make it so clear. He seems anti-authoritarian by nature, democratic by virtue of character. His politics are as natural to him as breathing.

Hughes's commitment to the American ideal was deep felt

and abiding. He held on to it despite his acute awareness of
the inequities of democracy, and he seemed to feel that in
time justice would prevail, that the promises of the dream
would be fulfilled. His early poem, "I, Too" (*The Weary
Blues*, 1926), is testimony to his faith.

> I, too, sing America.
>
> I am the darker brother.
> They send me to eat in the kitchen
> When company comes,
> But I laugh,
> And eat well,
> And grow strong.
>
> Tomorrow,
> I'll be at the table
> When company comes.
> Nobody'll dare
> Say to me,
> "Eat in the kitchen,"
> Then.

The later long poem, "Freedom's Plow," written during
World War II and having about it something of a patriotic,
wartime flair, is no less an expression of the poet's basic
feeling.

> America!
> Land created in common,
> Dream nourished in common,
> Keep your hand on the plow! Hold on!
> If the house is not yet finished,
> Don't be discouraged, builder!
> If the fight is not yet won,
> Don't be weary, soldier!
> The plan and pattern is here,

Woven from the beginning
Into the warp and woof of America . . .

In an essay titled "My America" (included in *The Langston Hughes Reader*) Hughes attempted to express his complex feelings about the United States. The essay begins, "This is my land America. Naturally, I love it—it is home—and I am vitally concerned about its mores, its democracy, and its well-being." The piece concludes with another testament of faith: ". . . we know . . . that America is a land in transition. And we know it is within our [black people's] power to help in its further change toward a finer and better democracy than any citizen has known before. The American Negro believes in democracy. We want to make it real, complete, workable, not only for ourselves—the fifteen million dark ones—but for all Americans all over the land."

As optimists generally do, Langston Hughes and Walt Whitman lacked a sense of evil. This (and all it implies) puts Hughes in a tradition with other American writers. He stands with Whitman, Emerson, Thoreau, and later Sandburg, Lindsay, and Steinbeck, as opposed to Hawthorne, Poe, Melville, James, Faulkner, and Eliot. This is not to say that he did not recognize the existence of evil, but, as Yeats says of Emerson and Whitman, he lacked the "Vision of Evil." He did not see evil as inherent in the character of nature and man, hence he felt that the evil (small *e*) about which he wrote so frequently in his poems (lynchings, segregation, discrimination of all kinds) would be eradicated with the passage of time. Of course the Hughes of *The Panther and the Lash* (1967) is not as easily optimistic as the poet was twenty or twenty-five years before. Hughes could not have written "I, Too" or even "The Negro Speaks of Rivers" in the sixties. But the evidence as I see it has it that though he does not speak so readily about the fulfillment of the American ideal for black people, and though something of

the spirit of having waited too long prevails, still the optimism remains. This is evidenced by his choosing to include
the poems with an optimistic bias in his last two volumes
of verse, *Selected Poems* and *The Panther and the Lash*.

Montage of a Dream Deferred (1951), included in *Selected
Poems*, describes the dream as deferred, not dead nor incapable of fulfillment. There is a certain grimness in the poem,
for example in its most famous section "Harlem" which begins, "What happens to a dream deferred?/ Does it dry up/
like a raisin in the sun?" but the grimness is by no means
unrelieved. There is, as a matter of fact, a lightness of tone
throughout the poem which could not exist did the poet see
the ravages of racial discrimination as manifestations of Evil.

> On that day when the Savoy
> leaps clean over to Seventh Avenue
> and starts jitterbugging
> with the Renaissance,
> on that day when Abyssinia Baptist Church
> throws her enormous arms around
> St. James Presbyterian . . .
>
> Maybe it ain't right—
>   but the people of the night
>   will give even
>   a snake
>   a break.

The whole tone of *Montage of a Dream Deferred* is characterized by the well-known "Ballad of the Landlord." There
the bitter-sweet quality of Hughes's attitude toward his subject is clear.

The Panther and the Lash is the least cheerful, the least
optimistic of Hughes's volumes of poetry. Even this book,
however, is not devoid of hope.

Quick sunrise, come!
Sunrise out of Africa,
Quick, come!
Sunrise, please come!
Come! Come! [p. 13]

    Four little girls
Might be awakened someday soon
By songs upon the breeze
As yet unfelt among magnolia trees. [p. 47]

In some lands
Dark night
And cold steel
Prevail—
But the dream
Will come back,
And the song
Break
Its jail. [p. 63]

The past has been a mint
Of blood and sorrow.
That must not be
True of tomorrow. [p. 69]

It must be said in all truth that though Hughes's optimism remains, his faith is not so much in democracy, nor America, nor, for that matter, in any specifically stated program or system. *The Panther and the Lash* reveals a generalized hope and optimism very much dimmed, comparatively. There is in respect to optimism no poem the least bit like "I, Too."

Whitman and Hughes share a similar attitude toward the relation of the poet to poetic tradition. Neither looked to the past for the sake of discovering suitable or acceptable forms or subject matter. Both poets were thoroughly engaged in their time, were men of the present and the future and not primarily of the past. I say "primarily" because both used to some extent the methods of traditional poetry—rhyme, regular metrical structures, poetic diction. But their work gives the impression on the whole that they were more reliant on their own sense of what constitutes poetry, were more inclined to look inward than outward in creating poems. Both found free verse to be more compatible with their aims than more structured verse though Hughes probably relied more than did Whitman on traditional form. Even so, neither poet looked backwards for poetic examples —at least not as a common practice. Whitman, of course, is our most original poet even though he was influenced by others. Hughes looked to other poets, but to his contemporaries. In *The Big Sea* (p. 28) he says:

> Ethel Weimer [a high school English teacher] discovered Carl Sandburg for me. Although I had read of Carl Sandburg before . . . I didn't really know him until Miss Weimer in second-year English brought him, as well as Amy Lowell, Vachel Lindsay, and Edgar Lee Masters, to us. Then I began to try to write like Carl Sandburg.

(This is an extremely important passage in this context, for it suggests that Hughes was probably more influenced by Whitman's follower, Sandburg, than by Whitman himself. Hughes's introduction to Whitman must have come later.)

Whitman and Hughes were as unconventional in their subject matter as in their form, and both were attacked for their lack of delicacy, especially in matters related to sex. An anonymous reviewer of the 1855 and 1856 editions of *Leaves of Grass* wrote in *The Christian Examiner* (reprinted in *Whitman the Poet*, edited by John C. Broderick, p. 69),

"The book might pass for merely hectoring and ludicrous, if it were not something a great deal more offensive. We are bound in conscience to call it impious and obscene." Hughes's *Fine Clothes to the Jew* was called "trash" by *The Pittsburgh Courier* in 1927. In a defense of his poems, published in the same newspaper, he wrote the following:

> My poems are indelicate. But so is life.
>
> I write about "harlots and gin-bibers." But they are human. Solomon, Homer, Shakespeare, and Walt Whitman were not afraid or ashamed to include them.

Such attitudes as these are not inconsistent with the poets' general stance against the *status quo*. Both seek change in the American society, and both welcome change. Hence they are less bound than many others to institutional ways of perceiving and responding. "A Woman Waits for Me" must have been even more shocking to genteel readers in the nineteenth century than Hughes's "indelicacies" have been in the twentieth. But the salient point is that the two poets shared the same impulse: to write honestly and truly about what they saw around them, and not to allow considerations of propriety to obfuscate their vision.

Another similarity between them is their choosing to speak through a mask, a persona, Whitman more consistently than Hughes. The observation that the poet who speaks in *Leaves of Grass* and Walt Whitman the man are not one and the same is by now common knowledge.

In an essay, "Walt Whitman and the American Tradition" (*Virginia Quarterly Review*, Autumn 1955), Floyd Stovall speaks of Whitman's "hero-poet" and warns us to avoid the temptation to identify the speaker of the poem and the historical personage. Whitman's reasons for projecting into the poem a kind of mythical, larger-than-life hero are multifarious, but clearly enough he wished to convey the impression of a figure who in spirit would contain the essence of the American nation and, ultimately, of human-kind. Hughes's use of the persona is somewhat different though not always entirely dissimilar. The speaker, for example, of "I, Too" is obviously not an individual; his is a collective "I," the same representative figure who says, "I've known rivers" in "The Negro Speaks of Rivers." Whereas Whitman's persona is a single, fairly consistent, developing consciousness, Hughes assumes a multitude of personae. At one time he is the spirit of the race who represents Negro or Black Man. Then he is a shoeshine boy, a black mother, a black woman quarreling with her husband, a black man with-out a job or money, a prostitute, a slum tenant. Sometimes he is a consciousness whose role is incapable of determination. And sometimes he speaks, though comparatively rarely, as the poet.

In those poems about black life, thought, and character we could say that the persona is the same. It may well be that we are expected to see a commonality among the various experiences set forth in Hughes's poems of this type. If so, then we could say that a consistent persona speaks in a great number of Hughes's poems.

Most of the poems of Hughes and Whitman have an end beyond themselves, and they differ, therefore, from the poems of poets who seek to write poems beautiful in themselves and void of ideas. In writing poetry Hughes and Whitman felt they were performing a function beyond mere entertainment. Both intended to influence the thinking and actions of men; both intended to change the world through their poetry. Whitman's poetry is suffused with poems whose intention is to instill in men's minds the basic tenets of democracy. As-selineau tells us in *The Evolution of Walt Whitman: The Creation of a Personality* (Volume II, p. 149) that "the two democratic principles which Whitman proclaimed with the greatest enthusiasm as early as 1855 were Liberty and Equality." Hughes likewise wished to encourage men to know and love democracy. One of many such poems about democracy and the value of freedom and equality is Hughes's "I Dream a World," an aria in the opera, *Troubled Island*, by William Grant Still; libretto by Langston Hughes.

> I dream a world where all
> Will know sweet freedom's way,
> Where greed no longer saps the soul
> Nor avarice blights our day.
> A world I dream where black or white,
> Whatever race you be,
> Will share the bounties of the earth
> And every man is free . . .

Both had a pretty clear idea of what the function of poetry should be, and though both wrote some poems whose character is not in accordance with that notion, the large majority of their poems indicates a rather fair consistency between their ideas of the function of poetry and the poems they actually wrote.

Just as Emerson's ideas of what a poet should be (set forth in his essay, "The Poet," and published eleven years prior to the first edition of *Leaves of Grass*) seem uncannily to describe Whitman, so Whitman's statements about how poetry should be written seem to codify Hughes's ideas and practice. In the preface to *November Boughs* Whitman says, "No one will get at my verses who insists upon viewing them as a literary performance, or attempt at such performance, or as aiming mainly toward art or aestheticism." Clearly the same could be said about Hughes's verses. Likewise Whitman's following statements, quoted from *Whitman the Poet*, about the composition of verse describe, essentially, what were Hughes's practices.

> Rules for Composition—A perfectly transparent plate-glassy style, artless, with no ornaments or attempts at ornaments, for their own sake . . .

> Clearness, simplicity, no twistified or foggy sentences, at all —the most translucid clearness without variation.

> Common idioms and phrases—Yankeeisms and vulgarisms— cant expressions, when very pat only. [p. 55]

Hughes would have agreed with the sentiments expressed by Whitman in one of his conversations with Horace Traubel in regard to the nature of poetry.

> He [Whitman] continued: "The trouble is that writers are too literary—too damned literary. There has grown up— Swinburne I think an apostle of it—the doctrine (you have heard of it? It is dinned everywhere), art for art's sake: think of it—art for art's sake. Let a man really accept that . . . and he is lost. . . . Instead of regarding literature as only a weapon, an instrument, in the service of something larger than itself, it looks upon itself as an end—as a fact to be finally worshipped, adored. To me that's all a horrible blasphemy—a bad smelling apostasy." [p. 63]

Such areas of agreement as these are not incidental—they imply a whole orientation. We need simply compare Langston Hughes's poem on Walt Whitman (cited above) with Ezra Pound's called "A Pact."

> I make a pact with you, Walt Whitman—
> I have detested you long enough.
> I come to you as a grown child
> Who has had a pig-headed father;
> I am old enough now to make friends.
> It was you that broke the new wood,
> Now is a time for carving.
> We have one sap and one root—
> Let there be commerce between us.

The strong negativism of the tone of Pound's poem has at
base nothing to do with judgment of poetic value. What
Pound objects to is Whitman's orientation. He cannot abide
that largeness of spirit, that breaking of the wood, that
standing in opposition to tradition. The key lines in this
poem are the sixth and seventh—"It was you that broke the
new wood,/Now is a time for carving." "Breaking new
wood" means going against tradition, seeking out new territory, writing lines which critics declare are not poetry.
"Now is a time for carving" is at best condescension. The
final lines of the poem about "one sap and one root" grudgingly admit that the kind of poetry Whitman writes is at
least poetry. Hence the poem admits that all poetry is not
"pure" poetry. At the same time it says that the *best* poetry
is of a certain kind. Whitman wrote crude poetry, the poem
says, and what he did needs refinement. Hence Pound speaks
to Whitman as an inferior, as one worthy of detestation, but
not entirely. He does not consider the possibility that Walt
Whitman may not even *want* to make a pact with him.
Central to the difference Pound elucidates is the difference
between the two poets' politics. Pound's sympathies lay with
authoritarianism and Whitman's with democracy. The two
perspectives produce completely different poets. Hughes
wrote the kind of poetry that Walt Whitman wrote; he,
therefore, could write an unambivalent poem in praise of
Whitman. No poet so inclined toward authoritarianism could
write such a poem. The authoritarian, dictatorial perspective
is by definition opposed to Whitman's. The literary values of
Hughes and Whitman stand in marked contrast not only to
Pound's, but to the values of all those writers who see literary
art as being an end in itself. Writers such as Henry James
and T. S. Eliot, who are aristocratic in orientation and
authoritarian in politics, naturally scorn the comparatively

free styles and, indeed, the whole world view of a Whitman and a Hughes.

There are undoubtedly more parallels than I have pointed out between Whitman and Hughes, but it should also be noted that there are many, many differences as well. For one thing Hughes was not a mystic nor does his poetry, according to James Emanuel in his book *Langston Hughes* (p. 88), indicate any kind of supernatural belief. He was a naturalist and a humanist, and his attention was toward the world. This seems to me to relate to Hughes's little poem, "Personal."

> In an envelope marked:
>   *Personal*
> God addressed me a letter.
> In an envelope marked:
>   *Personal*
> I have given my answer.

The poem, written by a naturalist, a disbeliever, is ironic, and the irony and mild humor consist in the fact that the poet equates himself with God and tells Him, man to man, what he thinks of Him.

Much of his poetry, unlike Whitman's, was written to be read aloud. Hughes must have read to more people than any other twentieth-century poet. Some of his most apparently mundane and lifeless poems sparkled to life in his reading of them. Unlike Whitman's, many of his poems depend upon the reader's familiarity with black expressions, both urban and rural. Some readers simply cannot respond to much of his poetry because they do not understand the rhythms, pronunciations, and meaning of his language. In this regard, though Whitman often forced the language to his own purposes, Hughes is the less formal poet. Of course these observations do not apply to Hughes's more formal poems which are usually quite conventional.

Though Hughes was a great admirer of Whitman, it is doubtful that he knew how Whitman the man really felt about black people. Asselineau points out in detail Whitman's strong personal aversion to black people in the chapter, "Democracy and Racialism—Slavery," in his book, *The Evolution of Walt Whitman* (Volume II, pp. 179 ff). (I urge the reader to see this unusually sensitive treatment of the subject. Few, if any, white Americans could have written such a chapter. Asselineau sees subtleties which Whitman's critics have either failed to see or not bothered to see.) His publisher in 1860, Eldridge, says of Whitman's views that:

> Of the Negro race he had a poor opinion. He said that there was in the constitution of the Negro's mind an irredeemable trifling or volatile element, and that he would never amount to much in the scale of civilization. I never knew him to have a friend among the Negroes while he was in Washington, and he never seemed to care for them. . . . In defence of the Negro's capabilities I once cited to him Wendell Phillips' eloquent portrait of Toussaint L'Ouverture, the pure black Haytian warrior and statesman. . . . He thought it a fancy picture much overdrawn, and added humorously paraphrasing Betsy Prig in "Martin Chuzzlewit," "I don't believe there was no such nigger."

Asselineau reports that Whitman found it "curious to see Lincoln 'standing with his hat off' to a regiment of black troops 'just the same as the rest' as they passed by" and that Whitman "in 1872, in the course of a visit to his sister's home in Vermont, rejoiced at not seeing a single Negro." Asselineau also points out that Whitman all his life "continued to behave and react like a Long Island peasant whose grandparents had owned slaves."

These feelings were for the most part personally expressed and did not enter directly into *Leaves of Grass*. On the contrary Whitman must have recognized the grave contradiction between his personal feelings and his notions about liberty and equality and certainly did not wish the poet of the poems to appear to be a bigot. There is, however, no poem on the Emancipation Proclamation and only one allusion to emancipation in *Leaves of Grass*. It should be pointed out, in all fairness, that Whitman was not *simply* a bigot. He abhorred the fugitive slave law; he felt slavery to be degrading to slave and slave owner; and he several times depicts the horrors of slavery in *Leaves of Grass*. It is this latter aspect of Whitman's character which Hughes knew from *Leaves of Grass* and admired. Hence Hughes might have felt the same (or similarly) toward Whitman had he known of the good gray poet's personal repugnance toward black people. Walt Whitman the man might have been a bigot, but Walt Whitman the poet was a thoroughgoing equalitarian.

There are many more differences that might be pointed out. But suffice it to say that in Whitman the poet, Hughes found a compatible spirit, a man of large sympathy, of broad vision, and great faith in the potential of America and Americans. Hughes and Whitman would have disagreed on many things had they known and talked with each other, but on most basic issues, on matters basic to the sustaining of life, on matters having to do with the well-being of the majority of people, they would have found many points of agreement. And it is for this reason, it seems to me, that the two poets want comparison.

LANGSTON HUGHES AS PLAYWRIGHT

By Darwin T. Turner

Throughout his professional writing career of forty-six years, Langston Hughes maintained keen interest in theater. He published his first play, *The Gold Piece*, in 1921. In 1935, he had his first Broadway show—*Mulatto*, which established a record by remaining in production on Broadway longer than any other play which had been written by a Negro. During the thirties and early forties, he founded three Negro dramatic groups—The Suitcase Theater in Harlem, the Negro Art Theater in Los Angeles, and the Skyloft Players in Chicago. As late as 1963, Hughes was still polishing *Emperor of Haiti*, which had been produced as *Drums of Haiti* twenty-seven years earlier.

Langston Hughes took pride in his achievements in the theater. In addition to the record-setting *Mulatto* and *Simply Heavenly*, which appeared on Broadway in 1957, he wrote seven other plays which were produced professionally. He also wrote musicals, a movie script, radio drama, a passion play, and the lyrics for the musical version of Elmer Rice's *Street Scene*. Nevertheless, despite his extensive efforts, Hughes never became outstanding as a dramatist. The reasons for his failure are evident in a close examination of his works.

Produced in 1935, but written in 1930, *Mulatto* is an emotionally engaging drama, marred by melodrama, propaganda, and crudities common to inexperienced playwrights. Developed from a short story, "Father and Son," *Mulatto* dramatizes the conflict between Colonel Norwood, a wealthy white man, and Robert, his "yard child." Since he was seven years old, Robert has hated his father for refusing to recognize their relationship, of which he himself had been proud. During his summer's vacation from college, Robert has strained tension to a breaking point by defying the mores of his father and of the Georgia town in which they live. Finally, on the scheduled day of Bert's return to college, the tension snaps. Incensed to learn that Bert has defied a white woman, has sped past a white man, and has entered the front door of the house regularly, Norwood threatens to kill him. Bert, instead, kills his father and flees; but, chased by a posse, he returns to the house, where he kills himself.

Much of the power of the play derives from the subject itself. A traditional subject in drama, father-son conflict inevitably generates excitement and frequently produces memorable characters and confrontations: Polonius and Laertes, Theseus and Hippolytus are only a few. In this instance, the excitement was intensified for American audiences by the first professional dramatization of a conflict between a mulatto and his father.

The play gains strength also from Hughes's characterizations of Bert and Cora. Although he is obviously modeled on the proud and noble slaves of Negro literary tradition, Bert is an interesting character. His contempt for other Negroes, his stubborn insistence that he be recognized as a man, and his arrogant defiance of custom symptomize a fatal *hubris*. In his deliberate provocation of trouble, a manifestation of what seems almost a suicidal complex, he anticipates James Baldwin's protagonist in *Blues for Mr. Charlie*, written a generation later.

Cora too seems a familiar figure from American stories about the antebellum days. At first, she is merely the docile servant who, for many years, has lived with the master, nurtured him, and borne his children without concern for herself and without complaint. After Norwood's death, however, Cora assumes more significant dimensions. Revealing that love had caused her to excuse Norwood's faults and cling to him, she now repudiates him because his death threatens her son, who is even more precious to her. Unfortunately, as Hughes has written the scene, a reader is uncertain whether Cora is insane or is, for the first time, rationally aware of the manner in which she has been abused by Norwood. Regardless of the reason for her transformation, Cora, like all of Hughes's other heroines, appears more carefully delineated and more admirable than the male figures who dominate her life.

Even Colonel Norwood is interesting as a character. Although Hughes, writing protest drama, stereotyped him from racial bigots of his own day and slave masters of the previous century, Norwood gains reality in his final confrontation with Bert. Transcending racial identity, he becomes, like Hughes's own father, a man in conflict with his son. When Norwood cannot pull the trigger of his gun to kill Bert, Bert strangles him. Although Bert could only wonder why Norwood did not fire, a reader suspects, romantically perhaps, that, at the critical moment, Norwood realized that Bert was actually his flesh and blood, not merely a "yard child" whom he could ignore.

Despite the subject and the interesting characterizations of Bert and Cora, the play is weak artistically in plot structure, language, and thought. From the moment of Norwood's death, the action moves with the rapidity and inexorability of Greek tragedy. Prior to the death, however, it too frequently seems painfully slow and digressive. For example, Bert's sister Sally appears in Act I, talks, and then leaves for college.

Rather than contributing to the plot or background, she merely distracts the reader, who puzzles about the reason for her existence. One can almost argue artistic justification for the play's producer, who revised the play to cause Sally to miss her train in the first act and be raped in the third. Even though the producer was motivated by the commercial possibilities of sensationalism, he at least provided dramatic reason for Sally's presence and carried to their logical conclusion hints which Hughes planted casually and forgot.

Hughes forgot some other matters in the drama. From the opening scene onward, he reiterated the fact that Norwood does not permit Negroes to use the front door. Negro servants who haul a huge trunk down the front hall steps are required to carry it out the back door. When Norwood learns that Bert frequently enters through the front door, he threatens to break Bert's neck. Nevertheless, only a few moments after Norwood has voiced his threat, a Negro servant helps his master enter through the front door and leaves through the same portal. Nothing in the stage directions indicates that Norwood pays any attention to this dark transgression of his hallowed sill.

Because Hughes was a talented poet, it is difficult to understand his apparent insensitivity to language and to effective usage in *Mulatto*. His faults are various. "Kid" and "old man" seem inappropriate slang for rural Georgia of the early 1930's. Even more incongruous is the use of "papa." Norwood slapped seven-year-old Bert for calling him "papa." One wonders how the word came into Bert's vocabulary since no one else in the play uses it. Cora uses "daddy" and "pappy." Bert's brother says, "Pa." Norwood says, "Pappy." Even Bert himself fails to use the counterpart when addressing his mother. He calls her "Ma."

Other words are questionable. It is doubtful that a South-

erner would use "lynching" to describe an activity in which
he participated. It is improbable that Norwood would emphasize his own immorality by calling his son a bastard. It is
unnecessary for the overseer to inform the audience that he
will form a posse from *white* men.

Quibbling about words may seem petty criticism of a
writer. Nevertheless, one assumes that a poet, more than other
writers perhaps, would exercise care in selecting words. Occasionally but too infrequently, Hughes demonstrated ability
to use language effectively when he chose to. The most appealing scene in the play is that in which Cora, in a monologue, recalls her early relationship with Norwood. The
speech rings true in every respect. It is colloquial, faithfully
representative of the dialect of Southern Negroes, and poetic.
Hughes also demonstrated incisive use of language in the
ironic moment at which a Negro servant, disregarding Norwood's five Negro children, agrees with a white under-
taker's assertion that Norwood had no relatives.

Part of Hughes's difficulty with language resulted from his
desire to be certain that spectators understood the full implications of the characters' statements. In order to assure himself that no one would miss the point, Hughes sometimes
overstated it. For example, Norwood, explaining his financial
security, says that he has "a few thousand put away." A
wealthy man who is not boasting would probably say merely
that he has a few *dollars* put away. But Hughes wanted the
spectator to realize Norwood's wealth. Similarly, Higgins, a
white man, says, "All this postwar propaganda on the radio
about freedom and democracy—why the niggers think it's
meant for them." Psychologically, the statement is false. A
bigot would not verbalize his awareness of a difference between the condition of the Negro and America's promise to
its citizens. In fact, he probably would not be aware of any

difference. But Hughes, using a white man as mouthpiece, wanted to emphasize the discrepancy in the minds of his audience.

Finally, in *Mulatto*, Hughes slipped into improbable contradictions which sometimes are amusing. For instance, to emphasize the sacredness of the Colonel's library, Cora says that even she has never been permitted to enter it in thirty years. Surely someone, however, cleaned the room at least once during that time. Certainly, Colonel Norwood was not a man to clean and dust a room; certainly also, the individual who most probably would be assigned the task would be Cora, the most trusted servant.

Not amusing, but even more improbable, is the picture of life in the Norwood house. Except for allusions to contemporary personalities and inventions, one might assume that the story was set in the antebellum South. For instance, there is never any mention of paying the servants. Surely, however, most working Negroes in Georgia in 1930 at least touched the money they earned even if they immediately handed it on to a creditor.

Little Ham, written during the thirties, is set in the Harlem Renaissance of the twenties. Webster Smalley, in the preface of *Five Plays by Langston Hughes*, has described it as a folk comedy. To a Negro reader, however, it is a slow-moving, frequently dull, artificial attempt to present within a single play all of the exotic elements which distinguish life in Harlem from life in the rest of America. Here, jumbled together like the animals in a box of animal crackers, are shoe shiners, beauticians, numbers runners, homosexuals, West Indians, followers of Father Divine, gangsters, middle-class Negroes. They cut, shoot, drink, make love, gossip, play numbers, flirt, but rarely utter a significant thought.

The slight and confused story, better suited for musical

comedy where it might be obscured by attractive songs and dances, recounts the adventures of Hamlet Hitchcock Jones, a "sporty" ladies' man. When Little Ham, who flirts with all women, meets fat Tiny Lee, a beauty parlor owner, his conversation ends in a promise to escort her to a Charleston contest the following evening. Soon afterwards, he purchases a stolen coat for his new girlfriend, wins $645 playing the numbers and is given a job as a numbers runner. When he visits Tiny at her shop, he is surprised to find Mattie Bea, his married girlfriend, who, expecting to accompany him, bought the contest tickets which Ham has given to Tiny and who believes that Ham will give her the stolen coat which he has already given to Tiny. When she discovers the true situation, she attacks Tiny; but Ham is arrested by the police, who assume that he is beating her. Later, Gilbert, Tiny's former boyfriend, visits her apartment to take her to the Charleston contest. His efforts are interrupted by the arrival of Ham, who has secured his release from jail by charming a female judge. To forestall trouble, Tiny hides Gilbert in a closet and locks him in. Still later, at the dance, Mattie Bea and Gilbert, both arriving late, threaten to continue their quarrels with Tiny and Ham. Coincidentally, however, it is revealed that Mattie Bea and Gilbert are husband and wife. Finding themselves together for a change, they become reconciled, and all the couples participate in a frenzied Charleston contest, which is won by Ham and Tiny.

A play with such insignificant action needs to be redeemed by characterization, language, humor, or thought. *Little Ham*, unfortunately, is weak in each of these.

The language probably is the most effective element of the play. In the Harlem dialect and slang, with which he was familiar, Hughes wrote more freely and more accurately than in *Mulatto*. The language constitutes a significant source for the humor of the play. Hughes wrote effective quips: "She is just a used blade, and I got a new razor"; "I don't duel, I duke"; "love is taking 'til you can't give no mo." Hughes also drew comedy from the strangeness of the Harlem dialect—"she-self," "perzactly"—and from such malapropisms as "reverted" (instead of "converted") and "prostitution" (instead of "prostration").

Like Zora Neale Hurston he assumed that non-Negro audiences would be amused by the colorful language of Negroes, especially the language of invective. This is effectively illustrated by Tiny's tirade directed towards Mattie Bea:

> Tiny: I'm a real good mama that can shake your
> peaches down. . . .
> I hear you cluckin', hen, but your nest
> must be far away. Don't try to lay no eggs
> in here.

Unfortunately, however, some of the expressions already had been overworked by the time Hughes wrote the play. Now they seem hackneyed: "I'm from Alabam, but I don't give a damn"; "God don't love ugly."

Hughes based his comedy almost as much on slapstick actions and situations, such as that in which Gilbert, locked inside a closet, quarrels with and shoots at Ham, who is outside. Hughes found humor in low comedy, such as the ridicule of the effeminate movements and cowardice of a homosexual and Tiny's accidental burning of the head of a middle-class woman who is her client. In general, the comedy is heavy rather than subtle.

The characterization too is heavy and stereotyped. Ham is a wise-cracking, fast-talking ladies' man. Tiny is fat, pleasant, and undistinguished. The other characters are such obvious types that Hughes frequently did not even name them. They are listed merely as "West Indian," "Staid Lady," "Youth," "Shabby Man," etc.

The action is heavily foreshadowed and overly dependent upon chance and coincidence. For example, the complicated love triangles of Tiny and Ham are eased by the improbable coincidence that their former lovers are married to each other. Motivation is puzzling. For example, although love is reputed to work marvels, a critical reader might wonder what attracts Ham to Tiny. Is he enchanted by her money, or is he conquered by her dominance? Without the necessary explanation, the incongruous pairing seems comic rather than sentimental.

Although serious ideas do not intrude upon the apparently continuous gaiety of the Harlemites, shadows of a troubled world appear at the edge of the gay and the comic. Such a shadow is the pathetic joy of the Shabby Man, who has secured a job for the first time in two years. Such a shadow appears in the wish-fantasies and self-delusions of the numbers players who, praying for the one wonderful windfall, overlook the vast sums which they are dribbling away by daily dimes and quarters. Shadowy too are social protests: a janitor's complaint about long hours, the silence of Madam Lucille and Ham when police, without a warrant, search the shoeshine parlor for evidence of gambling.

Don't You Want To Be Free? also written in the thirties, is a poetic drama—or, more appropriately, a pageant—which traces the history of the American Negro from the original enslavement to the Depression. The scenes are predictable—a slave auction, a slave rebellion which ends in massacre. Nevertheless, effective narration provides pride for Negro spectators by recounting Negroes who struggled for freedom— Nat Turner, Denmark Vesey, Harriet Tubman, Sojourner Truth. Furthermore, Hughes effectively underscored the emotion by using lyrics and melodies of spirituals and the blues. A product of the thirties, however, the pageant overemphasizes a call for a uniting of the workers of the world. In language and in thought, the play was the most artistic which Hughes had written, but its obvious aiming at a Negro audience made it unsuitable for commercial production on Broadway.

The Sun Do Move (1942) echoes, expands, individualizes, and dramatizes the thought which was narrated in *Don't You Want To Be Free?* After two Negro porters strip to reassume their identity as Africans, the play begins with the auction of two young Africans, Rock and Mary. After a period of time Rock is sold before he has time to see the birth of his child. On the new plantation, he becomes friends with Frog and resists the advances of Bellinda, who has been chosen as his new mate. When they attempt to escape, Frog is killed and Rock is recaptured. Meanwhile, on the other plantation, Mary, Rock's wife, has reared their son. When Little Rock attempts to protect his mother from her mistress's brutality, he is sent to another plantation, where he dies. Escaping again, Rock this time reaches Mary and, with her, flees to the North, where assisted by Quakers, they become free.

Despite structural weaknesses caused by cinematic flashes from scenes of Rock to those of Mary or Little Rock and despite Hughes's characteristic interpolations of irrelevant low comedy, the play is much more forceful and dramatically interesting than the earlier one. The dispassionate historicity of the pageant is emotionalized by Hughes's focus upon Mary and Rock, struggling to live as human beings rather than chattel.

Simply Heavenly (1957), designed for the commercial theater, reached Broadway in a state weaker than *Simple Takes a Wife*, the book upon which the play was based. The major sufferer in the adaptation is Jesse B. Semple himself. In the tales and dialogues of the Simple books, Jess assumes the dimensions of a folk hero. Even though he drinks, cavorts with women, has difficulty paying rent, talks ungrammatically and excessively, his foibles never detract from his dignity; for, like the Greek gods and the heroes of various myths, he is larger than life. It may be appropriate even to say that he, like Joseph Conrad's Kurtz, is remembered primarily as a voice, in this instance a voice which utters common sense even when the speaker seems emotional and illogical. Reduced to actable dimensions, however, Simple, losing his grandeur, shrinks into a more sincere, more conservative, and more thoughtful Ham. In the play, he peeks beneath his legs to watch Joyce, his fiancée, change clothes; he turns somersaults; he is thrown from a car to land on his "sit-downer"; he is propped comically in a hospital bed with his legs in traction; sentimentally and pathetically, he tries to reform and to win Joyce. In short, Simple's reality as the embodied spirit of the Negro working class is reduced to the Harlem barfly; the Chaplinesque Comic Hero shrinks to a farcical fall guy of the pattern of Stan Laurel and Lou Costello.

The second major injury resulting from the transformation from the book to the play is suffered by the material itself. Even though incidents occur in the book, they generally serve merely as acceptable devices to generate Simple's philosophizing. Consequently, what matters is not what happens but what reaction it stimulates from Simple. For a Broadway musical, however, it was necessary to emphasize action and to minimize Simple's reflections. As a result, undue attention is given to Simple's unsuccessful efforts to seduce Joyce, to the Watermelon Man's pursuit of Mamie, and to the domestic difficulties of Bodidilly and Arcie.

Judged merely in its own terms, however, without reference to the Simple material which it distorts and cheapens, *Simply Heavenly* is vastly superior to *Little Ham*. Simple is more likable than Ham. Joyce and Zarita are less grotesque than Tiny, whose type reappears in Mamie, a secondary lead.

Similarly, the ideas of *Simply Heavenly* have significance missing from *Little Ham*, where Harlemites seemed to concern themselves only with numbers, gossip, parties, sex, and killing. In fact, the differences in *Simply Heavenly* underscore the fact that *Little Ham* was intended as a commercial exploitation of Harlem's exoticism rather than as a presentation of its actuality. In *Simply Heavenly*, the people occupy the same socioeconomic level as those in *Little Ham*; they take interest in numbers, gossip, parties, and sex; but they also think and talk about racial problems, economic problems, and domestic problems.

Hughes reacted sensitively to the allegation that he had stereotyped the characters of his earlier books and plays. When a middle-class man says that the denizens of Paddy's Bar are stereotypes, Mamie, defender of the race, answers furiously:

> Why, it's getting so colored folks can't do nothing no more without some other Negro calling you a stereotype. Stereotype, hah! If you like a little gin, you're a stereotype. You got to drink Scotch. If you wear a red dress, you're a stereotype. You got to wear beige or chartreuse. Lord have mercy, honey, do-don't like no blackeyed peas and rice! Then you're a down-home Negro for true—which I is—and proud of it! I didn't come here to Harlem to get away from my people. I come here because there's more of 'em. I loves my race. I loves my people. Stereotype!

Nevertheless, it is true that Hughes generally created stereotypes. Even in *Simply Heavenly*, Hughes clung to gross, time-honored models. Joyce is a loving but prim heroine, who probably will become a shrew. A good-hearted, fun-loving girl, who wears her morals loosely, Zarita is from a tradition as old as literature itself.

Both comedy and language seem improved in *Simply Heavenly*. In addition to writing better quips, Hughes, writing lyrics for songs, was able to display his poetic talent more persuasively than in earlier plays. Using the contemporary idiom of Harlem, he created a free and natural dialogue, sometimes rising to colloquial eloquence, as in Simple's recollection of his aunt's efforts to reform him.

Despite the improvement, Hughes continued to relish sentimentality and farce which too frequently detract from the reality of the characters. For example, it is difficult to believe Boyd's honesty when he describes Simple's crying at night.

During the sixties, Hughes worked on his two best plays—*Emperor of Haiti* and *Tambourines to Glory*. *Emperor of Haiti* was a generation old. Hughes first presented it as *Drums of Haiti* (1936), rewrote it as *Troubled Island*, an opera, revised it further, and completed his final revisions in 1963, shortly before he presented a script to the Schomburg Collection in Harlem.

Emperor of Haiti is the story of Jean Jacques Dessalines' progress from slave to emperor to corpse. Beginning during the Haitian blacks' rebellion against their French masters and treating historical fact freely, the play focuses on the economic and personal problems of Dessalines' rule as emperor. Economically, the kingdom suffers because Dessalines refuses to require labor from the liberated blacks. When he finally realizes the need, they turn against him. Personally, Dessalines fails in Hughes's play because, after becoming emperor, he rejects his uneducated wife Azelea, who loves him. In her place, he takes Claire Heureuse, a pawn of the mulattoes who seek to overthrow him. The play climaxes and ends when, riding to crush a rebellion, Dessalines is killed in the trap set by mulattoes. Melodramatically, Azelea, now a penniless street seller, discovers his body and mourns his death while Claire flees with her mulatto lover, and two passing Haitians fail to recognize their emperor.

The play has artistic and historical flaws. As in much of Hughes's drama, low comic relief is overworked while the plot lags. For instance, prior to the climactic arrival of Dessalines at the trap, street sellers talk and joke interminably. Furthermore, history is distorted. Although Toussaint is mentioned, the play suggests that Dessalines is the only leader of the slaves' rebellion. Moreover, Dessalines' character is given a moral bath. The libertinism which characterized Dessalines after his becoming emperor is reduced to his affair with Claire Heureuse.

Nevertheless, the historical events provided Hughes with plot, thought, and character superior to those which generally emerged from his imagination. Although Azelea is perhaps idealized as a devoted, self-sacrificing wife, Dessalines is well-drawn, even in outline.

Hughes's final play, *Tambourines to Glory*, was adapted from his novel of the same name. It is a modernized morality play and, as such, is surprisingly good. To make money, Laura Reed, a gay girl like Zarita, persuades staid, religious Essie Johnson to join her in establishing a church. They are assisted and protected by Big-Eyed Buddy Lomax, who actually is the Devil. Gradually Laura slips further and further into sin as Buddy's mistress. She swells membership by giving tips on numbers; she sells tap water as holy water. Vainly, she tries to thwart Buddy's pursuit of Gloria, a singer, and Marietta, Essie's teen-aged niece. Finally, fearing him, Laura stabs Buddy. Essie is arrested but released when Laura confesses. Laura is charged with manslaughter.

There is more development in this plot than in any Hughes had written previously; and, although the action is tinged with melodrama, it is free from the irrelevant comedy and improbable coincidence which characterize most of Hughes's work. The characters are not new, but they are smoothly delineated—perhaps because Hughes's frequent recreation of the same types enabled him to know them fully. As has been explained, Laura is modeled after Zarita, and Essie is a quieter, more mature, less attractive Joyce.

More than in any work since *Don't You Want To Be Free?* Hughes used poetry to develop thought. Instead of being entertaining diversions, as in *Simply Heavenly*, the lyrics of the songs explain the motivation and personalities of the characters. For example, Laura sings her love for Buddy; Buddy sings the blues characterizing life in Harlem; Marietta sings her purity.

Perhaps the chief reason for Hughes's success is that the musical morality play permitted him to display his major talents without straining the credulity of the audience. Stereotyped characters and heavy underlining of ideas are accepted in morality plays, and colloquial poetry and broad comedy have a place in musicals.

As Webster Smalley has pointed out, Langston Hughes must be credited with establishing several all-Negro professional dramatic groups. In doing so, he contributed significantly to the development of American drama. In his own work, however, even though he continued to write and to be produced through two generations, he never developed the artistry of a first-rate playwright. Least successful when he catered to the predictable taste of Broadway audiences, he was most artistic when he wrote simply and lyrically of the history and aspirations of black people.

NOT WITHOUT LAUGHTER
BUT WITHOUT TEARS

By William Edward Farrison

James Mercer Langston Hughes first achieved prominence in
the school of fiction writers of the Harlem Renaissance when
Not Without Laughter, his first published novel, appeared in
1930. The history of the writing of this novel began more
than two years before it was published, while its author was
still a student at Lincoln University. As Hughes did not tell
in his account of the novel in his *The Big Sea* (pp. 303–306),
by the spring of 1928 he had written a considerable part of
an extremely realistic, if not naturalistic, story with his early
life as a background. He showed this work to the wife of
one of the Lincoln professors, a lady of sound though somewhat conservative literary interests. The lady urged him by
all means to refine it. This was the story which he rewrote
in 1928 and 1929 and developed into *Not Without Laughter.*
In the winter of 1929 and 1930 he made the final revisions
of it.

    Not Without Laughter has been generally favorably criti-
cized, although some weaknesses in it have been pointed out.
V. F. Calverton, an avant-garde critic of the era of the
Harlem Renaissance who was much better informed concerning Negro writers than many of his contemporaries, observed
in the *Nation* (August 6, 1930) that the characters in the

story enlivened it "with that quick and intimate reality which is seldom seen in American fiction." Calverton discovered, however, "no great situations in the novel, no high points of intensity to grip and overpower the reader," nor vigor in its style. "The Browsing Reader" in the *Crisis* (September, 1930) said that the story was "realistic and close to human beings," but that because of its emphasis on character rather than on plot, it was without the probability of holding "the sustained interest of most readers. It touches dirt," that reader continued, "but is not dirty," and "it is well written." Writing in *Opportunity: Journal of Negro Life* (September, 1930), Sterling A. Brown discerned in the novel "the simplicity of great art"; and with the exception of Tempy, who seemed to him "slightly caricatured," he considered all of the characters in the story "completely convincing."

Eleven years after publication, in his book, *Intellectual America: Ideas on the March* (p. 511), Oscar Cargill classified the novel as "one of the best fictional treatments of the Negro in American letters." Still later Hugh M. Gloster said that "the leading characters in the book are ably delineated." In his opinion, which he expressed in his book, *Negro Voices in American Fiction* (p. 187), "the chief merit of the novel, however, is its detached but sympathetic story of the life of a colored youth."

Probably the most superficial and the worst criticism accorded *Not Without Laughter* is found in Robert Bone's *The Negro Novel in America*. Bone's book, whose critical method is ridiculously mechanical—as if works of art can be measured with foot rules—suffers very badly from what may be called, after the manner of the pathologists, chronic symbolitis. Here, there, and almost everywhere else Bone saw symbols or illusions thereof in almost every work he attempted to discuss. His identification of illusory symbols reached the height of absurdity when he says of *Not Without*

Laughter that "Laughter is the central symbol of the novel—
the complex, ironic laughter which is the Negro's saving response to racial oppression. The characters cluster around
the poles of laughter and not-laughter"—whatever the hyphe-
nated word means. On the same page he says that "The
author [Hughes] sets out to make a defense of laughter."

Perhaps Bone knows who *the* Negro is, but there is ample
room for doubt that he does. The present writer has been
classified as a Negro all of his life, and he has known well
many Negroes, but he has never known anyone who could be
identified as the (typical?) Negro; nor has he known anyone
else classified as a Negro who could identify such a Negro.

Only want of information concerning the origin of the
title of *Not Without Laughter* insulated with a careless reading of it could have betrayed anyone into making the statements of Bone's quoted above. As Bone has perhaps never
known, the book was ready for the press before it was given
its present title. This is to say that while Hughes was writing
the story, he was not trying to symbolize anything about
laughter nor to develop laughter of any kind as a theme—
certainly not as a distinctive racial theme. For he knew
very well that throughout the history of civilization non-
Negroes as well as Negroes have often laughed in the face
of trouble to keep from crying as well as to express pleasure
and happiness.

Indeed, as has been said, it is not improbable that not
Hughes but one of his publisher's readers gave the book its
title, taking it from a teen-age reflection of Sandy Rogers (or
Rodgers), the principal character in the story. In his hometown Sandy had observed life for a short time in a pool
hall frequented by adventurers, vagabonds, denizens of the
town, and others. From them he had heard popular songs,
arguments, tall stories and the like always interspersed with
good-natured laughter. He supposed, therefore, apparently

without much regard for the logic of cause and effect, that the reason why "poverty-stricken old Negroes like Uncle Dan Givens [a nonagenarian frequenter of the pool hall] lived so long" was that "to them, no matter how hard life might be, it was not without laughter." From the context here it appears that Sandy was referring to laughter indicative of happiness.

About the same time Sandy heard his thrifty uncle-in-law assert dogmatically that Negroes were only minstrels, dancers, jazzers, and clowns, and that because of this fact they were poor. As Sandy thought later about his uncle-in-law's assertion, he disagreed with it. Taking an entirely different point of view, he came to believe that Negroes were "dancers because of their poverty; singers because they suffered; laughing all the time because they must forget." Apparently, here it was a matter of laughing to keep from crying. Nevertheless, on the basis of individual observations which were necesarily narrowly limited, neither Sandy nor his uncle-in-law nor their creator could have generalized convincingly about Negroes and laughter.

In the previously mentioned account of the novel in *The Big Sea*, Hughes explained that "I wanted to write about a typical Negro family in the Middle West, about people like those I had known in Kansas." He was cognizant, as he said, that his was not a typical Negro family. Accordingly, assuming that he had been a typical Negro boy, "for purposes of the novel," he said, in his autobiography, *The Big Sea* (pp. 303–304), "I created around myself what seemed to me a family more typical of Negro life in Kansas than my own had been." In doing this he followed the well-established practice of writers of fiction who drew their characters from actual life. He modeled his characters after persons he had known or heard of principally in Lawrence, Kansas, during his boyhood there. That was during most of the first fifteen years of the present century. In the story Lawrence is called Stanton.

Sandy Rogers was, of course, Hughes himself. He was of the same age as Hughes was. He "was the shade of a nicely browned piece of toast, with dark brown-black eyes and a head of rather kinky, sandy hair that would lie smooth only after a rigorous application of vaseline and water." Annjee (or Annjelica) Rogers, his mother, seemed to share with Hughes's mother the apparently "fixed idea that a son is born for the sole purpose of taking care of his parents as soon as possible." Both mothers thought that their sons should quit school and work in order to help their mothers financially. Jimboy Rogers, the guitar-playing husband of Annjee and father of Sandy, had at least one notable habit in common with Homer Clark, Hughes's stepfather. This was the habit of constantly wandering in quest of a satisfactory job and simultaneously ignoring the contingency of domestic happiness upon domestic responsibility.

The *mater familias* of the family Hughes created was Aunt Hager Williams, the mother of Annjee and two other daughters—Tempy, the oldest, and Harriett, the youngest. As Hughes's grandmother, Mrs. Mary Sampson Patterson Langston, a widow, did for him while his mother worked in various places, Aunt Hager, also a widow, took care of Sandy during most of his first thirteen years while Annjee worked in domestic service. After Aunt Hager died, Sandy's aunt Tempy kept him with her until his mother took him with her, just as Auntie and Uncle Reed of Lawrence kept Hughes with them after Mrs. Langston died, until his mother took him to live with her and her second husband. The Reeds, however, were not relatives but friends of Hughes's grandmother. Auntie Reed, who was a faithful churchwoman, compelled Hughes to go regularly to church with her, and thus her determination doubtless became the model for Aunt Hager's efforts to bring Sandy up in the church.

Mrs. Langston and Aunt Hager found themselves in similar impoverished circumstances in Lawrence and Stanton respectively, but they were altogether different kinds of persons with radically different backgrounds. Mrs. Langston, who was educated, had always been free. Her first husband, Sheridan Leary, was a cohort of John Brown in the raid on Harpers Ferry and was killed there. She was proud and independent in spirit. Although she was often in dire need, she neither washed nor cooked for white people, as many other Negro women in Lawrence did. On the contrary, Aunt Hager, who was not educated, had been a slave in the deep South until the Civil War ended slavery. Humble and lowly as she was, she supported her household in Stanton for many years by taking in washing. Although she knew that slavery was "no paradise," she remembered her antebellum life somewhat sentimentally and without ill feelings for either slaveholders or their descendants. She was all too aware of racism on the part of the white people in Stanton, but she was convinced that there were some good white people in the town.

Being practical-minded and thoroughly if primitively religious, Aunt Hager had learned well the New Testament philosophy of Christian love and had tried to implant it in the minds of her daughters. She had not succeeded at all in doing so, however, as far as Harriett, now a little more than sixteen years old, was concerned. Because of the active anti-Negro sentiment that pervaded Stanton, Harriett and other young Negroes in the town hated white people. Nevertheless, Aunt Hager was still endeavoring to instill the philosophy of Christian love in Sandy. Looking back on her life of "mighty nigh seventy years," she told him that "when you gets old, you knows they ain't no sense in gettin' mad an' sourin' yo' soul with hatin' peoples . . . Ever'thing there is but lovin' leaves a rust on yo' soul" (pp. 189, 194).

For Aunt Hager life had been not merely real and earnest, it had been exceedingly difficult. She had demanded but little from it for herself, however, and had made herself satisfied with what she got. She had tried very hard to bring her three daughters up right, but for reasons probably beyond her ken, all of them had fallen below her hopes. As a result of her prosperity and inordinate desire for social respectability, Tempy had become a snob, who was embarrassed to own her mother and sisters. In order to give the child she had conceived a legal surname, Annjee had been compelled to marry a man who loved playing a guitar and wandering more than he loved work, and who gave neither her nor their child anything but love—and not a great deal of that. Harriett had not only become antireligious but was also headed for the life of a show girl and membership for a while in Rehab's profession. Aunt Hager's ambition was now for her grandson, whom she wanted to get an education so that he might be a credit to his race, like Booker T. Washington or Frederick Douglass. All things considered, Aunt Hager emerges in the story as a sterling and admirable character who is rivaled in vividness and interest only by Sandy.

As Hughes himself must have realized, Aunt Hager's household typified only one class of Negro families, the class presently described as culturally deprived, or economically disadvantaged. Tempy and her husband, Arkins Siles, a railway mail clerk, represented a more fortunate but comparatively small class—the Negro middle class. Both of them owned real estate when they married, and their combined resources assured them a comfortable income. Their level of existence and their values were essentially the same as those of the white middle class. They had a bathroom with running water in it. Tempy had changed from the Baptist to the

Episcopal church; "she got her recipes from *The Ladies'
Home Journal*—and she never bought a watermelon" (p. 254).
Whether or not one considers her characterization unconvincing, as Brown did, it appears that Hughes intentionally
satirized in her some of the members of the Negro middle
class.

As has been indicated, Sandy is the principal character in
Not Without Laughter, although he has not always been
recognized as such. From the beginning of the action in
Stanton in his tenth year to its end in Chicago in his sixteenth
year, when he is not in the foreground, he is clearly in the
background. It is what he said and did and what was said
and done with reference to him that give continuity to the
story. At the beginning of the action, one afternoon while
Aunt Hager was at home alone with only Sandy, a cyclone
carried her front porch away, as a similar storm had once
done with Mrs. Langston's front porch. During the brief
and violent tempest, her little grandson's safety rather than
her own was Aunt Hager's chief concern.

Beginning with this event, the story carries Sandy through
six years of varied experiences incident to a Negro boy's
growing up early in the present century in a town in Kansas,
where Negro life was narrowly proscribed by racism, poverty, and conservatism. There were his learning experiences
with his playmates and schoolmates. Among these were
Jimmy Lane, who was three years older than he, and who
often led him astray; Willie-Mae Johnson, who partly educated him concerning "how girls were different from boys";
and Buster, who was more than half-white, and whose mulatto mother had difficulty keeping him colored. From his
experience with Pansetta Young, a beautiful high-school classmate with whom he thought himself in love for a while, he
learned that innocence was not always a companion of
beauty.

Sandy and other Negro children in Stanton were taught in separate schoolrooms by Negro teachers until they passed the fourth grade. In the fifth grade he and his Negro classmates were seated by their white teacher behind the white students and out of alphabetical order. One summer day, when he, Willie-Mae Johnson, and other Negro children tried to attend a free children's day party in a new amusement park, they were told that the party was for white children only. Buster, however, was taken for a white boy and was admitted to the party. Experiences both in and out of school impressed upon Sandy the cruelty of racial discrimination and prompted him to say that "Being colored is like being born in the basement of life, with the door to the light locked and barred—and the white folks live upstairs." The more he learned about racial matters in Stanton, the more sympathetically he viewed Buster's resolution to go to some big city in a few years and pass for white so that he might prosper economically. He would not need to worry about being smart, he assured Sandy, since he would be white. Buster's implication was that an incapable white man had better opportunities to succeed than a capable Negro. (Buster's resolution foreshadowed the story in "Passing" in Hughes's *The Ways of White Folks*.)

Sometimes, indeed, Sandy hated white people, as his Aunt Harriett said she did. Yet his occasional contact with Earl James, a white classmate and friend, and with one of his teachers of English reminded him that kindness did sometimes transcend race, and that there were some good white people in Stanton, as Aunt Hager said that there were. Such sobering reflections on Sandy's part, withal, were only transitory, for as far as he could see, whoever the good white people were, their goodness did nothing to eliminate discrimination against Negroes where jobs and civil rights were concerned. Had the action in *Not Without Laughter* been set in Stanton in the third quarter of the present century, Sandy might have identified most of the good white people in the town as members of what is now known as the good but silent and uninfluential majority.

It is somewhat surprising that Calverton with his critical insight did not discover any great situations or high points of intensity in the novel. Perhaps he was looking for what he should not have expected to find in it. In this realistic story of a Negro boy's growing up in a specific setting in place and time, the greatness and intensity of situations were necessarily determined by the boy's experiences and his reactions to them, not simply by the situations in themselves. Admittedly various occasions, whether new or old, have taught various duties, but frequently it has been the duties necessitated which have lent importance to the occasions rather than the other way around. Considered in the light of these facts, some of Sandy's situations were both great and intense—as great and intense as consistency in the story made possible.

One of these situations involved the Christmas story concerning a sled. Not long before Christmas, Sandy informed Annjee and Aunt Hager that he wanted Santa Claus to bring him one of the Golden Flyer sleds he had seen on display in a local hardware store. Because they had no money with which to buy a sled but did not want to disappoint him, Annjee and Aunt Hager had a carpenter to make him one gratis which looked embarrassingly homemade. Having seen it secretly the night before Christmas, he did not wish to see it on Christmas morning, but he had to hold back his tears, handle it, and conceal his unhappiness behind a smile. He knew that his mother and grandmother had no money with which to buy a Golden Flyer sled, and that they had done the best they could do for him. What now must he do—hurt their feelings by showing ingratitude or hurt himself by pretending to happiness which he did not feel? Instantly he acted wisely, heroically. He sacrificed his own feelings to theirs. " 'It's a nice sled, grandma,' he lied. 'I like it, mama.' " One can hardly imagine a more difficult moment for a boy of ten or twelve years than the trice in which Sandy repeatedly but unconvincingly assured his grandmother and mother that he liked the homemade sled.

Another situation possessed of a high point of intensity and of diabolical greatness, if of no other kind, was that which culminated in Sandy's quitting his job as bootblack and handy boy at the Drummer's Hotel. One winter night one of a group of white men in the hotel lobby, a drunk Mississippian, called Sandy names and tried to taunt him into dancing, foolishly assuming that all Negroes could dance. Sandy explained that he could not dance, and angered by the men's Negro jokes and the name-calling, he picked up his bootblack's box and started away from the group without collecting for having polished the Mississippian's shoes. Just then the Mississippian grabbed him roughly by an arm to detain him, whereupon with a loud yell he broke away and ran to the street entrance. There, before anyone could reach him, he turned, raised his bootblack's box high above his head, and hurled it furiously at the group, which had been laughing at him. As bottles of polish, cans, and brushes clattered across the lobby, Sandy disappeared in the darkness of the street. If Sandy's act in ending the encounter with the drunk Mississippian was not greatly heroic, it at least amounted to poetic justice.

When Hughes wrote *Not Without Laughter*, he had not yet had sufficient experience as an author to be a noteworthy prose stylist. Nor is it probable that he thought at the time of trying to be one. He simply tried, doubtless, to harmonize his ideas and his expression of them so as to make what he said clear and interesting. He did this very well, although certainly not perfectly.

To portray illiterate and semiliterate Negro characters, Hughes represented their speech with what is commonly called Negro dialect. In *Not Without Laughter,* as in ever so many other works, this amounts principally to mutilated spellings which represent nobody's actual speech. Such spellings, for example, as *ma* for both "mama" and "my," *yuh're* for "you are," and the exclamations *Umnhuh* and *Whoa* give no clear idea of how Hughes heard these words pronounced. Also, in omitting postvocalic *r* from such words as *boa'd, fo',* and *sho'* for "board," "four," and "sure" respectively, he differed from Midwestern pronunciation, where *r* in this position has long been commonly pronounced as a part of a centering diphthong in both standard and substandard English. This pronunciation has not been limited by race, for as philologists have long known, dialects are not scientifically distinguishable by race—whatever "race" means—but by regions and classes. Much better than Hughes's Negro dialect is his representation of substandard usage by grammatical peculiarities such as the use of *is* for the first and second person singular of the present tense of *to be,* of *were* for the first person singular of the indicative past tense of the same verb, and the addition of *-s* to the first and second persons singular of the present tense of many common verbs.

Everywhere in the novel the writing is distinguished by simplicity, by the absence of rhetorical flourishes. Here and there, however, occur graphic expressions such as "de Battle-Ax of de Lawd," an epithet which refers to a certain preacher, and the remarks that the social outcasts in Stanton "ceased to struggle against the boundaries between good and bad" and "hung no curtain of words between themselves and reality." There is some uncertainty, of course, about the pronunciations represented by *de* and *Lawd*, especially by the second word, in which *w* has been substituted for post-vocalic *r*. With the exception of a few instances, notably in Jimboy Rogers' songs, the novel is without humor apart from that generated by satire. The want of extensive humor, however, can hardly be considered a fault in a book, for except in an intentionally humorous work, an author is not bound to be humorous.

Strangely enough, criticism of *Not Without Laughter* has generally overlooked the fact that it is an important social document as well as a literary work. It is a boy's story but it is something more than that. It is a clear exposure of many of the ramifications of racism and of their traumatic effects especially upon children. It is thus an indirect but nonetheless obvious protest against racism. It is an argument by means of narration, which appeals as much to the intelligence and the conscience of the reader as to his emotions.

As far as matters racial were concerned, the Kansas of the time in which the action in the novel was set had much more in common with Mississippi than with Massachusetts—a fact which adds no luster to the history of Kansas. Moreover, at the time of the publication of the novel, various degrees of the kinds of racism exposed in it were common throughout the United States—as they still are in many parts of it. Racial discrimination was taken for granted by many and was not really considered an evil—or if an evil, a necessary evil about which little or nothing could be done earlier than halfway between then and never.

If *Not Without Laughter* had first appeared some twenty years later, after changes resulting in a large measure from World War II outmoded the doctrine of racial inferiority and emphasized anew the democratic ideal, it probably would have shared honors as a protest novel with much of the best-known fiction of this kind which has been published since

1950. If it had appeared while the case now known as *Brown* v. *the Board of Education of Topeka, Kansas,* was before the United States Supreme Court, and if its frank and objective portrayal of racial discrimination in the schools of Stanton (actually Lawrence) had been cited before the court, it would have helped to document the long-existing complaints of the petitioners in those cases.

On one occasion early in *Not Without Laughter,* Sandy heard the white woman for whom his mother cooked reprimand her for no very good reason. His mother answered quite humbly, but he became so angry that he cried without his mother's knowing why he cried. Some time later, when the fifth-grade teacher segregated him and his Negro classmates in the classroom, he felt like crying but did not cry, "because he was no longer a small boy." He was learning not to cry about racial discrimination, as Aunt Hager consolingly advised Willie-Mae Johnson not to do after the Negro children were refused admission to the new amusement park. Aunt Hager had long known, of course, that crying solved no problems, and that worthwhile daily living as well as occasional difficulties necessitated the best thought and actions one was capable of. These facts Sandy was also learning while he was learning about good and evil, about laughter and tears, and about life in general.

A WORD ABOUT SIMPLE

By Blyden Jackson

It is highly probable that Langston Hughes reached his most appreciative, as well as his widest, audience with a character whom he named, eponymously and with obvious relish, Jesse B. Semple. The *Jesse*, not too incidentally, clearly invited an abbreviation to Jess.

Simple made his bow to the world in the columns of the Chicago *Defender*, the Negro weekly which, in its heyday from early in World War I through the whole of World War II, circulated into virtually every nook and cranny of Negro America and, indeed, functioned as a sort of bible to many Negroes in every walk of Negro life. Via the columns of the *Defender*, then, Hughes addressed not so much the Negro elite, cultural or otherwise, but rather he spoke, powerfully and directly, to the very Negro of whom Simple was supposed to constitute an almost perfect replica. He spoke, that is, in great part to the black rank and file of our industrial Babylon, who may not be nearly so illiterate as their slave forebears, but who even now are still a far cry in their rapport with the world of books from the proverbial Harvard graduate.

Illiterate or not, however, these Negroes, a twentieth-century equivalent of Chaucer's fair field full of folk seem to have taken Simple to their hearts. They followed him week after week in the columns of the *Defender*. They gossiped about him with their associates. They found Simple understandable and comfortably convincing. True, they had not created Simple from an impulse originating in their own minds, nor made him what he became through arts which they had learned to practice, as, for instance, an earlier epoch of folk Negroes had created, and then, in effect, composed the Negro spiritual. In these senses, but only in these senses, Simple lacks the full authenticity of folk material. He was an adopted child, not a native son. Yet the attitude of his foster parents, the often so-called "common, ordinary" Negroes, toward him, their ready identification with him, suggests a special status of importance for his significance. Whether or not he is truly like most ordinary Negroes, he is certainly, in both form and substance, what many ordinary Negroes were at least once prepared to concede without rancor they thought they were. At least, to that extent, Simple must be accounted a folk Negro's concept of the folk Negro. Thus, too, he must be seriously considered a valuable specimen of Americana.

As such, it may well be noted first of Simple that he is a black man, highly visible with skin too dark, facial features too African, and hair too anything but lank, to be mistaken for an Aryan. He comes from Virginia, although in the days of his youth, when the Solid South (an admirable figure of speech) was still intact, there could be localities in Virginia as dismaying to Negroes as the worst counties in the heartland of the Old Confederacy. After a childhood in which he was, in his own words, "passed around" among his relatives—for, of his actual parents, he clearly never had much knowledge—he has gravitated to Harlem, with intermediate stops, during one of which he has married and "separated," that have qualified him for a true insider's view of a big-city Negro ghetto. Under the perspective of *multum in parvo*, indeed, his personal history typifies in several vital respects the sociological Negro of his class. He is the product of a broken home, out-migration from the South, and a disillusioning experience as a young and naïvely hopeful husband.

Put in the context of the environment forced upon him, Simple's efforts to express himself through the spoken word could hardly be expected to emanate from a well of English undefiled. As a matter of inescapable fact, he speaks a dialect. It is not that curious idiom, in which pronouns converted into "dises" and "dats" play a conspicuous role, so long associated with the synthetic Negro of blackface minstrelsy and the, until most recently, orthodox American dogmas about Negro behavior. That idiom, it probably should be observed, seemed determined to maintain the proposition that Negroes could not master the approved pronunciations of some English sounds either (or both) because of innate biological inadequacies in the organs of speech solely and irremediably attributable to the Negro's African blood, or (if not and) because the Negro ear, in its neurological inferiorities, simply could not properly hear the nuances of sound imparted to speech by a white tongue. But Simple talks as he does plainly because he has not had the benefit of living during his formative years where the people closest around him would have provided him with models of impeccable utterance. Nor has he had later much institutionalized linguistic aid that could have served as a corrective. In his own superbly succinct solecism, he has not been "colleged." He says usually (although puzzlingly enough, not invariably) "I were" for "I was." It is as if he has somehow established in his mind both an awareness of the interesting intelligence that verbs should be conjugated and an inclination so special to show his eagerness to comply with civilized procedures that he overdoes his willingness to inflect. Moreover, as with his peers whom one may encounter in such fictive haunts as those of *Invisible Man*, he has also a taste, as well as a positive knack, for either coining, or remembering, locutions that rhyme as they quip and that, in addition, are great fun to be savored as they are paraded over, and rolled around, the tongue.

Simple, in short, is a character who would clearly be something of a bull in a china shop in those purlieus of America frequented by the so-called best people. Nevertheless, even at his very worst he represents a great departure from the stereotypes of the Negro traditionally afloat in the common lore of the American mass intelligence. He is not Little Black Sambo grown up and existing half-wittedly in an urban setting beyond his resources to cope with, nor is he a brute, a demented apeman with a fearful affinity for lust and pillage, especially apropos the bodies and properties of persons more Nordic than himself. Indeed, quite to the contrary, he is an *ingénu* with very decent instincts, and a ruffian only in the sense that he is, underneath his gaucheries and his shortcomings, a diamond, unpolished and sometimes uncut.

He has, as has already been implied, reached maturity with little guidance after a childhood in humble circumstances. He did sojourn, as we have also seen, on his travels, in Baltimore long enough to have become involved with the wife from whom he has been estranged for a considerable time. His serious and sustained interest in the likable nice girl whom he is determined to wed, once he has secured the divorce the cost of which somewhat appalls him, testifies to his fundamental kinship with the Tom Joneses, rather than the Blifils, of this world. His vices might perturb an Anthony Comstock. They would hardly perturb an apostle of sweet reasonableness. He drinks a nightly beer. When he can get it, he is not averse to stronger stimulant. But he is, except on the rarest of occasions, only a mild inebriate, his addiction being controlled, indeed, both by his disposition and his purse. On the other hand, to speak the utter truth, he is also a great cadger of drinks, principally from the college-bred associate who is his boon companion at Simple's most accessible version of the Mermaid Tavern.

Even so, however, his addiction to the bottle, such as it is, is actually only the indulgence of a comradely spirit. At the bar, with the excuse of a slowly diminishing glass in his hand, and an attendant ear at his side, he assumes the role of genial philosopher which is his métier. For bitterness has not corroded him as it has Bigger Thomas in Wright's *Native Son* or Rufus Scott, Baldwin's victim in *Another Country*. It is a human comedy which Simple passes in review in his castle of indolence at his Harlem rendezvous, not an unrelieved panorama of hopeless gloom and horrors. Things happen in Simple's world sometimes for the best, all too often for the worst, although there is a tendency for the good things to come to good people just when the bad things are about to become unbearable, and, always, for the common lot of man, the good and the bad are tempered, and their deviations in any direction mediated toward a neutral ground, by laughter, the superb and therapeutic acknowledgment by the human intellect that frailties of many kinds are endemic to the human condition.

Nor is Simple's laughter an assault on others. It is, like his petty bibulousness, companionable. He laughs with his fellows, at their foibles, and at his own. When he recounts his wooing of his wife and the subsequent gradual disintegration of his marriage, he is at least as much the target of his own satirical thrusts as anyone else. When his young cousin just out of high school, Franklin D. Roosevelt Brown, appears, to discomfit him momentarily, and then to win his only apparently grudging approval, it is his own slack habits which he reviews for exposure to good-humored ridicule as much as his young cousin's impetuosities. Moreover, as it does develop that he rather likes playing the role of a father, or an older uncle, to his young kinsman, and, even, that he plays both roles rather well, the sardonic self-deprecations with which he dismisses his virtuous behavior confirm the verdict of his relations with the girl who is his intended, that he is essentially made of the salt of the earth, that his deeper instincts substantiate democracy's trust in the average man, that he even has dreams, big dreams of a noble nature, which, if he cannot always articulate them, or even admit publicly to their possession without some self-embarrassment, still are, after all is said and done, the things to which he truly clings.

Hughes with Simple is not, as is well-known, the first Negro writer to write about the Negro folk. Long before Simple, to take a justly conspicuous example, James Weldon Johnson in his *God's Trombones* renders old-time folk-Negro preaching into verse, a medium which he may well have chosen in the hope that it would impart to his black divines a longer and happier literary life, especially since the verse is not in dialect. Johnson probably wanted his preachers to be admired. For, just as Johnson expressly felt that the great wide world of conscious cultural recognition had failed to give due credit to the Negro spiritual, so he was correspondingly distressed at this same world's neglect of the art of the old-fashioned Negro preacher; an art which, moreover, he could see very clearly and surely was being contained within an epoch in Negro history which would not, and, indeed, could not, last. Johnson, then, with his preachers, was an advocate, not so much of the mere existence of a phenomenon as of a theory maintaining its special worth. But Hughes wanted Simple merely to be known. At the very heart of American racism there seems to be an assumption of the most dangerous import: to wit, that there are no Negroes who are average people. Moreover, this assumption for a long time exercised great sway over virtually all the American contemplation of Negro life. All Negroes were *exceptional*. A few, like Booker T. Washington in his time, and Ralph Bunche, later on, were *exceptionally* intelligent, usually because, probably, of an admixture of white blood. Also beneficent, as well as more understandable, since intellect is not the decisive factor for performing artists, but rather, some strange and peculiar organic or neurological accidents, were freaks like Blind Tom and Marian Anderson, Negroes who could play and sing not only their own *simple* Negro songs, but even compositions from the classical literature of *serious* music. But whether Negroes were tragic mulattoes or curious developments from their usually in some way defective African genes, in the final analysis, they were all freaks, even when of a beneficent kind.

Most Negroes, however, were not freaks of a beneficent kind. They were departures from nature in their lack of normal human attributes. So read, and still reads, the holy writ of American racism. Moreover, by an unfortunate coincidence, so read, in effect, the pronouncements of most Negro writers on Negro subjects. In all of Negro fiction the Negro who is unabashedly and simply an *average man* is as rare as once, in that same fiction, octoroons were disturbingly numerous. The best-known Negro novels, even *Invisible Man* (as, however, it must be admitted, its title implies), abound with grotesques, with people whose distinctive stigma is failure, so that the prevailing conclusion to a Negro's tale of Negro life is catastrophe—Bigger Thomas awaiting execution; Lutie Johnson, Ann Petry's heroine in *The Street*, fleeing the corpse of the would-be seducer she has just murdered; Bob Jones, in *If He Hollers Let Him Go*, on his

way to enforced military service; the Invisible Man sub-
merged, and lost, in his hole in the ground.

The motives of the Negro writer, of course, have not been
those of the white supremacists, nor has been the chain of
reasoning by which he has arrived at his conclusions. Negroes
have been maimed, the Negro writer has contended, by their
environment. The Negro characters of the Negro writer are
freaks, pitiably and depressingly so, say their Negro creators,
because the superimposed conditions of Negro life make them
what they are. Their environment is freakish. How can they
be otherwise? Yet, the plain truth is that men have never
conclusively resolved the conundrum of the true influence
of adversity upon the human psyche and that, moreover,
most Negroes in actual life are not awaiting execution, fleeing
murdered corpses, or living in sub-basements either for ritual
or fiscal reasons of an imperative nature.

What, then, are Negroes really like? This is the question
which Langston Hughes seems to ask with his portrait of
Simple. And his reply seems to be altogether different from
many of the chilling responses to that same question provided
by the apostles of a belief in the Negro *manqué*. Thus, in
Hughes's warm and sane definition of an average Negro,
Simple is no freak of any kind. He adores Jackie Robinson
and respects Ralph Bunche, but he is no superman like either
of them. Simple is an ordinary person who is a Negro. He
has an understandable distaste for white people who abuse
him merely because he is black or who commit acts which
contribute to the system that exists solely to perpetrate a
continuing series of such abuses. On the other hand, he takes
also a dim view of the nastiness often observable in Negroes.
His landlady, he has noted, is no angel of sweetness and light
and, indeed, he scathes a Negro girl who is clerking in a
white chain store for her rudeness and incompetence quite

as much as he does President Eisenhower for spending so much time playing segregated golf in segregated Georgia.

To Simple, quite obviously, the millennium is far, far in a distant future. His vision of the good life is a modest conception only remotely related to the heady doctrine of the perfectability of man, as articulated, let us say, by such an evangelist of a New Order as a Shelley or a Fourier. It is based upon a soberly realistic acceptance of human society in which due allowance is made for man's limitations as well as his potential for self-improvement. Nor is Simple unique in the art of Langston Hughes. Rather he is representative. He belongs to the same world as the Negro characters, more memorable for their ordinariness than anything else, in Hughes's one novel, *Not Without Laughter*. For Hughes never succumbed to the monstrous error of arguing that, because race prejudice is itself monstrous, it has made Negroes monsters.

American history proves Hughes right. In the 1860's there were some prophets who debated only the probable length of the period during which Negroes, freed to use their own resources, could manage even physical survival in the complex American environment. Some of these critics wondered, indeed, if the American Negro might not even be extinct by the end of the nineteenth century. The nineteenth century has been gone seventy years. At Emancipation, speaking generously, there were less than five and a half million Negroes in America. In the 1960's, speaking cautiously, there are at least four Negroes extant for every Negro alive when President Lincoln issued his history-making Proclamation. Moreover, gradually, and in spite of an occasional setback here and there, it has become unmistakably clear that the general direction of Negro welfare in America is up. The Negro has both survived, multiplied and improved his status in every respect.

He will never, however, be perfect. Nor will America. Most Americans, moreover, in the twenty-first century, as now, heretofore and forever hereafter, will continue to be average personalities. They will still, to an extent, get divorces, waste time, drink beverages stronger than tea, lose an occasional job, mistreat their fellows, shirk responsibilities, and commit crimes against the state and nature. But they will also, and probably to a relatively greater degree, sometimes fall ecstatically, beautifully, and nobly in love, aid their relatives, do good turns for friends and, now and then, even for strangers, and, at some rare, unforeseen and, to them, unavoidable moments, even rise above themselves to perform prodigies of heroism and gracious feats magnificent in their altruism. Black and white, that is, they will be like Simple. Thus, they will justify, as they demonstrate, Langston Hughes's faith in human nature and illustrate the soundness of his affirmations both about Negroes, America and humanity in general. These future Americans, that is, will join the Negro readers who, when Simple did appear in the *Defender*, rallied round him in such a manner as to indicate their conviction of his reality. They will give further incontrovertible proof, in their sentiments as well as their conduct, of the validity of Hughes's judgments on his chosen subject, the true character of the Negro Everyman. They will vindicate, in fact, the basic implications of our political and social creeds in America which argue that governments and communities exist not for the privileged few, but in the interest of everyone—even, and indeed most, for the Simples of this earth.

A PAIN IN HIS SOUL: SIMPLE AS EPIC HERO

By Eugenia W. Collier

By the time Jesse B. Semple had expounded his last deep point from the rotating stool at Paddy's Bar more than twenty years after his literary birth in the Chicago *Defender* in 1943, the *Simple* sketches had become the black American epic and Simple himself the epic hero.

An epic is a long poetic narrative which relates the adventures of a hero and which reflects the customs, mores and values of a culture. So it was with *Beowulf;* so it was with *The Song of Roland* and the *Nibelungenlied*. So it was with the sketches of Jesse B. Semple.

Now, I am not going to try to prove this point. Critics have already recognized Simple as the black Everyman, and if you have read enough of the Simple pieces to peruse this article about him, then you know the extent to which this bar-stool philosopher reflects black truth. So proof of Simple's epic quality is not necessary. Rather, I want to illustrate this quality by looking at the characters, the milieu, the Simple point of view and the artistry with which they are all presented. What I am really doing is grabbing a chance to talk about our mutual buddy-o, who has spoken so often to us.

The action of an epic occurs in a setting meaningful to

the people to whom it belongs. Homer's *Iliad* is set around
the ancient walled city of Troy at a crucial time in the long
Greco-Trojan war. The Greek camp, the battlefield, the
doomed city itself are clearly presented as the backdrop of
significant action. The setting of the *Simple* sketches is
Harlem, the black Mecca, a potent symbol of blackness.
All roads lead to Harlem. It is the enslaved sharecropper's
dream of freedom; it is also the dark spawning place of
invidious urban ills. Harlem is disillusionment and desperation and crime. It is opportunity. It is home. It is the place
where the brothers and the sisters converge and pool their
strength and joys and sorrow. Harlem produced the literary
flowering of the twenties, the *Amsterdam News* and Adam
Clayton Powell. It is no less a battleground than Troy; and
no less of humanity is at stake there.

In the *Simple* sketches Harlem is portrayed in all her
squalor and all her splendor: "Pavement hot as a frying pan
on Jennie Lou's griddle. Heat devils dancing in the air. Men
in windows with no undershirts on—which is one thing ladies
can't get by with if they lean out windows. Sunset. Stoops
running over with people, curbs running over with kids.
August in Harlem too hot to be August in hell. Beer is
going up a nickel a glass . . ." ("Midsummer Madness," *The
Best of Simple*, p. 125). The worriation of winter when the
radiators are cold and summer when the heat is smothering;
the sing-song cry of Watermelon Joe plying his wares; the
sight of laboring people going to work early and trudging
wearily back through littered streets at night—all the sights
and smells and sounds of the urban jungle are included.

Yet the warm black beauty of Harlem is even more vivid.
Harlem is a feeling: "I love Harlem. . . . It's so full of Negroes . . . I feel like I got protection. . . . You say the houses
ain't mine. Well the sidewalk is—and don't nobody push me
off. . . . Here I ain't scared to vote—that's another thing I

like about Harlem. . . . Sometimes I run into Duke Ellington on 125th Street and I say, 'What you know there, Duke?' Duke says, 'Solid, ole man.' He does not know me from Adam, but he speaks. . . . Folks is friendly in Harlem. I feel like I got the world in a jug and the stopper in my hand! . . . From Central Park to 179th, from river to river, Harlem is mine! Lots of white folks is scared to come up here, too, after dark" ("A Toast to Harlem," *Simple Speaks His Mind*, pp. 31–33).

Through Simple's perceptions we experience the joys of spring in Harlem, the neon lights of the bars offering fellowship and forgetfulness, the glory in the walk of a lovely black girl ("Girl, where did you get them baby-doll clothes? Whee-ee-oooo! . . . Hey Lawdy, Miss Claudy! Or might your name be Cleopatra?"), the wonder of the soul food ("All boiled down with a side of pork, delicious! Greens make my mouth water. I have eaten so many in my life until I could write a book on greenology—") and all the comfortable things that make a place home.

In the panorama of Simple's Harlem certain characters stand out sharply. On one level they are believable individuals because we have all known people like them. Some characters change through the years, grow, mature, mellow; others remain fairly well the same. On another level the Simple characters are something more than individuals. Like the Grecian soldiers and Trojan citizens in the *Iliad*, like the knights and courtiers in *Le Morte d'Arthur*, the Harlemites in the *Simple* sketches are significant in the interpretation of the culture which created them. The basic factor of Harlem is blackness; the key dimension of blackness is the response to racism and its effects. Simple's friends adjust in their individual ways to the psychological and economic trap in which they are caught by reason of their blackness in this America.

Take Cousin Minnie, for instance. (*Know* Cousin Minnie? Why, I *have* a Cousin Minnie, and so do you!) One day she appears at Simple's door in Harlem, looking like "the junior wrath of God" and introduces herself as "an offshoot from the family" (illegitimate child of Simple's Uncle Willie) ("Enter Cousin Minnie," *Simple Stakes A Claim*, p. 47). She has come North in search of freedom and has selected Harlem as her Valhalla. She is soon made aware of the harshness of life in the Mecca, but from beginning to end she is undefeated. In her way she triumphs, in spite of everything. Minnie is not beautiful: "Cousin Minnie's knees is farther apart than necessary. . . . In fact, [she] is so bowlegged she could not catch a pig. . . . Minnie is also homely, squat, shot, beat, and what not!" ("Minnie One More Time," *Simple Stakes A Claim*, p. 157.) She seldom works, but meets expenses (including such small luxuries as a wig) through her male acquaintances and through "borrowing" from Simple. Her motto is "Beg, borrow, and ball till you get it all—a bird in the hand ain't nothing but a man." Minnie is staunchly self-sufficient. She neither whines nor grovels, but simply takes direct action to solve her own problems: "She crowned him king of kings . . . not to mention lord of lords. When my Cousin Minnie hit that man with a beer bottle, he were conked and crowned all at once. Minnie raised a knot on his head bigger than the Koorinoor Diamond which, I hear, were the biggest diamond ever to be set in a crown. . . . When Rombow went to slap her, Minnie squatted. The blow went over her head. When Minnie come up, the nearest beer bottle were in her hand. With this Minnie christened, crowned, and conked Rombow all at once" ("Self-Protection," *Simple's Uncle Sam*, pp. 60–61).

Minnie has learned to weather the exigencies of life; fate has hurled her to the ground many times, but she has never broken. From her birth as a "side child" in rural Virginia, through poverty and ignorance and near despair, she has made it to the streets of Harlem. Now she is as tough as tempered steel. Yet she is never vicious nor dishonest. She wears her selfhood like a garment as she seeks light and comfort and financial support in the friendly bars. Minnie is lovable. She is admirable. She has endured.

Simples girlfriend, Joyce, who later becomes his wife, makes a different adjustment to the black-white thing. The identity confusion of the black person in a white world is clearly evident in her, but as the years pass Joyce grows and develops until she virtually resolves the identity problem. In the early years she rejects blackness to a large extent and pursues values which are basically white. She is saving her money to move out of Harlem into a nice suburban neighborhood. She drags Simple to all sorts of cultural events —operas, formal dances, lectures, banquets. She disapproves of low-class tastes. She disapproves of Cousin Minnie, who is a "lickerterian." She wants to have her name in the paper. She belongs to a high-tone club which has as one of its projects the urbanization of black immigrants from the South. Her ideal is Mrs. Sadie Maxwell-Reeves, the black society matron of the balloon bustline and lorgnette.

Yet we can love Joyce, too, because beneath her highly polished veneer is a very good, very black woman. Joyce works long hours, scrimps to put aside a little money, and keeps her man straight (but not too straight). Although she will not admit it, she loves chitterlings. And she loves Simple. At first Joyce does not know the beauty of blackness. She thinks that one must emulate high-society ways to be a complete human being. She has tremendous race pride, which manifests itself in her attempts at self-improvement and her being ashamed of the less "cultured" ways of black people. Yet like a colored woman with blonde hair, her roots are black. By the mid-sixties Joyce has found her black beauty: "Joyce thinks Greenwich Village is a fast place where colored are likely to forget race and marry white. My wife is opposed to intermarriage on the grounds of pride. Joyce says she is so proud of her African heritage she don't want nobody to touch it" ("Soul Food," *Simple's Uncle Sam*, p. 111).

Simple's writer friend Boyd, who narrates, functions in a similar way but on a more intellectual scale. The writer studies life "for literary purposes." He is "colleged" and a trifle pedantic, especially in the early sketches. He argues mildly in favor of integration, accuses Simple of being too much of a race man, and assures him that black people have made a great deal of progress. Yet, like Joyce, he is basically black. Folk expressions creep into his speech; he reveres black heroes and loves soul food. He is blacker than usual when he has had a few beers. His love of Harlem and his compassion for its denizens, his attraction to the fraternity of bar-dwellers and his willingness to treat Simple to an occasional beer—all these qualities bespeak blackness. And he is Simple's best friend.

The writer is the perfect foil for Simple. We constantly contrast the writer's book-learning with Simple's wisdom, the writer's naïveté about America's racism with Simple's realism, the writer's extremely proper (and pallid) diction with Simple's warm accents and colorful idioms. Moreover, the writer's innocuous voicing of the more popular clichés gives Simple the opportunity to refute them with humor and perfect logic:

> "Don't you think that it's great that the Supreme Court finally banned segregation in the public schools," I asked, "and has also decreed against Jim Crow on buses?"
>
> "It's about time," said Simple.

"You don't sound very enthused," I said. "Of course, the time is long overdue. But now that it's done, it *is* something of which democracy can be proud."

"I don't see nothing to be proud of—just doing what they ought to do," said Simple. "If white folks was doing something extra, yes, then be proud. But Negroes have a right to go to decent schools just like everybody else, also to set on buses. So what's there to be proud of in that they are just now letting us? They ought to be ashamed of themselves for Jim Crowing us so long. I might have had a good education myself had it not been for white folks. If they want something to be proud of, let them *pay* me for all the education I ain't got." ["Great but Late," *Simple Stakes a Claim*, p. 33]

Other characters come and go, people with the significance of epic characters in their reflection of the truths of a culture. Yet they are all people we know: Simple's parsimonious landlady who leaves signs around for the roomers ("NO CO. AFTER 10"); Zarita, the loud-mouthed nighttime girl; young F. D. (Franklin D. Roosevelt Brown); Simple's estranged wife Isabel, who later pays for one-third of the divorce. They are molded by the racism which has kept them poor and unlettered and hated. But they have endured and even triumphed. Their very endurance is triumph, and there is an epic grandeur about it.

Simple himself is the epic hero, as grandly heroic as Aeneas or Roland or Lancelot. An epic hero has fabulous adventures: Simple's life as a black man in America has been a series of adventures since his birth and childhood in Virginia. The narrative begins *in medias res* with Simple an adult Harlemite. In a series of flashbacks via his conversations with Boyd, Simple reconstructs his life to date with its treacherous pitfalls, most of which are due to his condition as an impoverished black orphan. Life itself is a battleground, and survival requires as much fortitude and sagacity as any epic hero has ever displayed. Moreover, Simple's quest for freedom in this Land of the Free is as holy a crusade as Galahad's quest for the Holy Grail.

An epic hero embodies the values of a culture. Simple is the ideal black folk hero. His name, Jesse B. Semple, implies the ruse which has enabled the folk black man to survive. Also, and more significantly, it implies the direct way in which Simple confronts his life, without phoniness and without false expectations. Yet Simple himself is extremely complex. He is a good man, warm, loving and generous. He is a strong man; he has never succumbed to alcoholism, narcotics, psychosis, or crime as a way out of the prison of the ghetto black. He is a wise man: his logic is perfect. If his statements seem humorous and incongruous, we soon realize that it is our culture that is out of tune.

> "Look here at these headlines, man, where Congress is busy passing laws. While they're making all these laws it looks like to me they ought to make one setting up a few Game Preserves for Negroes. . . . The government protects and takes care of buffaloes and deers—which is more than the government does for me or my kinfolks down South. Last month they lynched a man in Georgia and just today I see where the Klan has whipped a Negro within a inch of his life in Alabama. . . . That is what I mean by Game Preserves for Negroes—Congress ought to set aside some place where we can go and nobody can jump on us and beat us, neither lynch us nor Jim Crow us every day. Colored folks rate as much protection as a buffalo or a deer." ["There Ought to Be a Law," *Simple Speaks His Mind*, pp. 115-116]

This epic hero speaks to us in our own language, which has the dignity and grandiosity of epic style. I cannot actually analyze this language in terms of regional linguistics and accuracy; I leave that to the dialectitians—of which I am not hardly one, as Simple would say. I only know that he speaks to me in terms that I can understand and that his speech is *right*.

The truths that Simple utters are black realities. The scope of black American ghetto life is revealed in Simple's conversations.

The toil: "Once when I was a chauffeur and yard-man, also relief butler, for that rich old country white lady down in Virginia, she kept me working twenty-five hours a day. She could find something for me to do *all* the time." "In this life she [Aunt Lucy] had very little to look forward to —except some more hard work. So no wonder she said, 'Take all this world—but gimme Jesus!' " "Can't you tell by the shoes I wear—not pointed, not rocking-chair, not French-toed, not nothing but big, long, broad, and flat—that I been standing on these feet a long time and carrying some heavy burdens?"

The fluid family structure because of poverty and social disorganization: "When I was a wee small child . . . I had no place to set and think in, being as how I was raised up with three brothers, two sisters, seven cousins, one married aunt, a common-law uncle, and the minister's grandchild —and the house had only four rooms. I never had no place to set and think. Neither to set and drink—not even much of my milk before some hongry child snatched it out of my hand. I were not the youngest, neither a girl, nor the cutest. I don't know why, but I don't think nobody liked me much."

The undermining effects of a system which makes the woman more economically capable than the man: "They cut my wages down again. Then they cut my wages *out*, also the job. My old lady had to go cook for some rich white folks. . . . She said, '. . . Who is paying for this furniture? Me! Who keeps up the house rent? Me! . . . It looks like you can't even get on the W.P.A. But you better get on something, Jess. In fact, take over or take off.' Then it were that

I took off." (Conversation on the Corner," *Simple Speaks His Mind*, pp. 23–24)

The failure of so-called Negro leaders, white-chosen: "Dr. Butts, I am glad to read that you writ an article in the *New York Times*, but also sometime I wish you would write one in the colored papers . . . If you are leading me, lemme see. Because we have too many colored leaders now that nobody knows until they get from the white papers to the colored papers and from the colored papers to me who has never seen hair nor hide of you. Dear Dr. Butts, are you hiding from me—and *leading* me too?" ("Dear Dr. Butts," *Simple Takes A Wife*, pp. 225-226)

The ridiculousness of the black bourgeoisie: "Mrs. Sadie Maxwell-Reeves, Joyce's club lady friend . . . has done moved into a high class white neighborhood. But no sooner than she got there hardly, than another colored family moved in —which made her mad. Now, six more houses in the block have been sold to colored. Mrs. Maxwell-Reeves is beginning to think that she had just as well have stayed in Harlem and not tried to get outside the circle. Which I reckon she had, because she says it won't be no time now before the candy store on the corner is turned into a bar, and the jukebox will be playing 'Jelly! Jelly! Jelly!' " ("Vicious Circle," *Simple Stakes A Claim*, pp. 114-115)

The ironies of black life: "The Savage South has got the Wild West beat a mile. In the old days adventures was beyond the Great Divide. Today they is below the Color Line. Such adventures is much better than the Late Late Show with Hollywood Indians. But in the South nobody gets scalped. They just get cold cocked. Of course, them robes the Klan sports is not as pretty as the feathers Indians used to wear, but they is more scary. And though a Klan holler is not as loud as a Indian war whoop, the Klan is just as sneaky. In cars, not on horseback, they comes under cover of night.

If the young people of the North really want excitement, let them go face the Klan and stand up to it." ("Adventure," *Simple's Uncle Sam,* p. 67)

The ability of black people to endure: "Not only am I half dead right now from pneumonia, but everything else *has* happened to me! I have been cut, shot, stabbed, run over, hit by a car, and tromped by a horse. I have also been robbed, fooled, deceived, two-timed, double-crossed, dealt seconds, and mighty near blackmailed—but I am still here! . . . I have been fired, laid off, and last week given an indefinite vacation, also Jim Crowed, segregated, barred out, insulted, eliminated, called black, yellow, and red, locked in, locked out, locked up, also left holding the bag. I have been caught in the rain, caught in raids, caught short with my rent, and caught with another man's wife. In my time I have been caught—but I am still here! . . . I have been underfed, underpaid, undernourished, and everything but *undertaken*. I been bit by dogs, cats, mice, rats, poll parrots, fleas, chiggers, bedbugs, granddaddies, mosquitoes, and a gold-toothed woman. . . . In this life I been abused, confused, misused, accused, false-arrested, tried, sentenced, paroled, blackjacked, beat, third-degreed and near about lynched! . . . I done had everything from flat feet to a flat head. Why man, I was born with the measles! Since then I had smallpox, chickenpox, whooping cough, croup, appendicitis, athlete's foot, tonsillitis, arthritis, backache, mumps, and a strain—but I am still here. Daddy-o, I'm still here!" (Final Fear," *Simple Speaks His Mind,* pp. 112-113)

The whole epic is infused with the sad-happy, tragic-funny, laughing-crying humor which has grown from the black man's suffering and strength.

No wonder we feel that Simple is someone we know! He takes off from the pages and becomes a warm, alive human being with love in his heart, wisdom in his head, and beer on his breath. And actually Simple *is* real, not only because of the way he plays back our lives, but also because he is the alter ego of his creator, Langston Hughes. Not Boyd the writer, but Simple himself utters the truths that Hughes has gleaned from a lifetime of compassionate observing and experiencing and writing. It is likely that Langston Hughes's greatest contribution to American culture is this black epic, centering around the adventures of a gentle ebony hero, who is really the mirror image of this loving, wise, strong, simple man.

RHETORICAL EMBELLISHMENT IN HUGHES'S SIMPLE STORIES

By Harry L. Jones

It is regrettable that the term "rhetoric" applied to speech or some written discourse suggests today that the discourse is at best bombastic or empty, and at worst, that it is deceptive or fraudulent. To the average person, rhetoric today is synonymous with meaningless talk. It is unfortunate that this is the case, for such an understanding of the term represents a semantic degeneration of a term that has a long and honorable history and tradition.

From the time of the ancient Greeks and Romans, through the medieval period, and well into the modern age, rhetoric was, as Quintilian defined it in the *Institutio Oratoria bene dicendi scientia*, the science (or art) of speaking (or writing) well. Rhetoric is the orator's art, the writer's art, and it embraces the selection of some subject for presentation, constructing a plan of organization, and finding a style appropriate to the audience, purpose, and occasion for speaking or writing. Since the time of the *Rhetoric* of Aristotle, it has been granted by most writers on the subject that moral suasion is the ultimate aim of rhetoric. The characteristic area of concern of rhetoric, therefore, has been those questions of justice and injustice, equity and inequity, of desirable and undesirable, good and bad, right and wrong. As Cicero put it in *De Oratorio*, "What function is so kingly, so worthy of the free, so generous, as to bring help to the suppliant, to raise up those that are cast down, to bestow security, to set free from peril, to maintain men in their civil rights?"

Knowing that the power to move men's minds through language is not one to be taken lightly, the ancients gave almost as much time to the character of the orator as they did to the nature of the speech. Plato openly criticized those rhetoricians who bastardized their art by presenting the merely convincing rather than being genuinely concerned about truth and justice. In his *Rhetoric*, Aristotle evidenced that he understood that the *ethos* or character of the speaker was a main ingredient in his ability to effect moral suasion, and he wrote of the rhetor, "We might almost affirm that his character is the most potent of all the means of persuasion."

In the *Phaedrus*, Plato has Socrates give some attention to the art of composing a speech; taking into account, as rhetoric must, the nature of the audience addressed, Socrates says the speaker ". . . must settle and order his discourse, addressing to the many-sided soul a varied speech that touches every chord, a simple to a simple one. Not till then can discourse be artistic, be controlled by art for the purpose of instruction or persuasion." Making the discourse artistic, that is, different from ordinary speech, was a primary concern of the medieval rhetoricians who considered rhetoric mainly as a means of finding appropriate kinds of stylistic embellishment.

To say that Langston Hughes wrote the *Simple* stories with a stack of books on rhetoric at hand or even with a conscious awareness of the rhetorical tradition which he followed would be to state that which is beyond demonstration. However, it is demonstrable that the stories do make full use of the best prescriptions and proscriptions of the best writers on rhetoric through the ages. Anyone who has read the stories grants that they are superb literary creations. Everyone can see that the stories are humorous because of the main character's posture and attitude about the truths of life presented in them. Few readers, however, recognize that Simple is completely a creation of his own words, his own rhetoric, and that all of the reader's impressions of what Simple is like—his moral nature, his hopes, dreams, and fears —are derived not with reference to an external universe but only with reference to the structured context in which Simple lives and moves and has his being. In the stories, there are few descriptions and few references to actions. As it works out in the context, the narrator, Boyd, sees Simple in a bar or on a street corner or sitting on the stoop in front of the place where Simple lives, and all of these encounters give rise to speeches by Simple. The reader hears and believes, laughs at, sympathizes with and trusts the things which Simple says. These effects are produced through Hughes's presentation of his character and by the series of rhetorical devices and types of embellishment that Hughes employs.

In the foreword to *The Best of Simple* (all references in this essay are to this work), Langston Hughes describes this character as one who tells his tales "mostly in high humor, but sometimes with a pain as sharp as the occasional hurt of that bunion on his right foot. Sometimes, as the old blues say, Simple might be 'laughing to keep from crying.'" Here Hughes sounds like a reader reacting to Simple rather than his creator. It may be that Hughes has done his artistic job so well that he has come to believe in the character as created rather than as conceived, and that he has forgotten all of the art that went into the creation.

Once Simple is created, it reflects to the excellence of the creation that Hughes and many others can point to a thousand Simple models, for Simple, as an artifact, does indeed image forth several transplanted Southern folk types. But Simple is a product of art, not life. Albeit, as a character, he has acquired some urban sophistication of Harlem and he has a great love for that city, in his language, the only means by which we know Simple at all and by which we discover his views and values, Simple is still very much "down-home." But this reflection of folk types does not mean that Simple is real; it merely hides the artistic or rhetorical problems of how Hughes has rendered a Southern folk Negro a universally believable person, one with whom others, black and non-black, can identify.

Hughes's rhetoric seeks to resolve the problems not by making Simple a perpetual clown—for who could believe a clown is sincere?—but by drawing his character in terms so broad that Simple becomes human in the universal sense of that term. What becomes evident beyond locale and beyond color is the fact that Simple is the traditional orator or rhetor, that is, a good man skilled in speaking. Despite Hughes's suggestion to the contrary, much in Simple is not humorous, nor is it intended to be. Episodes like "A Veteran Falls," where Simple begins, "It's a sad and sorry thing to see how some of these fellows come back from the war all wounded and crippled up, ain't it?" are not marked by any of the devices or embellishments which Hughes uses to produce humor, and are not, therefore, something that a reader laughs at. The same is true for episodes like "Last Whipping," "Seven Rings," "A Million—and One," and "Christmas Song," all of which are devoid of humor-producing devices. These are episodes in which Simple is talking about matters of grave concern to him, and the style is plain, straightforward, and unembellished. They serve as a canon against which to measure the humorous passages, and the total effect for the character of Simple emerging from the serious passages in the plain style is honesty and sincerity.

These serious episodes serve to lend credibility to Simple and to set him forth as a good man, and his plain style is not only an evidence of character, it becomes the canon against which the embellished humorous style can be gauged. It is precisely this tension between the plain style and the embellished style that makes Simple's language so effective.

In the stories there are three voices, Hughes's, Boyd's, and Simple's, and there are three styles. Hughes, in his own voice as writer-narrator, occasionally uses poetry in the grand style to set scenes. One of the best examples of the poetic introduction appears in "What Can a Man Say?"

> Sweep, rain, over the Harlem rooftops. Sweep into the windows of folks at work, not at home to close the windows. Wet the beds in side bedrooms almost as narrow as the bed against the window. Sweep, rain! Have fun with the brownstone fronts of rooming houses full of people boxed in *this* room, *that* room, seven rings, two rings, five, nine.
>
> Turn into a spring equinox, rain, and blow curtains from Blumstein's until they flop limp-wet.

Items like these are, however, examples of an unstructured aesthetic, that is, presented for their own sakes and not because they contribute anything beyond scene setting and their own beauty to what is to follow.

Boyd's language is different since it functions organically within the frame of each of the narrative episodes. In contrast to Simple's urban folk speech, Boyd's language is educated. But being educated is no excuse for Boyd's use of the unnecessarily elevated and somewhat stilted style which is so often characteristic of him. For instance, he says to Simple, "So, my dear fellow, I trust you will not let your rather late arrival on our contemporary stage distort your perspective." The point in calling attention to this typical remark is that no one, educated or not, sitting in a

Harlem bar and drinking beer, speaks normally this way. Boyd, too, is an artistic creation, and his primary artistic function is to play straight man for Simple, to feed lines which Simple can either distort or put down. Simple, as has already been suggested, employs two linguistic styles: a plain, serious, unadorned style, and an embellished comic style. It is in connection with the latter style that Boyd functions as straight man.

Conceived originally as weekly columns for the Chicago *Defender*, the *Simple* stories are necessarily episodic. They are a series in the loosest sense of that term since it is only the characters of Simple and Boyd (with certain recurrent thematic material) that tie the stories together. Each tale is rather like a vaudeville act where the performer has to decide not only on an opening but a way of concluding or "getting off." In a collection such as *The Best of Simple*, since there is neither temporal sequence or thematic order, each episode presents the problem of how to conclude. To solve this problem, Hughes developed a closing formula for the episodes. As it works, Boyd gives a line or raises a question the response to which serves as the clincher or punch line which closes the episode. For instance, after the speech in "Income Tax," Simple says, "My place is at the bar." "Of Justice?" Boyd asks. Simple's concluding punch line is, "Justice don't run no bar." In another instance, after Simple has related how he has suffered about every calamity known to man or beast, Boyd asks, "Having survived all that, what are you afraid of?" Simple answers, "I'm afraid that I will die before my time." Again, when Simple has suggested the possibility of marrying Joyce without his final decree from his first wife, Boyd remarks, "But if you go in for bigamy, you will end up in the arms of justice." To which Simple replies, "Any old arms are better than none."

The closing formula, however, has a function beyond

merely rounding off an episode. Despite the overall impression of high humor that the stories create, the fact is that in general the subject matter always is in those areas characteristic of the concerns of rhetoric: justice and injustice, equity and inequity, desirable and undesirable, right and wrong, good and bad. These are hardly humorous matters. Simple's stance regarding all of these is uncompromisingly militant, and there is always a danger that the discussion will slide over the line from good-natured humor to bitterness. The closing formula serves to provide a humorous release from the tension built up by the nature of the preceding discussion.

While Boyd's "colleged" speech serves as a foil for Simple in the closing formula, Simple oftentimes relies on Boyd's greater knowledge of language to ask questions about words he doesn't understand. When his ego is not involved, he can even ask Joyce, who functions like Boyd, "What do you mean by all that language?" But usually it is to Boyd he turns to ask about words. When Joyce leaves word with her landlady that she has gone on vacation for a fortnight, Simple asks Boyd, "What's a fourth night?" On another occasion, he asks, "What's a chastisement?" But no matter what the circumstance, language play tends to be comic and turned against Boyd's linguistic style. For instance, when Simple tells Boyd about how Joyce fussed with him about gnawing a pork chop bone away from the table, Boyd drops a French phrase, saying, "It is not a crime but it is a *faux pas. Faux pas* is a French phrase." Simple responds, "Then, now I know how to say 'gnawing a bone' in French."

Simple himself is a past master of language, as a rhetorician should be, and he can make words do anything he wants them to do. Yet in almost every instance in the stories where speech is structured to yield a comic effect, Boyd is involved. Part of this is due to the nature of rhetorical speech as addressed.

Boyd serves in one respect as Simple's immediate audience, although in actuality he is consubstantial with Simple, that is, Simple and Boyd share the same value scheme, attitudes, hopes, and aspirations for the justice, truth, honesty, and racial equity which Simple promulgates over and over again. Boyd is the more moderate, less militant, Simple. In a larger sense, however, Boyd is representative of Simple's wider audience, and he reflects Hughes's assumptions that people of the United States and of the world subscribe to Simple's ideas about peace, freedom, and brotherhood; in a word, that the world constitutes an audience which is consubstantial with Simple, a world which is, therefore, able to appreciate Simple's essential humanity.

Against this general background, one can examine some of the types of rhetorical embellishments that Hughes uses to lift Simple's ordinary urban folk speech to the level of art. In addition to the devices already mentioned, Hughes achieves his effects in Simple's language through a whole host of phonologic devices, the most obvious of which is rhyme. Simple's language is replete with rhyme patterns: "it's not right to fight"; "at Calvary way back in B. C."; "Bartender, two beers for two steers"; "By the time Congress convenes, I'll be without means." Simple can be aphoristic with rhyme as in "Midsummer madness brings winter sadness, so curb your badness"; or "Duty cannot be snooty"; or "If you can't be nice, take advice. If you don't think once, you can't think twice." When he is jiving the girls on the street corner, Simple says, "Hey, Lawdy, Miss Claudy! You must be deaf—you done left! I'm standing here by myself."

Since rhyme is a standard ingredient in the jive talk of urban folk speech, Hughes is aware that rhyme might not constitute elevating embellishment. He makes this clear when, on one occasion, Simple is talking about a letter he received from Joyce. Because he is feeling good, Simple remarks, after Boyd suggests that Simple and Joyce must "be back on an even keel," "If *keel* means back in the groove, then there's nothing left to prove. Come seven, manna from heaven! Cool, fool." For once Boyd has the comeback, "Dispense with the hep talk. You're not at Birdland."

But Simple's rhymes are not always jive or hep talk. He may be jiving when he says to a pretty girl on the street, "Baby, if you must walk away, walk straight—and don't shake your tail-gate," but he is not jiving when he says, "If you don't take me as I am, damn!" or when he describes F. D.'s father as one who was always "bawling and brawling, drinking and not thinking." Sometimes rhyme functions in a simple descriptive fashion, as when Simple says that Zarita is an after-hours gal who is "great when the hour is late, the wine is fine, and mellow whiskey has made you frisky." Sometimes the rhyme is a means of accolade, as when Simple speaks glowingly of Joyce as "sweet, I mean! In my heart she is a queen! My desire, my fire, my honey—the only women who ever made me save my money!" He is not jiving or shucking when he talks about his ugly cousin Minnie's ability to attract men and get their money. Of one old dude he says, "His payday is her heyday!"

Nonetheless, since rhyme is too near hep talk to be considered real embellishment by a black audience, Hughes resolves the problem by giving Simple alliterative patterns or combinations of rhyme and alliteration. Once Simple suggests to Boyd that they go up to Sugar Hill "where the barmaids are beautiful and the barflies are belles." Speaking of a woman he met on his vacation, Simple says, "I would not tell you a word of lie; she wanted to latch on to me for life." He says of cold weather, "Winter is a worriation," and of tickets he and Joyce purchased for one of Mrs. Maxwell-Reeves' affairs, "a deuce of three-dollar ducats." Ugly Minnie is mentioned again in her ability to attract men in, "You would never think that Minnie could attract a chimpanzee, let alone a chump."

In malapropisms and word play, Hughes combines the phonologic and the semantic for effect. No one who has ever read Simple is likely to forget the comic effect resulting from the word play and *double entendre* in the famous letter to Dr. Butts, but in the other stories the word play tends to be a bit more subtle. Sometimes Simple is reduced to out-and-out malapropism which has no end other than the comic effect it produces. Once he reports on an affair he attended where some woman sang "O Carry Me Homey," which Boyd quietly corrects to "O Caro Nome." Another time Simple says he had no "alternity." More often than not, however, seeming word play and malapropisms overlap so that the item in question does double semantic duty and yields a more appropriate meaning. Such a case occurs when Simple says, "Joyce took me to a pay lecture to hear some Negro hysterian . . ." "Historian," says Boyd, but the correction doesn't take. Simple ignores it and continues, ". . . hysterian speak, and he laid our Negro race low."

Simple relies on Boyd's greater vocabulary only when it is artistically necessary. When the artistic end demands something else for comic effect, Simple either ignores Boyd's words or plays with them. For instance, Simple mentions that he took his income tax form to one of "them noteriety republicans." Boyd's correction has no effect, for since Simple is a staunch Democrat, the malapropism is a much more meaningful structure. The same thing holds true for the description which Simple gives of Trilby, a dog known for biting people, as a "thorough-bred-pedigreedy-canine dog."

Phonologic devices constitute only one class of the types of embellishment that Hughes uses in the *Simple* stories. Even more important are the semantic structures where the effects are determined by what the words mean rather than by how they sound. Hughes produces desired effects through parallel patterning or parataxis. In "Bop," for example, the closing formula is a paratactic structure. Boyd: "Your explanation depresses me." Simple: "Your nonsense depresses me." In "Sometimes I Wonder," the closing formula is: Boyd: "Sometimes I wonder what makes you so race-conscious." Simple: "Sometimes I wonder what made me so black." This kind of parataxis can be combined with word play, as it is when Boyd says to Simple, "You're a kind of displaced person yourself." Simple: "I would be a *displeased* person if I had to live down South again."

Parallel patterning is often expanded to produce the comic list. The list usually begins with items of equal importance, but sometimes the last item is ridiculously out of place. Spring, for instance, "is the time when flowers come out of their buds, birds come out of their nests, bees come out of their hives, and Negroes come out of their furnished rooms." One of the fullest presentations of the list is the description of what happened when Zarita's pocketbook flew open:

> Well, you know how many things a woman carries in her pocketbook. Zarita lost them all: compact busted open, powder split, mirror, key ring with seven keys, lipstick, handkerchief, deck of cards, black lace gloves, bottle opener, cigarette case, chewing gum, bromo-quinine box, small change, fountain pen, sunglasses, big old silver Box-Dollar for luck, address books, fingernail file, three blue poker chips, matches, flask, also a shoehorn.

It is in images, however, that one finds the prime matter of poetic embellishment. The images set forth in the metaphors, similes, and comparisons in the *Simple* stories, apart from the other kinds of embellishment, would be enough to demonstrate Hughes's rhetorical art. Since Hughes is so very consistent in the kind of language he assigns to Simple, the metaphors and similes seem to come naturally from him, out of the background and survival experiences which Simple has had. They are never forced; they are consummate art without being arty. They come from almost all of the areas of Simple's life.

In Simple's language beautiful women are often presented in food or dessert images. One girl looked to him "like chocolate icing on a wagon-wheel cake," and another, "like lemon meringue on a Sunday pie." Ugly women receive a variety of images, some sense and some nonsense. Zarita's unkempt hair looks "like a hurrah's nest," and another woman has a shape "like a pyramid upside down." Trilby, an ugly dog, looked "like she were made up for Halloween," and Simple's ugly cousin Minnie sometimes looks "like the junior wrath of God." The winner of Simple's "Ugly Contest" would have to look "like King Kong's daughter plus the niece of Balaam's off-ox."

Few things escape Simple's image-making powers. When Joyce gets angry, she is "as touchous as a mother hen done lost her chicks." And Joyce once bought an evening gown which was "cut so low it looks like she is trying to show how little she can wear and not catch pneumonia." As for the weather, in the summer, "the sun is so hot it makes even a cold snake mad," and in winter, the chilly wind, called "the Hawk" or Hawkins in urban speech, evokes from Simple: "Hawkins is talking like the rent man does on the fifteenth, when you should have paid your rent on the first." Since money is a perennial problem, some figures touch on the cost of living. According to Simple, "a formal costs almost as much as a funeral," and prices in general are "as high as a cat's back in a dogfight." With money enough so that he wouldn't have to work, Simple says he would "respect work just like I respect my mother and not hit her a lick." But only in fancy can Simple afford to travel so that "the sky is his roadway and the stars his stopping place." Only the young, like F. D., can "wear Harlem for a sport coat."

Simple has his frustrations, such as the night he returned to his room and found that Zarita had brought over her whole birthday party "unannounced, uninvited, and unwanted." His room is smelling "like womens, licker, mens, and a Night in Paris." Zarita is talking so loud "you could hear her in Buffalo," and she grabs Simple "as close as paper on a wall" and begins to dance. But times like these are matched by those when Simple, because of Joyce's love, feels so good he says, "Like the camel, I have been threaded through the eye of a needle and come out a new man." He is "loose as a goose," and he adds, "Like a sow's ear, I am a silk purse; like the Liberty Bell, I ring for freedom," and he is "liable to explode like firecrackers on the Fourth of July." Both happiness and frustration fit perfectly into the kind of adjustment Simple has made to the business of living. He knows, for instance, that "Days are like stair-steps. If you stumble on the first day yesterday, you liable to be falling tomorrow."

Langston Hughes's *Simple* stories have been translated into several of the languages of the world. Such popularity is due to Simple's growth from a transplanted Southern black man caught up in the urban centers of this country to a kind of universal folk-type, schooled in life and wise in the ways of the world. Simple has insights and perceptions that others wished they had, and in the hands of Hughes, Simple has the ability to verbalize in high humor truths that lie too deep for tears. Through the repeated use of traditional types of embellishment, Hughes has sold the world a good man skilled in speaking. Perhaps the Danes' description of Simple as the "black philosopher of the bar-stool" says as adequately as anything could how well Langston Hughes has wrought.

THE SHORT FICTION
OF LANGSTON HUGHES

By James A. Emanuel

Justly esteemed for his versatility and competence as a writer, especially as a poet and humorist, Langston Hughes deserves close study as the author of sixty-six published short stories. Although at Central High School in Cleveland, Ohio, he wrote his first short story, "Mary Winosky," to fulfill an English assignment in 1918, his first published stories were those that seem appropriately named the West Illana Series in *The Short Stories of Langston Hughes*, my unpublished dissertation completed at Columbia University in 1962. Printed in 1927 by *The Messenger*, they are "Bodies in the Moonlight" (April), "The Young Glory of Him" (June), and "The Little Virgin" (November), a trilogy about the bawdy crew of the freighter *West Illana*, closely reflecting Hughes's own six months in 1923 as a mess boy on the S.S. *Malone*. His other early stories—the semifictional, tableau-like "Burutu Moon," published in the *Crisis* of June, 1925, and "Luani of the Jungles," a tale of compulsive interracial love printed in *Harlem* in November, 1928—combine with the West Illana Series both to complete Hughes's fictional treatment of Africa and the sea, with only three later exceptions, and to forecast much of his characteristic style.

Hughes's deep involvement with the short-story form began in February, 1933, in the New Moscow Hotel, where he had accumulated enough surplus rubles from articles on Asia sold to *Izvestia, International Literature,* and other Moscow publications to return to America via Korea, China, Japan, and Hawaii. A night or two after reading two stories by D. H. Lawrence that brought "cold sweat and goose pimples" to his body, he found himself, upon sitting down to typewrite an article on Tashkent, beginning a short story. And although Hughes was separated from Harlem by thousands of miles of ocean and Asian soil, he discovered himself involuntarily writing about Negroes there. After thus immersing himself in the story, "Slave on the Block," to be followed in the Moscow group by "Mother and Child," "A Good Job Gone," "Poor Little Black Fellow," and "Cora. Unashamed," he made a conscious choice to turn his career into the unconventional, risky path of writing honest stories about his own race. He knew that magazines seldom bought such stories, considering them, he records in *I Wonder as I Wander,* "exotic, in a class with Chinese or East Indian features." But his desire to live as a professional writer had to adjust itself to his esteem for his own people, and to his understanding of their profound need for true representation.

The rest of his stories were often written in comfort and with the help of generous friends. Noel Sullivan in California, for example, allowed him a year's use of "Ennesfree," his cottage at Carmel-by-the-Sea, in 1933-1934, and again arranged for similarly convenient months of short-story writing in a cottage edging his Hollow Hills Farm in Carmel Valley near Monterey, in 1940-1941. On the other hand, he sometimes revised stories while on the road during poetry reading or lecture tours. Some early fiction was written in a segregated Reno boardinghouse, some in a cheerful flat in Mexico City; many later tales came from his typewriter near his apartment window, third-floor rear, overlooking a Harlem back yard on East 127th Street. The numerous stories thus created between 1926 and 1962 (the year his often-revised "Blessed Assurance" appeared as "Du, Beine Zuversicht" in Hamburg's *Konkret*) have been printed in America in at least two dozen magazines and in just as many anthologies; in European, African, Asian, and South American countries, they have been published in about a dozen periodicals and in nine or ten book-length collections. Fifty-one of Hughes's narratives have appeared in his own three short-story collections: *The Ways of White Folks* (1934), *Laughing to Keep from Crying* (1952), and *Something in Common and Other Stories* (1963).

No reasoned estimate of Hughes's total accomplishments in these stories—other than the aforementioned dissertation and the relevant sections of *Langston Hughes*, Volume 123 of Twayne's United States Authors Series—has been made. Yet, recent and current works of some magnitude, centering upon other genres of his, or adopting other approaches, forecast increased study of Hughes's short fiction: Donald C. Dickinson's *A Bio-Bibliography of Langston Hughes: 1902-1967* (1967); Webster Smalley's *Five Plays by Langston Hughes* (1963); French-language studies of his poetry by Jean Wagner in 1963 and Raymond Quinot in 1964; and a projected dissertation on his poetry. The present ferment over the possibilities of a Black Aesthetic, the thrust of emerging coteries and publications dedicated to the encouragement of racial art, and the deepening cry for Afro-American critics all augur a reversal of the neglect suffered by Hughes's fiction.

In the meantime, it is fitting that his achievements as a short-story writer be publicly rehearsed. The ninety-odd reviews of *The Ways of White Folks* and the less numerous brief critical notices of his other collections of stories record as their main consensus that Hughes's style is natural, humorous, restrained and yet powerful. The naturalness is largely found in his characters' talk, which merges incident, personality, and racial history into recurrent patterns. The dialogue is particularly true to facts of race, which authentically control cadences, accents, and ductile phrases. The realism and pathos in much of his work are not adequately recognized in published commentary; nor is his characteristic irony—a point of view that Negro reviewers have best understood. At least twenty-five other typical traits of the stories, including their linguistic play, lyrical exuberance, juxtapositions, and repartee, have been relatively unnoticed. Their rhythm even, not to mention their tension and imagery, has barely been subjected to analysis. Hughes's interspersed songs and Chekhovian endings, which suggest both racial history and modern impasses in social progress, enhance his virtues of style.

The comprehensiveness of his stories has been generally admitted, although not usually detailed. Using settings as different as Harlem and Hong Kong, Havana and Africa, Hollywood and the Midwest, Alabama and New England, and in the main limiting himself to "ordinary" Negroes, Hughes reflects all the crucial factual realities and psychological depths of Negro experience, especially in urban communities. The variety of themes, images, and symbols through which he mounts this large picture can be indicated by a few statistical and analytical references. Of his forty-odd distinct themes, his main theme is racial prejudice (the focus of thirty-eight stories); his much less intense thematic purposes are to present usually delinquent fathers, affection-seeking women, interracial love, the faddish misconceptions of Negroes by whites, religion and morality, the life of the artist, and jealousy. His images, classifiable into sixteen general types, are most vivid when he is treating nature, physical

violence, and weariness. His symbols, usefully introduced
in at least seventeen different varieties, into material approached with uncluttered directness, most effectively employ crosses, Negro voices and laughter, snow, coal, and
steel.

Hughes's skill in plotting and in creating character demands some comment. The easy and lively movement of "A
Good Job Gone" exemplifies what Sherwood Anderson
meant in calling him a "natural story teller." Hughes's plots
are never complicated, and flashbacks are usually handled
with grace. Some of his plots are mere gossamer, as in the
sketches that he calls his "prose-poems"; some are rather
mechanical, like that of "One Friday Morning," which he
judges his most "contrived" story; and some are skillfully
unified, like that of "Little Dog." Some tales invite the risi-
bilities in the manner of sure-fire anecdotes, like "Tain't
So." Only in such uncollected narratives as "Saved from
the Dogs" does the usual interest lag.

Not ordinarily concerned with fully rounding his characters, Hughes intimately develops only ten (Cora Jenkins of
"Cora Unashamed," Mr. Lloyd of "A Good Job Gone,"
Oceola Jones of "The Blues I'm Playing," Clara Briggs of
"Little Dog," Colonel Norwood and Bert of "Father and
Son," Carl Anderson of "On the Way Home," and Professor Brown, Charlie Lee, and Flora Belle Yates in three
other stories); and some details of appearance, activities,
background, and range of emotion and attitude are missing
even in these portraits. Characterization is Hughes's primary
technical consideration, however: he said conversationally in
1961, "I do not analyze what goes into the story from the
standpoint of emotion, but in terms of whoever I am writing
about." Racially, his characters are rather well balanced,
despite a few claims to the contrary. One Negro newspaper
review of *The Ways of White Folks* asserts that "Hughes's

characters are no Uncle Toms"; but old Sam in "Father and Son," complete with multiple *yes, sah*'s, chattering teeth, popping eyes, and moaning, justifiably fits the mold—and more are stationed in Colonel Norwood's kitchen. And the pompous Dr. Jenkins in "The Negro in the Drawing Room" impressively qualifies. It is true, however, that Hughes almost never subjects Negroes to his own ridicule; and he never attributes any unmitigated felonious activity to them.

Regarding his characterization of whites, which has been usually termed compassionate, even "generous," the author clarified his view in a letter to me in 1961:

> I feel as sorry for them as I do for the Negroes usually involved in hurtful . . . situations. Through at least one (maybe *only* one) white character in each story, I try to indicate that "they are human, too." The young girl in "Cora Unashamed," the artist in "Slave on the Block," the white woman in the red hat in "Home," the rich lover in "A Good Job Gone" helping the boy through college, the sailor all shook up about his "Red-Headed Baby," the parents-by-adoption in "Poor Little Black Fellow," the white kids in "Berry," the plantation owner in "Father and Son" who wants to love his son, but there's the barrier of color between them. What I try to indicate is that circumstances and conditioning make it very hard for whites, in interracial relationships, each to his "own self to be true."

Hughes's sense of personal identification with specific characters in "Slave on the Block," "Father and Son," "On the Way Home," and five other stories, explained in the same letter, increases the importance of characterization to his reshaping of experience into fiction.

Hughes's demonstrable sympathetic characterization of whites stands in revealing conjunction with the bitterness observed by about one-fifth of the reviewers of the 1934 collection and by a somewhat smaller percentage of those commenting upon *Laughing to Keep from Crying* in 1952. This bitterness, emphasized in a *Phylon* review by the perceptive John W. Parker in 1952 as "unwavering pessimism," is generalized by another Negro critic, Blyden Jackson, in 1960 in *CLA Journal*, as the impoverishing "ogre" of the ghetto-ridden substance of Negro fiction. The fact that it coexists, in the not unusual case of Hughes, with restraint of style—a characteristic attributed to *The Ways of White Folks* almost as often as bitterness—should invite psychologically oriented critics to explore ways in which Negro writings illuminate the creative process itself.

The nature of the bitterness in Hughes's stories throws light upon his art, his wisdom, and his realism. In the forty-one narratives in his first two collections, only two characters have personalities substantially weighted with bitterness: Bert in "Father and Son" and Charlie Lee in "Powder-White Faces." Both kill because of it. The bitterness in four other characters is modified: Johnny Logan, in "Trouble with the Angels," gives in, only at the end, to a bitterness that is bound to subside into resignation; the bitterness of Bill, in "Sailor Ashore," and of little Maurai, in "African Morning," is too dispirited to merit the name, and is evanescent. The bitterness of the Columbia University-trained secretary, in "The Negro in the Drawing Room," means less to him than his stewardship of the papers of an important man, and is merely occasional stimulation for his sense of virtue.

There remains only the bitterness of circumstance. Into this tight corner is pushed the meaning of what commentators have felt with a clarity often sharper than their powers of explanation. It is here that one understands how fully Hughes has accomplished what he stated as his purpose: "to explain and illuminate the Negro condition in America." The bitterness spreads throughout that condition, not as a definable mood of Negroes in the stories (and Hughes knows that the healthy mind cannot long sustain pure bitterness, however rational that attitude might be), but as a stern, incessant truth suffused through the countenance of factual life.

Ugly truth, when recorded by Negro authors, usually raises the blanket indictment of "protest writing," the persistent balderdash which Hughes disposes of in a reply to Rochelle Girson for one of her "This Week's Personality" features in the *Saturday Review* after the publication of *Laughing to Keep from Crying:*

> I have . . . often been termed a propaganda or a protest writer. . . . That designation has probably grown out of the fact that I write about what I know best, and being a Negro in this country is tied up with difficulties that cause one to protest naturally. I am writing about human beings and situations that I know and experience, and therefore it is only incidentally protest—protest in that it grows out of a live situation.

Some of Hughes's narrative sketches in his books about Jesse B. Semple that qualify as short stories ("A Dog Named Trilby," a few pieces on Cousin Minnie, "Banquet in Honor," and "A Veteran Falls") ably combine social protest with humor, artistic restraint, and the bright accumulations of energetic word play for which Simple is famous.

A nighttime and pre-dawn writer who composed his average first draft in three days and his second and third drafts in an additional day or more, Hughes has reflected in his short stories his entire purpose as a writer. Early in his career, he knew what he wanted to accomplish in his art: to interpret "the beauty of his own people," a beauty, he wrote in 1926 in the *Nation*, that they were taught either not to see or not to take pride in. He sought to portray their "soul-world." Above the weaknesses of his stories (didacticism, dialogue from unseen "white folks" and other voices, and too many exclamations and parentheses) rise his humanity, his faithful and artistic presentation of both racial and national truth—his successful mediation, that is, between the beauties and the terrors of life around him.

One becomes alive to the vigor and delicacy, the fun and somber meaning, in Hughes's short stories only by reading them attentively. But it would be helpful to read or reread his best works mindful of certain themes, technical excellences, or social insights. "Slave on the Block," available in *The Langston Hughes Reader* (1958), for example, a simple though vivid tale, reveals the lack of respect, and even human communication, between Negroes and those whites whose interest in them is only modishly superficial. "Poor Little Black Fellow," found in *The Ways of White Folks*, satirizes religious, rather than social cant in race relations, treating corrosive varieties of self-deceit with a subtle complexity—although its consistent point is merely that Negroes, even little ones, want only to be treated like everyone else.

Hughes's best stories include four that portray racial violence, but his more comprehensive revelation of prejudices is woven, for the most part, into eleven other tales of uneven quality. Among the eleven, "Professor," which is in *Something in Common and Other Stories*, excels in its use of irony and ambiguity, and in its solid but artful attack on discrimination in education; "Powder-White Faces" and "Sailor Ashore," reprinted in the same collection, deserve close reading too, the former for its meditative picture of the chaos that prejudice can swell in a Negro's mind, the latter for its exploration of a uniquely baneful government-tolerated prejudice, that suffered by military men.

Among the four well-written stories containing racial violence (all except "Home" reprinted in *Something in Common*), two employ religious themes and events. "On the Road" is a story perfectly conceived as both fantasy and reality, and poetically executed, using intense patterns of wintry images to join Christ and a black hobo in a brief adventure against systematized, prejudiced religion. "Big Meeting," less artistically ingenious than "On the Road" but richer in racial meaning, pursues the theme of Negro identification with Christ more emotionally and picturesquely, using a green-coated, big revival preacher whose timing and histrionics are masterful. "Home," published in *The Ways of White Folks*, ends with a savagery that tends to obscure the profound interplay between life and art which thematically deepens the action; the sensitive, gifted little Negro violinist who finds the world too "rotten" for his survival, is a doomed purveyor of beauty into the midst of European decay and hometown American racism. In "Father and Son," Hughes works at a number of themes (psychopathic Southern violence, sexual exploitation of Negro women, Negro miseducation, and religious abuses) and uses effective symbols and striking arrays of atmospheric images; but the title itself underscores his strongest theme: the climactic encounters of steel will and frustrated love between a white father and his mulatto son.

One of Hughes's best stories, "The Blues I'm Playing" (collected in *The Ways of White Folks*), addresses itself not only to the Harlem "cult" of the Negro in the twenties, but to the exploration of American Negritude as conceived by Hughes in that decade. Although this story, like "Home," written in the same month, September, 1933, closely pictures the conflict between life and art, the blues-playing heroine represents life more so than art precisely because she is so much of a Negro, so close to the roots of art—the blues— in her own racial community experience. The last few pages of the story, almost chart-like in their clarity, support Negritude as an insistence upon the black artist's preservation of personal and racial integrity.

Two of Hughes's top stories, "A Good Job Gone" and "Little Dog," both available in *Something in Common*, cross the color line on the wings of interracial love. The former fast-moving tale, in which a "sugar-brown" with a suppressed hatred of bigots drives a promiscuous rich white man insane, remains as popular as the "hugging and kissing" with which Harlem's updated Luani of the Jungles works her charms. "Little Dog" is distinguished by Hughes's adept characterization of a lonely white spinster who falls in love with a "big and brown and kind looking" Negro janitor; the formidable task of presenting a wasted life without minimizing its integrity or ridiculing its belated humanity is handled admirably. "Red-Headed Baby," reprinted in *The Langston Hughes Reader*, tells of a white sailor's carelessly destructive amours; it is unique for its ably used stream-of-consciousness passages, not attempted again, however, until twenty-eight years later, in "Blessed Assurance."

Two essentially nonracial stories, "Cora Unashamed" and "On the Way Home," are among Hughes's best narratives. The former, twice published the same year, in *The Ways of White Folks* and *Best Short Stories of 1934*, shows the ignoble defeat of both parental and carnal love; its tragedy is moderated only by the earth-rooted strength of a Negro maid whose simple thoughts ("And there ain't no reason why you can't marry, neither—you both white") free her of all but natural impulses. "On the Way Home," reprinted in *Something in Common*, suggestively employing various images of wine and water understandingly describes a young man's ambivalent responses to his mother's death; trapped in both guilty exhilarations and anguish, the dutiful son—who is never racially identified—struggles to be reborn.

Traveling throughout the world, Langston Hughes was always a man of the people, equally at home eating camel sausage in an Asian desert or tasting strawberries in a Park

Avenue penthouse. He once said that he had lived much of his life in basements and attics. Metaphorically, his realism and his humanity derive from this fact. Moving figuratively through the basements of the world, where life is thickest and where common people struggle to make their way, he remained close to his vast public. At the same time, writing in attics like the one he occupied in Harlem for twenty years, he rose to the long perspective that enabled him to shine a humanizing, beautifying, but still truthful light on what he saw. His short stories form a world of fiction built with truth and a special love—a little civilization shaped by high purpose and steadfast integrity.

LANGSTON HUGHES AS TRANSLATOR

By John F. Matheus

In approaching the study of Langston Hughes as a translator of French and Spanish speaking poets one remembers certain verities which have not yet become platitudinous. These have been well expressed by Edna St. Vincent Millay in the "Preface" to her and George Dillon's rendering into English verse of Baudelaire's *Les Fleurs du Mal*.

> Poetry should not, [she writes] and indeed cannot properly be translated except by poets. But there is more to it than that; it is as complicated as blood-transfusion. . . .
>
> The poet best fitted, technically, to translate the work of a foreign poet, is the accomplished and disciplined craftsman in his own tongue, who possesses also a comprehensive knowledge of the language from which he is translating. All his skill, however, will not avail him, if he is not sufficiently in sympathy with the poem he is translating, to feel that he might have written it himself. . . . He must be able to fill the veins of the poem, nearly emptied through the wound inflicted by translation, with his own blood, and make the poem breathe again.

Langston Hughes met Miss Millay's standards in such lofty degree that the critic marvels at the fecund versatility of his creative gift. In *The Big Sea*, story of his life, Hughes tells of his interest in his French class at Central High School in Cleveland, Ohio. "I never will forget the thrill," he wrote, "of first understanding the French of de Maupassant. . . . I think it was de Maupassant who made me really want to be a writer and write stories about Negroes, so true that people in far-away lands would read them—even after I was dead."

Hughes was taken by his father to Mexico where he learned to understand and speak Spanish. During a second sojourn in Mexico, after graduation from Central High School, he increased his knowledge of Spanish to the extent of reading Blasco Ibáñez's *Cuentos Valencianos* and *Canos y Barro*.

He picked up German from Fran Schultz, a widow who landed in Mexico with a daughter leaving other family members in Germany. She became his father's housekeeper and eventually his second wife.

With this brief preliminary examination of our translator's linguistic background, it is fitting that we begin with the earliest Spanish poetical form which intrigued his attention. In 1924, the most popular poet of the Iberian collectivity began his *Romancero gitano, Gypsy Ballads*. Federico García Lorca, a native of Granada, then at the age of twenty-six devoted three years to their composition. He chose the Gypsy as symbol of the two great forces in the Spanish libido, death and sex.

In 1937 Langston Hughes came to Spain by way of Barcelona and Valencia with Nicolás Guillén, the Cuban poet, to become a correspondent for the Spanish Civil War. When they finally arrived in Madrid, which was being bombed by the Falangists, they found rooms at the "Alianza de Escritores," a writers' and artists' club. It was here that he did most of his translation of the *Ballads*, aided by the poets Rafael Alberti, Manuel Altolaguirro and other friends of Lorca.

While attending Columbia University in 1945 in New York, he revised them with the help of Miguel Covarrubias. On June 10, 1951, the final copy was ready for publication. He had checked the translation with three Spanish friends and had also made comparisons with French and Italian translations.

Further he describes vividly, shortly after arriving in Madrid, his first hearing of La Niña de los Peines, queen of the Gypsy ballad singers, Pastora Pavon, the "old Girl with the Combs" on the stage with a background of Gypsy guitarists and clapping dancers:

> Shortly, without any introduction or fanfare, she herself sat up very straight in her chair and, after a series of quavering little cries, began to half-speak, half-sing a *solea*—to moan, intone and cry in a Gypsy Spanish I did not understand, a kind of raw heartbreak rising to a crescendo that made half the audience cry aloud with her after the rise and fall of each phrase. The guitars played behind her, but you forgot the guitars and heard only her voice rising hard and harsh, wild, lonely and bitter-sweet from the bare stage of the theater with the unshaded house lights on full. This plain old woman could make the hair rise on your head, could do to your insides what the moan of an air-raid siren did, could rip your soul-case with her voice [*I Wonder as I Wander: An Autobiographical Journey*, pp. 332-33].

This is what Federico García Lorca put in his *Gypsy Ballads*. This is why all Spanish-speaking peoples in all continents adore them. This is what Langston Hughes caught and redistilled into English.

The Hughes translation of Lorca's *Gypsy Ballads* was published by Beloit College, Beloit, Wisconsin, in the fall of 1951, in the *Beloit Poetry Chapbook* No. 1. It contains fifteen of the eighteen ballads in the original text.

The most difficult problem was adapting the octosyllabic

ballad meter to English words. Some lines from the following
ballad show how well the English version is true to the
original, while the English vowels, less in number than the
Spanish, give the impression of the original.

In the first ballad, Lorca wrote:

> La luna vino a la fragua
> con su polisón de nardos.
> El niño la mira mira.
> El niño la está mirando.
> En el aire conmovido
> mueve la luna sus brazos
> y enseña, lúbrica y pura,
> sus senos de duro estaño.
> Huye luna, luna, luna.

> The moon came to the forge
> with her bustle of spikenards.
> The child looks, looks.
> The child is looking.
> In the trembling air
> the moon moves her arms
> showing breast hard as tin,
> erotic and pure
> Fly, moon, moon, moon.

Again in "La Monja Gitana," "The Gypsy Nun," there is
that deftly balanced melody of similar sounds.

> Silencio del cal y mirto
> Malvas en las hierbas finas.
> La monja borda alhelíes
> sobre una—tela pajiza.
> Vuelan en la araña gris
> siete pájaros del prisma.

> Silence of lime and myrtle.

Mallow among the herbs.
The nun embroiders gilliflowers
    on a straw-colored cloth
Seven rain birds
    fly through the grey chandelier.

In Hughes's translation of "The Faithless Wife," "La ca-
sada infiel," he reveals a more accurate rendering of the
original Spanish than, for example, the New Directions
translation . . .

En las últimas esquinas
toqué sus pechos dormidos, [as]

In the farthest street corners
I touched her sleeping breasts.

Hughes says, "At the farthest corners, I touched her sleeping breasts." Again, three of Lorca's last four lines are:

y no quise enamorarme
porque teniendo marido
me dijo que era mozuela

Hughes translates:

But I didn't want to fall in love with her
for, having a husband, she told me she was
single

This is closer than—

And I did not fall in love for although
she had a husband, she told me she was a
maiden.

There is not too great a variance, but there is some.
    The eighth ballad, "San Miguel" (Granada), has the haunt-
ing Spanish lines . . .

> Se ven desde las barandas
> por el monte monte, monte,
> mulos y sombres de mulos
> cargados de girasoles,
> Sus ojos en las umbri'as
> se empañan de immensa noche.
> En los recodos del aire
> Cruje la aurora salobre.

The melody still haunts and lingers in the poet's English . . .

> You see from your railing
> in the mountain, mountain, mountain,
> mules and the shadows of mules
> loaded down with sunflowers
> are blurred with vasty night
> at the corners of the air
> the salt dawn crackles.

Unfortunately such a small number was printed of the Beloit publication of this English version by Hughes of Lorca's ballads, so tremendously popular in the Spanish world, that it is most difficult to find a copy.

After much searching, here and there, a copy was discovered in the Howard University Library's Reference Division. So rare and valuable is this copy that it is not allowed to circulate. Xerox reprints are available, however, and are quite adequate.

In 1961, New Directions published a paperback book as *The Selected Poems of Federico García Lorca*, edited by his brother Francisco, and Donald M. Allen. In the preface signed by Francisco García Lorca, the statement is made that, "In making the present selection from the whole published verse of the poet, the editors have sought to choose poems they consider to be most representative of the many very different facets of the poet's varied and complex work. They feel that the translations included are faithful to the text of the Spanish poems and, more often than not, to the spirit as well, in so far as this is possible in the incredibly difficult matter of translating poetry."

On pages 80–85, Hughes's translation of the "Romance de Emplazado" appears under the English title, "Ballad of One Doomed to Die." In the ten years intervening between the Beloit publication of this ballad and the more recent book, Hughes has made some changes which reveal his continued search for perfection in his translations.

BALLAD No. 14–ROMANCE DEL EMPLAZADO

Donde se aleja tranquilo
un sueño de trece barcos.
Sino que, limpios y duros
escuderos desvelados,
mis ojos miran un nortre
de metales y peñascos
donde mi cuerpo sin venas
consulta naipes helados.

Beloit Version 1951	New Directions Version 1961
Where a dream of thirteen boats quietly disappear in the distance instead, shields of wakefulness, my eyes clean and hard look toward a north of metals and of cliffs where my veinless body consults decks of frozen cards.	Where quietly disappears a dream of thirteen boats. Instead, clean and hard, squires of wakefulness, my eyes look for a north of metals and of cliffs where my veinless body consults frozen playing cards.

Los densos bueyes del agua
embisten a las muchachos
    que se bañan en las lunas
de sus cuernos ondulados.

Heavy water oxen charge Boys who bathe in the rippling moons of their horns.	Heavy water oxen charge boys who bathe in the moons of their rippling horns.

Y agujas de cal mojada
te morderán los zapatos.

And needles of wet lime Eat at your shoe leather.	And needles of wet lime will bite into your shoes.

Será de noche, en lo oscuro,
por los montes imantados
donde los bueyes del agua
beben los juncos soñando.

It will be night, in the dark,
in the mountains of magnet
Where water oxen drink
in the dreaming reeds.

It will be night, in the dark
in the magnetic mountains
where water-oxen drink
in the reeds, dreaming.

Espadón de nebuloso
Mueve en el aire Santiago
Grave silencio de espalda
Manaba el cielo combado.

Santiago moved his misty
sword in the air
Behind him heavy with silence
the curved sky flowed.

Santiago moved his misty
sword in the air,
Dead silence flows over
the shoulder of the curved sky.

The English sound in "Dead silence flows over the shoulder of the curved sky," translates more accurately the rhythm and music of the Spanish.

On the other hand both versions give a magnificent equivalent to the tremendous crescendo of the original—

Y la sábana impecable,
de duro acento romano,
daba equilibrio a la muerte
con las rectas de sus paños.

And the impeccable sheet
with its hard Roman accent
gave death a certain poise
by the rectitude of its folds.

Through the generosity of Dr. Ben Frederic Carruthers, former professor of Spanish at Howard, I was able to borrow his only copy of his collaboration with Langston Hughes in translating Nicolás Guillén's collection of poems, bearing the title of *Cuba Libre*, 1948; only 500 copies were printed and these have long since vanished. Dr. Carruthers met the famous Cuban poet, Guillén, from his acquaintance with Señorita

Eusebia Cosme, the gifted *diseuse* who charmed the Spanish circles from Miami to New York in the thirties.

After attending the Anniversary of Havana in 1940 he met Langston Hughes. They obtained the consent of Guillén for an English translation.

To quote from Dr. Carruthers' letter:

> Upon my return to Howard in 1941 I began my own translations and when I moved to New York in 1944 I met Langston again and began to compare notes. We found that a few but not many of our translations were of the same poem but that there were many which I had finished which Langston thought good enough to stand as they were and many others which Langston had completed without my having touched them. We collaborated completely on the final editing and polishing and Langston secured the publisher and the artist, Gar Gilbert.

This collection, *Cuba Libre: Poems by Nicolás Guillén*, consisted of fifty poems from Guillén's early publications *Motivos de son* (1930), *Sóngoro cosongo*, (1931), and *Sones para turistas y cantos para soldados* (1937). It contained much Cuban Negro dialect, which the authors turned into American Negro dialect (Carruthers) and Negro folk idiom (Hughes). An example is "Blade":

> Knife-toting, sweet-man
> become a knife himself:
> whittling chips of the moon
> until the moon runs out,
> whittling chips of shadow
> until the shadows run out,
> whittling chips of song
> until the song runs out—
> and then,
> sliver by sliver, the dark body
> of his no-good gal.

Six translations by Langston Hughes are included in the *Anthology of Contemporary Latin-American Poetry*, edited by Dudley Fitts. Four are from the Spanish of Nicolás Guillén—"Execution," "Dead Soldier," "Cantaliso in a Bar," and "Wake for Papa Montero." Two are from the French of the Haitian poet, novelist, and patriot, Jacques Roumain. The subjects are "When the Tom-Tom Beats . . . ," and "Guinea."

Editor Fitts in his "Preface" pays the following tribute to the translator: "And I am obligated to Mr. Langston Hughes for his unselfishness in sharing with me his fine creative interest in the poetry of which he has long been an outstanding interpreter."

In 1949, Langston Hughes joined Arna Bontemps in editing an anthology, *The Poetry of the Negro, 1746–1949*. To this monumental work Hughes contributed fourteen original poems and eleven translations, three from the French and eight from the Spanish.

In 1945 Gabriela Mistral won the Nobel Prize for literature and became the first Latin-American author to receive this international honor. In 1957, the Indiana University Press published a book entitled *Selected Poems of Gabriela Mistral*, translated by Langston Hughes. This is the only English translation of her works in book form and includes seventy-four of her best poems.

Hughes received high praise from the reviewers of this volume. A comparison of the original with the translation of a short poem and one half of another reveals the skill and genius of the translator.

Meciendo—Cradle Song

El mar sus millares de olas
  mece, divino,
Oyendo a los mares amantes
  mezo a mi niño.
	The sea cradles
	its millions of stars divine.
	Listening to the seas in love,
	I cradle the one who is mine.

El viento errabundo en la noche
  mece a los trigos
Oyendo a los vientos amantes
  Mezo a mi niño.
	The errant wind in the night
	cradles the wheat.
	Listening to the winds in love,
	I cradle my sweet.

Dios Padre sus miles de mundos   God Our Father cradles
mece sin ruido   His thousands of worlds
sintiendo su mano   without sound.
en la sombra,   Feeling His hand in the darkness,
  Mezo a mi niño.   I cradle the babe I have found.

Ausiencia—Absence

Se va de tí mi cuerpo gota a gota.   My body leaves you drop by drop,
Se va mi cara en un oleo sordo   my face leaves in a silence, of the
Se van mis manos en azoque suelto;   oil of death;
Se van mis pies en los tiempos   my hands leave in live mercury;
  de polvo.   my feet leave in two puffs of dust.
¡Se te va todo, se nos va todo!   All leaves you, all leaves us!

Se va mi voz que te hacia   My voice leaves that you make
  campana   a bell,
cerrada a cuanto no somos nosotros   silent when we are not ourselves.
Se van mis gestos que se devanaban, Expression leaves, dizzily entangled
en lazaderas, debajo tus ojos.   in knots and bows before your eyes.
Y se te va la mirada que entrega,   And the glance that I gave you
cuadan te mira,   leaves as I look at you, juniper
el enebro y el olino.   and elm.

On August 18, 1944, Jacques Roumain died in Port-au-
Prince mourned by hundreds to whom he was the intransigent
symbol of Haiti. Less than a month before, he had completed
his masterpiece, a novel, *Gouverneurs de la Rosée, Masters of
the Dew.*

During this period Dr. Mercer Cook was Supervisor of
English in the National Schools of Haiti under "La Commis-
sion Coopérative Haitiano-Americane d'Education." Dr.
Cook—to quote from a communication from him—did "the
basic translation in Port-au-Prince with help from the author's
Haitian friends and admirers."

Dr. Cook submitted his translation to at least two publishers
who rejected it. "Doubleday thought it 'too thin.'" Then
the late James H. Whyte suggested Reynal and Hitchcock.

"They liked the work but decided it needed considerable
revision. The language had to be more 'popular.' Remembering that Langston and Roumain were old friends, I wrote him
asking that he put the finishing touches on the translation.

"With the aid of Dr. René Piquion, Langston did the

revision and did it beautifully. He found the correct rhythm in English for the prose of his Haitian friend."

Here lay the supreme test of his translation power in his innate poetical gift of rhythm to convert into English Roumain's story of the Haitian people so close to earth, told in the melodious cadences of their speech.

Continues Dr. Cook, "Sometimes merely by changing the position of a word, Langston produced the desired effect. For example in the introduction to the novel, I had quoted Jean F. Brierre: 'Oh Jacques, Jacques!' This Langston improved to 'Jacques, oh Jacques!' "

Further examples may be supplied of Hughes's uncanny sense of diction in transposing into English the eloquent and musical turn of phrases either given directly in Creole Patois or in Roumain's masterful rendering of peasant speech in popular French to the height of literature.

The following furnish examples in contrasting the original text with the final English translation:

Original Text	*English Translations*
1. Elle fait: oui, mais de mauvaise grace.	Unwillingly she answered "Yes."
2. nègre à moué	Honey
3. Ses yeux ont une lumière de source.	Her eyes had an inner glow.
4. Ou délà des bayahondes une vapeur s'élève ou perd dans un dessin brouillé, la ligne a moitié effacéedes mornes lointains. Le ciel n'a pas une fissure. Ce n'est qu'une plague de tole brulante.	
	Back of the thorn acacias a hot haze distorted the half-hidden silhouette of far-off mountains. The sky was a gray-hot sheet of corrugated iron.
5. —la tamarinier lançait soudain comme une poignée de graviers un tourbillonnement criard de corneilles.	
	—the tamarind tree suddenly let fly a noisy swirl of crows like a handful of gravel.

The leading examples of Langston Hughes's contribution to the growing literature of translation have been culled from all available sources. In editing anthologies, particularly of

African creative writers, he has contributed translations of the writings of French-speaking native poets and creators of prose.

For example, in *Poems from Black Africa*, Mr. Hughes translated the French poem, "Flute Players," by Jean-Joseph Rabéarivelo, the most famous poet of Madagascar who died in Tananarive, a suicide.

Also, he put into English two French poems by the Senegalese David Diop who was lost with his wife in a plane wreck over the Atlantic in 1960. The English titles are "Those Who Lost Everything" and "Suffer, Poor Negro."

And now that our beloved interpreter has gone from us, "disparu dans le monde inconnu," mayhap he yet translates on higher planes the sorrows, the joys, the heartaches of those who dwell still in the shadows of Harlem; in the woebegone ghettos of our super cities.

In *Cuba Libre*, Ben Frederic Carruthers has translated Guillén's "Federico," a requiem for the great poet buried in an unmarked grave by his murderers in Granada. It is quoted in part here to paraphrase its closing refrain:

> I knock at the door of a romance.
> "Is Federico not here?"
> A parrot answers:
> "No, he has gone."
>
> I knock at the door of a gypsy.
> "Is Federico not here?"
> No one answers, no one speaks . . .
> "Federico! Federico!"
>
> *He left on Sunday at nine,*
> *he left on Sunday, at night,*
> *he left on Sunday, and never came back!*
>
> [Is it permitted to paraphrase here?]

Where are you, Langston?
Where are you, that you don't come?
Langston! Langston!
Where are you that you don't come?
Where are you that you don't come?

THE LITERARY EXPERIMENTS OF
LANGSTON HUGHES

By James A. Emanuel

Hanging almost out of sight, on the wall of an alcove at the corner of Langston Hughes's memento-crowded working-room in his attic apartment in Harlem, was a plaque engraved with the details of his election in 1961 to the National Institute of Arts and Letters. Among his achievements noted on the plaque was his success as an innovator. That imaginative work, especially the blues and jazz poetry, has been partially explored by the few critics who have deeply penetrated Hughes's style and substance. But the poet who published "Jazzonia" in 1923 and "Homesick Blues" in 1926 (experimental pieces that did not balk commentators) also published *Ask Your Mama* in 1961, a venturesome long poem updating Hughes's original efforts of the 1920's with a leap in technique that has out-distanced critical perceptions. When his dramatic, musical, and racial sensitivities happily merged in the gospel song-play, best exemplified in *Black Nativity*, Hughes established the dimensions of a new artistic form that analytical minds have accepted more as pleasure than as challenge. Although "the Poet Laureate of the Negro People" has been praised as an innovator, his innovations and experiments—not to mention his best works in all the major literary forms—have just begun to attract scholarly study.

Literary criticism, whether inspired by an awakening in the Establishment or by careful nurturing of Black Aestheticism, should closely examine Hughes's stylistic experiments, especially in his plays, his humorous prose, his short stories, and his poetry. In the drama, his union of tragicomedy and fantasy in *Soul Gone Home* suggests a kind of inquiry worthy of attention. In his humorous works, the language of Jesse B. Semple so tickles and startles students of literature that they have not fully appreciated the ingenuity behind its presentation. Whether that ingenuity is to be credited mostly to Hughes—as it should be—or mostly to the Negro folk diction to which his ear was so authentically tuned, there remains the task of assessing it as a contribution to literary art in America.

Technical experimentation in the author's short fiction, mentioned in discussions of his many stories in my dissertation, *The Short Stories of Langston Hughes* (Columbia University, 1962), becomes inseparable from personal style as the reader grows accustomed to Hughes's interspersed songs, parenthetical tableaus, and recurrent, racially significant images. Some unusual passages, however, are clearly experimental. Chief among them are his uses of interior monologue, limited to "Red-Headed Baby" and "Blessed Assurance." The rarity of stream-of-consciousness writing in Hughes's fiction rouses speculation about the occurrence of it even in those two stories, published twenty-eight years apart. A brief inspection of the contexts in which these passages of interior monologue appear may throw light on the problem of craftsmanship which they were meant to resolve.

In July, 1961, Hughes told me of the source of "Red-Headed Baby": "The background was from my own merchant marine days, and those dreary ports that coastwise ships go into; and they make several trips to the same port. A sailor could very well be the father of a child." The story, written in Carmel, California, in 1933 and first published the next year in *The Ways of White Folks*, recounts the brief visit of a red-headed sailor, Clarence, from his tramp steamer to the hut of Betsy, the Florida Negro girl he had enjoyed for a price three years earlier. While drinking with Betsy and her mother, the sailor is surprised by the appearance of what he calls "a damn runt of a red-headed baby," a deaf mute named Clarence, he soon discovers. Angered by the stares of the child, the sailor violently departs.

After the midpoint of this story, told almost completely through the fragmented thoughts of the predatory white sailor, Clarence takes on his lap the girl who three years before was a church-going teetotaler, but who now drinks liquor "strong enough to knock a mule down." He thinks:

> Soft heavy hips. Hot and browner than the moon—good licker. Drinking it down in little nigger house Florida coast palm fronds scratching roof hum mosquitoes night bug flies ain't loud enough to keep a man named Clarence girl named Betsy old woman named Auntie from talking and drinking in a little nigger house on Florida coast dead warm night with the licker browner and more fiery than the moon.

Near the end of the story, the sailor, thoroughly startled by the features of the child ("over two years old," says Betsy's mother, "and can't even say, 'Da!' "), vigorously insists on the baby's removal from the room:

> A red-headed baby. Moonlight-gone baby. No kind of yellow-white bow-legged goggled-eyed County Fair baseball baby. Get him the hell out of here pulling at my legs looking like me at me like me at myself like me red-headed as me.

The third and final passage, on the last page of the story, reveals the sailor's thoughts as he stumbles out of the shack:

> Knocking over glasses by the oil lamp on the table where the night flies flutter where skeleton houses left over from

> boom sand in the road and no lights in the nigger section
> across the railroad's knocking over glasses at edge of town
> where a moon-colored girl's got a red-headed baby deaf as
> a post like the dolls you wham at three shots for a quarter in
> the County Fair half full of licker and can't hit nothing.

In this story—a favorite of Hughes's—why does the author forsake standard exposition in these three passages? He is expert with dialogue, whether it is spoken by one of the Negro characters ("That chile near 'bout worries de soulcase out o' me. Betsy spiles him, that's why") or by the sailor ("Hey! Take your hands off my legs, you lousy little bastard!"). And expository sentence fragments elsewhere effectively convey the careless but sentient rush of the sailor's movements. The probable answer credits Hughes with an artistic deliberation that has seldom been recognized, linked with a humanity that, on the contrary, is widely acknowledged. Hughes must get inside the mind of Clarence, now slightly muddled with liquor but nevertheless—and perhaps for that very reason—keenly aware on a nonverbal level of its meandering fusions of personal and racial responses. The knowledge that he is white and that he is a father—and that he momentarily is both these things under the wrong conditions and in the face of the wrong consequences—unsettles him with a shock that defines a predicament of twentieth-century white America.

Hughes catches all the meaning, none of which would be as effective if rendered in coherent, rational prose. In the first passage, one senses the rough comforts of a sailor ashore: voluptuousness; brown skin turned into brown liquor; humming sounds that ward off a "scratching" world and unite three people with names instead of races in a carousal subconsciously ritualistic with its "Auntie" and "nigger" setting. The disruptive truth appears and controls the second passage, which appropriately begins with hints of ambivalent paternal pride and masculine sternness. In the middle of that natural response obtrudes awareness of race ("looking like me at me like me"), which is the signal for racial unreason and its stylistic counterpart, syntactical incoherence. That incoherence properly dominates the final passage. One should estimate Hughes's feeling for the sailor—as a father, not as a white man—in the complex of sensations and ideas blurred in the paragraph: blind, almost fearful, escape; perception of economic and political injustice; and guilt-ridden violence accentuated by a sense of failure (the failure of bawdy virility fathering only a "baby deaf as a post," a "baseball baby" whose rollicking sire in his sexual life "can't hit nothing"). Asked whether the stream-of-consciousness style was deliberately chosen as a necessary effect in "Red-Headed Baby," Hughes wrote to me in July, 1961, "Yes—like what goes through the characters' minds in the room."

A year later, the author presented me with a typescript of another story, inscribed "14th and Final Draft (I hope)." Written and revised seven times in July, 1961, and much altered the following winter, the version of it dated October 9, 1962, became his final story, "Blessed Assurance," and in America was first printed in *Something in Common and Other Stories* (1963). The six-page story concentrates on the Spring Concert of the Tried Stone Baptist Church, where the protagonist-father's anguish over his son Delmar's occasional femininity culminates. When Dr. Manley Jaxon, Minister of Music, who has written an anthem for the concert and assigned the female lead to "Delly," faints and falls off his organ stool as the boy hits a sweet high note, the father's "I'll be damned" concedes his moment of worst despair.

As in "Red-Headed Baby," three passages of interior monologue detail the protagonist's crucial bewilderment. The first one offers a glimpse of the thoughts of John, the father, when his seventeen-year-old son chooses spectacles with exaggerated rims: " 'At least he didn't get rhinestone rims,' thought John half-thought didn't think felt faint and aloud said nothing." The second passage pictures John wondering about Delmar after the boy starts to grow a beard in imitation of certain beatniks he has seen in Greenwich Village:

> "God, don't let him put an earring in his ear like some," John prayed. He wondered vaguely with a sick feeling in his stomach should he think it through then then think it through right then through should he try then and think it through should without blacking through think blacking out then and there think it through?

Instead of thinking it through, John ponders Delmar's remark that he would like to study at the Sorbonne in Paris—not at Morgan, the Negro university that is his own alma mater. After the embarrassment at the Spring Concert, John wonders about the Sorbonne: "Does it have dormitories, a campus? In Paris he had heard they didn't care about such things. Care about such what things didn't care about what?"

Again, why does Hughes not employ standard exposition? Dealing this time with a Negro father and son whose race is essentially irrelevant to their dilemma—rather than with a white sailor whose race exacerbates his predicament—the author must again illuminate a perversion of feeling by reaching psychological depths where the whirl of things remembered and feared constitutes a disorder frightfully coherent to the unsteady mind but resistant to the shaping powers of traditional syntax. John's thinking and not thinking—that is, his thinking about his son and half-thinking or not thinking about himself—are captured in the first passage with an economy not available to ordinary prose. In the second passage, interior monologue makes almost kaleidoscopic the changing patterns of the father's unstated past failures and his present weakness—the patterns of causation and time, as modified by doubts about the laws of heredity, being strictly controlled by the juxtapositions "then then" and "then and there." In the third passage, the knuckle-rapping self-administered by the father sharply opposes consciousness and conscience in this man struggling to be honest with himself. That struggle, according to a letter that Hughes wrote to me on September 19, 1961, represents to the author the plight of "one afraid to fully face realities." (And the dilemma of Clarence in "Red-Headed Baby," the same letter indicates, is meant to show that white people "are human, too.")

The relatively unknown experimental techniques that add interest to many of Hughes's poems are too numerous to record in a brief essay. Yet, their categories can be fairly represented, some by example and others by descriptive reference. Examples are necessary in the case of Hughes's topographical and emblematic experiments—forms having antecedents in seventeenth-century England and America, and ultimately related to the acrostic verse of early Greek and Latin poets. His "Angels Wings" is a good example:

> The angels wings is white as snow,
>   O, white as snow,
>   White
>   as
>   snow.
> The angels wings is white as snow,
>   But I drug ma wings
>   In the dirty mire.
>   O, I drug ma wings
>   All through the fire.
> But the angels wings is white as snow,
>   White
>   as
>   snow.

The grammar of the first line brings the poem into the domain of Jesse B. Semple; and the zest and imagery of the Negro folk sermon possessively move through what would otherwise seem an emblematic verse by the pious English rector, George Herbert, shaped like the angel's wings that it praises.

Another kind of experimental thrust by Hughes is represented by "Jitney," a poem topographical in conception, intended to convey the reader almost physically on the jump-seat of a jitney cab making two round trips up and down South Parkway in Chicago. The first half of the poem follows:

> Corners
> Of South Parkway:
> Eeeoooooo!
> Cab!
> 31st,
> 35th,
> 39th,
> 43rd,
> Girl, ain't you heard?
> *No, Martha, I ain't heard.*
> I got a Chinese boy-friend
> Down on 43rd.
> 47th,
> 51st,
> 55th,
> 63rd,
> Martha's got a Japanese!
> Child, ain't you heard?
> 51st,
> 47th,
> Here's your fare!
> Lemme out!

I'm going to the Regal,
See what this week's jive is all about:
The Duke is mellow!
Hibbler's giving out!
43rd,
39th,
Night school!
Gotta get my teaching!
35th,
31st,
Bless God!
Tonight there's preaching!
31st! All out!
Hey, Mister, wait!
I want to get over to State.
I don't turn, Madam!
Understand?
Take a street car
Over to the Grand.

The form itself is meant to capture the single-street route, endlessly turning back upon itself; the numbers indicate the bouncing speed; and the distortions of rumor—realistically introduced after the 43rd Street intersection and continued only after Martha has left the cab—are thoughtfully mixed with references to educational ambition as well as entertainment among South Side Negroes.

An additional type of poem expressing the innovative bent of Hughes at work on total form is exemplified by "The Cat and the Saxophone/(2 A.M.)," which merges a swinging Negro lyric with a traditional but Harlem-toned dramatic dialogue. The first half reads as follows:

EVERYBODY
Half-pint,—

> Gin?
> No, make it
> LOVES MY BABY
> corn. You like
> liquor,
> don't you, honey?
> BUT MY BABY
> Sure. Kiss me,
> DON'T LOVE NOBODY
> daddy.
> BUT ME.

Hughes's modernity in 1926 (when this poem appeared in *The Weary Blues*), evident in the advanced form as well as in the typography of the title and the final line of the poem (consisting of a single exclamation point), anticipates modes common to poets of the 1960's. The flow of meaning between the phrases of the lyric and the contiguous dialogue ably accentuates the poet's ingenuity.

A number of stylistic ventures in other poems merit attention. The use of folk diction and of urban slang from the milieu of jazz and be-bop, like certain characteristics of his short stories, so often informs Hughes's poetic styles that familiarity wears down the reader's surprise, if not his satisfaction. Phrases like "birthing is hard" in "Advice," and "put de miz on me" in "Brief Encounter," and "don't ig me" in "Midnight Chippie's Lament," all poems from the 1940's, are examples. In his work of the 1950's, when the dawn "bops bright" in "Chord," when a "cool bop daddy" goes by in "Dead in There," and when boys are "copping a thrill" in "Up-Beat," the innovative language is still part of the life style of Hughes's Harlem models.

Other experimental devices found in the poet's work owe less to racial sources, although Hughes adapts them to his racial materials. The kind of stylistic freedom widespread among American poets in the 1920's and strengthening among writers of fiction is particularly apparent in such poems of Hughes's as "Ballad of the Landlord," which uses newspaper captions as lines of verse. A related technique, employed almost twenty years later in "Neon Signs" (in *Montage of a Dream Deferred*, 1951), yields a poem almost totally comprised of the names of Harlem bars and nightclubs. As if toying with a concept of medley and miscellany, Hughes writes "Deferred" a few years later, using twelve voices besides his own. In the same decade, his "Good Morning" and "In Explanation of Our Times" use unpunctuated series of geographical and personal names to bring new fluidity into his images and to make phrasal units out of groups that sociologically or economically are bound together. This same technique is practiced with greater virtuosity in the later *Ask Your Mama*.

Hughes's final book of poems, *The Panther and the Lash* (1967)—distinguished partly for its reprinting of that passionately brave and artful poem of 1931 that nearly caused a riot at the University of North Carolina, "Christ in Alabama"— contains three poems relevant to this sketch of Hughes as innovator. "Elderly Leaders," "Go Slow," and "Stokely Malcolm Me" all elaborate upon a technique forecast forty years earlier in "The Cat and the Saxophone/(2 A.M.)." The final lines of each poem appear on the page as follows:

["Elderly Leaders"]	["Go Slow"]	["Stokely Malcolm Me"]
$$$$$	????	
$$$$	???	???
$$$	??	??
$$	?	?
$		

The structural authenticity of the ending of each of the first two poems can be estimated by its obvious summation of the meaning discernible even in the title. The ending of the third poem is emphatic, but less functional.

These last poems connect Hughes the stylist with LeRoi Jones and other young poets who are reaching in many directions for style strong enough to control the fervor of their substance. Every reader of poetry, in perusing the work of Hughes, connects solidly with him many times, in the plain truth of his utterance, in the warmth or gaiety of the life that he pictures, or in the freshness of his style. It is the responsibility of the critics to sift among Hughes's poems, stories, and other productions to preserve his best art, to strengthen in his countrymen what the novelist Joyce Cary has called "the bridge between souls."

LANGSTON HUGHES AND AFRO–AMERICAN FOLK AND CULTURAL TRADITION

By George E. Kent

Langston Hughes's literary career began with a commitment to black folk and cultural sources as one important basis for his art. The folk forms and cultural responses were themselves definitions of black life created by blacks on the bloody and pine-scented Southern soil and upon the blackboard jungle of urban streets, tenement buildings, store-front churches, and dim-lit bars. Thus the current generation of black writers, who are trying to develop artistic forms that reflect a grip upon realities as they exist from day to day in black communities, discover that Langston Hughes is an important pioneer, in his non-ideological way, who has already "been there and gone."

Hughes's commitment to folk and cultural tradition forces us to look more searchingly for the *significance* of the folk literature and art that derives from centuries of confrontation of black lives with the ambiguities of their universe and that of American culture.

From the animal tales to the hipsterish urban myth-making, folk tradition has *is-ness*. Things are. Things are funny, sad, tragic, tragicomic, bitter, sweet, tender, harsh, awe-inspiring, cynical, other-worldly, worldly—sometimes alternately expressing the conflicting and contradictory qualities; sometimes, expressing conflicting qualities simultaneously. Thus a Brer Rabbit story is full of the contradictions of experience—an expression of the existing order of the world and Brer Rabbit's unspecific sense of something "other." And there are times in Brer Rabbit stories during which the existing order and Brer Rabbit's "other" have almost equal validity. (See especially "Brer Rabbit and Sis Cow" and "Why Brer Rabbit Wears a 'Round-'Bout" in Hughes and Bontemps, *The Book of Negro Folklore* [New York, 1958], pp. 4-6. In this discussion of folk and folk tradition, I have been particularly influenced by Ralph Ellison, *Shadow and Act* [New York, 1964], and by conversations with my colleague, Professor Charles Long, of the Divinity School of the University of Chicago.) The black preacher can be a revered personage, but also a figure of comedy, and the oppressed can be sad as victim but comic as a person. As creative artist, Langston Hughes had more of an instinctive, than intellectual, sense of the folk acceptance of the contradictory as something to be borne, climbed on top of, confronted by the shrewd smile, the cynical witticism, the tragicomic scratch of the head, the tense and sucked-in bottom lip, the grim but determined look beyond this life, and, more familiarly, the howl of laughter that blacks have not yet learned to separate from the inanities of minstrel tradition.

Thus, upon entering the universe of Langston Hughes, one leaves at its outer darkness that *type* of *rationality* whose herculean exertions are for absolute resolution of contradictions and external imposition of symmetry. For at many points, though not at all points, Hughes is full of the folk.

And in the face of the stubborn contradictions of life, the folk could frequently call upon their spirits and selves to mount on up a little higher, and simply acknowledge: "It be's that way."

Failure to understand the instance in which the folk do

more to move their spirit than to move "objective" reality can lead the critic of the folk and Hughes into a fantasia of misinterpretation. Thus blues critic Samuel Charters in *The Poetry of the Blues* (p. 33) complains because blues singer Bessie Smith's "Long Old Road" expresses great determination to stand up to the terrors of life's journey and to shake hands at journey's end with a friend, but ends in a futility that eliminates the value of the journey: "Found my long lost friend, and I might as well stayed at home." However, Bessie's resolution is in the face-up-to-it spirit, a tone of pathos, outrage, and defiance mingled, not in the rhetoric of formal rationality.

And thus Robert Bone in his work of criticism, *The Negro Novel in America* (pp. 76-77), makes neat, clever remarks about ideological confusion in Hughes's novel, *Not Without Laughter*, upon discovering that the story advocates both "compensatory" laughter in the face of life's pain and achievement based upon "the protestant ethic." But expressions such as "the success drive," and "the protestant ethic" simply flatten out into lifeless categories the rich density of the folk hope, which is better expressed by its own terms: "being somebody" and "getting up off your knees." The folk tend to be community oriented; thus in *Not Without Laughter* Aunt Hager and Aunt Harriett (representative of the religious and blues traditions, respectively) tend to see the central character's achievement possibilities in the form of community uplift. It is Aunt Tempy who more nearly represents something that could be called "protestant ethic," and she is rejected. As will be seen later in the essay, the novel does have problems, but it is unlikely that they would be resolved under the neat dichotomies with which Bone deals.

A third major quality that folk tradition reflects in its less self-conscious form is an *as ifness*. Whereas one feels behind self-conscious black literature the unarticulated knowledge that America for blacks is neither a land of soul nor of bread, a good deal of folklore suggests a complete penetration of its universe, a possession of the land and self in a more thoroughgoing way than that expressed by white American literature. Spirituals, for example, suggest a complete mining of their universe. Many of the animal tales and general folk stories also suggest that a universe has been possessed and defined. The *blues*, however, as a more self-conscious folk form achieves this confident embracement only in specific songs, since so many of them feature a wanderer and throw such terrible weight upon the individual self. What Langston Hughes and Claude McKay (and possibly Jean Toomer in *Cane*) were able to retain, though sometimes insecurely, were a bounce and warm vitality whose fragile supports are everywhere apparent even when the entire work seems to be devoted to their celebration. The sudden appearance of aggressive symbols of the white world would bring many of the celebrations to a halt or reveal, at least, the high cost of soul. As a result, some black novels end in an otherwise inexplicable romanticism.

Despite the difficulties, Langston Hughes chose to build his vision on the basis of the folk experience as it had occurred in the South and as it appeared modified in the modern industrial city. Judging from his autobiography, *The Big Sea*, his choice proceeded from the center of his being. He liked black folks. He liked their naturalness, their sense of style, their bitter facing up, their individual courage, and the variety of qualities that formed part of his own family background. He was also in recoil from the results of his father's hard choices of exile, hatred of blacks, self-hatred, and resulting dehumanization. His manifesto of 1926, "The Negro Artist and the Racial Mountain," revealed that choosing the life of the black folk was also a way of choosing himself, a way of possessing himself through the rhythms and traditions of black people. His choice enabled him to allow for prevailing ideologies without being smothered by them, since folk vision could suddenly shift from tenderness to biting cynicism and since within its womb a pragmatic embracement of ideological impulses that promised survival was a secure tradition. Thus, whereas pre-1920's black writers, devoid of a land of soul and a land of bread, found themselves completely at the mercy of that complex of ideas in the social arena known as the American Dream, Hughes brings in aspects of the Dream at will, but so many bitter notes accompany it that he can hardly be said to put much confidence in it. I speak, of course, in the light of the large number of poems that are devoted to other matters. The individual poems, such as "I, Too," which speak of an America that will come to its senses are scattered here and there among poems that discharge the sudden drop of acid. Hughes prized decency in the individual person and could not look with compassion upon those corrupted delusions and systematized prejudice, but in several poems he responded with outrage, bitterness, anger, and threat.

It is easily forgotten that one part of "I, Too" speaks of eating well and growing strong, so that no one would *dare* say to the black, "Eat in the kitchen." In *Selected Poems*, bitterness and desperation are especially apparent in the sections entitled "Magnolia Flowers" and "Name in Uphill Letters," but also directly and indirectly in individual poems among the other sections. In the two sections mentioned, the poems "Roland Hayes Beaten" and "Puzzled" convey the sense of a coming explosion. But one needs merely to range over the body of published poems, in order to sense within Hughes a very powerful ambivalence. Nevertheless, he adopted a psychological approach for his readings to black audiences, described in his second autobiographical book, *I Wonder as I Wander* (pp. 56-60), which allowed for laughter, then serious and grim situations, and finally the hopeful and stoical stance. Such poems as "I, Too" and "The Negro Mother" gave the positive note without shoving aside the ogres that threatened.

In Langston Hughes's vision, both in regard to the folk and to himself, the most nearly consistent focus is upon a lifesmanship that preserves and celebrates humanity in the face of impossible odds. In regard to himself, Hughes is the most modest of persons. Even his apparent frankness in the autobiographies *The Big Sea* and *I Wonder as I Wander* is deceptive, since his emotional responses are frequently understated or their nuances undramatized. Missing is the closeup focus of the protracted relationship that threatens to reveal the soul or the total person. Thus there are unforgettable pictures—Hughes's relationship to his father and mother, his brief companionship with a refugee girl while down and out in Paris, his conflict with Russian officials over the production of a movie on race relationships in America, etc. But the man behind the picture remains somewhat elusive.

What does emerge is transcendent moments amidst the chaos that society and human nature tend to create. Two or more people getting through to each other, the seizure of richness from surrounding rottenness or confusion, the sudden appearance of the rainbow after the storm, the individual retaining his focus upon the human—the foregoing comprise the stuff of the autobiographies, which are frequently comparable to the episodic experiences of lyrics and convey only the slimmest hint of the single broad meaning that would impose the illusion of unity upon human experience. In all the autobiographical approaches, Hughes is consistent with what I have called the *is-ness* of folk vision and tradition—life is lived from day to day and confronted by plans whose going astray may evoke the face twisted in pain or the mouth open in laughter. The triumph is in holding fast to dreams and maintaining, if only momentarily, the spirit of the self.

As to the folk, Hughes was early captivated by their stubborn lifesmanship. Through his grandmother he had early learned the heroic side of black life, and he had experienced the rituals of the black church and pretended to be saved. As he encountered the urban folk, he was taken in by the full-bodied warmth of their lives, the color, the bounce, the vitality. But he also knew the harshness of their existence in the huge city, since he had spent a summer during adolescence on South State Street in Chicago when his mother was employed by a dress shop. In *The Big Sea: An Autobiography* (p. 33) he says:

> South State Street was in its glory then, a teeming Negro street with crowded theaters, restaurants, and cabarets. And excitement from noon to noon. Midnight was like day. The street was full of workers and gamblers, prostitutes and pimps, church folks and sinners. The tenements on either side were very congested. For neither love nor money could you find a decent place to live. Profiteers, thugs, and gangsters were coming into their own.

Like Sandy in *Not Without Laughter*, Hughes walked bewildered among the new sights. But the harshness within the black community was not the sum of the situation. When he wandered beyond it, he was beaten by hostile whites.

This early awareness of the embattled situation of folk existence in the Northern city and the direct brutality of the Southern life that drove blacks to urban questing probably protected Hughes from the falsification of folklife that James Weldon Johnson found in the poetry of Paul Laurence Dunbar (see his comments in the two prefaces in *The Book of American Negro Poetry*). Instead of the idyllic, Hughes could portray honestly a people caged within a machine culture, sometimes feeding upon each other, sometimes snarling at the forces without, and sometimes rising above tragedy by the sheer power of human spirit. A people responding to existence through cultural forms and traditions derived from so many terrible years of facing up and demanding, at the same time, a measure of joy and affirmation: the dance, jazz, blues, spirituals, the church. Across the water in France, he found:

> Blues in the rue Pigalle. Black and laughing, heartbreaking blues in the Paris dawn, pounding like a pulse-beat, moving like the Mississippi!
>
> *Lawd, I looked and saw a spider*
> *Goin' up de wall.*
> *I say, I looked and saw a spider*
> *Goin' up de wall.*
> *I said where you goin', Mister Spider?*
> *I'm goin' to get my ashes hauled!*
> [*The Big Sea*, p. 162]

The variety of life and its relationship to the self was expressed in simple symbols that allowed for the whole gamut of stances toward existence.

Later, amidst the phoniness that he found in black middle-class Washington society, he was again to encounter the triumphant spirit of the "low-down folks." They served as an inspiration:

> I tried to write poems like the songs they sang on Seventh Street—gay songs, because you had to be gay or die; sad songs, because you couldn't help being sad sometimes. But gay or sad, you kept on living and you kept on going. Their songs—those of Seventh Street—had the pulse beat of the people who keep on going. [*The Big Sea*, p. 209]

Hughes speaks of the "undertow of black music with its rhythm that never betrays you, its strength like the beat of the human heart, its humor, and its rooted power." On

Seventh Street, he encountered both the "barrel houses," suppliers of the gay, naughty, and wise music, and the black churches full of song and intense religious experience. It is good to keep in mind the ceremonies of humanity which Hughes found in the folk even when reading of his non-black experiences, since he seems to have sought the same qualities in all people.

The above approach applies to Hughes's writings that are not in folk forms and are not about the folk. He seldom takes up a form that could not express the folk or that expresses *forms of response* to existence that are foreign to their sensibility. This is to say that Hughes was sensitive to the implications of form. Thus he early allied himself with free verse forms that acknowledge, as Walt Whitman long ago pointed out, the flexibility, sweep, and unstructured aspects of life and the dynamic quality of American society. The blues form, with its sudden contrasts, varied repetitions, resolution areas, allows for the brief and intense expression of the ambiguities of life and the self, and for sharp wit and cynicism. The jazz, bebop, and boogie-woogie rhythms achieve a free swing away from Western constraints. One could add comments on the significance of the traditional work songs, the influence of spirituals, shouts, the gospel song, the prayer, the testimonial, and the sermon. Suffice it here to say that they move us into an immediate recognition of a black experience that is at the center of a long tradition, convey attitudes and forms of response to existence, and often give the illusion of confronting us, not merely with lines upon a page, but with a participant of a particular ritual.

Now as James A. Emanuel has ably pointed out in his book, *Langston Hughes* (pp. 137, 146) it is difficult to gain the total blues experience or the musical experience of jazz and other rhythms from the printed page, since the writer is deprived of the embellishments used by the blues singer and the musician. However, the handicap of the printed page should alert us to compensations available to the writer, to other dangers that bestride his path, and to Hughes's variation from the standard path of the Western artist. In the first place, it is seldom really of value simply to duplicate a folk form, since the folk artist has already pushed the form to its greatest heights of expressiveness. In mere repetition, the self-conscious artist usually runs the risk of merely echoing achievements that have had the advantage of generations of responsive audiences. His real opportunity is in capturing the spirit of the art, in adapting techniques, in adding to folk forms an articulation of assumptions which the folk artist merely had to hint at because his audience was so closely akin to him (or he was so closely akin to his audience). Thus the self-conscious artist is not necessarily being praised for a very high achievement when the critic points to his creation of a perfect blues or spiritual form.

The above principles regarding the folk artist and the self-conscious writer are true if the printed page is to be the sole basis of judgment, a handicap that Hughes often hurdled by reading his poems directly to audiences (with or without musical accompaniment) and by his close relationship to the black community. He, therefore, to a degree, evaded the confinement to the printed page that is the fate of the alienated or abstracted standard Western artist. Thus he could read the mulatto's statement in the poem "Cross" to an audience that had lived with the white enforced miscegenation that forms the subject of the poem, and deliver a powerful impact. He did not, for example, have to dramatize or explain the changes within the mulatto, who merely states them as conclusions. This kind of compensation, however, was not available for every poem by Hughes, and therefore, he must frequently face the question as to whether he is not operating too close to the folk form.

Any criticism of Hughes must thus also face the instances and the degree to which he varied from the traditional stance of the Western artist. Much of his work is very little reflective of a concern to be *universal* and *timeless*. Instead, the topicality of numerous pieces reflects Hughes's satisfaction in giving the issues of the community an immediate and striking voice.

A more concrete demonstration of Hughes's relationship to folk and cultural tradition may be gained from selected fiction, poetry, and drama. Although he became famous during the 1920's as a poet, Hughes reveals the spread of his concerns and their hazards more clearly in literary types that provided considerable sweep, rather than brief lyrical intensity. *Not Without Laughter*, Hughes's first novel, is therefore the starting point, for strategic reasons peculiar to this essay, and its discussion will be followed by an examination of representative poems and plays.

Not Without Laughter portrays a family that is very close to the folk, and reveals styles of confronting the disorder and chaos that attempted to hammer its way into the precariously held sanctuary of black family life. The novel portrays the tensions of a generation that came to adulthood not long after the hopes of blacks for freedom had been fully brought low throughout the land. (The first reference to time is a letter postmarked June 13, 1912.) The mainstay and would-be shepherd of this generation is Aunt Hager, whose life is an epic of labor over the washtub. Getting ready to meet adulthood as the third generation is her grandson, Sandy, a witness to the perilous hold on life managed by his family: the grandmother; his mother, Anjee; his wandering father, Jimboy; and his aunts, Tempy and Harriett. Although the events controlling the life of each member of the family absorb a goodly portion

LANGSTON HUGHES: BLACK GENIUS

of the novel, the development and fate of the boy Sandy and especially the extent to which the lives of his elders provide him with a usable resource form the big question mark in the novel.

Aunt Hager, the grandmother, represents the religious tradition begun in the secret "praise" meetings of slavery and further developed in the little whitewashed churches that once dotted the countryside and the small towns.

And here we must beware of the oversimplified versions of black religion, since the race's religious experience, like all other black experiences, requires reevaluation in its own terms, one which will release it from the oversimplified categories of escapism and otherworldliness that were developed by analogy with what is required in duplicating the Faustian quest of whites. Aunt Hager's religion, as Hughes presents it, reflects solemn moments, dogged persistence, and an ability to love and forgive, that give magnitude to the humblest. It places man against the sky. It allows Aunt Hager, according to her report, to pray for whites that she doesn't like, but she is still pragmatic and unworshipful towards them (unlike Faulkner's Dilsey of *The Sound and the Fury*). In her eyesight, whites, in their relationship with blacks, are good as far as they *see* but they do not see far. This is not to say that Aunt Hager fully grasps or brings into a single focus the hard realities of a racially oppressive system that primarily values her as a workhorse and twists the lives of her children into shapes that can grasp joy only by refusing to be stifled by disaster. Since Hughes is aware of her limitations, he counterpoints her determined optimism by the bitter and sinister reports of Jimboy, Sister Johnson, and Harriett, and by portraits of racial injustice.

What impresses Hughes and Sandy is the passionate spiritual power that sustains faith in life and in a day of overcoming. She would like for Sandy to be a Booker Washington and a Frederick Douglass: "I wants him to know all they is to know, so's he can help this black race of our'n to come up and see de light and take they places in de world. I wants him to be a Fred Douglass leadin' de people, that's what, an' not followin' in de tracks o' his good-for-nothin' pappy . . ." (*Not Without Laughter*, p. 146).

This folk sense of making something out of oneself has a lasting impact upon Sandy, but there are also available to him the jazz and blues tradition through his father Jimboy and his Aunt Harriett. Hughes plays very warmly and lovingly the notes of the tradition that involve a bouncing vitality and a defiant celebration of the sweets, joys, and pains of life, and Sandy finds himself drawn to the people who demand that life yield its more soulful fruits. However, Hughes has a very complex awareness, one that he cannot fully render within the novel. He is also an honest and realistic writer. Therefore, he can not make of Jimboy's situation a very simple triumph and must report the cost of Jimboy's joy, charm, and exuberance. It is the increased deprivation of his family and some rather painful childhood experiences of Sandy that register the cost of Jimboy's bounce and spontaneity. Thus, despite Hughes's distancing of Jimboy's wide-ranging amours, explanations of the systematic oppression that tends to reduce black men, the portrayal of him as a "rounder" who works and holds good intentions, and dramatization of his ability to transform the atmosphere of his surroundings, Jimboy is never quite clear of the dubious stature which Aunt Hager very early in the novel confers upon him. Jimboy is, after all, *boy*.

Thus the sensitive youth Sandy can only share moments of the tradition represented by his father, can only feel that the swing and bounce that he represents ought, somehow, to be a part of the richness of any life.

Hughes's complex awareness of what the folk were up

against in the attempt to assert the free life spirit is also apparent in his portrait of Harriett, who learns through her intermittent bouts with prostitution and utter destitution the price-tag placed by a machine culture upon spontaneity. Near the end of the novel, she seems to be on the way to fame and fortune, but Hughes was too familiar with the instabilities that hovered about the success of the black actors, actresses, and entertainers of this period. For most, it was an up and down sort of life, and the "down" area was often slimy.

Since Aunt Tempy's choice of a bloodless imitation of white society represented for Hughes an obvious surrender of soul, her life represented little that could promise richness to Sandy.

In the end, Sandy is thrown back upon the dreams of Aunt Hager. Although the metaphor seems awkward when applied to her, she too was a dancer of the spirit and held dreams of his becoming the dancer who overshot the un-ambiguous hazards that, for the folk, skyrocketed the price of soul. Perhaps one need not literally repeat the folk forms of dancing, the folk existence; perhaps one might achieve fulfillment if one could conceive of Booker Washington and Frederick Douglass as dancers of the spirit, too. Perhaps one could retain much of the folk spirit and attitude as one transformed their dances.

> A band of dancers. . . . Black dancers—captured in a white world. . . . Dancers of the spirit, too. Each black dreamer a captured dancer of the spirit. . . . Aunt Hager's dreams for Sandy dancing far beyond the limitations of their poverty, of their humble station in life, of their dark skins. [*Not Without Laughter*, p. 313]

Other than folk responses to existence, the novel contains such forms as blues, folk aphorisms, slave narratives and a slave tall story, dances, and spirituals. Especially significant is the spiritual that comes at the very end, "By an' by when de mawnin' comes . . ." The spiritual ends with the line, "An' we'll understand it better by an' by!" It tells of overcoming, suggests a determined struggle which cannot be easily conceptualized or understood, and is being sung in the big, raw city of Chicago. As Hughes has said, it is the music of a "people on the go," who are somehow to break free from their cage. The vague aspirations, but settled determination, of Sandy are a fitting part of the ending.

The novel, of course, has its problems. Sandy's consciousness does not develop dramatically, and there are contradictory statements about his degrees of innocence. Jimboy's moral lecture to Sandy comes abruptly, and, seemingly, out of character, and Harriett's insistence upon the vision of Aunt Hager needs stronger foreshadowing. Finally, the ending does not dramatically impose itself upon the reader, although it is logically the right one. Much of the source of the forgoing deficiencies seems to be Hughes's complex awareness of the hard and stubborn realities, which the characters will somehow have to overcome. He is almost too aware of the uncertainties of black life.

On the other hand, the novel makes clear the sensibility that created the poems which preceded it and followed it, and looks forward to the rough urban responses provided by his short stories, the *Simple* sketches, and the plays. For *Not Without Laughter* emphasizes Hughes's awareness of the overwhelming oppression that dancers of the spirit faced in both rural and urban cages of the American machine culture, the limitations in the major forms of folk culture, and the increasing difficulty of asserting the triumph of the spirit, as will be reflected by the poems and plays that form the remainder of this discussion.

In his essay, "The Harlem of Langston Hughes' Poetry,"

in *Phylon*, XIII (Fourth Quarter, 1952), Arthur P. Davis has cogently pointed out the increasing desperation and the decreasing emphasis upon joy in poems devoted to urban Harlem reflected in the major collections of poetry from *The Weary Blues* through *Montage of a Dream Deferred*. The volumes represent the adaptation of the folk spirit to the big urban surroundings, and the attempt to transform the threatening pressures of city machine culture into a poetry responsive to the spirit and often to transcend by defiant assertion of spirit. On the one hand are the tough and soulful blues, the cabarets and jazz bands, the singers, and sparkling personalities; on the other, the stark upcreep of weariness and the varieties of offenses to the human spirit unleashed by the city. To these may be added other urban poems that do not deal with Harlem, the more rural Southern poems, or poems on the general theme of the South, and poems on the general theme of the qualities and dilemmas of blacks. Finally, there are the poems that address themselves to life, without regard to race. The variety of categories makes possible a variety of notes and attitudes.

Hughes's most obvious and original innovation was the introduction of blues form and attitudes as part of the art of poetry. The uses of such blues devices as swift contrasts, sharp wit, voice tones, and folk imagery frequently create striking effects, despite the lack of musical accompaniment and gesture that were available to the blues singer. "Midwinter Blues," which first appeared in *Fine Clothes to the Jew*, seems to me to catch the essential folk spirit adapted to an urban setting and to contain the literary possibilities of the form. The poem, taken from *Selected Poems of Langston Hughes*, begins:

> In the middle of the winter,
> Snow all over the ground.

> In the middle of the winter,
> Snow all over the ground—
> 'Twas the night befo' Christmas
> My good man turned me down.

The conjunction of the cold of the winter with the associations we have with Christmas and the contrasting actual response of "my good man" get the poem off to an incisive start and combine narrative and blues techniques. However, the second stanza has the sudden turn of wit and irony of attitude more closely associated with the blues.

> Don't know's I'd mind his goin'
> But he left me when the coal was low.
> Don't know's I'd mind his goin'
> But he left when the coal was low.
> Now, if a man loves a woman
> That ain't no time to go.

The third and fourth stanzas, unfortunately, lack the power of the first two, but the third stanza does bring in a new response of the *contradictory self*. Despite the somewhat snide remarks in the first two lines of the second stanza, the "good man" is acknowledged as "the only man I'll/ Love till the day I die." The fourth stanza states a general attitude that requires the voice of the blues singer to maintain intensity and to assert the toughness of spirit characteristic of the blues. Frequently, the last stanza seems to lose intensity, simply because we do not have the ingenious use of triumphant tone that the actual blues singer is able to render.

Thus "Young Gal's Blues" has three closely knit stanzas by written literary standards. The fourth is related to the other three in an associational way, but an actual blues singer would bring home both its power and relatedness. On the other hand, "Down and Out," which first appeared in *Shakespeare in Harlem*, 1942, maintains its unity, sings itself, and provides an interesting effect by an *apparently* anti-climactic arrangement and the repetition of the last line for emphasis.

> Baby, if you love me
> Help me when I'm down and out.
> If you love me, baby,
> Help me when I'm down and out,
> I'm a po' gal
> Nobody gives a damn about.
>
> The credit man's done took ma clothes
> And rent time's nearly here.
> I'd like to buy a straightenin' comb,
> An' I need a dime fo' beer.
>
> I need a dime fo' beer.

As a song, "Down and Out" would lend itself to a variety of singing styles. As a written work, the concision of the first verse and the suggestiveness regarding the blues attitudes in the second verse allow for the activity of the creative reader. Several poems (all poems quoted hereafter are found in *The Selected Poems of Langston Hughes*) provide both this unity and suggestiveness: "Lament over Love," "Stony Lonesome," "Miss Blues'es Child," and "Hard Daddy," for example. Obvious literary unity, however, does not always produce the powerfully expressed folk spirit, since, in its own style, the poem must compete with the folk blues poem whose black audiences hold assumptions in common with the singer—a fact that permits him to impose a unity not based upon simple logical structure but upon his total performance. The following lines by Blind Lemon Jefferson as I have been able to gather them from Samuel Charters' edited record, *The Country Blues*, will illustrate the non-logical structure with which the blues singer is free to operate. Jefferson gives

it a powerful rendering by his damn-my-hard-luck-soul
variations in tone:

> I'm gwine to de river
> Walk down by the sea (Repeated)
> I got those tadpoles and minnows
> Arguing over me.

> Settin' here wonderin'
> Will a match-box hold my clothes (Repeated)
> Ain't got so many matches
> But I got so far to go.

> Lord, mama, who may your manager be?
> Hey, hey, mama, who may your manager be?
> You ask so many questions, can't you
> Make 'rangements for me?

> I got a girl way cross town
> She chrochet all the time (Repeated)
> Baby, if you don't stop chrocheting
> You goin' lose your mind.

> I wouldn't mind marrying,
> But I can't stand settlin' down
> Wouldn't mind marryin'
> But, Lord, settlin' down
> I'm goin' act like a preacher
> An' ride from town to town.

> I'm leaving town
> Cryin' won't make me stay,
> I'm leavin' town, woo-oo
> Cryin' won't make me stay,
> The more you cry, baby,
> The more you drive me away.

The blues lyric has behind it enough audience assumptions

regarding the singer's message to make a discussion for a separate essay: the gritty circumstances that inform the mood; the appearance of the prostitute in the third stanza; the implications concerning the girlfriend in the fourth stanza "chrocheting" (sexual intercourse); views of marriage and the preacher; attitudes of lovers; the character of the roving "rounder," etc. I leave the analysis of imagery, the associational development, and *apparent* difficulty of the images of the *river* and the sea, to the reader.

My point is that the conscious literary artist runs the risk of appearing second-rate when he is compared with the blues artist at his best, if he simply tries to mine exactly the same ore. In the "Match-Box Blues," the challenge resides even in the blues poem as literary lyric, since its images and associational development allow it to penetrate so suggestively the privacy and complexity of a particular black experience. (This associational development is greatly admired when it appears in a poem by T. S. Eliot.) It is perhaps not too much to say that even on a purely literary basis Hughes has trouble matching the authority wielded here by Blind Lemon Jefferson, in the poems that follow strictly the validated blues form.

I would tentatively say that Hughes is best when he attempts to capture the blues spirit and varied forms of response to existence in a poem that uses non-blues devices. Among such poems would be "Reverie on the Harlem River," "Early Evening Quarrel," "Mama and Daughter," and especially, "Lover's Return." Such poems can combine the simplicities of free verse, the free dramatizing of concrete situations, the folk tendency to hold in suspension contradictory attitudes, the incisive folk definition, and various formal resources of literary technique, for the effective rendering that is more available to the self-conscious and relatively isolated artist.

In an overall way, it may also be said that Hughes gains a good deal from experimentation with blues form. One certainly could not imagine his having to buy a Bessie Smith record, as James Baldwin reports that he once did, in order to get back to how blacks actually express themselves or to recapture the sound patterns of their speech. Hughes seldom strikes a false note with black sound patterns, and these are apparent also in non-blues poems. His poems are also full of the hard complex attitudes of the people stubbornly "on the go," whom he mentions in his autobiography, *The Big Sea*. He is seldom at the mercy of forms that immediately evoke experiences whose essentials are not those of the black experience, a dilemma that sometimes catches up with Claude McKay as we hear him crowded by the romantic tradition and the sudden notes of Byron or Shelley.

It is, of course, possible to credit too much to his contact with a single form, and to overlook the fact that Hughes was drawing from the whole of black culture. Suffice it to say that the self confronting defiantly the enemy at home and abroad is amply evident in his blues and blues toned poems.

There is evidence in Hughes's poetry of his capturing the forms of response of the folk implied by the religious tradition and its cultural modes of expression: the spirituals, gospel songs, and the sermon. In most of such poems the concentration is not on the close duplication of form that is sometimes encountered in the blues poems, but upon mood, definitions, motifs, and the determination and persistence provided by having a friend not made of earth. Such approaches to life can sometimes be rendered through dramatization of personalities who sometimes mention God—but not always. Such poems as "Aunt Sue's Stories," "The Negro Mother," "Mother to Son," and even the poem that strikes the blues note, "Stoney Lonesome," convey a sense of standing erect upon the earth by means of a quiet but deep relationship to something more than this world.

Perhaps the closest that Hughes came to attempting to catch the immediate bounce and beat of a form is the emphasis upon the gospel music form and beat found in the poem, "Fire," which begins:

> Fire,
> Fire, Lord!
> Fire gonna burn ma soul!

The beat of the gospel music can be heard, and if one has been exposed to the musical accompaniment, it too can be heard. But it is only necessary to read a few gospel songs or to hear Mahalia Jackson render one in the ecstatic modulations that have made her famous to realize that Hughes is trying neither to mount to the heights or to give the typical resolution of conflict that is usually essential to the form. In the spiritual tradition, Hughes is better at rendering the quieter moments, even when they involve desperation, which may be found in such poems as "Sinner," "Litany," "Feet of Jesus," and "Judgment Day," although he can mount to the ecstatic by combining well-established lines and images drawn from tradition with other literary resources as he does in "Spirituals."

Hughes's spectacular effort in the vein of the folk sermon is "Sunday Morning Prophecy," but he makes no effort to exploit the full sermon form: the conventional apology for ineptitude, the clear statement and explanation of text, and the movement into ecstatic seizure by the spirit. The ecstatic seizure and eloquent imagery characteristic of the folk sermon are utilized, but the emphasis is finally upon the powerful condemnation of things of this world and the minister's final plea:

Come into the church this morning,
Brothers and Sisters,
And be saved—
And give freely
In the collection basket
That I who am they shepherd
Might live.

Amen!

The associations that people have with the urbanized folk minister of Cadillac fame can raise issues concerning the interpretation of the poem, if one is also acquainted with the rural or small town folk minister who was expected by the congregation to make the same plea for his meager remuneration. If Hughes is thinking of the Cadillac preacher, then the effect is irony, but somewhat grotesque and the means seem out of proportion to the effect. It seems more effective to consider the poem in line with the folk tendency to balance apparent contradiction without feeling the urge for logical symmetry.

More important for Hughes is his sense of the power to persist, and perhaps eventually to prevail, which the religious impulse and definitions provide. To persist, that is, with human personality and its full range refusing to be destroyed and determined to overcome "some day." Here Hughes is dealing with a cultural dimension that deeply reflects the desperate history of a people caged in a machine culture. It is, in its urban setting, in accord with the ending of the novel *Not Without Laughter*, in which Sandy finds in Chicago his people hard embattled but retaining that dance of the spirit which they insisted upon amidst the ravages of slavery. In the poetry of Hughes, the dance moves sometimes in a deeply contemplative slow drag, sometimes in the fast triumphal pace inescapable in gospel music.

In a modified folk tradition also are poems which fit into no particular category, but represent depths of lives, nonetheless. "Railroad Avenue" celebrates the transforming power and spirit of laughter; "Me and the Mule" expresses stubborn self-acceptance and defiance; and "Mama and Daughter," the male-female attraction and resentment. Other poems touch upon a wide range of topics: defiance in the face of discrimination, the potential sudden explosion of put-upon people, the African heritage, the on-the-go impulse in the face of oppression, police brutality, etc. And still others range over topics that cannot be said to have a direct relation to folk and cultural tradition.

Finally, there are the published plays (*Five Plays by Langston Hughes*, edited by Webster Smalley), some of which yield their full depths only when related to folk and cultural tradition. The play version of *Mulatto* is a tragedy, whose title suggests a focus upon the mulatto Robert, the son of the white Georgia plantation owner Colonel Norwood and his black housekeeper, Cora. However, the deeper aspects of the play derive from Cora and the narrow range of choices within which the plantation folk have had to make their definition of the possibilities of life. After submitting to sexual advances by Norwood in a seduction involving both her fear and attraction, Cora, at the age of fifteen, received her plantation mother's definition of her situation:

> Then I cried and cried and told ma mother about it, but she didn't take it hard like I thought she'd take it. She said fine white mens like de young Colonel always took good care o' their colored womens. She said it was better than marryin' some black field hand and workin' all your life in de cotton and cane. Better even than havin' a job like ma had, takin' care o' de white chilluns.

Within this narrow margin of something "better," Cora has tried to move her relationship with Norwood from that of simple sexual exploitation into one in which natural claims of fatherhood and motherhood could prevail. Norwood has been married, but Cora is the sole source of his fatherhood, his only resource for rising above the mere category of *whiteness*. Cora's deepest pride is in the potential magnitude of her role. Otherwise, she has to be content with the fact that by force of personality she has compelled Norwood to educate his children, an act that strains and goes beyond the customary code governing miscegenation in the Georgia county. Thus, on the one hand Norwood strains the white code until it and its compulsions overtake him; on the other, Cora has strained the folk code, which only promised, in the definition provided by her mother, relief from brute labor. The clash between the claims of whiteness and the claims of the rhythms of natural fatherhood produces Norwood's tragedy: in the final analysis, he cannot exist without the validation of whiteness, a situation expressed by his participation in a lynching and the remorseful aftermath, his beating of his son for publicly calling him father, and the line he draws between Cora and himself: "There was no touchin' Bert, just like there was no touchin' you [Norwood]. I could only love him, like I loved you." The situation collapses completely as the mulatto son Robert chokes his father to death and then destroys himself to prevent being lynched by the mob. Robert acted after Norwood had drawn a pistol, in an attempt to force Robert to act, not like the son he demanded to be, but like a plantation darky.

The one-act play "Soul Gone Home" presents a mother crushed by the pressures of the city and self-betrayals, one result of which is the death of her illegitimate son from undernourishment and tuberculosis. By allowing the dead son and the mother to argue the essential realities of their lives, Hughes breaks through the simple realistic form which would merely have rendered a picture of environmental determinism.

The reader is kept off balance, since no simple categories will sum up the density of the folk reality in the urban city as rendered by the dramatic structure. The folk element may be summed up by the compulsions of the mother: the emphasis upon all aspects of the decorum demanded by death —passionate mourning, the proper appearance of the dead, the set role of the bereaved mother, and the motif of the uneasy and troubled spirit. Within this frame, we learn, unsentimentally, of the tragedy of the mother, who has been reduced to prostitution in her effort to survive, and that of the boy—both the child to whom she, in her own way, has been attached and partially the premature instrument of her efforts to survive.

The remaining published plays in *Five Plays by Langston Hughes* are comedies which deserve more comment than can here be given to them. "Little Ham," "Tambourines to Glory," and "Simply Heavenly" all have their settings in Harlem.

The world of "Little Ham" is a bit beyond the folk, but involves cultural traditions and adaptations: the hipster, the actress who engages in high-level prostitution, the numbers men, the operators of shoeshine and beauty parlors, and the promoters of the latest dances. Hughes is interested in what his smart personalities retain from the blues and jazz traditions: the fierce vitality, the insistent celebration of joy, and the frank and skilled seizing upon the fruits of existence. Laughter. Hughes gives effective rendering to those qualities by allowing nothing to become too serious: guns are drawn but do not kill, women begin to fight but do not maim, a disgruntled lover is comically locked away, and two-timing mates cast new and warm glances upon each other. Then, too, the pressures of the white world are cooled out before being released. One does not, however, escape entirely the awareness that a few touches of hard realism would turn the celebrators into sullen puppets of the gangsters and corrupt police who control the fat that permits the celebration. The play, nonetheless, has power and charm.

In the play, "Tambourines to Glory," Hughes again keeps the white world on the periphery while he unites the traditions of the blues and the spirituals in the struggles of Laura and Essie, who, from different motives, become religious evangelists. Laura requires money and the presence of a flesh and blood comforter right here on earth, who can minister to her loneliness. She engages in a struggle to control the affections of Big-Eyed Buddy Lomax, a pimp-like figure with contacts that reach into the underworld. In the course of her losing struggles, she evokes the man-woman struggle that harks back to the folk ballads and folklore. Her struggle finally ends in her murdering Lomax, since her bouncing energy does not provide her with the power over the rampaging male that she admired in her North Carolina mother. Essie, on the other hand, triumphs through a simple Christian love and her desire to uplift the people. She is able also to bring forward representatives of a newer generation with brighter hopes and dreams. The play is filled with gospel songs, spirituals, folk and hipsterish definitions.

In a quieter vein, Simple of "Simply Heavenly," more famous as the Southern migrant and curbstone philosopher of Hughes's sketches, manages finally to get his divorce from his first wife and prepares to marry his church-going respectable girlfriend, Joyce. The play is filled with the varieties of song and character. Simple does not have quite the salty wit that he displays in the sketches, but retains his character as Hughes's ordinary black man with uncommon common sense and perception.

The works discussed offer a wide range of the manner and methods of Langston Hughes with black folk and cultural tradition, and they reflect a good deal of his achievement as a writer. It is difficult to imagine having to conceive both the battles and the joys of black life without him. His great value is in the range of notes that he was able to play regarding the souls and strivings of black folks. Moving so frequently with a strong sense of definitions and responses derived from the intense struggles that cryptically flash forth from folk and cultural traditions, his representations of black life usually carry the ring of the true metal, whether he is responding to the topic of the day or trying to reach deeply into the heart of being. His gift was also to catch the shifting tones of the times and to sense the continuity of old things among the new. Thus he always seems current with the newer forces that arise with each decade. Like the folk in their assertion of spirit over circumstance, he usually gives the impression of being "on top of it," an achievement that actually came from constant experimentation and work.

Now it is a commonplace that Hughes is uneven. I have suggested that a part of this "unevenness" derives from his lack of the concentrated Western concern about the immortality of the writer and his works. Hughes was often the social poet, committed to the tasks of the time. Perhaps a more serious criticism is that his awareness on many occasions seems more complex than the art which he can command to render it. His works in the folk medium remain closer to the folk definitions in their original form than the self-conscious artist can afford to be, since he lacks the folk artist's well-defined audience. The consequence is that we look in vain for a few works that radiate with the big vision. On the other hand, it is apparent today that he almost always worked the right ground and broke and tilled it. So that today those who follow will find a field clearly marked out and in readiness for deeper harvesting.

LANGSTON HUGHES: A SELECTED CLASSIFIED BIBLIOGRAPHY

By Therman B. O'Daniel

Twenty years ago, one of the early attempts at "A Langston Hughes Bibliography" appeared in what was then the official publication of The College Language Association. Again in June, 1968, when the Association dedicated a special number of its *CLA Journal* to the memory of the noted author, it published a revised and updated version of the previous Langston Hughes bibliography. In the bibliography which follows, most sections of the 1968 compilation have been reprinted with only minor changes and additions. Sections XXV, XXVI, and XXVIII are three exceptions. To the first of these, "A Few Articles by Langston Hughes," twenty-four more selected pieces from Hughes's pen have been added. Section XXVI, however, "A Few Books and Articles About Langston Hughes," has been expanded to more than twice its original length by the addition of many previously omitted old works and by a large number of recent studies on Hughes. Section XXVIII, "Reviews of Books About Langston Hughes in the *CLA Journal*," which concludes the bibliography, is completely new.

As in the two earlier CLA versions of *Langston Hughes: A Selected Classified Bibliography*, chronological order has been maintained only where feasible. Moreover, no attempt has been made to list the hundreds of miscellaneous Hughes pieces which systematically appeared in a variety of publications in this country and abroad over a period of four decades. Excluded also from this bibliography are data regarding various editions and reprints of listed titles. Persons interested in more comprehensive data should consult *A Bio-Bibliography of Langston Hughes, 1902-1967*, by Donald C. Dickinson, and James A. Emanuel's *Langston Hughes* (1967), in Twayne's United States Authors Series.

I. POETRY

The Weary Blues. New York: Alfred A. Knopf, 1926.

Fine Clothes to the Jew. New York: Alfred A. Knopf, 1927.

Dear Lovely Death. Poems Privately Printed. Amenia, New York: Troutbeck Press, 1931.

The Negro Mother. New York: Golden Stair Press, 1931.

The Dream Keeper and Other Poems. New York: Alfred A. Knopf, 1932.

Scottsboro Limited. Four Poems and a Play. New York: Golden Stair Press, 1932.

A New Song. New York: International Workers Order, 1938.

Shakespeare in Harlem. New York: Alfred A. Knopf, 1942.

Freedom's Plow. New York: Musette Publishing Company, 1943.

Jim Crow's Last Stand. n.p.: Published by Negro Publication Society of America, 1943.

Lament For Dark Peoples and Other Poems. Holland, anonymously published, 1944.

Fields of Wonder. New York: Alfred A. Knopf, 1947.

One-Way Ticket. New York: Alfred A. Knopf, 1949.

Montage of a Dream Deferred. New York: Henry Holt and Company, 1951.

Selected Poems of Langston Hughes. New York: Alfred A. Knopf, 1959.

Ask Your Mama: 12 Moods For Jazz. New York: Alfred A. Knopf, 1961.

The Panther and the Lash: Poems of Our Times. New York: Alfred A. Knopf, 1967.

II. NOVELS

Not Without Laughter. New York: Alfred A. Knopf, 1930.
Simple Speaks His Mind. New York: Simon and Schuster, 1950.
Simple Takes a Wife. New York: Simon and Schuster, 1953.
Simple Stakes a Claim. New York: Rinehart and Company, 1957.
Tambourines to Glory. New York: The John Day Company, 1958.
Simple's Uncle Sam. New York: Hill and Wang, 1965.

III. CHILDREN'S STORY

Popo and Fifina: Children of Haiti. By Arna Bontemps and Langston Hughes. New York: The Macmillan Company, 1932.

IV. SHORT STORIES

The Ways of White Folks. New York: Alfred A. Knopf, 1934.
Laughing to Keep From Crying. New York: Henry Holt and Company, 1952.
Something in Common and Other Stories. New York: Hill and Wang, 1963.

V. AUTOBIOGRAPHIES

The Big Sea: An Autobiography. New York: Alfred A. Knopf, 1940.
I Wonder as I Wander: An Autobiographical Journey. New York: Rinehart and Company, 1956.

VI. BIOGRAPHIES FOR YOUNG PEOPLE

Famous American Negroes. New York: Dodd, Mead and Company, 1954.
Famous Negro Music Makers. New York: Dodd, Mead and Company, 1955.
Famous Negro Heroes of America. New York: Dodd, Mead and Company, 1958.

VII. HISTORIES FOR YOUNG PEOPLE

The First Book of Negroes. New York: Franklin Watts, 1952.

The First Book of Rhythms. New York: Franklin Watts, 1954.

The First Book of Jazz. New York: Franklin Watts, 1955.

The First Book of the West Indies. New York: Franklin Watts, 1956.

The First Book of Africa. New York: Franklin Watts, 1960.

VIII. HISTORIES

A Pictorial History of the Negro in America. By Langston Hughes and Milton Meltzer. New York: Crown Publishers, 1956.

Fight For Freedom: The Story of the NAACP. By Langston Hughes. New York: W. W. Norton and Company, 1962.

Black Magic: A Pictorial History of the Negro in American Entertainment. By Langston Hughes and Milton Meltzer. Englewood Cliffs, New Jersey: Prentice-Hall, 1967.

IX. TRANSLATIONS

Masters of the Dew [*Gouverneurs de la Rosée*]. By Jacques Roumain. Translated by Langston Hughes and Mercer Cook. New York: Reynal and Hitchcock, 1947.

Cuba Libre. Poems by Nicolás Guillén. Translated from the Spanish by Langston Hughes and Ben Frederic Carruthers. Los Angeles: Anderson and Ritchie: The Ward Ritchie Press, 1948.

Gypsy Ballads. By Federico García Lorca. Translated by Langston Hughes. *Beloit Poetry Chapbook*, No. 1. Beloit, Wisconsin: Beloit College, 1951.

Selected Poems of Gabriela Mistral [Lucila Godoy Alcayaga]. Translated by Langston Hughes. Bloomington: Indiana University Press, 1957.

"Those Who Lost Everything" and "Suffer, Poor Negro." Poems by David Diop. Translated by Langston Hughes. In *Poems from Black Africa*, edited by Langston Hughes. Bloomington: Indiana University Press, 1963, pp. 143-145.

"Flute Players." Poem by Jean-Joseph Rabéarivelo. Translated by Langston Hughes. In *Poems from Black Africa*, pp. 131-132.

"When the Tom-Tom Beats" and "Guinea." Poems by Jacques Roumain. Translated by Langston Hughes. In *Anthology of Contemporary Latin-American Poetry*, edited by Dudley Fitts. Norfolk, Connecticut: New Directions, 1942, pp. 191, 193.

"Opinions of the New [Chinese] Student." Poem by Regino Pedroso. Translated by Langston Hughes. In *Anthology of Contemporary Latin-American Poetry*, pp. 247, 249. Also in *The Poetry of the Negro, 1746-1949*, edited by Langston Hughes and Arna Bontemps. Garden City: Doubleday and Company, 1949, pp. 372-373.

"Really I Know," "Trite Without Doubt," and "She Left Herself One Evening." Poems by Léon Damas. Translated by Langston Hughes. In *The Poetry of the Negro, 1746-1949*, pp. 371-372.

X. PHOTO ESSAYS

The Sweet Flypaper of Life. By Roy DeCarava [Photographer] and Langston Hughes. New York: Simon and Schuster, 1955.

Black Misery. By Langston Hughes. Illustrations by Arouni. New York: Paul S. Ericksson, Inc., 1969.

XI. ANTHOLOGIES OF HIS OWN WRITINGS

The Langston Hughes Reader. New York: George Braziller, 1958.

Selected Poems of Langston Hughes. New York: Alfred A. Knopf, 1959.

The Best of Simple. New York: Hill and Wang, 1961.

Five Plays by Langston Hughes. Edited by Webster Smalley. Bloomington: Indiana University Press, 1963.

XII. EDITED ANTHOLOGIES

Four Lincoln University Poets. Edited by Langston Hughes. Lincoln University, 1930.

The Poetry of the Negro, 1746-1949. An Anthology Edited by Langston Hughes and Arna Bontemps. Garden City: Doubleday and Company, 1949.

Lincoln University Poets. Edited by Waring Cuney, Langston Hughes, and Bruce McM. Wright. New York: The Fine Editions Press, 1954.

The Book of Negro Folklore. Edited by Langston Hughes and Arna Bontemps. New York: Dodd, Mead and Company, 1959.

An African Treasury: Articles, Essays, Stories, Poems By Black Africans. Selected by Langston Hughes. New York: Crown Publishers, 1960.

Poems from Black Africa. Edited by Langston Hughes. Bloomington: Indiana University Press, 1963.

New Negro Poets: U. S. A. Edited by Langston Hughes. Bloomington: Indiana University Press, 1964.

The Book of Negro Humor. Selected and Edited by Langston Hughes. New York: Dodd, Mead and Company, 1966.

The Best Short Stories by Negro Writers: An Anthology from 1899 to the Present. Edited and with an Introduction by Langston Hughes. Boston: Little, Brown and Company, 1967.

Voices: A Quarterly of Poetry. Negro poets issue. Edited by Langston Hughes, winter, 1950.

XIII. FULL-LENGTH PLAYS

Mulatto. Three-Act Tragedy. Produced at the Vanderbilt Theatre on Broadway, 1935. Year on Broadway, eight months on road. (Original version produced by the Gilpin Players of Cleveland, Ohio, 1939.) First published in English in the author's original version, in *Five Plays by Langston Hughes,* edited by Webster Smalley. Bloomington: Indiana University Press, 1963, pp. 1-35.

Little Ham. Three-Act Comedy. Produced and twice revived by the Gilpin Players of Cleveland, Ohio, 1935. In *Five Plays by Langston Hughes,* pp. 43-112.

*Troubled Island.** Three-Act Tragedy. Produced by Gilpin
Players of Cleveland, and Roxanne Players of Detroit, 1935-
1936.

When the Jack Hollers. Three-Act Comedy. By Langston
Hughes in collaboration with Arna Bontemps. Produced by
the Gilpin Players, 1936.

Joy to My Soul. Three-Act Comedy. Produced by the Gilpin
Players, and once revived, 1937.

Front Porch. Three-Act Comedy-Drama, with happy or tragic
ending. Produced by the Gilpin Players, 1938.

The Sun Do Move. Full-length Music Drama. Produced by the
Skyloft Players of Chicago, Illinois, 1942.

Simply Heavenly. Originally presented by Stella Holt at 85th
Street Playhouse in New York City on May 21, 1957.
Moved to Playhouse on Broadway on August 20, and to the
Renata Theatre in the Village on November 8. Produced in
Hollywood on February 14, 1958. An English production
toured the provinces, then opened at the Adelphia Theatre
in London on May 20, 1958. A Two-Act Comedy with
Music. Book and Lyrics by Langston Hughes. Music by
David Martin. Acting Edition, New York: Dramatists Play
Service, Inc., 1959. Also in *Five Plays by Langston Hughes*,
pp. 113-181; and *The Langston Hughes Reader*, pp. 244-313.

Tambourines to Glory. A Two-Act Gospel Singing Play,
Adapted from His Novel. By Langston Hughes. Music by
Jobe Huntley. New York City at The Little Theatre, in
November, 1963. In *Five Plays by Langston Hughes*, pp.
183-258.

XIV. ONE-ACT PLAYS

Soul Gone Home. One-Act Fantasy. Produced by the Cleveland
Federal Theatre and various amateur groups across the
country. Published in *One Act Play Magazine* (July, 1937).
Also in *Five Plays by Langston Hughes*, pp. 37-42.

Don't You Want to Be Free. Long One-Act Play. Historical

---

* Also billed and performed under the titles of *Emperor of Haiti* and
Drums of Haiti.

Drama-Panorama. Published in *One Act Play Magazine* (October, 1938), 359-393. Produced by Negro amateur groups in New York (1936-1937), Chicago, Los Angeles, St. Louis, Washington, New Orleans, Atlanta, and elsewhere, in 1938 and the years following. The New York Suitcase Theater set a record, at that time, with 135 performances of the play.

XV. GOSPEL SONG-PLAYS

Gospel Glow. A Song-play, performed in Brooklyn, New York, in October, 1962.

Black Nativity. A Christmas Song-Play [in Two Acts]. Produced at New York's 41st Street Theater, 1961. Later produced at the York Playhouse, New York City; at the Festival of the Two Worlds at Spoleto, Italy, 1962; and at the Lincoln Center in New York in 1962 during the Christmas season. On tour in England and on the Continent of Europe during 1962, 1963, 1964, and 1965; with American tours during 1963 and 1964.

Jericho-Jim Crow. A Song-play produced at The Sanctuary, 143 West 13th Street, New York City, December 28, 1963, and ran through April, 1964.

The Prodigal Son. Produced at the Greenwich Mews Theater, 141 West 13th Street, New York City during May, 1965. On tour abroad, beginning in the fall of 1965.

XVI. CHRISTMAS CANTATA

The Ballad of the Brown King. Music by Margaret Bonds. Performed at the New York YMCA's Clark Auditorium on December 11, 1960.

XVII. LYRICS FOR DRAMATIC MUSICALS

Street Scene. Based on Elmer Rice's play. Music by Kurt Weill. Book by Elmer Rice. Lyrics by Langston Hughes. Presented at the Adelphi Theatre in New York on January 9, 1947. Score published by Chappell and Company, New York, 1947.

Just Around the Corner. Two-Act Musical. Book by Abby Mann and Bernard Drew. Music by Joe Sherman. Lyrics by Langston Hughes. Performed in 1951 at the Ogunquit Playhouse in Maine.

XVIII. OPERA LIBRETTOS

Troubled Island. An Opera in Three Acts. Poetic version set to music by William Grant Still. Produced at City Center by the New York City Opera Company. World premiere, Thursday Evening, March 31, 1949. Libretto by Langston Hughes, published by Leeds Music Corporation, RKO Building, Radio City, New York, 1949.

The Barrier. Full-length Opera with Musical Score by Jan Meyerowitz. Libretto by Langston Hughes. Produced by the Columbia University Opera Workshop, January 18, 1950. Broadhurst Theatre, then on tour.

Esther. Opera with music by Jan Meyerowitz. Libretto by Langston Hughes. Produced by the University of Illinois in March, 1957. Again produced by the New England Conservatory of Music in 1958, in Boston.

Port Town. One-Act Opera. Music by Jan Meyerowitz. Libretto by Langston Hughes. Performed at Tanglewood, Lenox, Massachusetts, in August, 1960.

XIX. SCREENPLAY

Way Down South. Hollywood Film (1942). Screenplay by Langston Hughes and Clarence Muse.

XX. RADIO SCRIPTS

Brothers. Written for the Writers War Board. Performed in New York and released to Local Stations, 1942.

Freedom's Plow. Blue Network-National Urban League Program, with Paul Muni and Golden Gate Quartet, 1943. Published by Musette Publishers, New York, 1943.

In the Service of My Country. WNYC—Written for the Writers War Board. War Script Extra for January, 1944.

The Man Who Went to War. British Broadcasting Company.

Transcribed in New York with Ethel Waters, Paul Robeson, Josh White, and the Hall Johnson Choir. Spring, 1944.

Pvt. Jim Crow. Published in *Negro Story Magazine*, May-June, 1945.

Booker T. Washington at Atlanta. CBS—Pursuit of Happiness Show with Rex Ingram. Published in *Radio Drama in Action*, edited by Erik Barnouw. New York: Farrar and Rinehart, 1945.

XXI. RADIO SCRIPTS IN COLLABORATION

Jubilee. CBS—Showcase Program From a Theatre Script by Langston Hughes and Arna Bontemps, 1941.

John Henry Hammers It Out. NBC—Labor For Victory with Paul Robeson and Kenneth Spencer. Script by Peter Lyons. Lyrics for bridges and final song, "Will Hammer It Out Together," by Langston Hughes. Music by Earl Robinson, 1943.

Swing Time at the Savoy. Written with Noble Sissle for Lucky Millinder's Band. Summer Musical Series, NBC, 1949.

XXII. TELEVISION SCRIPT

Strollin' Twenties (1966). Produced by Harry Belafonte. Script by Langston Hughes.

XXIII. LYRICS FOR SONGS

Shake Your Brown Feet, Honey. Composer: John Alden Carpenter. Publisher: G. Schirmer.

The Cryin' Blues. Composer: John A. Carpenter. Publisher: G. Schirmer.

That Soothin' Song. Composer: John A. Carpenter. Publisher: G. Schirmer.

Jazz Boys. Composer: John A. Carpenter. Publisher: G. Schirmer.

The Breath of a Rose. Composer: William Grant Still. Publisher: G. Schirmer.

Songs to A Dark Virgin. Composer: Florence Price. Publisher: G. Schirmer.

The Negro Speaks of Rivers. Composer: Margaret Bonds. Publisher: Handy Brothers Music Company.

Freedom Train. Composer: Sammy Heyward. Publisher: Handy Brothers.

Golden Brown Blues. Composer: W. C. Handy. Publisher: Handy Brothers.

Go and Get the Enemy Blues. Composer: W. C. Handy. Publisher: Handy Brothers.

Freedom Road. Composer: Emerson Harper. Publisher: Musette Publishers, Inc.

That Eagle. Composer: Emerson Harper. Publisher: Musette Publishers.

This Is My Land. Composers: Harper and Tullos. Publisher: Musette Publishers.

The Founding Fathers. Composers: Harper and Tullos. Publisher: Musette Publishers.

A New Wind A-Blowin'. Composer: Elie Seigmeister. Publisher: Musette Publishers.

Love Is Like Whiskey. Composer: Roger Segure. Publisher: Exclusive Publications.

African Dance. Composers: Bemis and Muse. Publisher: Exclusive Publications.

Louisiana. Composer: Clarence Muse. Publisher: Exclusive Publications.

Night Song. Composer: Howard Swanson. Publisher: Weintraub Music Company.

Pierrot. Composer: Howard Swanson. Publisher: Weintraub Music Company.

Joy. Composer: Howard Swanson. Publisher: Weintraub Music Company.

The Negro Speaks of Rivers. Composer: Howard Swanson. Publisher: Weintraub Music Company.

A Black Pierrot. Composer: William Grant Still. Publisher: Leeds Music Corporation.

Song For A Dark Girl. Composer: Silvestre Revueltas. Publisher: Marks Music Corporation.

Sea Charm. Composer: Frederic Piket. Publisher: Associate Music Publishers.

Sad Song in de Air. Composer: Jacques Wolfe. Publisher: Robbins Music Corporation.

Moan. Composer: Edward Harris. Publisher: J. Fischer and Brothers.

Lovely Dark and Lonely One. Composer: H. T. Burleigh. Publisher: G. Ricordi and Company.

Suicide's Note. Composer: Cleo Allen Hibbs. Publisher: Richard Drake Saunders.

Sharecroppers. Composer: Joseph Rubel. Publisher: Trans-Continental Music.

Sea Charm. Composer: Ray Green. Publisher: New Music Society of California.

Gypsy Man. Composer: Harvey Enders. Publisher: Galaxy Music Corporation.

Night Time. Composer: Roger Segure. Publisher: Sherman Clay and Company.

Let My People Go Now. Composer: Chappie Willet. Publisher: Text Music Company.

For This We Fight. Composer: Haufrecht. Publisher: Negro Freedom Rally.

On the Dusty Road. Composers: Harper and Johnson. Publisher: Carl Fisher, Inc.

At the Feet of Jesus. Composers: Harper and Johnson. Publisher: Carl Fisher, Inc.

Glory Around His Head. Composer: Jan Meyerowitz. Publisher: Broude Brothers.

On a Pallet of Straw. Composer: Jan Meyerowitz. Publisher: Broude Brothers.

Four Songs. Composer: Jean Berger. Publisher: Broude Brothers.

NOTES ON VARIOUS SONGS

African Dance was in the motion picture, *Stormy Weather*. *Lou Lou Louisiana* and *Good Ground* were in the motion picture, *Way Down South*. *Night Time* was the radio theme song for Midge Williams on the Blue Network for over a year. *Freedom*

Road, a war song, was featured on *The March of Time, Labor For Victory*, and many other radio programs during World War II. *Going Mad With a Dime* was in Duke Ellington's West Coast Revue, *Jump For Joy*. A satirical song called *Hollywood Mammy* was in Otis Renee's West Coast revue. Over the years, Nellie Lutcher, Juanita Hall, Burl Ives, Dolly Rose, Patti Page, Benny Goodman, Teddy Wilson, Freddy Martin, Johnny Mercer, Josh White, Midge Williams, Harry Belafonte, Lotte Lenya, Abbey Lincoln, June Christy, Martha Schlamme, Muddy Waters, and others have recorded songs by Langston Hughes, and Louis Armstrong's band and other bands have played them. On the concert stage his lyrics have been performed by Lawrence Tibbett, Marian Anderson, Paul Robeson, Eva Gautier, Roland Hayes, Muriel Rahn, Etta Moton, Helen Thigpen, Kenneth Spencer, Betty Allen, William Warfield, Lawrence Winters, the Westminster Choir, the Hampton Choir, and others.

XXIV. RECORDINGS

Simple Speaks His Mind. Folkways Records FP 90 [1952]. Poems read by the author. Biographical notes by Arna Bontemps inserted in slipcase.

The Story of Jazz. Folkways Records FP 712 [1954]. The First Album of Jazz for Children with Documentary Recordings from the Library of Folkways Records. With narration by the author.

The Dream Keeper and Other Poems. Folkways Records FP 104 [1955]. Recordscript read by the author.

Rhythms of the World. Folkways Records FP 740 [1955]. Narrated by the author with dubbed documentary sounds. Based on the author's *The First Book of Rhythms*.

The Glory of Negro History. Folkways Records FP 752 [1955]. Documentary narrated by the author. Includes the voices of Ralph Bunche and Mary McLeod Bethune, with incidental music dubbed from recordings issued by Folkways Records.

The Weary Blues and Other Poems. MGM Record LPs E3697 [1958]. Thirty-three poems read by author. Jazz background provided by Charles Mingus and others. Program notes by Martin Williams and Leonard Feather on slipcase.

Tambourines to Glory. Folkways Records FG3538 [1958]. Gospel Songs by Langston Hughes and Jobe Huntley. Porter Singers with instrumental accompaniment. Hugh E. Porter, Conductor. Words by Langston Hughes. Recorded in New Canaan Baptist Church, New York City, October 3, 1958.

Did You Ever Hear the Blues? United Artists [1959]. Eleven blues by Langston Hughes, recorded by Clarence H. "Big" Miller.

Jericho-Jim Crow. Folkways Records FL 9671 [1964]. The Langston Hughes musical performed by the Hugh Porter Gospel Singers, with piano, organ, and percussion.

A Night at the Apollo. Commentary. Vanguard Records.

The Best of Simple. Folkways Records 9789.

Simply Heavenly. Columbia Records. The Langston Hughes Musical—Original Cast.

Street Scene. Columbia Records. Musical—Original Cast. Lyrics by Langston Hughes.

Anthology of Negro Poetry. Edited by Arna Bontemps. Folkways Records FP 91. Langston Hughes, Sterling Brown, Claude McKay, Countee Cullen, Gwendolyn Brooks, and Margaret Walker reading their own poems.

Sterling Brown and Langston Hughes. Folkways Records 9790.

A Gathering of Great Poetry for Children. Caedmon Records TC 1235 LP. Volume I—Julie Harris, Cyril Ritchard, and David Wayne. Includes poems by Langston Hughes.

Meditations for the Modern Classroom. Caedmon Records TC 2029 LP. Judith Anderson and Ed Begley. Includes poems by Langston Hughes.

XXV. A FEW ARTICLES BY LANGSTON HUGHES

"The Negro Artist and the Racial Mountain," *Nation*, CXXII (June 23, 1926), 692-694.

"Our Wonderful Society: Washington," *Opportunity*, V (August, 1927), 226-227.

"Letter to the Editor," in "The Outer Pocket," *Crisis*, XXXV (September, 1928), 302.

"A Cuban Sculptor," *Opportunity*, VIII (November, 1930), 334.

"Brown America in Jail: Kilby," *Opportunity*, X (June, 1932), 174.

"Richard Allen: Founder of a Church," *Crisis*, XLI (December, 1933), 605-607.

"To Negro Writers," *American Writers' Congress*, ed. Henry Hart. New York: International, 1935, pp. 139-141.

"Love in Mexico," *Opportunity*, XVIII (April, 1940), 107-108.

"Harlem Literati in the Twenties," *Saturday Review of Literature*, XX (June 22, 1940), 13-14.

"Songs Called the Blues," *Phylon*, II (Second Quarter, 1941), 143-145.

"My America," *The Journal of Educational Sociology*, XVI (February, 1943), 334-336.

"Is Hollywood Fair to Negroes?" *Negro Digest*, I (April, 1943), 19-21.

"My Most Humiliating Jim Crow Experience," *Negro Digest*, III (May, 1945), 33-34. (See also *The Langston Hughes Reader*, pp. 488-489.)

"Simple and Me," *Phylon*, VI (Fourth Quarter, 1945), 349-353.

"My Adventures as a Social Poet," *Phylon*, VIII (Third Quarter, 1947), 205-212.

"When I Worked for Dr. Woodson," *Negro History Bulletin*, XIII (May, 1950), 13. Also, XXX (October, 1967), 17.

"How to Be a Bad Writer (In Ten Easy Lessons)," *The Harlem Quarterly* (Spring, 1950), 13-14. (See also *The Langston Hughes Reader*, pp. 491-492.)

"Some Practical Observations: A Colloquy" [By Langston Hughes and the Editors], *Phylon*, XI (Fourth Quarter, 1950), 307-311.

"Ten Ways to Use Poetry in Teaching," *CLA Bulletin*, VII (Spring, 1951), 6-7. (Reprinted in the *CLA Journal*, XI [June, 1968], 273-279.)

"Sweet Chariots of the World," *Negro Digest*, IX (April, 1951), 58-62. (See also *The Langston Hughes Reader*, pp. 494-498.)

"The Influence of Negro Music on American Entertainment,"

Theatre Spotlight (September, 1955), 6, 15. (Originally appeared in the *New York Age-Defender*.)

"Speech at National Assembly of Authors and Dramatists Symposium: 'The Writer's Position in America,' " *Mainstream*, X (July, 1957), 46-48. (See also *The Langston Hughes Reader*, pp. 483-485.)

"Ten Thousand Beds," *The Langston Hughes Reader*. New York: George Braziller, Inc., 1958, pp. 489-491. (Originally appeared in the Chicago *Defender*.)

"Memories of Christmas," *The Langston Hughes Reader*, pp. 485-488. (Originally appeared in the *Circuit Magazine*.)

"The Fun of Being Black," *The Langston Hughes Reader*, pp. 498-500.

"Jazz as Communication," *The Langston Hughes Reader*, pp. 492-494. (Originally appeared in the Chicago *Defender*.)

"Jolly Genius of Jazz," *Popular Album News* (July, 1958), 9, 13. (On Fats Waller.)

"Writers: Black and White," *The American Negro ·Writer and His Roots*. New York: American Society of African Culture, 1960, pp. 41-45.

"Problems of the Negro Writer" [Langston Hughes, LeRoi Jones, and John A. Williams], *Saturday Review*, XLVI (April 20, 1963), 19-20, 40.

"My Early Days in Harlem," *Freedomways*, III (Summer, 1963), 312-314. (Reprinted in *Harlem, U.S.A.*, ed. John Henrik Clarke, Berlin, Germany: Seven Seas Books, 1964, pp. 76-79.)

"Gospel Singing: When the Spirit Really Moves," New York: *The Sunday Herald Tribune Magazine* (October 27, 1963), 12-13.

"Down Under in Harlem," *New Republic*, CX (March 27, 1964), 404-405.

"Hold Fast to Dreams," *Lincoln University Bulletin*, LXVII (Langston Hughes Issue, 1964), 1-8.

"Tribute to W. E. B. Du Bois," *Freedomways*, V (Winter, 1965), 11.

"That Boy LeRoi," the Chicago *Defender* (January 11, 1965.)

"The Task of the Negro Writer as an Artist," *Negro Digest*, XIV (April, 1965), 65.

"*Ebony's* Nativity: An Evaluation From Birth," *Ebony*, XXI (November, 1965), 40-42, 44-46.

"The Twenties: Harlem and Its Negritude," *African Forum*, I (Spring, 1966), 11-20.

XXVI. A FEW BOOKS AND ARTICLES ABOUT LANGSTON HUGHES

Adams, Russell L. *Great Negroes Past and Present*. Chicago: Afro-Am Publishing Company, Inc., 1965, p. 127.

Adoff, Arnold, Editor. *I Am the Darker Brother*. New York: Macmillan Company, 1968.

Allen, Samuel W. "Négritude and Its Relevance to the American Negro Writer," *The American Negro Writer and His Roots*. New York: American Society of African Culture, 1960, pp. 8-20.

Allen, William. "*The Barrier:* A Critique," *Phylon*, XI (Second Quarter, 1950), 134-136.

Arvey, Verna. "Langston Hughes: Crusader," *Opportunity*, XVIII (December, 1940), 363-364.

Babb, Inez Johnson. "Bibliography of Langston Hughes, Negro Poet." Unpublished Master's Thesis, Pratt Institute Library School, 1947.

Bardolph, Richard. *The Negro Vanguard*. New York: Rinehart, 1959.

Barton, Rebecca. *Witnesses for Freedom*. New York: Harper Brothers, 1948.

"Birth of a Poet," *Milwaukee Journal* (February 5, 1945). See also *Negro Digest* (April, 1945), 41-42.

Bone, Robert A. *The Negro Novel in America*. New Haven: Yale University Press, 1958.

Bontemps, Arna. "The Two Harlems," *American Scholar*, XIV (Spring, 1945), 167-173.

——. "The Harlem Renaissance," *Saturday Review of Literature*, XXX (March 22, 1947), 12-13, 44.

——. "Negro Poets, Then and Now," *Phylon*, XI (Fourth Quarter, 1950), 355-360.

——. "Langston Hughes: He Spoke of Rivers," *Freedomways*, VIII (Spring, 1968), 140-143.

Brawley, Benjamin. *The Negro Genius*. New York: Dodd, Mead & Company, 1937.

——. "The Negro Literary Renaissance," *Southern Workman*, LVI (April, 1927), 177-180.

Britt, David D. "The Image of the White Man in the Fiction of Langston Hughes, Richard Wright, James Baldwin, and Ralph Ellison," *Dissertation Abstracts*, XXIX (1968), 1532A.

Brooks, A. Russell. "The Comic Spirit and the Negro's New Look," *CLA Journal*, VI (September, 1962), 35-43.

Brooks, Gwendolyn. "Langston Hughes" [Editorial], *Nation*, CCV (July 3, 1967), 7.

Brown, Lloyd W. "Black Entitles: Names as Symbols in Afro-American Literature," *Studies in Black Literature*, I (Spring, 1970), 16-44.

Brown, Sterling, Arthur P. Davis, Ulysses Lee, eds. *The Negro Caravan*. New York: Dryden Press, 1941.

Brown, Sterling A. "Not Without Laughter," *Opportunity*, VIII (September, 1930), 279-280.

——. *The Negro in American Fiction*. Bronze Booklet Number 6. Washington: The Associates in Negro Folk Education, 1937.

——. *Negro Poetry and Drama*. Bronze Booklet Number 7. Washington: The Associates in Negro Folk Education, 1937.

"Browsing Reader, The," *Crisis*, XXXVII (September, 1930), 321.

Burroughs, Margaret. "Langston Hughes Lives!" *Negro Digest*, XVI (September, 1967), 59-60.

Calverton, V. F. "This Negro," *The Nation*, CXXXI (August 6, 1930), 157-158.

——. *The Liberation of American Literature*. New York: Charles Scribner's Sons, 1932, p. 147.

——. "The Negro and American Culture," *Saturday Review of*

Literature, XXII (September 21, 1940), 3-4, 17-18.

Cargill, Oscar. *Intellectual America: Ideas on the March*. New York: Macmillan Company, 1941, p. 511.

Carmen, Y. "Langston Hughes: Poet of the People," *International Literature*, No. 1 (1939), 192-194.

Carrington, Glenn. "The Harlem Renaissance—A Personal Memoir," *Freedomways*, III (Summer, 1963), 307-311.

Cartey, Wilfred. "Four Shadows of Harlem," *Negro Digest*, XVIII (August, 1969), 22-25, 83-92.

Chamberlain, John. "The Negro as Writer," *Bookman*, LXX (February, 1930), 603-611.

Chandler, G. Lewis. "A Major Problem of Negro Authors in Their March Toward Belles-Lettres," *Phylon*, XI (Fourth Quarter, 1950), 383-386.

Chapman, Abraham. "The Harlem Renaissance in Literary History," *CLA Journal*, XI (September, 1967), 38-58.

——. *The Negro in American Literature and A Bibliography of Literature By and About Negro Americans*. Oshkosh, Wisconsin: Wisconsin Council of Teachers of English, 1966.

——. "Introduction," *Black Voices*, ed. Abraham Chapman. New York: A Mentor Book. The New American Library, 1968.

Clarke, John Henrik, Editor. *Harlem U.S.A.* Berlin: Seven Seas Publishers, 1964.

——. "The Origin and Growth of Afro-American Literature," *Negro Digest*, XVII (December, 1967), 54-67.

——. "Langston Hughes and Jesse B. Semple," *Freedomways*, VIII (Spring, 1968), 167-169.

Combecher, Hans. "Zu einem Gedicht von Langston Hughes: 'Minstrel Man,'" *Die Neueren Sprachen*, XV (1966), 284-287.

——. "Interpretationen fur den Englischunterricht: Langston Hughes, F. R. Scott, T. S. Eliot," *Neueren Sprachen*, n.s., XVII (October, 1968), 506-514.

Cook, Mercer. "President Senghor's Visit: A Tale of Five Cities," *African Forum*, II (Winter, 1967), 74-86.

Cook, Mercer and Stephen E. Henderson. *The Militant Black Writer in Africa and the United States.* Madison: The University of Wisconsin Press, 1969, pp. 102-107.

Cuban, Larry. *The Negro in America.* Glenview, Illinois: Scott, Foresman and Company, 1964.

Cullen, Countee. "Our Book Shelf: Poet on Poet," *Opportunity,* IV (March, 1926), 73.

Davis, Allison. "Our Negro Intellectuals," *Crisis,* XXXV (August, 1928), 268-269.

Davis, Arthur P. "The Harlem of Langston Hughes' Poetry," *Phylon,* XIII (Fourth Quarter, 1952), 276-283.

——. "Jesse B. Semple: Negro American," *Phylon,* XV (First Quarter, 1954), 21-28.

——. "The Tragic Mulatto Theme in Six Works by Langston Hughes," *Phylon,* XVI (Fourth Quarter, 1955), 195-204.

——. "Integration and Race Literature," *Phylon,* XVII (Second Quarter, 1956), 141-146.

——. "Langston Hughes: Cool Poet," *CLA Journal,* XI, 4 (June, 1968), 280-296.

Davis, Charles T., and Daniel Walden, Editors. *On Being Black: Writings by Afro-Americans from Frederick Douglass to the Present.* Greenwich, Connecticut: Fawcett Publications, Inc., 1970, pp. 27, 38, 159, 179.

Diakhaté, Lamine. "Langston Hughes, conquerant de l'espoir," *Presence Africaine,* LXIV (1967), 38-46.

Dickinson, Donald C. *A Bio-Bibliography of Langston Hughes, 1902-1967.* Hamden, Connecticut: Archon Books. The Shoe String Press, Inc., 1967.

——. "Langston Hughes and the Brownie's [*sic*] Book," *Negro History Bulletin,* XXXI (December, 1968), 8-10.

Dodat, Francois. "Situation de Langston Hughes," *Presence Africaine,* LXIV (1967), 47-50.

Drew, Fraser. "Langston Hughes and My Students," *Trace,* XXXII (June-July, 1959), 22-25.

Du Bois, W. E. B., and Alain Locke. "The Younger Literary Movement," *Crisis,* XXVII (February, 1924), 161-163.

Ellison, Martha. "Velvet Voices Feed on Bitter Fruit: A Study of American Negro Poetry," *Poet and Critic*, IV (Winter, 1967-1968), 39-49.

Emanuel, James A. "Langston Hughes' First Short Story: 'Mary Winosky,'" *Phylon*, XXII (Third Quarter, Fall, 1961), 267-272.

——. "The Short Stories of Langston Hughes." Unpublished Ph.D. Dissertation, Columbia University, 1962.

——. *Langston Hughes*. New York: Twayne Publishers, Inc., 1967.

——. "'Soul' in the Works of Langston Hughes," Book Excerpt, *Negro Digest*, XVI (September, 1967), 25-30, 74-92.

——. "'Bodies in the Moonlight': A Critical Analysis," *Readers and Writers*, I (November-January, 1968), 38-39, 42.

——. "The Short Fiction of Langston Hughes," *Freedomways*, VIII (Spring, 1968), 170-178.

——. "The Literary Experiments of Langston Hughes," *CLA Journal*, XI (June, 1968), 335-344.

——. "America Before 1950: Black Writers' Views," *Negro Digest*, XVIII (August, 1969), 26-34, 67-69.

Emanuel, James A., and Theodore L. Gross, Editors. *Dark Symphony: Negro Literature in America*. New York: The Free Press, 1968, pp. 191-203.

Embree, Edwin. *Thirteen Against the Odds*. New York: Viking Press, 1944, pp. 117-138.

Evans, Mari. "I Remember Langston," *Negro Digest*, XVI (September, 1967), 36.

Fields, Julia. "The Green of Langston's Ivy," *Negro Digest*, XVI (September, 1967), 58-59.

Filatova, Lydia. "Langston Hughes: American Writer," *International Literature*, No. 1 (1933), 103-105.

Ford, Nick Aaron. "I Teach Negro Literature," *College English*, II (March, 1941), 530-541.

——. "The Negro Novel as a Vehicle of Propaganda," *Quarterly Review of Higher Education Among Negroes*, IX (July, 1941), 135-139.

———. "Battle of the Books: A Critical Survey of Significant Books by and About Negroes Published in 1960," *Phylon*, XXII (Summer, 1961), 119-134.

———. "Search for Identity: A Critical Survey of Significant Belles-Lettres by and About Negroes Published in 1961," *Phylon*, XXIII (Summer, 1962), 128-138.

Furay, Michael. "Africa in Negro American Poetry to 1929," *African Literature Today* (Formerly *Bulletin of the Association for African Literature in English*), No. 1 (1968); No. 2 (January, 1969).

Gayle, Addison. "Langston Hughes: A Simple Commentary," *Negro Digest*, XVI (September, 1967), 53-57.

Gibson, Donald, Editor. *Five Black Writers: Essays on Wright, Ellison, Baldwin, Hughes, and LeRoi Jones*. New York: New York University Press, 1970, pp. XXIII-XXV, 167-189.

Glicksberg, Charles. "Negro Fiction in America," *South Atlantic Quarterly*, XLV (October, 1946), 477-488.

Gloster, Hugh M. *Negro Voices in American Fiction*. Chapel Hill: University of North Carolina Press, 1948, pp. 219-222.

Gross, Seymour L., and John Edward Hardy, Editors. *Images of the Negro in American Literature*. Chicago: University of Chicago Press, 1966, pp. 16-17, 194-203, 308-309.

Guillén, Nicolás. "Le souvenir de Langston Hughes," *Presence Africaine*, LXIV (1967), 34-37.

Hampton, Bill R. "On Identification with Negro Tricksters," *Southern Folklore Quarterly*, XXXI, 55-65.

Hawthorne, Lucia S. *A Rhetoric of Human Rights as Expressed in the "Simple Columns" by Langston Hughes*. University Park, Pennsylvania: Unpublished Ph.D. Dissertation at The Pennsylvania State University, 1971, pp. 1-206.

Hentoff, Nat. "Langston Hughes, He Found Poetry in the Blues," *Mayfair* (August, 1958), 26-27.

Hill, Herbert, Editor. *Soon One Morning*. New York: Alfred A. Knopf, 1963, p. 106.

———. *Anger, and Beyond*. New York: Harper and Row, 1966, pp. 14, 16, 18 ff.

Holmes, Eugene. "The Legacy of Alain Locke," *Freedomways*, III (Summer, 1963), 293-306.

Holmes, Eugene C. "Langston Hughes: Philosopher-Poet," *Freedomways*, VIII (Spring, 1968), 144-151.

"Hommage à Langston Hughes," *Presence Africaine*, LXIV (1967), 33.

Hudson, Theodore R. "Langston Hughes' Last Volume of Verse," *CLA Journal*, XI (June, 1968), 345-348.

"Hughes at Columbia," *New Yorker*, XLIII (December 30, 1967), 21-23.

Isaacs, Harold. "Five Writers and Their African Ancestors," *Phylon*, XXI (Third Quarter, Fall, 1960), 247-254.

Jackson, Blyden. "An Essay in Criticism," *Phylon*, XI (Fourth Quarter, 1950), 338-343.

——. "The Continuing Strain: Resumé of Negro Literature in 1955," *Phylon*, XVII (First Quarter, 1956), 35-40.

——. "Recognition of an Undramatic Task" [Review-Article], *Phylon*, XXII (Spring, 1961), 98-99.

——. "A Word About Simple," *CLA Journal*, XI (June, 1968), 310-318.

——. "The Negro's Image of the Universe as Reflected in His Fiction," *CLA Journal*, IV (September, 1960), 22-31.

——. "A Golden Mean for the Negro Novel," *CLA Journal*, III (December, 1959), 81-87.

Jahn, Janheinz. *Neo-African Literature: A History of Black Writing*. New York: Grove Press, Inc., 1969.

Johnson, Charles S. "Jazz, Poetry and Blues," *Carolina Magazine*, LVIII (May, 1928), 16-20.

——. "The Negro Renaissance and Its Significance," *The New Negro Thirty Years Afterward*, ed. Rayford Logan, Eugene Holmes, and G. Franklin Edwards. Washington: Howard University Press, 1955.

Johnson, James Weldon. *Black Manhattan*. New York: Alfred A. Knopf, Inc., 1930, pp. 271-273.

——, Editor. *The Book of American Negro Poetry*. New York: Harcourt, Brace and Company, 1931, pp. 232-234.

Jones, Eldred. "'Laughing To Keep From Crying': A Tribute to Langston Hughes," *Presence Africaine*, LXIV (1967), 51-55.

Jones, Harry L. "A Danish Tribute to Langston Hughes," *CLA Journal*, XI (June, 1968), 331-334.

——. "Black Humor and the American Way of Life," *Satire Newsletter*, VII (Fall, 1969), 1-4.

Kaiser, Ernest. "The Literature of Harlem," *Freedomways*, III (Summer, 1963), 276-291.

——. "Selected Bibliography of the Published Writings of Langston Hughes," *Freedomways*, VIII (Spring, 1968), 185-191.

Kamp, Stella. "Langston Hughes Speaks to Young Writers," *Opportunity* XXIV (April, 1946), 73.

Killens, John Oliver. "Broadway in Black and White," *African Forum*, I (Winter, 1966), 66-76.

King, Jr., Woodie. "Remembering Langston Hughes," *Negro Digest*, XVIII (April, 1969), 27-32, 95-96.

Kinnamon, Kenneth. "The Man Who Created Simple," *Nation*, CCV (December 4, 1967), 599-601.

Kramer, Aaron. "Robert Burns and Langston Hughes," *Freedomways*, VIII (Spring, 1968), 159-166.

"Langston Hughes," *Publishers' Weekly*, 191, No. 24 (June, 1967), 37.

"Langston Hughes Dies at Sixty-Five," *Negro History Bulletin*, XXX (October, 1967), 16. Reprinted from *The Washington Post* (May 24, 1967).

"Langston Hughes and the Example of 'Simple,'" *Black World* [Formerly *Negro Digest*], XIX (June, 1970), 35-38.

Larkin, Margaret. "A Poet of the People—A Review," *Opportunity*, V (March, 1927), 84-85.

Lash, John S. "The American Negro and American Literature: A Check List of Significant Commentaries," *Bulletin of Bibliography*, XIX (January-April, 1946), 12-15, 33-36.

——. "The American Negro in American Literature: A Selected Bibliography of Critical Materials," *Journal of Negro Education*, XV (Fall, 1946), 722-730.

——. "What Is Negro Literature," *College English*, IX (October, 1947), 37-42.

——. "The Race Consciousness of the American Negro Author: Toward a Reexamination of an Orthodox Critical Concept," *Social Forces*, XXVIII (October, 1949), 24-34.

——. "A Long, Hard Look at the Ghetto: A Critical Summary of Literature by and About Negroes in 1956," *Phylon*, XVIII (First Quarter, 1957), 7-24.

——. "Dimension in Racial Experience: A Critical Summary of Literature by and About Negroes in 1958," *Phylon*, XX (Second Quarter, 1959), 115-131.

Lieberman, Laurence. "Poetry Chronicle," *Poetry*, CXII (August, 1968), 339-340.

Littlejohn, David. *Black on White: A Critical Survey of Writing By American Negroes*. New York: Grossman Publishers, Inc., 1966, pp. 51-55, 144-147.

Locke, Alain, Editor. *The New Negro: An Interpretation*. New York: Albert and Charles Boni, 1925, pp. 4-5, 416.

——. *Four Negro Poets*. New York: Simon and Schuster, 1927. (McKay, Cullen, Toomer, and Hughes.)

——. "The Negro Poets of the United States," *Anthology of Magazine Verse for 1926 and Yearbook of American Poetry*, ed. William Stanley Braithwaite. Boston: B.J. Brimmer, 1927, pp. 143-149.

——. "The Negro's Contribution to American Art and Literature," *Annals of the American Academy of Political and Social Science*, CXL (November, 1928), 234-247.

——. "The Negro in American Culture," *Anthology of American Negro Literature*, ed. V.F. Calverton. New York: Modern Library, 1929, pp. 248-266.

——. "This Year of Grace: Outstanding Books of the Year in Negro Literature," *Opportunity*, IX (February, 1931), 48-51.

——. "We Turn to Prose: A Retrospective Review of the Literature of the Negro for 1931," *Opportunity*, X (February, 1932), 40-44.

——. "Black Truth and Black Beauty: A Retrospective Review of the Negro for 1932," *Opportunity*, XI (January, 1933), 14-18.

——. "Deep River; Deeper Sea: Retrospective Review of the Literature of the Negro for 1935," *Opportunity*, XIV (January, 1936), 6-10; (February, 1936), 42-43, 61.

——. "The Negro: 'New' or Newer: A Retrospective Review of the Literature of the Negro for 1938," *Opportunity*, XVII (January, 1939), 4-11; (February, 1939), 36-42.

——. "Dry Fields and Green Pastures" [Review of Negro Literature for 1939], *Opportunity*, XVIII (January, 1940), 4-10, 28; (February, 1940), 41-46, 53.

——. "Of Native Sons: Real and Otherwise," *Opportunity*, XIX (January, 1941), 4-9; (February, 1941), 48-52.

——. A Contribution to American Culture," *Opportunity*, XXIII (October-December, 1945), 192-193, 238.

——. "The Negro Minority in American Literature," *English Journal*, XXXV (June, 1946), 315-319.

——. "From *Native Son* to *Invisible Man*," A Review of the Literature of the Negro for 1952," *Phylon*, XIV (First Quarter, 1953), 34-44.

Loveman, A. "Anisfield-Wolf Awards," *Saturday Review*, XXXVII (April 17, 1954), 20.

Lucas, Bob. "The Poet Who Invented Soul," *Los Angeles Sentinel* (June 8, 1967), D-1.

MacLeod, Norman. "The Poetry and Argument of Langston Hughes," *Crisis*, XLV (November, 1938), 358-359.

Maloff, S. "Death of Simple," *Newsweek*, LXIX (June 5, 1967), 104.

Margolies, Edward. *Native Sons: A Critical Study of Twentieth Century Negro American Authors*. Philadelphia and New York: J. B. Lippincott Company, 1968, pp. 35-38.

Matheus, John F. "Langston Hughes as Translator," *CLA Journal*, XI (June, 1968), 319-330.

Mayfield, Julian. "Langston," *Negro Digest*, XVI (September, 1967), 34-35.

Meltzer, Milton. *Langston Hughes: A Biography*. New York: Thomas Y. Crowell, 1968.

Miller, Johnnine Brown. "The Major Themes in Langston Hughes's *Not Without Laughter*," *The CEA Critic*, XXXII (March, 1970), 8-10.

Mintz, Lawrence E. "Langston Hughes's Jesse B. Semple: The Urban Negro as Wise Fool," *Satire Newsletter*, VII (Fall, 1969), 11-21.

Mitchell, Loften. *Black Drama: The Story of the American Negro in the Theatre.* New York: Hawthorn Books, Inc., 1967, pp. 97, 145-147, 204-205.

——. "In Memoriam to Langston Hughes," *New York Amsterdam News* (May 27, 1967), 1, 29.

——. "For Langston Hughes and Stella Holt: An Informal Memoir," *Negro Digest*, XVII (April, 1968), 41-43, 74-77.

Moore, Richard B. "Africa Conscious Harlem," *Freedomways*, III (Summer, 1963), 315-334. [Reprinted in *Harlem, U.S.A.*, pp. 56-75.]

Morris, Lloyd. "The Negro 'Renaissance,'" *Southern Workman*, LIX (February, 1930), 82-86.

Myers, Elisabeth P. *Langston Hughes: Poet of His People.* Champaign, Illinois: Garrard Publishing Company, 1970, pp. 1-144.

Nichols, Lewis. "Langston Hughes Describes the Genesis of His 'Tambourines to Glory,'" *New York Times* (October 27, 1963), Sect. 2, 3.

Noble, Enrique. *Nicolás Guillén y Langston Hughes.* Habana, Cuba, 1962.

O'Daniel, Therman B. "A Langston Hughes Bibliography," *CLA Bulletin*, VII (Spring, 1951), 12-13.

——. "Lincoln's Man of Letters," *Lincoln University Bulletin*, LXVII, 2 (Langston Hughes Issue, 1964), 9-12.

——. "Langston Hughes: A Selected Classified Bibliography," *CLA Journal*, XI (June, 1968), 349-366.

Orlenin, D. "Lengston X' juz-poèt cernoj Ameriki, 'Xèppening'—prodolzenie 'total'nogo' teatra?" *Grani*, LXVII, 190-202.

Ovington, Mary White. *Portraits in Color.* New York: Viking Press, 1927, pp. 194-204.

Parker, John W. "Tomorrow in the Writing of Langston

Hughes," *College English,* X (May, 1949), 438-441.

Patterson, Lindsay. "Langston Hughes—An Inspirer of Young Writers," *Freedomways,* VIII (Spring, 1968), 179-181.

Patterson, Louise Thompson. "With Langston Hughes in the USSR," *Freedomways,* VIII (Spring, 1968), 152-158.

Piquion, René. *Langston Hughes: Un Chant Nouveau.* Introduction par Arna Bontemps. Port-au-Prince, Haiti: Imprimerie de l'État, 1940, pp. 1-159.

Pool, Rosey E. "The Discovery of American Negro Poetry," *Freedomways,* III (Fall, 1963), 511-517.

Presley, James. "The American Dream of Langston Hughes," *Southwest Review,* XLVIII (Autumn, 1963), 380-386.

Randall, Dudley. "Three Giants Gone," *Negro Digest,* xvi (November, 1967), 87.

Redding, Saunders. *To Make A Poet Black.* Chapel Hill: University of North Carolina Press, 1939, pp. 113-117.

Rive, Richard. "Taos in Harlem: An Interview with Langston Hughes," *Contrast,* XIV (1967), 33-39.

Rollins, Charlemae H. *Black Troubadour: Langston Hughes.* Foreword by Gwendolyn Brooks. Chicago: Rand McNally & Company, 1970, pp. 1-143.

Salkey, Andrew. "To Langston Hughes," *Presence Africaine,* LXIV (1967), 56.

Shelton, Robert. "Theatre" ["*Black Nativity* at Philharmonic Hall"], *Nation,* CXCVI (January 5, 1963), 20.

Spencer, T. J. and Clarence Rivers. "Langston Hughes: His Style and Optimism," *Drama Critique,* VII (Spring, 1964), 99-102.

Staples, Elizabeth. "Langston Hughes: Malevolent Force," *American Mercury,* LXXXVIII (January, 1959), 46-50.

Stewart, Donald Ogden, Editor. *Fighting Words.* New York: Harcourt, Brace and Company, 1940, pp. 58-63.

Thurman, Wallace. "Negro Artists and the Negro," *New Republic,* LII (August 31, 1927), 37-39.

——. "Nephews of Uncle Remus," *The Independent,* CXIX (September 24, 1927), 296-298.

——. "Negro Poets and Their Poetry," *The Bookman*, LXVII (July, 1928), 555-561. (Reprinted in Addison Gayle, ed. *Black Expression*. New York: Weybright and Talley, 1969, pp. 70-81.)

Turner, Darwin T. "Langston Hughes as Playwright," *CLA Journal*, XI (June, 1968), 297-309.

——. "*The Negro Novel in America:* In Rebuttal," *CLA Journal* X (December, 1966), 122-134.

——. "The Negro Dramatist's Image of the Universe, 1920-1960," *CLA Journal*, V (December, 1961), 106-120.

——, Compiler. *Afro-American Writers*. Goldentree Bibliographies in Language and Literature. New York: Appleton-Century-Crofts, 1970, pp. 6, 12, *et passim.*

Turpin, Waters E. "Four Short Fiction Writers of the Harlem Renaissance—Their Legacy of Achievement," *CLA Journal*, XI (September, 1967), 59-72.

Wagner, Jean. "Langston Hughes," *Information and Documents*, No. 135, Paris (January 15, 1961), 30-35.

——. *Les Poètes Nègres des Etats-Unis*. Paris: Librairie Instra, 1963, pp. 423-533.

Walker, Margaret. "New Poets," *Phylon*, XI (Fourth Quarter, 1950), 345-354.

Wertz, I. J. "Langston Hughes: Profile," *Negro History Bulletin* (March, 1964), 146-147.

Williams, Kenny J. *They Also Spoke: An Essay on Negro Literature in America, 1787-1930*. Nashville, Tennessee: Townsend Press, 1970, pp. 250-251, 267-268.

Winslow, Vernon. "Negro Art and the Depression," *Opportunity*, XIX (February, 1941), 40-42, 62-63.

Yoseloff, Thomas, Editor. *Seven Poets in Search of An Answer*. A Poetic Symposium. New York: B. Ackerman, Inc., 1944.

XXVII. REVIEWS OF LANGSTON HUGHES'S BOOKS IN THE *CLA JOURNAL*

Farrison, W. Edward. *Simple's Uncle Sam*, IX (March, 1966), 296-300.

——. *The Book of Negro Humor*, X (September, 1966), 72-74.

——. *The Best Short Stories by Negro Writers*, X (June, 1967), 358-360.

——. *The Panther and the Lash: Poems of Our Times*, XI (March, 1968), 259-261.

——. *The Sweet Flypaper of Life*. By Roy DeCarava and Langston Hughes. XI (March, 1968), 261-263.

——. *Black Magic: A Pictorial History of the Negro in American Entertainment*. By Langston Hughes and Milton Meltzer. XI (June, 1968), 367-369.

——. *Black Misery*. By Langston Hughes. Illustrations by Arouni. XIII (September, 1969), 87-88.

Lee, Ulysses. *Ask Your Mama: 12 Moods for Jazz*, VI (March, 1963), 225-226.

Long, Richard A. *Tambourines to Glory*, II (March, 1959), 192-193.

——. *Poems From Black Africa*, VII (December, 1963), 176.

——. *Something in Common and Other Stories*, VII (December, 1963), 177.

Parker, John W. *Simple Stakes a Claim*, I (November, 1957), 46-47.

——. *The Book of Negro Folklore*. Edited by Langston Hughes and Arna Bontemps. II (March, 1959), 185-186.

——. *The Best of Simple*, V (December, 1961), 155-157.

Turpin, Waters. *Five Plays by Langston Hughes*. Edited by Webster Smalley. VII (December, 1963), 180-181.

XXVIII. REVIEWS OF BOOKS ABOUT LANGSTON HUGHES IN THE *CLA JOURNAL*

Farrison, W. Edward. James A. Emanuel's *Langston Hughes*, XII (December, 1968), 168-169.

——. Donald C. Dickinson's *A Bio-Bibliography of Langston Hughes, 1902-1967*, XII (December, 1968), 170-172.

——. Milton Meltzer's *Langston Hughes: A Biography*, XIII (September, 1969), 85-86.

——. Elisabeth P. Myers's *Langston Hughes: Poet of His People,* XIV (June, 1971).

——. Charlemae H. Rollins's *Black Troubadour: Langston Hughes,* XIV (June, 1971).

NOTES ON CONTRIBUTORS

EUGENIA W. COLLIER, a graduate of Howard and Columbia Universities, teaches English at the Community College of Baltimore where, in collaboration with four colleagues, she co-authored *A Bridge to Saying It Well*, a freshman textbook. Her research articles have appeared in *Phylon* and the *CLA Journal*, and her fiction and poetry in the *Negro Digest* and *Black World*. Her 1969 *Negro Digest* short story, "Marigolds," won the fiction prize in the first Gwendolyn Brooks Literary Awards.

ARTHUR P. DAVIS, Professor of English at Howard University, holds the B.A., M.A., and Ph.D. degrees from Columbia University. He is the author of *Isaac Watts: His Life and Works*, first published in 1943, and republished in England in 1948 to mark the 200th anniversary of the death of the great hymnologist. Professor Davis is the author of numerous research articles, newspaper columns, and short stories; co-editor, with Sterling Brown and the late Ulysses Lee, of *The Negro Caravan*; and co-editor, with Saunders Redding, of *Cavalcade: Negro American Writing from 1760 to the Present*.

JAMES A. EMANUEL, author of *Langston Hughes* in Twayne's United States Authors Series, is Professor of English at the City College of the City University of New York. He became interested in doing research on Langston Hughes while studying at the Graduate School of Columbia University, and earned a

Ph.D. degree there by writing a dissertation on "The Short Stories of Langston Hughes." He is the author of many scholarly articles, book reviews, and poems, and co-editor, with Theodore L. Gross, of *Dark Symphony: Negro Literature in America*.

WILLIAM EDWARD FARRISON, Professor Emeritus, North Carolina Central University, is author of the definitive biography, *William Wells Brown: Author and Reformer*, and editor of The Citadel Press edition of *Clotel or, The President's Daughter*. A *magna cum laude* graduate of Lincoln University in Pennsylvania, he holds the M.A. degree from the University of Pennsylvania, and the Ph.D. degree from Ohio State University. A frequent contributor of articles and book reviews to scholarly publications, Professor Farrison is also co-editor, with Hugh M. Gloster and the late Nathaniel P. Tillman, of *My Life, My Country, My World: College Readings for Modern Living*. Currently, he is preparing a new edition of Brown's *The Negro in the American Rebellion*.

DONALD B. GIBSON, Professor of English at the University of Connecticut, is author of *The Fiction of Stephen Crane* and editor of *Five Black Writers: Essays on Wright, Ellison, Baldwin, Hughes, and LeRoi Jones*. After earning two degrees at the University of Kansas City and a Ph.D. at Brown University, Professor Gibson was a Fulbright Lecturer in American Literature at Jagiellonian University, in Cracow, Poland, for two years, and a summer lecturer, in 1965, at the American Studies Seminar in Falkenstein, Germany. His latest book, *Black and White: Short Stories of Modern America*, is now on press.

BLYDEN JACKSON, Professor of English at the University of North Carolina at Chapel Hill, is a graduate of Wilberforce University and holds M.A. and Ph.D. degrees from the University of Michigan. A former president of the College Language Association and a frequent contributor to the *CLA Journal*, his research articles have also appeared in *Phylon* and the *Michigan Alumni Review*. Recently, he was chosen by the National Council of

Teachers of English as one of its four Distinguished Lecturers for 1971.

HARRY L. JONES, Professor of English at Morgan State College, holds B.A. and M.A. degrees from Howard University, and a Ph.D. degree from Catholic University of America where he wrote his dissertation on Jones Very. He is a former lecturer in World Literature at the International Peoples' College, in Elsinore, Denmark. A frequent contributor to the *CLA Journal*, Dr. Jones's articles and book reviews have been published in *Satire Newsletter* and other periodicals.

GEORGE E. KENT, Professor of English at the University of Chicago, is a graduate of Savannah State College and holds M.A. and Ph.D. degrees from Boston University. The author of poems, essays, and fiction, Dr. Kent's byline appears regularly in *CLA Journal*. At present he is editing some of his literary criticisms for publication, and is writing a book on William Faulkner.

NANCY B. McGHEE holds the Avalon Foundation Endowed Professorship of Humanities and is also Chairman of the English Department at Hampton Institute. A graduate of Shaw University, she holds the M.A. degree from Columbia University, the Ph.D. degree from the University of Chicago, and has studied at both the University of London and Cambridge University. Professor McGhee has been the recipient of many fellowships and honors; has traveled widely in the British Isles, Europe, and West Africa; and has published articles and book reviews in *The Journal of Negro Education*, *The Midwest Journal*, *Phylon*, the *CLA Journal*, and other publications.

JOHN F. MATHEUS, Professor of Modern Languages at Kentucky State College, has had a distinguished career as a teacher and appointed government official at home and abroad. He received his B.A. degree, *cum laude*, from Western Reserve University, and his M.A. degree from Columbia University, after which he pursued further studies at the Sorbonne and the University of Chicago. A creative writer as well as a teacher and scholar, he has been awarded first prize for the short story by *Opportunity* magazine, and is the author of numerous articles, plays, and short stories. In collaboration with Professor W. N. Rivers, he edited Alexander Dumas' *Georges* for use as an intermediate French reader.

THERMAN B. O'DANIEL, editor of this volume, is Professor of English at Morgan State College. One of the founders of the *CLA Journal,* he has been its only editor. A graduate of Lincoln University in Pennsylvania, he holds the M.A. degree from the University of Pennsylvania, and the Ph.D. degree from the University of Ottawa (Canada). He has studied also at Harvard University and the Pennsylvania State University, and has been a General Education Board Fellow at the University of Chicago, and a Ford Foundation Fellow at the University of Ottawa. His articles on Cooper, Melville, Emerson, Hughes, Baldwin, Ellison, and other writers have appeared in *Phylon,* the *CLA Journal,* and other publications. Recently, he wrote the introduction to Collier Books' reprint edition of Wallace Thurman's *The Blacker the Berry.*

DARWIN T. TURNER, Professor of English at the University of Michigan, has published critical studies on Afro-American literature, drama, American literature, and literary criticism in the *CLA Journal, Southern Humanities Review, Massachusetts Review, Mississippi Quarterly, Negro Digest* and other publications. A Phi Beta Kappa graduate of the University of Cincinnati, he received his M.A. degree there, and a Ph.D. degree from the University of Chicago. He is co-editor of *Images of the Negro,* author of Study Guides to *The Scarlet Letter* and *Huckleberry Finn,* compiler of *Afro-American Writers,* a bibliography, and author of *Katharsis,* a volume of verse. Recently, he edited three companion volumes for Black Studies: *Black American Literature: Essay, Black American Literature: Fiction,* and *Black American Literature: Poetry.*

JAMES TWINING

The Geneva Deception

HARPER

HARPER

HarperCollins*Publishers*
77–85 Fulham Palace Road, Hammersmith, London W6 8JB

www.harpercollins.co.uk

Published by HarperCollins*Publishers* 2009

2

Copyright © James Twining 2009

James Twining asserts the moral right to
be identified as the author of this work

A catalogue record for this book
is available from the British Library

ISBN: 978 0 00 723043 3

Set in Meridien by Palimpsest Book Production Limited,
Grangemouth, Stirlingshire

Printed in Great Britain by
Clays Ltd, St Ives plc

Mixed Sources

Product group from well-managed
forests and other controlled sources
www.fsc.org Cert no. SW-COC-1806
© 1996 Forest Stewardship Council

FSC is a non-profit international organisation established
to promote the responsible management of the world's forests.
Products carrying the FSC label are independently certified
to assure consumers that they come from forests that are managed
to meet the social, economic and ecological needs
of present and future generations.

Find out more about HarperCollins and the environment at
www.harpercollins.co.uk/green

To Jack, Jill and Herbie. Vegas, baby.

'There is a house in New Orleans
They call the Rising Sun
It's been the ruin of many a poor boy
And me, Oh Lord! was one'

Traditional American folk song

Historical background

This story was inspired by a Carabinieri raid on a warehouse in the Geneva Freeport in 1995 and their discovery within it of over ten thousand illegally excavated antiquities worth over $35 million. The resulting investigation implicated the mafia and raised questions over the role of some of the world's largest museums, collectors and auction houses in the multi-million-dollar international trade in illicit cultural artefacts.

All descriptions and background information provided on works of art, artists, thefts, antiquities smuggling, 'orphans', illegal excavation practices, and architecture are accurate, apart from the Desposito Eroli in Rome, which I have altered to suit my purpose.

For more information on the author and on the fascinating history, people, places, art and artefacts that feature in *The Geneva Deception* and the other Tom Kirk novels, please visit www.jamestwining.com

Extract from the Amherst Papyrus, original court records from the reign of Ramses IX (−1110 BC); translated by J. H. Breasted, *Ancient Records of Egypt,* **Book IV (1904)**

We opened their coffins and their coverings in which they were. We found this august mummy of this king . . . Its coverings were wrought with gold and silver, within and without; inlaid with every splendid costly stone.

We stripped off the gold, which we found on the august mummy of this god, and its amulets and ornaments which were at its throat, and the coverings wherein it rested. [We] found the King's wife likewise; we stripped off all that we found on her likewise. We set fire to their coverings. We stole their furniture, which we found with them, being vases of gold, silver, and bronze.

We divided, and made the gold which we found on these two gods, on their mummies, and the amulets, ornaments and coverings, into eight parts.

Extract from letter written by Thomas Bruce, the seventh Earl of Elgin, to Giovanni Lusieri, 1801

I should wish to have, of the Acropolis, examples in the actual object of each thing, and architectural ornament – of each cornice, each frieze, each capital of the decorated ceilings, of the fluted columns – specimens of the different architectural orders and of the variant forms of the orders – of metopes and the like, as much as possible. Finally everything in the way of sculpture, medals and curious marbles that can be discovered by means of assiduous and indefatigable excavation.

PROLOGUE

'I see wars, terrible wars, and the Tiber foaming with blood'

Virgil, *The Aeneid*, Book VI, 86

Ponte Duca d'Aosta, Rome
15th March – 2.37 a.m.
The cold kiss roused him.

A teasing, tentative embrace, it nibbled play-fully at his ear and then, growing in confidence, slipped down to nuzzle against his naked throat.

Eyes screwed shut, cheek pressed against the wooden decking, Luca Cavalli knew that he should enjoy this moment while it lasted. So he lay there, cradled by the darkness, the gentle swell of the river rocking him softly, concentrating on keeping the steady cadence of his breathing constant. So they wouldn't notice he was awake.

Ahead of him, near the bow, a small pool of rainwater had gathered. He could hear it sloshing from side to side under the duckboards as the boat swayed, smell the rainbow shimmer of engine oil dancing across its surface, the heady scent catching in the back of his throat like an exotic perfume.

He had a strange, uncontrollable urge to swallow, to taste the raw truth of this moment while he still could.

The momentary stutter in his breathing's rhythmic beat was all it took. Immediately, the thin lips resting against his skin parted with a snarl, and the sharp teeth of the knife's serrated edge bit into him savagely. He was hauled upright, eyes blinking, shoulders burning where his wrists had been zip-locked behind his back.

There were three of them in all. One at the helm, his slab hands gripping the wheel. One perched on the bench opposite, a gun wedged into the waistband of his jeans and a cigarette balancing on his lip. One hugging him close, the knife he had caressed his cheek with only a few moments before now pressed hard against his belly.

They were silent, although there was something noisily boastful about their lack of disguise, as if they wanted him to know that they would never be caught, never allow themselves to be picked out from some Questura line-up. Perhaps because of this, the longer he gazed at them, the more featureless they appeared to become, their cruel faces melting into black shadows that he imagined travelled on the wind and lived in dark places where the light feared to go.

Instead, he was struck by their almost monastic serenity. Mute, their eyes fixed resolutely on the horizon, it was as if they had been chosen to complete some divinely ordained quest. Part of him envied their solemn determination, their absolute certainty in their purpose, however base. These were not people whose loyalty could be bought or trust swayed. They were true believers. Perhaps if he'd shared their unswerving faith, he might have avoided his present damnation.

Cavalli gave a resigned shrug and glanced over the side. The river was engorged and running fast, the sharp ripples on the water's ebony surface betraying the occasional patches of shallower ground where the current tripped and dragged against the muddy bed. Above them the street-lights glowed through the trees that lined the embankments on both sides, casting their skeletal shadows down on to the water. The roads appeared quiet, the occasional yellow wash of a car's head-lights sweeping through the gloom overhead as it turned, like a distant lighthouse urging him to safety.

Cavalli realised then that the engine wasn't running, and that this whole time they had been carried forward noiselessly on the river's powerful muscle as it flexed its way through the city. Peering behind them, he could see that because of this, and like some infernal, enchanted craft, they had left no wake behind them, apart from a moment-ary fold in the river's dark velvet that was just as soon ironed flat again.

The gallows creak of the trees as they passed

under the Ponte Cavour interrupted his thoughts. He glanced up fearfully and caught sight of the cylindrical mass of the Castel Sant'Angelo up ahead, the blemishes in its ancient walls concealed by the sodium glare of the lighting that encircled it. To its rear, he knew, was the Passetto, the corridor that had for centuries served as a secret escape route from the Vatican to the castle's fortified sanctuary. For a moment, he allowed himself to imagine that he too might yet have some way out, some hidden passage to safety. If only he could find it.

Still the current carried them forward, steering them towards the Ponte Sant' Angelo and the carved angels lining its balustrades, as if gathered to hear his final confession. It was a strangely comforting thought, although as they drew closer, he realised that even this harmless conceit was to be denied him. The pale figures all had their backs to the river. They didn't even know he was there.

Abruptly, the helmsman whistled, violating the code of silence that had been so religiously observed until now. Up ahead a light flashed twice from the bridge. Someone was expecting them.

Immediately the engine kicked into life as the helmsman wrestled control from the current and steered them towards the left-hand arch. The two other men jumped up, suddenly animated, one of them readying himself with a rope, the other tipping the fenders into place along the port gunwales. As they passed under the arch, the helmsman jammed the throttle into reverse and expertly edged the boat against the massive stone pier, the fenders squealing in protest, the rattle of the exhaust echoing noisily off the vaulted roof. He nodded at the others and they leapt forward to secure the boat to the rusting iron rings embedded in the wall, leaving just enough play for the craft to ride the river's swell. Then he switched the engine off.

Instantly, a bright orange rope came hissing out of the darkness, the excess coiling in the prow. The helmsman stepped forward and tugged on it to check it was secure, then found the end and held it up. It had already been tied into a noose.

Now, as he understood that there was to be no last-minute reprieve, that this was how it was really going to end, Cavalli felt afraid. Desperate words began to form in his mouth, screams rose from his stomach. But no sound came out, as if he had somehow been bound into the same demonic vow of silence that his captors seemed to have taken.

Hauling him out of his seat, the two other men dragged him over to where the helmsman was looping the surplus rope around his arm, and forced him on to his knees. Cavalli gave him a pleading look, gripped by some basic and irrational need to hear his voice, as if this final and most basic act of human communion might somehow help soften the ordeal's cold, mechanised efficiency. But instead, the noose was simply snapped over his head and then jerked tight, the knot biting into the nape of his neck. Then he was silently lifted to the side and carefully lowered into the freezing water.

He gasped, the change in temperature winding him. Treading water, he looked up at the boat, not understanding why they had tied the rope so long, its loose coils snaking through the water around him. The three men, however, hadn't moved from the side rail, an expectant look on their faces as if they were waiting for something to happen. Waiting, he realised as he drifted a few feet further away from the boat, for the current to take him.

Without warning, the river grabbed on to him, nudging him along slowly at first and then, as he emerged out from under the bridge, tugging at his ankles with increasing insistence. He drew further away, the rope gently uncoiling in the water, the steep angle of the cord where it ran down from the bridge's dark parapet getting closer and closer to him as the remaining slack paid out.

It snapped tight. Choking, his body swung round until he was half in and half out of the water, the current hauling at his hips and legs, the rope lifting his head and upper body out of the river, the tension wringing the water from the fibres.

He kicked out frantically, his ears flooding with an inhuman gurgling noise that he only vaguely recognised as his own voice. But rather than free himself, all he managed to do was flip himself on to his front so that he was face down over the water.

Slowly, and with his reflection staring remorselessly back up at him from the river's dark mirror, Cavalli watched himself hang.

PART ONE

'The die has been cast'

Julius Caesar
(according to Suetonius, *Divus Julius*,
paragraph 33)

ONE

**Arlington National Cemetery,
Washington DC 17th March – 10.58 a.m.**
One by one, the limousines and town cars drew
up, disgorged their occupants on to the sodden
grass, and then pulled away to a respectful
distance. Parked end-to-end along the verge, they
formed an inviolable black line that followed the
curve of the road and then stretched down the hill
and out of sight, their exhaust fumes pinned to
the road by the rain as they waited.

A handful of secret service agents were
patrolling the space between the burial site and
the road. Inexplicably, a few of them were wearing
sunglasses despite the black clouds that had sailed
up the Potomac a few days ago and anchored
themselves over the city. Their unsmiling presence
made Tom Kirk feel uncomfortable, even though
he knew it shouldn't. After all, it had been nearly
two years now. Two years since he'd crossed over

to the other side of the law. Two years since he'd teamed up with Archie Connolly, his former fence, to help recover art rather than steal it. Clearly it was going to take much longer than that to shake off instincts acquired in a lifetime on the run.

There were three rows of seats arranged in a horseshoe around the flag-draped coffin, and five further rows of people standing behind these. A pretty good turnout, considering the weather. Tom and Archie had stayed back, sheltering under the generous spread of a blossoming tree halfway up the slope that climbed gently to the left of the grave.

As they watched, ceremony's carefully choreographed martial beauty unfolded beneath them. The horse-drawn caisson slowly winding its way up the hill, followed by a single riderless horse, its flanks steaming, boots reversed in the stirrups to symbolise a fallen leader. The immaculate presenting of arms by the military escort, water dripping from their polished visors. The careful securing and transport of the coffin to the grave by a casket party made up of eight members of the 101st Airborne, Tom's grandfather's old unit. The final adjustments to the flag to ensure that it was stretched out and centred, the reds, blues and whites fighting to be seen through the tenebrous darkness.

From his vantage point, Tom recognised a few of the faces sheltering under the thicket of black umbrellas, although most were strangers to him and, he suspected, would have been to his grandfather too. That figured. Funerals were a vital networking event for the DC top brass – a chance to talk to the people you normally couldn't be seen with; a chance to be seen with the people who normally wouldn't talk to you. Deals were done, handshakes given, assurances provided. In this city, death was known to have breathed life into many a stuttering career or stalled bill.

There was perhaps, Tom suspected, another, more personal reason for their presence too. After all, like them, Trent Clayton Jackson Duval III had been an important man – a senator, no less. And as such it was in their shared interest to ensure that he got a proper send off. Not because they cared about him particularly, although as a war hero, 'Trigger' Duval commanded more respect than most. Rather because they knew, as if they were all party to some secret, unspoken pact, that it was only by reinforcing these sorts of traditions that they could safeguard their prerogative to a similarly grand send off when their own time came.

'Who's the bird?' Archie sniffed. In his mid-forties, about five foot ten and unshaven with close cropped blond hair, Archie had the square-shouldered, rough confidence of someone who didn't mind using their fists to start or settle an argument. This was at odds with the patrician elegance of his clothes, however; a three-

buttoned, ten-ounce, dark grey Anderson &
Sheppard suit, crisp white Turnbull and Asser
shirt, and woven black silk Lewin's tie hinting at
a rather more considered and refined temperament. Tom knew that many struggled to reconcile this apparent incongruity, although the truth
was that both were valid. It was only a short
distance from the rain-lashed trestle tables of
Bermondsey Market to Mayfair's panelled auction
rooms, but for Archie it had been a long and difficult journey that had required this expensive
camouflage to travel undetected. Tom rather
suspected that he now deliberately played off the
contradiction, preferring to keep people guessing
which world he was from rather than pin him
down to one or the other.

'Miss Texas,' Tom answered, knowing instinctively that his eye would have been drawn to the
platinum blonde in the front row. 'Or she was a
few years ago. The senator upgraded after
meeting her on the campaign trail. He left her
everything.'

'I'll bet he did, the dirty old bastard.' Archie
grinned. 'Look at the size of those puppies! She'd
keel over in a strong wind.'

The corners of Tom's mouth twitched but he
said nothing, finding himself wondering if her dark
Jackie O glasses were to hide her tears or to mask
the fact that she had none. The chaplain started
the service.

'You sure you don't want to head down?' Archie was holding up a Malacca-handled Brigg umbrella. A gold identity bracelet glinted on his wrist where his sleeve had slipped back.

'This is close enough.'

'Bloody long way to come if all we're going to do is stand up here getting pissed on,' Archie sniffed, peering out disconsolately at the leaden skies. 'They invited you, didn't they?'

'They were being polite. They never thought I'd actually show. I'm not welcome here. Not really.'

The empty caisson pulled away, the horses' hooves clattering noisily on the blacktop, reins jangling.

'I thought he liked you?'

'He helped me,' Tom said slowly. 'Took me in after my mother died, put me through school, recommended me to the NSA. But after I left the Agency . . . well. We hadn't spoken in twelve years.'

'Then tell me again why the bloody hell we're here?' Archie moaned, pulling his blue overcoat around his neck with a shiver.

Tom hesitated. The truth was that, even now, he wasn't entirely sure. Partly, it had just seemed like the proper thing to do. The right thing to do. But probably more important was the feeling that his mother would have wanted him to come. Expected it, insisted on it. To him, therefore, this was perhaps less about paying his respects to his grandfather than it was a way of remembering her.

'You didn't have to come,' Tom reminded him sharply.

'What, and miss the chance to work on my tan?' Archie winked. 'Don't be daft. That's what mates are for.'

They stood in silence, the priest's faint voice and the congregation's murmured responses carrying to them on the damp breeze. Yet even as the service droned mournfully towards its conclusion. 'Let us Pray' people lowered their heads, a man stepped out from the crowd and signalled up at them with a snatched half-wave, having been waiting for this opportunity, it seemed. Tom and Archie swapped a puzzled look as he clambered up towards them, his shoes slipping on the wet grass.

'Mr Kirk?' he called out hopefully as he approached. 'Mr Thomas Kirk?'

Short and worryingly overweight, he wore a large pair of tortoiseshell glasses that he was forever pushing back up his blunt nose. Under a Burberry coat that didn't look as though it had fitted him in years, an expensive Italian suit dangled open on each side of his bloated stomach, like the wings on a flying boat.

'I recognised you from your photo,' he huffed as he drew closer, sweat lacquering his thinning blond hair to his head.

'I don't think . . .?' Tom began, trying to place the man's sagging face and bleached teeth.

'Larry Hewson,' he announced, his tone and eagerly outstretched hand suggesting that he expected them to recognise the name.

Tom swapped another look with Archie and then shrugged.

'Sorry, but I don't . . .'

'From Ogilvy, Myers and Gray – the Duval family attorneys,' Hewson explained, almost sounding hurt at having to spell this out. '*I* sent you the invitation.'

'What do you want?' Archie challenged him.

'Meet Archie Connolly,' Tom introduced him with a smile. 'My business partner.'

Below them, the chaplain had stepped back from the casket, allowing the senior NCO and seven riflemen to step forward and turn to the half right, their shoulders stained dark blue by the rain, water beading on their mirrored toecaps.

'Ready,' he ordered. Each rifleman moved his safety to the fire position.

'It's a delicate matter,' Hewson said in a low voice, throwing Archie a suspicious glance.

'Archie can hear anything you've got to say,' Tom reassured him.

'It concerns your grandfather's will.'

'Aim,' the NCO called. The men shouldered their weapons with both hands, the muzzles raised forty-five degrees from the horizontal over the casket.

'His will?' Archie asked with a frown. 'I thought he'd left the lot to Miss 32F down there?'

'Fire.'

Each man quickly squeezed the trigger and then returned to port arms, the sharp crack of the blank round piercing the gloom, the echo muffled by the rain. Twice more the order to aim and fire came, twice more the shots rang out across the silent cemetery. Hewson waited impatiently for their echo to die down before continuing.

'The senator did indeed alter his will to ensure that Ms Mills was the principal beneficiary of his estate,' he confirmed in a disapproving whisper. 'But at the same time, he identified a small object that he wished to leave to you.'

A bugler had stepped forward and was now playing Taps, the mournful melody swirling momentarily around them before chasing itself into the sky. As the last note faded away, one of the casket party stepped forward and began to carefully fold the flag draped over the coffin, deliberately wrapping the red and white stripes into the blue to form a triangular bundle, before respectfully handing it to the chaplain. The chaplain in turn stepped over to where the main family party was seated and gingerly, almost apologetically it seemed, handed the flag to the senator's wife. She clutched it, rather dramatically Tom thought, to her bosom.

'I believe it had been given to him by your mother,' Hewson added.

'My mother?' Tom's eyes snapped back to Hewson's, both surprised and curious. 'What is it?'

'I'm afraid I don't know,' Hewson shrugged as the ceremony ended. The congregation rapidly thinned, most hurrying back to their cars, a few pausing to conclude the business they had come there for in the first place, before they too were herded by secret service agents towards their limousines' armour-plated comfort. 'The terms of the will are quite strict. No one is to open the box and I am to hand it to you in person. That's why . . .'

'Tom!' Archie interrupted, grabbing Tom's arm. Tom followed his puzzled gaze and saw that a figure had appeared at the crest of the hill above them. It was a woman dressed in a red coat, the headlights of the car parked behind her silhouetting her against the dark sky in an ethereal white glow.

'That's why I sent you the invitation,' Hewson repeated, raising his voice slightly as Tom turned away from him. 'I've taken the liberty of reserving a suite at the George where we can finalise all the paperwork.'

'Isn't that . . .?' Archie's eyes narrowed, his tone at once uncertain and incredulous.

'Otherwise I'm happy to arrange a meeting at our offices in New York tomorrow, if that works better,' Hewson called out insistently, growing increasingly frustrated, it seemed, at being ignored. 'Mr Kirk?'

'Yes . . .' Tom returned the woman's wave, Hewson's voice barely registering any more. 'It's her.'

TWO

Via del Gesù, Rome
17th March – 5.44 p.m.

Ignoring her phone's shrill call, Allegra Damico grabbed the double espresso off the counter, threw down some change and stepped back outside into the fading light. Answering it wouldn't make her get there any quicker. And if they wanted her to make any sense after the day she'd just had, she needed the caffeine more than they needed her to be on time. Shrugging with a faint hint of indignation, she walked down the Via del Gesù then turned right on to the Corso Vittorio Emanuele, cupping the coffee in both hands and blowing on it, her reflection catching in the shop windows.

She owed her athletic frame to her father, an architect who had met her mother when he was working as a tour guide in Naples and she, a Danish student, was backpacking across Europe. As a result, Allegra had contrived to inherit both his olive skin and quick temper and her mother's high cheekbones and the sort of curling strawberry blonde hair that the rich housewives who stalked the Via dei Condotti spent hundreds of euros trying to conjure from a bottle. Nowhere was this genetic compromise more arrestingly reflected than in her mismatched eyes – one crystal blue, the other an earthy brown.

Lifting her nose from the cup she frowned, suddenly aware that despite the time of day, dawn seemed to be breaking ahead of her, its golden glow bronzing the sky. Sighing, she quickened her pace, taking this unnatural event and the growing wail of sirens as an ominous portent of what lay in wait.

Her instincts were soon proved right. The Largo di Torre Argentina, a large rectangular square that had once formed part of the Campo Marzio, had been barricaded off, a disco frenzy of blue and red lights dancing across the walls of the surrounding buildings. A swollen, curious crowd had gathered on one side of the metal railings, straining to see into the middle of the square, some holding their mobile phones over their heads to film what they could. On the other side loomed a determined cordon of state police, some barking at people to stay back and go home, a few braving the baying masses in a valiant attempt to redirect the backed-up traffic along the Via dei Cestari. A police helicopter circled overhead, the bass chop of its blades mingling with the sirens' shrill treble to form a deafening and discordant choir. A single searchlight shone down from its belly, its celestial beam picking out a spot that Allegra couldn't yet see.

Her phone rang again. This time she answered it.

'*Pronto*. Yes sir, I'm here . . . I'm sorry, but I came as soon as I could . . . Well, I'm here now . . . Okay, then tell him I'll meet him at the north-east corner in three minutes . . . *Ciao*.'

She extracted her badge from her rear jeans pocket and, taking a deep breath, plunged into the crowd and elbowed her way to the front, flashing it apologetically in the vague direction of the muffled curses and angry stares thrown her way. Once there, she identified herself and an officer unhooked one of the barriers, the weight of the crowd spitting her through the gap before immediately closing up behind her.

Catching her breath and pulling her jacket straight, she picked her way through a maze of haphazardly parked squad cars and headed towards the fenced-off sunken area that dominated the middle of the square. She could see now that this was the epicentre of the synthetic dawn she had witnessed earlier, a series of large mobile floodlights having been wheeled into place along its perimeter, the helicopter frozen overhead.

'Lieutenant Damico?'

A man had appeared at the top of a makeshift set of steps that led down to the large sunken tract of land. She nodded and held out her ID by way of introduction.

'You're a woman.'

'Unless you know something I don't.'

'I know you're late,' he snapped.

About six foot three, he must have weighed seventeen stone, most of it muscle. He was wearing dark blue trousers, a grey jacket and a garish tie that could only have been a gift from his children at Christmas. She guessed he was in his late fifties; his once square face rounding softly at the edges, black hair swept across his scalp to mask his baldness and almost totally grey over his ears. A scar cut across his thick black moustache, dividing it into two unevenly sized islands separated by a raised white ribbon of skin, like a path snaking through a forest.

For a moment she thought of arguing it out with him. Not the fact that she was late, of course: she was. Which, to be honest, she always was. Rather that she had an in-tray full of reasons to be late. But for once she held back, suspecting from his manner that he wouldn't be interested in her excuses. If anything, his anxious tone and the nervous twitch of his left eye suggested that he was wasn't so much angry, as afraid.

'So everyone keeps telling me.'

'Major Enrico Salvatore –' he grudgingly shook her hand – 'Sorry about . . . we don't see too many women in the GICO.'

She just about managed to stop herself from rolling her eyes. GICO – properly known as the Gruppo di Investigazione Criminalità Organizzata – the special corps of the Guardia di Finanza that dealt with organised crime. And by reputation an old-school unit that frequented the same strip joints as the people they were supposedly trying to lock up.

'So what's the deal?' she asked. Her boss hadn't told her anything. Just that he owed someone a favour and that she should get down here as soon as she could.

'You know this place?' he asked, gesturing anxiously at the sunken area behind him.

'Of course.' She shrugged, slightly annoyed to even be asked. Presumably they knew her background. Why else would they have asked for her? 'It's the "Area Sacra".'

'Go on.'

'It contains the remains of four Roman temples unearthed during an excavation project ordered by Mussolini in the 1920s,' she continued. 'They were built between the fourth and second centuries BC. Each one has a different design, with . . .'

'Fine, fine . . .' He held his hands up for her to stop, his relieved tone giving her the impression that she had just successfully passed some sort of audition without entirely being sure what role she was being considered for. He turned to make his way back down the steps. 'Save the rest for the boss.'

The large site was enclosed by an elegant series of brick archways that formed a retaining wall for the streets some fifteen or so feet above. Bleached white by the floodlights' desert glare, a forensic search team was strung out across it, inching their way forward on their hands and knees.

Immediately to her right, Allegra knew, was the Temple of Juturna – a shallow flight of brick steps leading up to a rectangular area edged by a row of travertine Corinthian columns of differing heights, like trees that had been randomly felled by a storm. They were all strangely shadowless in the artificial light. Further along the paved walkway was the Aedes Fortunae Huiusce Diei, a circular temple where only six tufa stone Corinthian columns remained standing, a few surviving bases and mid-sections from the other missing pillars poking up like rotting teeth.

But Salvatore steered her past both of these, turning instead between the second and third temples and making his way over rough ground scattered with loose bits of stone and half-formed brick walls that looked like they had been spat out of the earth. Here and there cats, strays from the animal shelter located in the far corner of the Area Sacra, glanced up with disdainful disinterest or picked their way languidly between the ruins, meowing hopefully for food.

With a curious frown, Allegra realised that Salvatore was leading her towards a large semi-permanent structure made of scaffolding, covered in white plastic sheeting.

Wedged into the space between the rear of the second and third temples and the retaining wall, she immediately recognised it as the sort of makeshift shelter that was often erected by archaeologists to protect an area of a site that they were excavating or restoring.

'I'd stay out of the way until the colonel calls you over,' Salvatore suggested as he paused on the threshold to the shelter, although from his tone it sounded more like an order.

'The colonel?'

'Colonel Gallo. The head of GICO,' Salvatore explained in a hushed tone.

She recognised the name. From what she remembered reading at the time, Gallo had been parachuted in last year from the AISI, the Italian internal security service, after his predecessor had been implicated in the Mancini corruption scandal.

'He'll call you over when he's ready.'

'Great.' She nodded, her tight smile masking a desperate urge to make some pointed observation about the irony of having been harried halfway across the city only to now be kept waiting.

'And I'd lose that if I were you, too,' he

muttered, nodding at her cup. 'It's probably better he doesn't know you stopped off for a coffee.'

Taking a deep breath, she theatrically placed the cup on the ground, then looked up with a forced smile. It wasn't Salvatore's fault, she knew. Gallo clearly orbited his waking hours like a small moon, the gravitational pull off his shifting favour governing the ebb and flow of Salvatore's emotions. But that didn't make him any less annoying.

'Happy now?'

'Ecstatic.'

Greeting the two uniformed men guarding the entrance with a nod, Salvatore held a plastic flap in the sidewall open and they stepped inside. It revealed a long, narrow space, the scaffolding forming a sturdily symmetrical endoskeleton over which the white sheeting had been draped and then fixed into place. In one place some of the ties had come loose, the wind catching the sheet's edges and snapping it against the metal frame, causing it to chime like a halyard striking a mast.

Salvatore motioned at a crumbling pediment, his gesture suggesting that he wanted her to sit there until she was called forward, then made his way towards a small group of people standing in a semi-circle fifteen or so feet in front of her – all men, she noted with a resigned sigh. Making a point of remaining standing, she counted the minutes as they ticked past – first one, then three, then five. Nothing. In fact no one had even turned round to acknowledge that she was there. Pursing her lips, she decided to give it another few minutes and then, when these too had passed, she made an angry clicking noise with her tongue and set off towards them. Busy was one thing, rude was another. She had better things to do than sit around until Gallo deigned to beckon her over like some sort of performing dog. Besides, she wanted to see for herself whatever it was they were and discussing so intently.

Seeing her approaching, Salvatore frantically signalled at her to stay back. She ignored him, but then stopped anyway, the colour draining from her face as a sudden gap revealed what they had been shielding from view.

It was a corpse. A man. A half-naked man. Arms spread-eagled, legs pinned together, he had been lashed to a makeshift wooden cross with steel wire. Allegra glanced away, horrified, but almost immediately looked back, the gruesome scene exercising a strange, magnetic pull. For as if drawn from some cursed, demonic ritual, the cross had been inverted.

He had been crucified upside down.

THREE

Arlington National Cemetery, Washington DC
17th March – 11.46 a.m.

'You sure about this?' Special Agent Bryan Stokes stepped out of the car behind her, his tone making his own doubts clear.

'Absolutely,' Jennifer Browne nodded, surprised at the unforced confidence in her voice as she watched Tom set off towards them, his short brown hair plastered down by the rain. He had seemed pleased to see her, his initial surprise having melted into a warm smile and an eager wave. That was something, at least.

'So what's the deal with you two?' Stokes wedged a golf umbrella against his shoulder with his chin and flicked a manilla file open. Medium height, about a hundred and seventy pounds, Jennifer guessed that Stokes had been born frowning, deep lines furrowing a wide, flat forehead, bloodless lips pressed into a concerned grimace. In his early forties, he was dressed in a severe charcoal suit and black tie that had dropped away from his collar, revealing that the button was missing.

'There is no deal,' she said quickly, looking away in case he noticed her smile.

'Then how do you know him?'

'We've worked a couple of cases together, that's all.'

Tom was navigating his way towards them through the blossom scatter of white gravestones like a skiff through a storm, tacking first one way and then the other as he plotted a route up the hill. Not for the first time she noted that despite his tall, athletic frame, there was something almost feline about the way he moved – at once graceful and fluid and yet strong and sure-footed.

'It says here he was Agency?'

'Senator Duval was on the Senate Intelligence Committee and recommended him,' she explained, picking her words carefully. FBI Director Jack Green had made it crystal clear that the specific circumstances in which Tom had joined and left the CIA were highly classified. 'They recruited him into a black op industrial espionage unit. When they shut it down five years later, Kirk went into business for himself, switching from technical blueprints and experimental formulas to fine art and jewellery.'

'Was he any good?'

'The best in the business. Or so they said.'

'And the guy with him?'

'Archie Connolly. His former fence. Now his business partner. And his best friend, to the extent he allows himself to have one.'

There was a pause as Stokes consulted the file again. It had been Jennifer's idea to come here, of course. INS had flagged Tom's name up when he'd landed at Dulles and it hadn't taken her much to figure out where he'd be headed. But now that she was actually here, she was surprised at how she was feeling. Excited to be seeing Tom again after almost a year, certainly. But there was also a nagging sense of nervousness and apprehension that she couldn't quite explain. Or perhaps didn't want to. It was always easier that way.

'And now they've gone straight?' There was the suggestion of suppressed laughter in Stokes's voice.

'I'm not sure that someone like Tom can ever go straight,' she mused. 'Not in the way you and I mean it. The problem is, he's seen too many supposedly straight people do crooked things to think those sorts of labels matter. He just does what he thinks is right.'

'And you're sure about this?' Stokes pressed again, her explanation seeming to have, if anything, heightened his initial misgivings.

She didn't bother replying, hoping that he would interpret her silence in whichever way made him most comfortable. Instead she stepped forward to greet Tom, who had reached the final incline that led up to where they were waiting. Tom, however, hesitated, his eyes flicking to Stokes and then back to her. He was clearly surprised that she hadn't come alone.

'Tom –' She held out her hand. It felt all wrong, too formal, but with Stokes hovering she didn't exactly have much choice. Besides, what was the alternative? A hug? A kiss? That also didn't seem right after eleven months.

'Special Agent Browne,' Tom shook her hand with a brief nod, having clearly decided to ape her stilted greeting. He looked healthier than when she had last seen him, his handsome, angular face having lost some of its pallor, his coral blue eyes clear and alive.

'This is Special Agent Stokes.'

'Agent Stokes,' Tom nodded a greeting.

Stokes grunted something indistinct in reply and glanced nervously over his shoulder, as if he was worried about being seen out in the open with him.

'Come to pay your respects?'

'We need some help on a case,' Jennifer began hesitantly.

'You mean this wasn't a coincidence?'

Despite his sarcastic tone, she sensed a slight

tension lurking behind his smile. Annoyance, perhaps, that she was only there because she wanted something. Or was that just her projecting her own guilty feelings?

'*I* need your help,' she said.

There was a pause, his smile fading.

'What have you got?'

'Why don't we get in . . .' She held the Suburban's rear door open. Tom didn't move. 'There's something I want to show you. It'll only take a few minutes.'

Tom hesitated for a moment. Then, shrugging, he followed Jennifer into the back, while Stokes climbed into the driver's seat.

'Recognise this?'

She handed him a photograph sealed inside a clear plastic evidence bag. Tom smoothed the crinkles flat so that he could see through it. It showed a nativity scene, an exhausted Mary clutching her belly and staring blankly at the Christ child lying on the straw in front of her, an angel plunging dramatically overhead. Unusually, in the foreground a spiky-haired youth, his back to the viewer and one foot touching the baby, has turned to face an aged Joseph, his face tortured by a mischievous disbelief.

Tom looked up, a puzzled smile playing across his lips. Outside, the sky had darkened even further, the rain thrashing the roof, the water running off the windscreen in sheets like rolled steel off a mill.

'Where did you get it?'

'Do you recognise it?' Stokes repeated, although Jennifer could already tell from Tom's face that he did.

'Caravaggio. *The Nativity with San Lorenzo and San Francesco*,' he pointed at the two other men in the painting gazing adoringly at the infant. 'Painted in 1609 for the Oratory of San Lorenzo in Palermo, Sicily. Missing since 1969. Where did you get it?'

It was Tom's turn to repeat his question.

Jennifer looked to Stokes and took his muted sigh and faint shrug as agreement to continue.

'Special Agent Stokes is from our Vegas field office,' she explained. 'A week ago he took a call from Myron Kezman.'

'The casino owner?' Tom asked in surprise.

'The photo arrived in his personal mail.'

'It had a New York City post mark,' Stokes added. 'We've checked the envelope for prints and DNA. It was clean.'

'There was a cell-phone number on the back of the photo,' Jennifer continued; Tom turned it over so he could see it. 'When Kezman called it there was a recorded message at the other end. It only played once before the number was disconnected.'

The windows had started to fog up. Stokes

started the engine and turned the heating on to clear them, a sudden blast of warm air washing over them.

'What did it say?'

'According to Kezman it made him a simple offer. The painting for twenty million dollars. And then a different cell-phone number to dial if he was interested in making the trade.'

'That's when Kezman called us in,' Stokes took over. 'Only this time we taped the call. It was another message setting out the instructions for the exchange. The denominations for the cash. The types of bags it should be in. The meet.'

'And then they called you?' Tom turned to Jennifer.

'The Caravaggio is on the FBI Art Crime team's top ten list of missing art works, so it automatically got referred our way,' she confirmed. 'I got pulled off a case to help handle it. I've been camping out in an office here in DC, so when I saw that you'd been flagged up at Dulles . . .'

'You thought that maybe I could handle the exchange for you.'

'How the hell did you . . .?' Stokes eyed him suspiciously.

'Because you've never dealt with anything like this before.' Tom shrugged. 'Because you're smart and you know that these types of gigs never go down quite like you plan them. Because you know I might spot something you won't.'

There was a pause as Stokes and Jennifer both swapped a look, and then laughed.

'That's pretty much it, I guess.' Stokes nodded with a grudging smile.

'When's this happening?'

'Tonight in Vegas. On the main floor at the Amalfi.'

'Kezman's joint?'

'Yep,' Stokes nodded.

'That's smart. Busy. Exposed. Plenty of civilian cover. Multiple escape routes.'

'So you'll do it?' Jennifer asked hopefully.

There was a sharp rap on the window. Tom lowered it and Archie peered in, the rain dripping off his umbrella.

'Very bloody cosy,' he observed with a wry smile. 'Not interrupting anything, am I?'

'I don't think you two have ever actually met before, have you?' Tom asked, sitting back so Jennifer could lean across him and shake his hand.

'Not properly.' She smiled.

'What do you want with my boy this time?' Archie sniffed, eyeing her carefully.

'The *Nativity* has turned up,' Tom answered for her. 'They want me to fly to Vegas with them to help handle the exchange.'

'I'll bet they do. What's our take?'

Tom looked searchingly at Jennifer and then at Stokes, who shrugged sheepishly.

'Looks like the usual fee,' he said with a smile. 'Attaboys all round.'

'Well, bollocks to that, then,' Archie sniffed. 'You and I are meant to be meeting Dom in Zurich tomorrow night to see a real client. One that pays and doesn't try and lock you up every five seconds.' He gave first Jennifer, then Stokes, a reproachful glare.

Tom nodded slowly. Having given up on the Swiss police, the curator of the Emile Bührle Foundation wanted their help recovering four paintings worth a hundred and eighty million dollars taken at gunpoint the previous month. Archie had a point.

'I know.'

A pause. He turned back to Jennifer.

'Who'll handle the exchange if I don't?'

'Me, I guess,' she replied with a shrug. 'At least, that was the plan until you flashed up on the system.'

There was a long silence, Tom looking first at Jennifer, then Stokes. He turned back to Archie.

'Why don't I just meet you in Zurich tomorrow.'

'Oh, for fuck's sake, Tom,' Archie protested. 'I don't know why I bother sometimes.'

'One night. That's all,' Tom reassured him. 'I'll be on the first flight out.'

'Fine,' Archie sighed. 'But you can deal with Hewson.' Archie stepped back and pointed down the slope towards a lonely figure who appeared to be patiently waiting for them to return. 'He's doing my bloody head in.'

'Whatever he's got for me, it's waited this long –' Tom sat back with a shrug – 'it can wait a day longer.'

FOUR

Largo di Torre Argentina, Rome
17th March – 6.06 p.m.
Allegra could just about make out one of the men's low voices. A pathologist, she guessed.

'Cause of death? Well, I'll only know when I open him up. But at a guess, oedema of the brain. Upside down, the heart continues to pump blood through the arteries, but because the veins rely on gravity, his brain would have become swollen with blood. Fluid would then have leaked out of his capillaries, first causing a headache, then gradual loss of consciousness and finally death, probably from asphyxiation as the brain signals driving respiration failed. Terrible way to go.'

'How long has he been here?' the man next to him asked. From his flinty, aggressive tone, Allegra knew immediately that this had to be Gallo.

'All day. Possibly longer. It was a cold night and that would have slowed decomposition.'

'And no one saw him until now?' Gallo snapped, his voice both angry and disbelieving. She could just about detect the vestiges of a Southern accent, presumably carefully discarded over the years. After all, provincial roots were not exactly something you advertised if you wanted to get ahead. Not in Rome.

'No one works here at the weekend,' Salvatore explained in an apologetic tone. 'And you couldn't see him from the street.'

'Terrible way to go,' the pathologist repeated, shaking his head. 'It would have taken hours for him to die. And right until the end he would have been able to hear people walking around the site and the cars coming and going overhead, and not been able to move or call for help.'

'You think I give a shit about how this bastard died?' Gallo snorted dismissively. 'Don't forget who he was or who he worked for. All I want to know is who killed him, why they did it here and why like this. The last thing I need is some sort of vigilante stalking the streets of Rome re-enacting Satanic rituals.'

'Actually, Colonel, it's Christian, not Satanic,' Allegra interrupted with a cough.

'What?' Gallo rounded on her, looking her up and down with a disdainful expression. He was six feet tall and powerfully built, with a strong, tanned face covered in carefully trimmed stubble. About forty-five or so, she guessed, he was wearing the full dress uniform of a colonel in the Guarda di Finanza and had chin-length steel-grey hair that parted down the centre of his head and fell either side of his face, forcing him to sweep it back out of his eyes every so often. He also had on a pair of frameless glasses with clear plastic arms. From the way he adjusted them on his nose, she sensed that these had only recently been prescribed and that he still resented wearing them, despite having done what he could to make them as unobtrusive as possible.

'The inverted crucifixion,' she explained, ignoring the horrified look on Salvatore's face. 'It's taken from the Acts of Peter.'

'The Acts of Peter?' Gallo snorted. 'There's no such book in the Bible.'

'That's because it's in the Apocrypha, the texts excluded from the Bible by the church,' she replied, holding her temper in check. 'According to the text, when the Roman authorities sentenced Peter to death, he asked to be crucified head down, so as not to imitate Christ's passing.'

Gallo said nothing, his eyes narrowing slightly as he brushed his hair back.

'Thank you for the Sunday school lesson, Miss . . .'

'Lieutenant. Damico.'

'The antiquities expert you asked for, Colonel,' Salvatore added quickly.

'You work at the university?' It sounded like a challenge rather than a question.

'I used to be a lecturer in art and antiquities at La Sapienza, yes.'

'Used to be!' he spluttered, glaring at Salvatore.

'The university passed me on to the Villa Giulia. One of the experts there recommended her,' Salvatore insisted.

'Now I'm in the TPA,' she added quickly, spelling out the acronym for the Nucleo Tutela Patrimonio Artistico, the special corps within the Carabinieri tasked with protecting and recovering stolen art. He looked her up and down again, then shrugged.

'Well, you'll have to do, I suppose,' he said, to Salvatore's visible relief. 'I take it you know who I am?'

She nodded, although part of her was itching to say no, just to see the look on his face. Ignoring the other two men standing there, which she assumed meant that he did not consider them important enough to warrant an introduction, Gallo jabbed his finger at the man next to him.

'This is Dottore Giovanni la Fabro from the coroner's office, and this is, or was, Adriano Ricci, an enforcer for the De Luca family.'

Allegra nodded. The GICO's involvement was suddenly a lot clearer. The De Luca family were believed to run the Bande della Magliana, one of Rome's most notorious criminal organisations.

Gallo clearly thought this was some sort of professional hit.

He stepped back and introduced the corpse with a sweep of his hand. Even dead, she could tell that Ricci had been overweight, loose skin sagging towards the ground like melted wax on the neck of a bottle. He was bare-chested with a large Lazio football club tattoo on his left shoulder, and was still wearing a striped pair of suit trousers that had fallen halfway down his calves. His wrists and ankles were bleeding where the chicken wire used to bind him to the cross had bitten into his flesh.

'Why am I here?' she asked with a shudder, glancing back to Gallo.

'This –' He led her forward to the body and snapped his flashlight on to illuminate its face.

For a few moments she couldn't make out what he was pointing to, her attention grabbed by Ricci's staring, bloodshot eyes and the way that, from the shoulders up, his skin had turned a waxy purple, like marble. But then, trapped in the light of Gallo's torch, she saw it. A black shape, a disc of some sort, lurking in the roof of Ricci's mouth.

'What is it?' she breathed.

'That's what you're meant to be telling me,' Gallo shot back.

'Can I see it, then?'

Gallo snapped his fingers and la Fabro handed him a pair of tweezers. To Allegra's horrified fascination, he levered the object free as if he was prising a jewel from an ancient Indian statue and then carefully deposited it inside an evidence bag, holding it out between his fingertips as if it contained something mildly repellent.

'Knock yourself out,' he intoned.

'I thought it might be some sort of antique coin,' Salvatore suggested eagerly over her shoulder as she turned it over in the light. 'It seems to have markings etched into it.'

'The ancient Romans used to put a bronze coin in the mouths of their dead to pay Charon to ferry their souls across the Styx to the Underworld,' she nodded slowly. 'But I don't think that's what this is.'

'Why not?'

'Feel the weight, it's lead. That's too soft to be used in everyday coinage.'

'Then what about the engraving?' Gallo asked impatiently.

She traced the symbol that had been inlaid into the coin with her finger. It showed two snakes intertwined around a clenched fist, like the seal from some mediaeval coat of arms.

'I don't know,' she said with an apologetic shrug. 'But whatever this is, it's not an antique nor, I would say, particularly valuable.'

'Well, that was useful.' Glaring angrily at Salvatore, Gallo turned his back on Allegra as if she had suddenly vanished.

'I'm sorry,' Salvatore stuttered. 'I thought that . . .'

'We've wasted enough time. Let's just get him bagged up and out of here so the forensic boys can move in,' Gallo ordered as he turned to leave. 'Then I want a priest or a cardinal or somebody else in sandals down here to tell me more about . . .'

'It can't be a coincidence though, can it, Colonel?' Allegra called after him.

Gallo spun round angrily.

'I thought you'd gone?'

'It can't be a coincidence that they killed him here?' she insisted.

'What the hell are you talking about?'

'In Roman times, this entire area was part of the Campus Martius, a huge complex of buildings that included the Baths of Agrippa to the north, the Circus Flaminius to the south and the Theatre of Pompey to the west,' she explained, pointing towards each point of the compass in turn. 'The Senate even met here while the Curia was being rebuilt after a fire in 54 BC –' she pointed at the floor – 'in a space in the portico attached to the Theatre of Pompey.'

'Here?' Gallo looked around him sceptically, clearly struggling to reconcile the fractured ruins at his feet with the imagined grandeur of a Roman theatre.

'Of course, the one drawback of this spot was that the Campus Martius stood outside the sacred *pomerium*, the city's official boundaries, meaning that, although it was quieter than the Forum, it was not subject to the same restrictions against concealed weapons.'

'What's your point?' Gallo frowned wearily, and she realised that she was going to have to spell it out for him.

'I mean that Ricci isn't the first person to be killed here,' she explained, a tremor of excitement in her voice. 'I mean that in 44 BC, Julius Caesar was assassinated on almost this exact same spot.'

FIVE

**The Getty Villa, Malibu, California
17th March – 10.52 a.m.**

Verity Bruce had been looking forward to this day for a while. For nearly three years, to be precise. That's how long it had been since she had first been shown the dog-eared Polaroid in a smoky Viennese café, first been winded by the adrenaline punch of excitement at what was on offer and chilled by the fear of possibly losing out.

She'd shaken on the deal there and then, knowing that the director would back her judgement. The trustees had taken a little more convincing, of course, but then they didn't know the period like she did. Besides, once they'd understood the magnitude of the find, they'd bitten and bitten hard, sharing her mounting frustration at the years lost to the scientists as test upon test had heaped delay upon deferral until she was sure they must have finished and started all over again. And then, of course, the lumbering and self-perpetuating wheels of international bureaucracy had begun to turn, a merry-go-round of sworn affidavits, authentication letters, legal contracts, bank statements, money transfer forms, export and import licences and Customs declarations that had added months to the process. Still, what was done was done. Today, finally, the waiting ended.

She positioned herself in front of the full-length mirror she'd had bolted to the back of her office door. Had the intervening years between that first breathless, absinthe-fuelled encounter and today's unveiling aged her? A little, perhaps, around her fern-green eyes and in the tiny fissures that had begun to fleck her top lip like faint animal tracks across the snow. Ever since she'd turned forty-five, the years seemed to weigh a little heavier on her face, as if they were invisibly swinging from grappling hooks sunk into her skin. She could have had surgery, of course – God knows everyone else her age in LA seemed to have had work done – but she hated anything fake or forced like that. Highlights in her long, coiled copper hair were one thing, but needles and knives . . . Sometimes, nature had to be allowed to run its course.

Besides, she reminded herself as she put the

finishing touches to her makeup, it wasn't as if she'd lost her looks. How else to explain the fact that that gorgeous thirty-two-year-old speech writer she'd met at a White House fund-raiser the other month was pestering her to travel up to his place in Martha's Vineyard next fall? And she still had great legs, too. Always had. Hopefully always would.

'They're ready for you.'

One of the Getty PR girls had edged tentatively into the room. Verity couldn't remember her name, but then all these girls looked the same to her – blonde, smiley, skinny, jutting tits that would hold firm in a 6.1 – as if the city was ground zero in some freakish cloning experiment. Even so, the girl's legs still weren't as good as hers.

'Let's do it,' she said, grabbing her leather jacket off the chair and slipping it over a black couture Chanel dress that she'd bought in Paris last year. It was an unlikely combination, but one deliberately chosen to further fuel the quirky image that she'd so carefully cultivated over the years. It was simple really. If you wanted to get ahead in the hushed and dusty corridors of curatorial academia without waiting to be as old as the exhibits themselves, it paid to get noticed. She certainly wasn't about to tone things down now, despite the occasion, although she had at least upgraded from flats to a vertiginous pair of scarlet Manolos that matched her lipstick. After all, this was a ten-million-dollar acquisition and the *Los Angeles Times* would be taking pictures.

The small group of donors, experts and journalists that she and the director had hand-picked for this private viewing to guarantee maximum pre-launch coverage was already gathered expectantly in the auditorium. The figure had been draped, rather melodramatically she thought, in a black cloth and then placed in the middle of the floor so that people had to circle, brows furrowed in speculation, around it. Snatching up a glass of Laurent-Perrier Rosé from a tray at the door, Verity swept inside and began to work the room, shaking the hands of some, kissing the cheeks of others, swapping an amusing anecdote here and clutching at a shared memory there. But she was barely aware of what she was saying or what was being said to her, her excitement slowly building as the minutes counted down until she could hear only the pregnant thud of her heart.

'Ladies and gentlemen . . .' The director had stepped into the middle of the room. 'Ladies and gentlemen, if I could have your attention please,' he called, ushering the audience closer. The lights dimmed. 'Ladies and gentlemen, today marks the culmination of a remarkable journey,' he began, reading from a small card and then pausing for effect. 'It is a journey that began over 2,500 years ago in ancient Greece. And it is a journey that ends, here, in Malibu. Because today, I am delighted to unveil the Getty Villa's latest acquisition and, in my opinion, one of the most important works of art to enter the United States since the Second World War.'

With a flourish, the cloth slipped to the floor. Under a lone spotlight stood a seven foot tall marble sculpture of a young boy, his left foot forward, arms at his sides, head and eyes looking straight ahead. There was a ripple of appreciative, even shocked recognition. Verity stepped forward.

'This uniquely preserved example of a Greek kouros has been dated to around 540 BC,' Verity began, standing on the other side of the statue to the director and speaking without notes. 'As many of you will undoubtedly know, although inspired by the god Apollo, a kouros was not intended to represent any one individual youth but the *idea* of youth itself, and was used in Ancient Greece both as a dedication to the gods in sanctuaries and as a funerary monument. Our tests show that this example has been hewn from dolomite marble from the ancient Cape Vathy quarry on the island of Thassos.'

Talking in her usual measured and authoritative style, she continued her description of the statue, enjoying herself more and more as she got into her stride: its provenance from the private collection of a Swiss physician whose grandfather had bought it in Athens in the late 1800s; the exhaustive scientific tests that had revealed a thin film of calcite coating its surface resulting from hundreds, if not thousands of years of natural lichen growth; the stylistic features linking it to the Anavysos Youth in the National Museum in Athens. In short, a masterpiece that was yet further evidence of the Getty's determination to build the pre-eminent American collection of classical antiquities.

Her speech drew to a close. Acknowledging the applause with a nod, she retreated to allow people forward for a closer look, anxiously watching over the figure like a parent supervising a child in a busy playground.

At first all went well, a few people nodding appreciatively at the sculpture's elegant lines, others seeking her out to offer muted words of congratulations. But then, without warning, she sensed the mood darkening, a few of the guests eyeing the statue with a strange look and whispering excitedly to each other.

Thierry Normand from the Ecole Française d'Athène was the first to break ranks.

'Doesn't the use of Thassian marble strike you as rather . . . anomalous?'

'And what about the absence of paint?' Eleanor Grant from the University of Chicago immediately added. 'As far as I know, all other kouroi, with the possible exception of the Melos kouros, show traces of paint?'

'Well, of course we considered . . .' Verity began with a weak smile, forcing herself not to sound defensive even though she could hardly not feel insulted by what they were implying.

'I'm sorry, Verity,' Sir John Sykes, the highly respected Lincoln Professor of Classical Archaeology and Art at Oxford University interrupted with an apologetic cough. 'It just isn't right. The hair is pure early sixth-century BC, as you say, but the face and abdomen are clearly much later. And while you can find similarly muscular thighs in Corinth, I've only seen feet and a base like that in Boeotia. The science can only tell you so much. You have to rely on the aesthetics, on what you can see. To me, this is almost verging on the pastiche.'

'Well, I'm sorry, Sir John, but we couldn't disagree more . . .' Verity began angrily, looking to the director for support but seeing that he appeared to have retreated to the periphery of the group.

'Actually, Sir John, the word I'd use,' Professor Vivienne Foyle of the Institute of Fine Arts at New York University added, pausing to make sure everyone was listening, 'is *fresh*.'

The loaded meaning of the word was clear. Foyle was suggesting that the statue was in fact a forgery, that it had been knocked up in some backstreet workshop and never been in the ground at all. Verity was reeling, but the mood in the room was now such that she knew she had no chance of sensibly arguing her case.

The interrogation continued. Why didn't the plinth have a lead attachment like other kouroi? Couldn't the degradation of the stone have been caused deliberately by oxalic acid? How was it that such an exceptional piece had only surfaced now? What due diligence had been carried out on it's provenance?

She barely heard them, her ears filled with the dull pulse of her mounting rage. Her face white and cold as marble, she nodded and smiled and shrugged at what seemed opportune moments, not trusting herself to open her mouth without swearing. A further ten minutes of this torture had to be endured before the director, perhaps sensing that she might be about to erupt, finally saw fit to bring an end to her ordeal.

'Fresh? I'll give that senile old bitch fresh,' she muttered angrily as she stalked back to her office. 'Sonya?'

'I'm Cynthia,' the PR girl chirped, skipping to keep up with her.

'Whatever. Get me Faulks on the phone.'

'Who?'

'Earl Faulks. F-A-U-L-K-S, pronounced like

folks. I don't care where he is. I don't care what he's doing. Just get him for me. In fact, I don't want just to speak to him. I want to see him. Here. Tomorrow.'

SIX

Over Nebraska
17th March – 8.43 p.m.
Normally used to scoop whales into the casino's deep-throated net, Kezman's private jet was a potent introduction to the Vegas experience: snow-white leather seats with a gilded letter 'A' embroidered into the head-rests, leopard-skin carpets, polished mahogany panelling running the length of the cabin like the interior of a pre-war steamer, a small glass bar lit with blue neon. At the front, over the cockpit door, hung a photo of Kezman, all teeth and tan, gazing down on them benevolently like the dictator of some oil-rich African state.

Tom, lost in thought, had immediately settled back into his seat, politely declining the offer of a drink from the attentive stewardess whose skirt seemed to have been hitched almost as high as her top was pulled low. Head turned to the

window, gaze fixed on some distant point on the
horizon, he barely noticed the plane take off, let
alone Jennifer move to the seat opposite him.

'You're still wearing it then?' she asked, head
tilted to one side so that her curling mass of black
hair covered the top of her right shoulder.

He glanced down at the 1934 stainless steel
'Brancard' Rolex Prince on his wrist. It had been
a gift from the FBI for Tom's help on the first case
he'd worked on with Jennifer, although Tom
suspected that the decision to offer it to him, and
the choice of watch, had been all hers.

'Why?' He turned to face her with a smile. 'Do
you want it back?'

Five feet nine, slim with milky brown skin, she
had a lustrous pair of hazel eyes and was wearing
her usual office camouflage of black trouser suit
and cream silk blouse. Her 'Fuck You' clothes, as
she'd once described them, as opposed to the 'Fuck
Me' outfits that some of the other female agents
favoured, only to wonder why they got asked out
all the time but never promoted. The truth was
that the odds of a woman succeeding in the
Bureau, let alone a black woman, were stacked
so heavily against her, that she had to load the
dice any way she could just to be given a fair spin
of the wheel. Then again, from what he'd seen,
Jennifer knew what it took to play the game,
having risen from lowly field agent in the Bureau's
Atlanta Division to one of the most senior members

of its Art Crime Team. That didn't happen by accident.

'Not unless you're having second thoughts.'

'Should I be?'

'You just seem a bit . . . distracted,' she ventured.

'Not really.' His gaze flicked back to the window. 'I guess I was just thinking about today.'

'About your grandfather?'

'About some of the people there. About my family, or what's left of it. About how little I know them and they know me.'

'You're a difficult person to get to know, Tom,' she said gently.

'Even for you?' He turned back to her with a hopeful smile.

'Maybe especially for me,' she shot back, an edge to her voice that was at once resigned and accusing.

He understood what she meant, although she had got closer to him than most over the years. Not that things had started well between them when they had first met, necessity strong-arming their initial instinctive mutual suspicion into a grudging and fragile working relationship. And yet from this unpromising beginning a guarded trust, of sorts, had slowly evolved which had itself, in time, built towards a burgeoning friendship. A friendship which had then briefly flowered into something more, their growing attraction for each other finding its voice in one unplanned and instinctive night together.

Since then, the intervening years and a subsequent case had given them both the opportunity at different times to try and revive those feelings and build on that night. But for whatever reason, the other person had never quite been in the same place – Tom initially unwilling to open up, Jennifer subsequently worried about getting hurt. Even so, the memory had left its mark on both of them, like an invisible shard of metal caught beneath the skin that they could both feel whenever they rubbed up against someone else.

'How have you been?' Tom asked, deliberately moving the focus of the conversation away from himself. Jennifer glanced over his shoulder before answering, prompting Tom to turn in his seat and follow her wary gaze. Stokes was asleep, his legs stretched out ahead of him, his head lolling on to his shoulder, two empty whisky miniatures on the table in front of him. The stewardess had retreated into the limestone-floored toilet cubicle with her make-up bag.

'Were you annoyed I came?' Jennifer answered with a question of her own.

'I was disappointed you didn't come alone,' he admitted, almost surprising himself with his honesty.

'This is Stokes's case,' she explained with an apologetic shrug. 'I couldn't have come without him.'

'That's not what I meant.'

A pause.

'You should have told me you were coming.'

'I didn't know I was until I was on the plane,' he protested.

'You could have called,' she insisted.

'Would you have called me if you hadn't needed my help?'

Another, longer pause.

'Probably not,' she conceded.

It was strange, Tom mused. They weren't dating, hadn't spoken in almost a year, and yet they seemed to be locked into a lovers' awkward conversation, both of them fumbling around what they really wanted to say, rather than risk looking stupid.

There was a long silence.

'Why did you agree to come?' Jennifer eventually asked him, her eyes locking with his.

'Because you said you needed my help,' he said with a shrug.

'You were going to say no,' she pointed out. 'Then something changed.'

'I don't really . . .'

'It was because I said I would handle the exchange myself if you didn't, wasn't it?'

A smile flickered across Tom's face. He'd forgotten how annoyingly perceptive she could be.

'What do you know about this painting?' Tom picked up the photo from the table between them and studied it through the plastic.

'It was one of four that Caravaggio completed in Sicily in 1609 while he was on the run for stabbing someone to death,' she said. 'We have it down as being worth twenty million dollars, but it would go for much more, even in today's market.'

'What about the theft itself?'

'October sixteenth, 1969,' she recited from memory. 'The crime reports say that the thieves cut it out of its frame over the altar of the Oratory of San Lorenzo in Palermo with razor blades and escaped in a truck. Probably a two-man team.'

'I'd guess three,' Tom corrected her. 'It's big – nearly sixty square feet. I'm not sure two men could have handled it.'

'At the time, people blamed the Sicilian mafia?' Her statement was framed as a question.

'It's always looked to me like an amateur job,' Tom replied with a shake of his head. 'Couple of local crooks who'd thought through everything except how they were going to sell it. If the Sicilian mafia have got it now, it's because no one else was buying or because they decided to just take it. The Cosa Nostra don't like people operating on their turf without permission.'

'And no one's ever seen it since?'

'I've heard rumours over the years,' Tom sighed. 'That it had surfaced in Rome, or maybe even been destroyed in the Naples earthquake in 1980. Then a few years ago, a mafia informer claimed to have rolled it up inside a rug and buried it in an iron chest. When they went to dig it up, the chest was empty.'

'What do you think?'

'If you ask me, it's been with the Cosa Nostra the whole time. Probably traded between *capos* as a gift or part payment on a deal.'

'Which would mean that the mafia are behind the sale now?'

'If not the mafia, then someone who has stolen it from them,' Tom agreed. 'Either way, they'll be dangerous and easily spooked. If we're lucky, they'll just run if they smell trouble. If we're not, they'll start shooting.' A pause. 'That's why I came.'

'I can look after myself,' she said pointedly; irritated, it seemed, by what he was implying. 'I didn't ask you here to watch my back.'

'I'm here because I know how these people think,' Tom insisted. 'And the only back that will need watching is mine.'

SEVEN

Amalfi Hotel and Casino, Las Vegas
17th March – 9.27 p.m.
Ever since going freelance, Kyle Foster had never met or even spoken to his handler. It was safer that way. For both of them. Besides, what would have been the fucking point? All he needed was a name, a photograph and fifty per cent of his fee in his Cayman Islands account. Why complicate things with a face or a voice when he could just email the details through and save them both the trouble? Assuming the handler was a guy, of course. There was no real way of knowing. A broad in this line of business? Not unheard of, but rare. Maybe he should suggest a meet after all?

His PDA vibrated on the glass table in front of him, breaking into his thoughts. Swinging his feet to the floor he sat forward, muting the TV so he could concentrate on the message rather than the squeals of the girl being screwed by her twin sister wearing a strap-on.

It was the photo he noticed first, his boulder-like face breaking into something resembling a smile at life's occasional burst of comic irony; he knew this person, or rather he'd come across them before on a previous job. Beneath it was a simple message:

Target confirmed arriving LAS tonight. Terminate with extreme prejudice.

Good, he thought, climbing on to the bed. He hated being kept waiting, especially now the mini-bar was running dry and he'd cycled through both the porn channels.

Unscrewing the ceiling grille, he lifted down a black US Navy Mark 12 Special Purpose Rifle from where he'd hidden it inside the AC duct and began to disassemble it. This weapon was a recent issue to US Special Forces in the Middle East and he liked what they had done with it, producing a rifle with a greater effective range than an M4 Carbine, while still being shorter than a standard-issue M16. He especially appreciated that although it had been chambered for standard NATO rounds, it performed much better with a US-made Sierra Bullets MatchKing 77-grain hollow-point boat-tail bullet, although for jobs like this he preferred using his own bespoke ammunition.

Stripped down, the dismembered weapon parts lay on the crisp linen sheets like instruments on a surgeon's tray. Laying a white hand-towel down next to them, he carefully arranged the pieces on it and then rolled it into a tight bundle that he secured shut by wrapping duct tape around it several times. Shaking the trussed-up towel hard to make sure nothing rattled, he placed it in his backpack.

Draining the last of the whisky, he turned his attention to his uniform, pulling on his red jacket and ensuring that his buttons were straight and done up right under his chin. Not quite as smart as the Army Green hanging in his wardrobe back in Charlotte, carefully positioned so you could see the gold flash of his Rangers badge through the plastic, but it would serve its purpose. He doubted the dry-cleaning company had even noticed that it had been taken from its store-room, and as for the waiter whose security pass he'd stolen and doctored . . . well, he wouldn't be missing anything anytime soon.

Finally, he smoothed down his light brown hair, almost not recognising himself without his straggly beard. That was one thing that had thrown him about Vegas. You could walk around in an Elvis suit or with a twelve-foot albino python around your neck and nobody would give you a second look. But wander more than twenty feet down the strip with a beard and people would stare at you like you were a freak in a circus side-show.

In the end, he'd had no choice but to shave it off. How else to blend in with the casino staff? How else to get where he needed to be, to take the shot?

EIGHT

**McCarran International Airport, Nevada
17th March – 10.37 p.m.**

'Kezman's laying it on pretty thick,' Tom observed as the plane taxied to a halt and the stairs folded down. A stretched white Hummer emblazoned with a gilded letter 'A' was waiting to greet them, its neon undercarriage staining the apron blue. 'First the jet. Now this. What does he want?'

'A friendly word with the Nevada Gaming Control Board,' Stokes growled, as he pushed past Tom and stepped through the doorway. An unmarked FBI escort vehicle was drawn up behind the limo and he gestured at them to follow. 'One of his pit bosses was caught dealing ecstasy to some college kids out here on spring break and he doesn't want to lose his gaming licence.'

An envelope was waiting for them on the white leather seat, together with three glasses and a bottle of Cristal on ice. To Jennifer's surprise, it was addressed to her. She opened it with a puzzled frown which relaxed into a slow nod as she realised what it was.

'Status update from my other case,' she explained as she flicked through it, guessing that someone in the escort vehicle must have been entrusted with it to pass on to her. Nodding, Stokes shuffled further along the seat towards the driver and reached for his phone.

'Bad news?' Tom asked eventually, his question prompting her unconscious scowl to fade into a rueful smile.

'Isn't it always?' she replied, placing the typed pages down next to her.

'Anything I can help with?'

She paused, her eyes locked with his. Discussing a live investigation with a civilian, let alone a civilian with Tom's flawed credentials, wasn't exactly standard procedure. Then again, her case wasn't exactly standard either, and she had learned to value his opinion. Besides, who would know? Certainly not Stokes, whom she could overhear noisily checking on the money and making sure that Las Vegas Metro weren't playing their usual jurisdictional games.

'A few weeks ago the Customs boys over in Norfolk got a tip-off about a shipment of car parts out of Hamburg,' she began in a low voice, leaning in closer. 'When they opened the container everything looked fine, but something weird showed up on the X-ray.'

'A marzipan layer?' Tom guessed.

'Exactly. Car parts stacked at the front and round the sides. A smaller crate hidden in the middle filled with furniture.'

'Furniture?' Tom frowned.

'Eileen Gray. Ten to fifteen million dollars' worth.'

Tom whistled, echoing her own surprise when she'd first understood what they were dealing with. Eileen Gray art deco furniture was apparently as rare as it was expensive.

'They boxed it back up and then followed the shipment via a freight-forwarding service to an art dealer in Queens, an Italian who moved here in the seventies. He started squealing the minute they kicked down the door. It turns out he thought they were a hit squad. I don't think anyone's ever been so relieved to see a badge.'

'Who did he think had sent them?'

'It turns out that he's been smuggling pieces for a high-end antiquities trafficking ring for years. The furniture was a little side-deal he'd cooked up for himself. He thought they'd found out.'

'What sort of antiquities?' Tom asked.

'Statues, vases, plates, jewellery, even entire frescoes. Most of it illegally excavated from Roman and Etruscan tombs. One of their favourite tricks was to cover objects in liquid plastic and then paint them so that they looked like cheap souvenirs. That's when they called me in.'

'My mother used to be an antiquities dealer,' Tom sighed. 'I remember her once describing grave-robbing as the world's second oldest profession.

'You're talking about tomb robbers?'

'In Italy they call them *tombaroli*, in Peru *huaceros*,' Tom nodded. 'Mexico, Cambodia, China, Iraq – The truth is that as long as there are people prepared to buy pieces without asking difficult questions about where they've come from, there'll be others only too happy to dig them up.' But Italy is ground zero, the *Terra Santa* of the tomb-robbing world. It's got over forty UNESCO World Heritage Sites and the remains of about five different civilisations.' A pause. 'Did your guy ID any of his buyers?'

She gave a firm shake of her head.

'His job was just to get the stuff through Customs. He never had any idea where it was coming from or going to. But he did give us another name. Someone from within the organisation who had apparently broken cover a few weeks before, looking to bring something across. We passed it on to the Italians and they said they'd check him out.' She tapped the file next to her in annoyance. 'The State Department's been working on them to make sure they keep us in the loop, but so far they're playing hard to get.'

'Does this outfit have a name?'

'We're not sure. Have you ever heard of the Delian League?'

Tom frowned.

'League as in club?'

'When we went through his trash, we found two bags of shredded paper,' she explained. 'Most of it was unusable, but the lab were able to piece together one yellow sheet, because the coloured strips stood out from everything else. It was mainly covered in doodles and practice runs of his signature; the sort of thing you do when you're on the phone to someone. But in one corner he'd written the words Delian League and then sketched out a sort of symbol underneath. Two snakes wrapped around a clenched fist.'

'Means nothing to me,' Tom shook his head.

'Well, it means something to him because he's clammed up since we showed it to him. Won't even talk to his attorney. But we found his bank records too and I think that the Delian League is –'

She broke off as Stokes ended his call and shuffled back down towards them.

'The money's ready and Metro are playing ball. Looks like we're all set.'

They turned on to Las Vegas Boulevard, a grinning cowboy on an overhead billboard welcoming them to the home of the seven-day weekend, the streets teeming with nocturnal creatures who, like vampires it seemed, were only now venturing outside to feed.

It was Jennifer's first time in Las Vegas, and even as they'd circled prior to landing she'd found herself struck by the almost unnatural way that this concrete oasis seemed to have been cut out of the desert's soft belly, its neon heartbeat pulsing hungrily, its wailing lungs breathing expensively chilled air.

The view from the ground wasn't much better, the different hotel resorts galloping past in a single garish streak of light, like an overexposed photograph of a merry-go-round. The Pyramids, Arthurian England, New York, Paris, Lake Como, Venice – she had the sudden, disorientating sensation of travelling without moving, of time and space having been folded in on itself so as to meet at this one point in the universe.

The strange thing was that while there was something undeniably intoxicating, perhaps even gorgeous, about the multi-million-dollar light shows, the balletic fountain displays and the smell of sulphur from the half-hourly volcanic eruptions, she had the strong sense that if she were to reach out and try to grasp anything, it would dissolve under her touch. She realised then that this was a city of hyper-reality, of carbon-fibre monuments, plastic trees and contrived experiences. A copy of everywhere and yet nowhere all at once, the desperate striving for authenticity only serving to reveal its essential falsehood. A non place. She hoped they wouldn't have to stay here long.

'We're here,' Stokes called as the limo turned

in under a monumental arch topped by two rearing lions.

Despite its name, the Amalfi seemed to have been inspired by Florentine rather than Neapolitan architecture, although rendered on such a scale as to make the Duomo look like a concession stand. It was the Palazzo Strozzi on steroids, a massive, fortress-like structure made from Indiana lime-stone and Ohio sandstone, the soaring arched windows covered with portcullis-like iron grilles that only added to its impregnable appearance.

Rather than pull round to the covered main entrance, their car headed to the left and then dipped into an underground car park.

'The high-rollers' entrance,' Stokes explained. 'Some of these guys don't want to risk getting jumped between the car and hotel.'

Tom laughed.

'They're more likely to be robbed inside than out there.'

NINE

The Pantheon, Rome
18th March – 6.58 a.m.

Different day. Different place. And yet it seemed to Allegra that there was something strangely familiar about the way things were playing out – the unexpected, and unwelcome, phone call. The barked summons. The police barricades across the streets. The swelling crowd. The fevered wailing of the sirens. The helicopter wheeling overhead. The TV crews prowling like hyenas around a kill. Her being late.

Even so, there was a subtle difference from the previous evening's events too. For if yesterday she had seen shock and curiosity on her way to the Area Sacra, today she had sensed outrage from the officers manning the barriers and mounting anger from the swelling crowd.

Returning her ID to her bag, she crossed the Piazza della Minerva and made her way on to the Piazza della Rotunda. Compared to the zoo she had just walked through, the square seemed eerily peaceful to her – the gentle chime of the fountain echoing off the massed walls, the hushed conversations of the officers and the muted fizz of their radios generating a faint hum that sounded like electricity on a power line on a wet day.

There was also a sense of dignified order here, perhaps even respect. For rather than being casually abandoned on the cobbles as appeared to have happened last night, the assembled police and other emergency service vehicles had been neatly parked next to each other along one side of the square.

As she walked it started to spit with rain, the sky huddling beneath a thick blanket of grey clouds, as if it didn't want to be woken. The Pantheon loomed ahead of her, the classical elegance of the three rows of monolithic granite columns which supported its front portico compromised by the hulking, barrel-shaped building behind it. Squat and solid, it appeared to sit in a small crater of its own invention, the streets encircling it as if it had fallen, meteor-like, from the sky, and buried itself between the neighbouring buildings.

Allegra walked up to the portico, stooping under the police tape that had been strung between the columns, and made her way inside the rotunda, her shoes squeaking on the ancient marble. Almost immediately she paused, her eyes drawn to the pale beam formed by the searchlight of the helicopter hovering overhead as it was funnelled through the circular opening at the apex of the coffered dome. A slanting column of light had formed between the ceiling and the altar, sparks of rain fluttering around it like fireflies trapped in a glass jar. It was a beautiful and unexpected sight.

'Are you coming in, or just going to stand there like a retard?' Salvatore crossed through the beam of light, sounding even more put upon than he had yesterday.

'"Hello" would be nice.'

'You're late.'

'Believe me, it takes years of practice to be this unreliable.'

'Gallo's not happy.'

'He doesn't exactly strike me as the happy type.'

He eyed her unblinkingly, looking both appalled and yet also slightly envious of her brazen tone. He gave a resigned shrug.

'Suit yourself.'

There were about fifteen, maybe even twenty people inside, some in uniform interrogating the security guards who'd been covering the night shift, others in hooded white evidence suits taking photographs or examining the floor around the altar, which itself was obscured by some makeshift screens. Gallo, in a suit this time, was waiting for her next to Raphael's tomb, his hands folded behind his back like a teacher readying himself to hand out a punishment. As Salvatore had warned

her, he was in a dark mood, and she found
herself wondering if the angry atmosphere she'd
noticed on the other side of the barricades was
in some strange way linked to his own emotional
barometer.

'Nice of you to show up.'

'Nice of you to ask me.'

Gallo paused, lips pursed, as if he couldn't quite
decide if he found her insolent or amusing.

'Where did you say you were from?' he asked,
taking his glasses off and polishing them on his tie.

'I didn't. But it's Naples,' she stuttered, his
question taking her by surprise.

'An only child?'

It was a simple question, but she could tell from
his tone that it was loaded with meaning – difficult, spoilt, selfish, stubborn. Pick your stereotype.

'That's none of your business.'

He paused again, then gave an apologetic nod.

'You're right. I'm sorry.'

Salvatore made a strangled noise next to her.
She wondered if this was the first time he'd ever
heard Gallo apologise.

'You say what you think, don't you?'

'Pretty much.'

'The difference between you and me is that you
can get away with it because you're a woman,'
Gallo sniffed. 'When I do it, I get called a rude
bastard.'

'I wouldn't say you were rude, sir.' The words

were out of her mouth before she even knew she was saying them.

His smile faded. Salvatore looked faint.

'What can you tell me about this place?' he snapped, motioning at her to follow him over to the altar.

'What do you mean?'

'The Pantheon. Is there anything I should know about it? Anything that might tie it to where we found Ricci's body last night?'

She ran her hand through her hair, desperately trying to dredge up the highlights of some long-forgotten lecture or text book.

'It was built by Hadrian in about 125 AD, so there's no obvious connection to Caesar, if that's what you mean?' she began with a shrug. 'Then again, although it's been a church since the seventh century, the Pantheon did used to be a pagan temple, just like the ones in the Area Sacra.'

'Hardly conclusive,' Gallo sniffed, patting his jacket down as if he was looking for cigarettes and eventually finding a packet of boiled sweets. 'I'm trying to give up,' he admitted as he popped one into his mouth. She noticed that he didn't offer her one.

'No,' she agreed with a firm shake of her head.

'Then what do you make of this?'

At a flick of his wrist, two forensic officers rolled away the screens. A body was lying on the altar, naked from the waist up. His bearded face was turned towards them, eyes gaping open with shock. Two gleaming white shop mannequins were standing at his head – one small and hunched, the other taller – staring down at the corpse with cold, vacant expressions. Both were unclothed, with moulded blank features and no hair, although the smooth hump of their breasts marked them out as female.

The taller mannequin had been carefully arranged so that her left hand was gripping the man's hair and the right holding a short sword. The sword itself was embedded in a deep gash in the victim's neck that had almost decapitated him. The blood had gushed from his wound, covering the altar and cascading to the floor where it had pooled and solidified into a brackish lake.

It was a carefully arranged, almost ritualistic scene. And one that, for a reason Allegra couldn't quite put her finger on, seemed strangely familiar to her.

'Who is it?'

'Don't you recognise him?' Salvatore, looking surprised, had ventured forward to her side. 'His brother's always on TV. He looks just like him.'

'Why, who's his brother?' she asked, wanting to look away and study the man's tortured features at the same time.

'Annibale Argento,' Salvatore explained. 'The Sicilian deputy. The stiff is his twin brother Gio, otherwise known as Giulio.'

'Hannibal and Julius,' Gallo nodded. 'There's your damn Caesar connection.'

'What's any of this got to do with me?' she interrupted, wondering if she still had time to untangle herself from this mess before the media got wind of it.

'We found this in his mouth –'

Gallo held up a clear plastic evidence bag. She knew, almost without looking, what it contained.

TEN

Amalfi Hotel and Casino, Las Vegas
17th March – 11.02 p.m.
Kezman's private elevator opened on to a tennis court-sized room, rainbows cloaking the lush tropical gardens that could be glimpsed through the open windows where the floodlights shimmered through a permanent cooling mist.

Glancing up, Tom could see that the soaring ceilings had been draped in what looked like black satin, three huge chandeliers flowering from within their luxuriant folds as if they were leaking glass. The only furniture, if you could call it that, was a 1926 Hispano-Suiza H6. Parked about two-thirds of the way down, it was a mass of gleaming chrome and polished black metal, the wheel arches soaring up over the front wheels and then swooping gracefully down towards the running boards, two dinner plate-sized headlights perched at the end of a massive bonnet like dragon's eyes.

'You're here. Good.'

A man had come in off the balcony, a radio in one hand, a mobile phone in the other. Short and wiry, his olive skin was pockmarked by acne scars, his black hair shaved almost to his skull. Rather than blink, he seemed to grimace every few seconds, his face scrunching into a pained squint as if he had something in his eye.

'Tom, this is Special Agent Carlos Ortiz.' They shook hands as she introduced them. 'I've borrowed him from my other case for a few days to help out.'

'Welcome.'

Ortiz's expression was impenetrable, although Tom thought he glimpsed a tattoo just under his collar – the number fourteen in Roman numerals. Tom recognised it as a reference to the letter 'N', the fourteenth letter of the alphabet, and by repute to the *Norteños*, a coalition of Latino gangs from Northern California. Ortiz had clearly taken a difficult and rarely trodden path from the violent street corners of his youth to the FBI's stiff-collared embrace.

'I hope you're half as good as she says you are,' Ortiz sniffed. Tom glanced questioningly at Jennifer, who gave him an awkward shrug. 'Did you get the envelope from the State Department?'

'Yeah.' She nodded. 'Let's talk about that later. How long have we got?'

'It's set for midnight so . . . just under an hour,'

he replied, checking his watch – a fake Rolex
Oyster, Tom noted, its second hand advancing with
a tell-tale staccato twitch rather than sweeping
smoothly around the dial as a real one would.

'Everyone's already in place,' Stokes added. 'I
got six agents on the floor at the tables and playing
the slots, and another four on the front and rear
doors. Metro and SWAT are holding back two
blocks south.'

'What about the money?' Tom asked.

'In the vault in two suitcases,' Stokes reassured
him. 'Unmarked, non-sequential notes, just like
they asked. They'll bring it out when we're ready.'

'Let's get you mike'd up.'

Ortiz led Tom over to the car, which Tom
suddenly realised had been turned into a desk,
the seats ripped out and the roof and one side cut
away and replaced with a black marble slab.

'I guess rich people are always looking for
new ways to spend their money, right?' Ortiz
winked.

'Some just have more imagination than others,'
Tom agreed.

Ortiz removed a small transmitter unit from the
briefcase and, as Jennifer turned away with a
smile, helped Tom fix it to his inner thigh, hiding
the microphone under his shirt.

'If anyone finds that, they're looking for a date
not a wire,' Ortiz joked once he was happy that
it was secure and working. He checked his watch

again. 'Let's go. Kezman asked to see you down-stairs before we hit the floor.'

'Any reason we didn't just meet down there in the first place?' Jennifer asked with a frown.

'He thought you might like the view.'

They stepped back inside the elevator and again it headed down automatically, stopping at the mezza-nine level, close to the entrance to the Amalfi's private art gallery.

'He suggested we wait for him inside,' Ortiz said, nodding at the two security guards posted either side of the entrance as he walked past.

The gallery consisted of a series of interlinked rooms containing maybe twenty or so paintings, as well as a number of small abstract sculptures on glass plinths. It was an impressive and expen-sively assembled collection, bringing to mind the recent newspaper headlines when Kezman had broken his own auction record for the highest amount ever paid for a painting. Tom's eyes sought out the Picasso he'd bought on that occasion in amongst the works by Cézanne, Gauguin, van Gogh, Manet and Matisse.

'Impressive, isn't it?' Jennifer said in a low voice, echoing his own thoughts. 'Although, I don't know, it feels a bit . . .'

'Soulless?' Tom suggested.

'Yes.' She nodded slowly. 'Soulless. Perhaps that's it.'

Tom's sense was that Kezman had been less

concerned with the paintings themselves than by who had painted them. To him these were trophies, specimens of famous names that he'd only bought so that he could tick them off his list, much as a big-game hunter might set out on safari intent on adding a zebra's head to the mounted antelope horns and elephant tusks that already adorned his dining-room walls.

'What do you know about him?'

'He's rich and he's smart. In thirty years he's gone from running a diner in Jersey to being the biggest player on the Strip.'

'He buys a place that's losing money, turns it around or knocks it down, and starts over,' Stokes added, having been listening in. 'As well as the Amalfi, he owns three other places in Vegas, two in Atlantic City and one in Macau.'

'And he's clean?' Tom asked.

'As anyone can be in this town,' Stokes replied with a smile. 'He mixes with a pretty colourful crowd, which always gets people talking, but so far he seems to check out.'

'He used to collect cars, but art is his new passion now,' Jennifer added. 'He's become a major donor to both the Met and the Getty.'

'Which is your favourite?'

Kezman had breezed into the room wearing sunglasses, a gleaming white smile and a tuxedo. He was closely flanked by an unsmiling male assistant clutching a briefcase in one hand and two gold-plated mobile phones in the other. From the way his jacket was hanging off his thin frame, Tom guessed that he was armed.

Kezman was in his mid-fifties or thereabouts, and shorter than Tom had expected. Although he was still recognisably the same person, the photo on his jet had clearly been taken several years before, his brown hair now receding and greying at the temples, the firm lines of his once angular face now soft and surviving only in the sharp cliff of his chin. The energy in his voice and movements, however, was undimmed, his weight constantly shifting from foot to foot like a boxer, his head jerking erratically as he looked around the room, as if it pained him to focus on any one thing for longer than a few seconds. He answered his own question before anyone else had a chance to respond.

'Mine's the Picasso, and not just because I paid a hundred and thirty-nine million dollars for it. That man was a genius. A self-made man. A true visionary.'

Tom smiled, the machine-gun rattle of Kezman's voice making it hard to know whether he was talking about himself or Picasso.

'Mr Kezman, this is . . .'

'Tom Kirk, I know.' He grinned. 'Luckily the FBI doesn't have a monopoly on information. At least not yet. I like to know who's on my plane.'

Tom stepped forward to shake his hand, but Kezman waved him back.

'Stay where I can see you, goddammit,' he barked.

Tom suddenly understood why Kezman was wearing sunglasses and moving his head so erratically – he was clearly blind, or very nearly so, his aide presumably there to help steer him in the right direction as he navigated through the hotel.

'Retinitis pigmentosa,' Kezman confirmed. 'The closer I get to things, the less I can see. And one day even that . . .'

His voice tailed off and Tom couldn't stop himself wondering if this explained Kezman's insistence that they should go up to his private apartment first, before meeting him down here. It was almost as if he'd wanted to give them some small insight into his shrinking world. A world where there was little point in furnishing a room he could barely see, but where a view was still there to be enjoyed. At least for now.

'I'm sorry,' Tom said. He didn't know Kezman, but he meant it all the same.

'Why? It's not your fault,' Kezman shrugged. 'Besides, in a way, it's a gift. After all, would I have started my collection if I hadn't known I was going blind? Sometimes, it's only when you are about to lose something that you really begin to understand what it's worth.'

There was a long silence, which Ortiz eventually broke with a forced cough.

'As I have discussed with your head of security,

the plan is for Mr Kirk to take the money down on to the casino floor and wait there for them to make contact.'

'It's unlikely they'll bring the painting with them,' Jennifer added. 'So we expect them to either provide us with a location, which we will then check out before handing over the money, or lead us to it so that we can make the exchange there.'

'Either way, we'll follow them to make sure we grab them, the painting and the money,' Stokes said confidently.

'Once again, Mr Kezman, the federal government is very grateful for your co-operation in this matter. We'll do what we can to ensure that your staff and customers . . .'

'Don't mention it,' Kezman waved Jennifer's thanks away with a sweep of his hand. 'You just make sure no one gets hurt.'

ELEVEN

**Amalfi Casino and Hotel Resort, Las Vegas
17th March – 11.22 p.m.**

It was funny how people conditioned themselves to only ever see what they wanted to, Foster mused. Ask anyone who wears a watch with Roman numerals how the number four is written on it and they'll say IV. All those years that they've been looking at it, checking the time, the numbers only a few inches from their stupid dumb-ass faces, and they've never actually noticed that it's IIII. That it's always IIII on a watch, because IV would be too easily confused with VI. That their brains have tricked them into seeing what they expect to, or rather not seeing what they should. It was pathetic really.

Like tonight. The security detail at the staff entrance had barely glanced at his badly fitting uniform and tampered badge before waving him through. He looked the part, so why see something that you've convinced yourself isn't there? That's why the beard had had to go in the end; that might have been the one thing that could have triggered a response.

He, on the other hand, had immediately picked out the FBI agents, uncomfortable in their civilian clothes as they loitered near the entrance, or perched unconvincingly in front of the slot machines. It was the half-hearted way they were feeding the money into the machine that was the killer tell – either you played the slots, or they played you.

He stopped next to an anonymous-looking red door. How many people had walked past it, he wondered, without ever asking themselves why, out of all the doors that lined this service corridor, this was the only one that warranted two locks. Without ever asking themselves what might possibly lie behind it that demanded the extra security. But then, that's what he'd noticed in civilians: a lack of basic human curiosity, a slavish, unquestioning acceptance of a life dropped into their lap like a TV dinner.

Quickly picking the locks, he opened the door on to a dimly lit stairwell that he slipped into, wedging a fire extinguisher between the base of the door and the bottom step of the metal staircase to stop anyone coming in after him. The staircase led up several flights to the observation deck – a series of cramped, interconnecting gantries hidden in the ceiling void that stretched over the entire casino floor.

Although in theory these were to allow maintenance staff to invisibly service the casino's complex lighting grid and vast network of A/C ducts, the careful positioning of two-way mirrors and air vents also allowed casino security to spy on people without being seen. Dealers watching the gamblers, boxmen watching the dealers, supervisors watching the boxmen, pit bosses watching the supervisors, shift managers watching the pit bosses . . . the entire set-up functioned on the assumption that everyone was on the make and on the take.

Not that the deck was used as often as it used to be – video cameras and advances in biometric technology that could flag-up suspicious changes in body heat and pupil dilation had seen to that. But Kezman was famously old-school and had insisted on having it there anyway, both as a low-tech back-up, and because he knew that sometimes you needed to get up there and sniff the floor to get a feeling for where the trouble was brewing.

As Foster had expected, the gantries were empty. He took up his position, removed the towel from his back-pack, and unrolled it. Piece by piece he began to reassemble his rifle, the parts sliding into place with a satisfying click echoed by the sound of the roulette ball skipping on the wheel below. With the infrared sight fitted he hesitated momentarily, toying with the suppressor before slipping it into his top pocket like a good cigar he was saving for the right moment.

No suppressor. Not tonight. He wanted everyone to hear the shot, to be paralysed by its angry roar, and then to run. To run screaming.

TWELVE

The Pantheon, Rome
18th March – 7.41 a.m.
Allegra was sheltering in the portico, grateful for
the coffee Salvatore had conjured up for her and
for the fresh air – there had been a strange, curdled
atmosphere inside that she had been glad to
escape.

The storm had now tethered itself directly overhead, rain lashing the square, lightning cleaving
the stygian sky only for the clouds to crash
thunderously back together. But it was the more
powerful storm brewing on the other side of the
barricades that worried her now. Rising out of
the warm waters of political scandal and feeding
on the lurid details of these murders, it would
quickly spin out of control, blowing them violently
towards the rocks until either the media lost
interest or they had all been dashed into pieces,
whichever came sooner. She wondered if Gallo's

men all knew this, and whether what she could sense inside, what she could almost taste, was their fearful anticipation of the hurricane that lay ahead.

'So it's the same coin?' Gallo had materialised at her side, lighting a cigarette.

'I thought you'd given up?'

'So did I.'

She was reassured that she wasn't the only one feeling the pressure.

'It's the same.' She nodded, not bothering to repeat that it wasn't a coin but a lead disc.

'So it's the same killer?'

'Are you asking me or telling me?'

'I'm asking.' As earlier, the hint of a smile was playing around his lips, as if she somehow amused him.

'There are some obvious similarities,' she began hesitantly, surprised that Gallo even cared what she thought. 'The lead discs. The proximity of the two murder scenes. The pagan temples. The connection to Caesar. But . . .'

'But what?'

'It's . . . the way they were killed. I'm not a profiler, but there's no consistency between the two murders. They look different. They feel different.'

'I agree. Two murders. Two killers.' Gallo held up photographs of the two crime scenes side by side as if to prove his point.

Allegra glanced at the photos and jumped. There

was something in the crime scenes, something she'd not noticed before, but which, when framed within the photographs' white borders, was now glaringly obvious.

'Where's your car?'

'Over there –' He pointed out a dark blue BMW.

'Come on!' She stepped out into the rain, then turned and motioned impatiently at him to follow when she realised he hadn't moved.

'Where to?'

'The Palazzo Barberini,' she called back, her hair darkening. 'There's something there you need to see.'

A few moments later, Gallo gunned out of the square down the Via del Seminario, the Carabinieri clearing a path for him through the crowd, Allegra shielding her face as the photographers and TV crews pressed their lenses up against their windows. As soon as they were clear, he accelerated through the Piazza San Ignacio and out on to the busy Via del Corso, his siren blazing as he carved his way through the rush-hour traffic. Reaching the Via del Tritone he turned right, racing down to where the palazzo loomed imposingly over the Piazza Barberini and then cutting up a side street to the main entrance at the top of the hill. The drive was chained off, although the museum was clearly open, those foreign tourists still able to swallow the euro's inexorable climb over the past few months already filtering through the gates.

'Damn these peasants,' Gallo muttered, leaning on his horn, until a guard appeared and let them through.

They lurched forward, the gravel spitting out from under their tyres as they shot round to the far side of the fountain.

'First floor,' Allegra called as she jumped out and headed through the arched entrance, not pausing on this occasion to admire the monumental Bernini staircase that led up to the Galleria Nazionale d'Arte Antica, the museum that now occupied this former papal residence.

'Police,' Gallo called, waving his badge at the astonished museum staff as they burst through the entrance and bypassed the queue waiting patiently at the ticket desk.

Allegra sprinted through first one room, then another, her eyes skipping over the paintings, not entirely sure where it was, but knowing it was here somewhere. Filippo Lippi, Piero de Cosimo . . . no, not here. Next room. Tintoretto, Bronzino . . . still nothing. Carry on through. Guercino . . .

'There,' she called triumphantly, pointing at the wall.

'*Ammàzza!*' Gallo swore, stepping past her for a closer look.

The large painting showed a bearded man being decapitated by a woman, a sword in her right hand, his hair firmly gripped in her left. He was naked, his face contorted into an inhuman scream, his body convulsed by pain, the blood spurting on to a white sheet. Next to the woman stood an old woman, her wrinkled face hungrily absorbing the man's death, her hands gripping the hem of her mistress's dress to keep it clear of the blood.

Gallo held the photograph of the Pantheon crime scene up next to it. There was no question it had been staged to mirror the painting's composition.

'It's the same.'

'*Judith and Holofernes*,' Allegra said slowly. 'It was only when I saw the photos that I made the connection.'

'And Ricci?'

'*The Crucifixion of Saint Peter* in the Cerasi Chapel in Santa Maria del Popolo,' she confirmed. 'That's what links your two murders, Colonel. The killers are re-enacting scenes from Caravaggio paintings.'

THIRTEEN

Amalfi Casino and Hotel Resort, Las Vegas
17th March – 11.56 p.m.

Tom had insisted on getting down on to the floor early, guessing that whoever had been sent to meet him would already be in position and that it would help if it looked as though he was keen to do the deal. More importantly, it gave them a chance to see the money, to see that this was for real. It was at Tom's feet now – twenty million in cash, neatly packed into two aluminium suitcases.

Twenty million dollars.

There was a time, perhaps, when he might have considered . . . But those days were behind him now, although you wouldn't have guessed it from the obvious reluctance with which Stokes had entrusted the cases to him, and his pointed reminder that they were electronically tagged. Then again, maybe Tom was naïve to have expected anything else. All Stokes had to go on was his file, and that told its own, damning story.

He looked around the blinking, cavernous floor to get his bearings, momentarily disoriented by the tumbrel-clatter of the roulette wheels, the dealers' barked instructions and the machines' remorseless chuckling. The place was packed. If Vegas was suffering from the economic slowdown that the press had been so gleefully reporting for the past few months, then it was hiding it well. Either that or it was still in denial.

He spotted Jennifer at the bar to his left, nursing a coke. Ortiz, meanwhile, was to his right, pretending to play video poker and losing badly. Stokes, he knew, was in the back with the casino's head of security, watching the screens and co-ordinating the other agents who had been posted around him. In front of him was a roulette table, the animated abandon with which a noticeably younger crowd were merrily flinging chips on to the baize contrasting with the silent, mesmerised application of the older people on the slots.

On cue, a woman wearing an *'I love Fort Lauderdale'* T-shirt waddled over to the machine next to him, the stool screeching under her weight. Resting a bucket full of quarters on her lap, she bowed her head briefly as if offering up a prayer, and then began to feed it with metro-nomic precision, the tips of her fingers stained black by the coins. A kaleidoscope of changing colours immediately skipped across her rapt face, her eyes gazing up at the spinning wheels with a mixture of hope and expectation.

Tom wondered if she knew that her faith was unlikely to be rewarded. In here, chance danced to the casino's tune. The roulette tables that paid out thirty-five to one, when the odds of winning were one in thirty-seven. The deliberate location of the premium slots next to the main aisles and blackjack tables, to lure people in. The lack of clocks and the suppression of natural light, so that everyone lost track of time. The careful variation in ceiling heights, lighting levels and music zones to trigger different emotional responses. The strategic location of the bathrooms, to minimise time off the floor. The purposefully labyrinthine layout, so that the sightlines provided neither a glimpse of a possible way out, nor allowed a potentially overwhelming view of the entire space. In this broad church, you were damned from the moment you walked through the door.

There. A man with his back to him at the neighbouring blackjack table, his head snapping back a little too fast to suggest the glance he had just given him had been accidental. And again, only this time he didn't break eye contact. He knew Tom had seen him. He was tipping the dealer, getting up. This was it.

'Blackjack table,' Tom muttered into his mike, hoping the others could hear him over the noise.

'White hair, black . . .' His voice tailed off as the man turned round and nodded.

Dressed in a black suit, he was about five feet ten with a curling mop of white hair and a farmer's sun-blushed cheeks that echoed the red hand-kerchief peeking out of a trouser pocket. But it was the white band encircling his neck that had drawn Tom's attention, its unexpected glare seeming to cast a bleaching wash over everything at the periphery of his vision.

'He's a priest,' Tom breathed in disbelief, as much to himself as anyone.

The man advanced towards him, Tom reassured that as Jennifer had predicted to Kezman earlier, he wasn't carrying anything that might have contained the painting. That would have marked him and whoever he was working for as amateurs, and amateurs were unpredictable and more easily spooked. Instead, slung over his left shoulder was a tired leather satchel.

They met in the middle of the main aisle. Saying nothing, the priest reached into his bag and handed Tom a series of photographs. They showed the *Nativity*, but in more detail this time, with close-ups of the faces and hands, always the hardest things to paint. From what Tom could tell, the brushwork looked genuine, and although the canvas had been slightly damaged over the years, overall the condition was very good, the faint reflection of a camera flash in a couple of the photos suggesting that it was being kept behind glass.

There was no sign of a signature, but Tom took that as further proof of the painting's probable authenticity. As far as he knew, Caravaggio had only ever signed one painting, *The Beheading of the Baptist*, where he had marked an M for Merisi, his family name, in the blood spilling from John the Baptist's neck.

'Is it close?' Tom asked.

'Close enough,' the priest replied, Tom detecting an Italian accent.

'I need to see it.'

'Is that the money?'

'Twenty million dollars,' he confirmed, tapping the case nearest to him with his foot. 'Unmarked, non-sequential bills, as requested.'

'*Bene, bene.*' The priest nodded. 'Good.' There was an anxious edge to the man's voice that surprised Tom. For a pro he seemed a little tense, although twenty million was enough to make most people tighten up.

'I need to see the painting first,' Tom reminded him.

'Of course,' the priest said. 'You have a car?'

'The painting's not here?'

'It's not far. Where's your car?'

'The money's going nowhere until I see the painting,' Tom warned him.

'Don't worry,' the priest immediately reassured

him. 'We have a deal, see –' He reached for Tom's hand and shook it energetically. 'You have the money, I have the painting, we have a deal, yes?'

'We have a deal,' Tom agreed.

'You want this painting, yes?'

'As much as you want the money,' Tom answered with a puzzled smile. It was a strange question to ask. Why else would he be there? 'My car's in the garage.'

'It has been a long time. You will be the first, the first in many years to see it.' His eyes flicked over Tom's shoulder as he spoke and then back again. 'It is beautiful, still beautiful, despite everything it has been through.'

Tom felt his stomach tightening. Something wasn't right. First a hint of nervousness. Now an abrupt shift from urgency to an almost languid calm as if . . . as if he was trying to waste time so that somewhere else . . .

A shot rang out, its whiplash crack cutting through the casino's raucous din. Tom staggered back, the world suddenly slowing, as if someone was holding the movie projector to stop the reel from turning – the individual frames crawling across the screen; a roulette ball, frozen in mid-flight; the soundtrack stretched into a low, slurring moan as words folded into each other.

Then, almost immediately, everything sprang forward, only sharper, louder and faster than before, as if time was overcompensating as it tried to catch up with itself. The ball landed, the winner cheered. But their celebration was drowned out by a terrified scream, one voice triggering another and that one two more until, like a flock of migrating birds wheeling through a darkening sky, a sustained, shrieking lament filled the air.

Tom glanced instinctively to his left. Jennifer was lying on the floor. Her blouse was blotted poppy red.

FOURTEEN

Institute for Religious Works,
Via della Statzione Vaticana, Rome
18th March – 8.08 a.m.

As the six men opposite him bowed their heads, Antonio Santos picked up his spoon and studied the hallmarks. To the left he recognised the symbol of the Papal State, and next to it the initials NL – Lorenzini Nicola, an Italian silversmith active in the mid eighteenth century, if he wasn't mistaken.

'Nos miseri homines et egeni, pro cibis quos nobis ad corporis subsidium benigne es largitus, tibi Deus omnipotens, Pater cælestis, gratias reverenter agimus . . .' Archbishop Ancelotti intoned grace, his voice rising and falling as if he was reciting some mediaeval incantation. Turning the spoon over, Santos smiled at the way its polished surface distorted his reflection.

'Simul obsecrantes, ut iis sobries, modeste, atque grate utamur. Per Iesum Christum Dominum nostrum. Amen.'

'Amen,' Santos agreed enthusiastically, carefully returning the spoon to its proper place before anyone had opened their eyes.

Ancelotti looked up and nodded at the two young priests standing near the door to serve breakfast. He was wearing a black simar with amaranth-red piping and buttons together with a purple fascia and zuchetto. A large gold pectoral cross dangled from his neck. The other five men sitting either side of him were similarly dressed, although, as cardinals, their buttons, sashes and skull-caps were scarlet.

'Thank you for coming, Antonio,' Ancelotti said, motioning with his finger to indicate that he wanted one, two, three spoonfuls of sugar. 'I apologise for the short notice.'

'Not at all, Your Grace,' Santos said with a generous shrug, holding his hand over his coffee as one of the priests went to add cream. 'I apologise for being late. The Carabinieri seem to have closed off half the city.'

'Nothing too serious, I hope,' Ancelotti enquired, brushing his hands together over his plate to dust some crumbs from his fingers.

'My driver told me that they've found a body in the Pantheon,' Cardinal Simoes volunteered, pushing his gold-rimmed glasses back up his nose.

'Dear, dear,' Ancelotti tutted, licking some jam from his thumb with a loud sucking noise. 'We live in such wicked times. Jam?'

'No, thank you.' Santos gave a tight smile. 'I don't eat breakfast.'

'You should, you should,' Ancelotti admonished him. 'Most important meal of the day. Now, does everyone have what they need?'

Seeing that they did, he waved at the two priests to retire to the outer room, then turned back to face Santos.

'I believe you know everyone here?'

He nodded. Cardinals Villot, Neuman, Simoes, Pisani and Carter. The Oversight Commission of the Istituto per le Opere di Religione. The Vatican Bank.

'Your eminences,' he said, bowing his head. Their murmured greetings were muffled by fresh croissants.

'Antonio, we asked you here today in our capacity as the largest shareholder in the Banco Rosalia,' Ancelotti began, sipping his coffee.

'Largest and most important shareholder,' Santos added generously. 'We are, after all, working to help finance God's work.'

'Ah yes, God's work.' Ancelotti clasped his hands together as if in prayer, pressing them against his lips. 'Which is, as I'm sure you understand, why we need to be especially vigilant.'

'I'm not sure I do understand, Your Grace,' Santos said with a frown, placing his cup back down on the table. 'Vigilant for what?'

'For anything that could harm the reputation of the Catholic Church, of course.'

'I hope you are not suggesting that –'

'Of course not, Antonio, of course not,' Ancelotti reassured him warmly, 'But after what happened before . . . well, we have to go through the motions, be seen to be asking the right questions.'

He was referring, Santos knew, to the huge scandal that had engulfed the Vatican Bank in the 1980s, when it had been implicated in laundering billions of dollars of mafia drug money. It was partly in response to this that the Oversight Commission had been set up in the first place.

'I fail to see how . . .'

'Your year-end accounts are almost a month overdue,' Cardinal Villot said in an accusing tone.

'As I've already explained to Archbishop Ancelotti, there are a number of small, purely technical matters that the auditors have . . .'

'We've also heard your liquidity position's deteriorated,' Cardinal Carter added, his voice equally sharp.

'Not to mention the provisions on your real estate portfolio,' Cardinal Neuman chimed.

Santos took a deep breath. So much for casting the money lenders out of the temple, he thought ruefully. Instead, armed with an MBA and a bible, the Oversight Commission seemed to be setting up shop right next to them.

'A number of banks have withdrawn their funding lines, yes, but that's to be expected with the squeeze that the whole market is feeling. We still have more than enough headroom, given our deposit and capital base. As for our real estate book, we've seen a slight uptick in bad debts like everyone else, but the provisions we took last year should be more than . . .'

'I think what we're suggesting is that a short, sharp financial review would help allay our concerns, in light of the extreme volatility of the markets and the rather bleak economic outlook,' Ancelotti said in a gentle tone.

'What sort of a financial review?'

'We'd probably start with a quick canter through your latest management accounts, bank statements and ALCO reports,' Ancelotti said breezily. 'We have a small team of accountants we like to use for this sort of thing. They'll be in and out in a few weeks. You won't even notice they're there.'

A pause. It wasn't as if he had any choice.

'When would you like them to start?'

'Is the day after tomorrow too soon?' Ancelotti asked with a casual shrug, although Santos noticed that the archbishop's eyes were locked on to his, as if to gauge his reaction.

'Of course not,' Santos replied with a confident smile. 'That gives me enough time to brief the team so that we can make sure that we have a room set aside and all the documentation prepared.'

'Excellent, excellent.' Ancelotti stood up to signal that the meeting was over and leant across the table to shake his hand. 'I knew you'd understand. By the way, I'm hosting a Mozart recital in Santa Sabina next month. You should come.'

'It would be my pleasure, Your Grace,' Santos smiled. 'Please forward on the details. Your Eminences . . .'

A few minutes later he was down on the street in the rain, angrily loosening his collar as he flicked a tin open and pushed one, then two pieces of liquorice into his mouth. Then he reached for his phone.

'We're fucked,' he barked into it the moment it was answered. 'Ancelotti and his performing monkeys want to audit the bank . . . I don't know what they know, but they must know something, and even if they don't, it won't take more than a few days for them to figure everything out . . . I need to bail. How much would I have if I liquidated everything? . . . No, not the property. Just whatever I can get out in cash by the end of the week . . . Is that it?' He swore angrily, earning himself a disapproving look from two nuns walking past. 'That's not enough,' he continued in an angry whisper. 'That's not even halfway to being enough . . . Hold on, I've got another call.' He switched lines, *'Pronto?'*

'It's done,' a voice rasped.

'Are you sure?' Santos stepped out of the rain and sheltered inside a doorway.

'It's done,' the voice repeated. The line went dead.

Smiling, Santos went to switch back to the first caller before pausing, a thought occurring to him. He helped himself to some more liquorice as the idea slowly took shape. It had only ever been part of the set-up, but why not? Why the hell not? The trick was getting to it, but if he could . . . the Serbians would take it off his hands. They were always in the market for that sort of thing.

'Spare some change?'

A beggar wearing a filthy army surplus over-coat, his face masked by a spade-like beard studded with raindrops, was holding a creased McDonald's cup up to him. Santos glanced up and down the street behind him. It was empty. With a flick of his wrist he knocked the cup into the air, the few, pathetic coins it contained scattering across the pavement. The beggar dropped moaning to his knees, his blackened fingernails scrabbling in the gutter.

'Spare *you* some change?' Santos spat. 'I'm the one who needs a handout.'

FIFTEEN

Amalfi Casino and Hotel Resort
18th March – 12.08 a.m.

Kicking their stools out from under them, people began to run, half-drunk cocktails collapsing to the floor and neatly stacked piles of chips swooning on to the baize as gamblers clambered over each other like calves trying to escape a branding pen.

Tom fought his way across to Jennifer's side, Ortiz only a few feet behind him. She was still alive, thank God, her eyes wide with shock, but still alive. He ripped her blouse open, saw the blood frothing from under her left breast.

'It's okay,' Tom reassured her, leaning close so she could hear him. She nodded, lifted her head as if to speak, then fell back.

'Where's she hit?' Ortiz fell on to his knees next to him as the fire alarm sounded.

'Get an ambulance here,' Tom shouted back over the noise, ripping his jacket off and folding it into a makeshift pillow. 'Press down —' He grabbed Ortiz's hand and jammed it hard against the wound, then leant across and snatched his Beretta out from under his arm.

'Where the hell are you going?' Ortiz called after him.

'To find the shooter.'

He leapt up on to the roulette table, knowing from the location of her wound and the direction she'd been facing that the gunman must have been positioned somewhere ahead of her. Scanning the floor, he suddenly noticed an unexpected shimmer of glass under the stampeding crowd's feet. He glanced instinctively up at the ceiling and saw that a single mirrored panel was missing from its reflective surface, the empty black square as obvious as a decaying tooth in an otherwise perfect smile.

'He's in the ceiling void,' Tom breathed.

He leapt down and grabbed a passing security guard who seemed more intent on saving himself than in stewarding anyone else to the exit.

'The observation deck,' Tom shouted. 'How do I get up there?'

The guard paused, momentarily transfixed by the gun gripped in Tom's left hand, then pointed unsteadily at a set of double doors on the other side of the floor.

'Through there,' he stuttered.

Snatching the guard's security pass off his belt, Tom fought his way through to the doors he had indicated and swiped them open. He found himself in a long white service corridor lit by overhead strip lighting and lined on both sides by a series of identical red doors. Cowering under the fire alarm's strident and persistent echo, a steady stream of people were half walking, half running towards him – casino staff ordered to evacuate the building, judging from their identical red Mao jackets and the confusion etched on to their faces.

Tom walked against the flow, scanning for a pair of shoes, or a uniform, or a face that didn't quite fit. Ahead of him, about two thirds of the way down the corridor, a door opened and a man wearing a baseball cap stepped out. Tom noticed him immediately. It was his studied calmness that gave him away. His calmness and the detached, almost curious expression on his face, as if he was taking part in some bizarre sociological experiment that he couldn't quite relate to.

He seemed to notice Tom at almost the same time because, grimacing, he turned and retreated back inside, locking the door behind him. Tom sprinted down the corridor after him, tried the handle and then stepped back and pumped four shots into the locks. With a firm kick, the door splintered open.

Carefully covering the angles above him, Tom made his way up the stairs into the shadows of the observation deck, his eyes adjusting to the darkness. He felt the shooter before he saw him,

the metal walkways shuddering under his heavy
step as he sprinted along the gantries away from
him. Tom took aim and fired three times, then
twice more, a couple of the bullets sparking
brightly where they struck the steel supports. But
the man barely broke his stride, turning sharply
to his left and then to his right.

Tom set off after him, trying to guess where
he'd turned, so that he wouldn't end up stranded
in a different section of the deck. Up ahead the
gunman paused and then in an instant was over
the side of the gantry and dangling down over the
suspended ceiling below. Tom again took aim, and
fired twice, this time catching him in his shoulder.
With a pained yell he let go, crashing through the
mirrored ceiling and vanishing from sight.

Tom sprinted across to the same point and then
lowered himself down as far as he could before
letting go and dropping through the hole on to a
blackjack table scattered with chips and fresh
blood.

'Where did he go?' Tom asked the dealer, who
was staring up at him open-mouthed.

The man pointed dumbly towards the exit. Tom
looked up and saw the gunman almost at the
door, his jacket burst open at the shoulder where
the bullet had passed through him. Tom again
pulled the trigger, the bullet skimming the man's
head and shattering a slot machine deliberately

positioned to tempt people into one final roll of the dice before heading outside. Next to it a bearded man in a *'Remember Pearl Harbor'* baseball cap carried on playing, gazing at the wheels as if he hated them.

Tom leapt down and followed the gunman outside, determined not to lose him. But rather than melt away into the panicked crowd that had swamped the forecourt, the man seemed to be waiting for him, backpack hitched over one arm. For an instant, no longer, they stood about twenty feet apart, their eyes locked, the swollen human flow parting around them like a river around two rocks. The gunman, clutching his shoulder, studied Tom with a detached curiosity; Tom, his gun raised, finger tested the trigger spring's resistance. But before he could take the shot, a powerful hand gripped his arm and pulled him back.

'Not here, for Chrissake,' Stokes yelled. 'Are you fucking crazy? You'll hit someone.'

Tom angrily shook him off, took aim and fired. The gun clicked, empty. With a wink, the killer turned and dived into the frothing sea of people.

In an instant, he was gone.

SIXTEEN

18th March – 12.23 a.m.

'Where's the backup? They need to set up a perimeter,' Tom ordered angrily.

'It's a little late for that,' Stokes shrugged helplessly at the untamed mob that had already spilled out on to the Strip, bringing the traffic to a standstill as they surged across the road, trying to get as far away from the Amalfi as they could.

Tom glared resentfully at the crowd, wanting Stokes to be wrong but knowing he wasn't. What made it worse was that the gunman had played him. He'd seen Tom was carrying a Beretta, counted the shots until he'd known it was empty, then waited for him. Taunted him.

With a violent jolt, Tom's thoughts snapped back to Jennifer.

'How is she?'

'The paramedics are with her now,' Stokes

reassured him, before lowering his gaze. 'She's lost a lot of blood.'

'Where is she?'

'They're taking her up on to the roof for a medevac to UMC.'

'Get me up there,' Tom barked.

They ran back into the casino and, using the card Tom had taken from the security guard, rode up to the top floor.

'What happened to the priest?' Tom asked as the levels pinged past.

'We lost him too,' Stokes admitted. 'Soon as everyone started running, he vanished. The money's safe, though.'

'You think I give a shit about the money?' Tom hissed.

The doors opened and they sprinted up the final two flights of the service staircase to a metal door that Tom swiped open. The helicopter was already there, its rotors buffeting them with a wash of hot, dusty air. Jennifer was being loaded into the rear by two paramedics, a drip attached to her arm and an oxygen mask over her face. Ortiz was crouching on the ground, his shirt covered in her blood, his head in his hands.

'I'm going with her,' Tom shouted over the throb of the engines.

'No way,' Stokes called back. 'You're the only person who can ID the gunman. I need you here.'

'I wasn't asking for your permission.'

Keeping his head down, Tom sprinted across the pad and hauled himself in behind the stretcher, slamming the door shut after him. The pitch of the engines deepened as the pilot throttled up and with a lurch they rose into the sky.

'How is she?' Tom called to one of the medics as they hooked her up to a mobile ECG, her pulse registering with a green blip on the screen and a sharp tone – Beep . . . beep . . . beep. Around them power and warning lights from other machines flashed and sounded intermittently.

'Who are you?'

'A friend.'

'She's lost a lot of blood . . . we need to get her into theatre ASAP.'

'Is she conscious?'

'In and out. Try talking to her. Keep her awake.'

Tom shuffled forward until he was sitting next to Jennifer's head. The glow of the ECG screen was staining her skin green. Her eyes flickered open and he was certain that he saw a smile of recognition tremble across her face.

'Hold on, Jen,' he whispered, pressing his lips to her ear. 'We'll be there soon.'

She nodded weakly. He brushed the hair out of her eyes, speaking almost to himself.

'You're going to be okay. I'll make sure you're okay.'

Beep . . . beep . . . beep.

He smiled at her reassuringly, glad that she

couldn't see the paramedics' grim-faced expression as they worked on the wound, the blood still oozing from her chest. He felt her hand reach for his, press something hard and rectangular into it, her grip tightening as she pulled him closer, her mouth moving under the oxygen mask.

He bent over her, straining to hear her voice against the chop of the rotors and the rhythmic pinging of the heart monitor. He caught something, the fragment of a word, perhaps more, and then her eyes closed again and her grip loosened, allowing him to slip what she had given him into his pocket.

'Come on, Jen,' Tom called, shaking her arm gently at first and then with increasing urgency. 'We're nearly there now. You're going to be okay. You just need to keep listening to me. Listen to my voice.'

He shook her again, more roughly this time. But there was no reaction and all he could hear was the gradual, almost imperceptible lengthening of the gaps between each tone of the ECG.

Beep . . . beep. Beep . . . . . . beep. Beep . . . . beep.

'Help her,' Tom shouted angrily to the paramedics. 'Do something.'

They swapped a glance, one of them wiping the back of his hand across his brow, smearing blood.

'We've done what we can.'

Far below, the city's neon carpet unravelled into

the distance. But from up here, Tom could see that it ended, that a black line had been drawn across the desert at the city's limits, and that beyond that was only darkness.

He leaned forward, his lips brushing against her cheek. He knew now that it was just him and her. Him and her and the hiss of the respirator and the unfeeling pulse of the ECG's electronic heart.

'Stay with me,' he whispered.

For a second he could have sworn that her breathing quickened. Then the machine gave a piercing shriek. The monitor showed a perfectly flat line.

PART TWO

'It is from the greatest dangers that the greatest glory is to be won.'
Thucydides, *History of the Peloponnesian War –*
Book 1, 144

SEVENTEEN

Via Galvani, Testaccio, Rome
18th March – 3.12 p.m.

The speaker crackled into life.

'Mitto tibi navem prora puppique carentem.'

Allegra hesitated, her mind racing. She understood the Latin, of course – I send you a ship lacking stern and bow. But what did it mean? How could a ship not have a stern and a bow? Unless . . . unless it was referring to something else. To the front and the back? The beginning and the end? The first and the last? Latin for ship was *navem*, so if it was missing its beginning and its end, its first and last letters perhaps . . .

'Ave,' she replied with a smile. Latin for hello.

'Ave, indeed,' the voice replied with a chuckle. 'Although I can't claim the credit this time. That was one of Cicero's.'

The door buzzed open and Allegra made her way to the lift, smiling. She'd first met Aurelio

Eco at La Sapienza, before heading off to Columbia
for her Masters, where he'd been a visiting
professor in the university's antiquities department. Before that, he'd spent fifteen years as the
Director of the Villa Giulia, Rome's foremost
Etruscan museum, during ten of which he had
also headed up the Ufficio Sequestri e Scavi
Clandestini, the Office of Clandestine Excavations
and Seized Objects. Unfortunately for her, these
posts seemed to have provided him with an in-
exhaustible supply of riddles, which he delighted
in asking her as a condition of entry to his apartment. A latter-day Sphinx to her Odysseus.

As usual the door was open and the kettle boiling.
She made herself a strong black coffee and Aurelio
an Earl Grey tea with lemon, an affectation of his
from a brief stint at Oxford in his twenties that he
had never been able, or wanted, to shake off.

He was waiting for her in his high-backed
leather chair, the split in the seat cushion covered
by a red-and-white *keffiyeh* purchased during an
exchange posting to Jordan. His dusty office was
full of such mementoes – photographs of him at
various digs over the decades, framed maps and
faded prints, prayer beads and inlaid boxes picked
up in dusty Middle-Eastern souks, fragments of
inscribed Roman tablets, shards of Etruscan
pottery, carved remnants of Greek statues. At times
it seemed to Allegra that his entire life was held
in this small room, each piece invested with a

particular meaning or memory that he only had to glance at or hold to live all over again.

And yet this primitive mental filing system was as chaotic as it was effective, pictures hanging askew, books stacked any which way on the shelves with dirty cups and glasses squeezed into the gaps, the floor covered in a confetti trail of newspaper cuttings and half-read books left face-down, alongside a stack of index cards inscribed with notes for a forthcoming lecture. And while a favoured few of his artefacts had been placed in a glass display cabinet, the rest were scattered indiscriminately around the room, some squeezed on to his desk and the marble mantelpiece, others lining the edges of the bookshelves like para-troopers waiting for the order to jump.

Despite his cheerfulness on the intercom, Aurelio now seemed to have sunk into what Allegra could only describe as a sulk, his bottom lip jutting out, brows furrowed. Funny, she thought, how old age seemed to have given him an almost childlike ability to flit between moods on a whim.

'Maybe you shouldn't come any more,' he sighed. 'Spend time with your real friends, instead, people your own age.'

'Don't start that again,' she sighed. 'I've told you, I'm too busy to have any friends. Besides, I like old things.' She winked. 'They smell more interesting.'

Approaching seventy, Aurelio had no family left now, apart from a distant cousin who only seemed to show up when he needed a handout. As they had got to know each other, therefore, Allegra had taken it upon herself to look in on him whenever she knew she would be in the area. And sometimes, like today, when she knew she wouldn't.

'But you said you'd be here for lunch,' he continued in a hurt tone, although she could sense that her reply had pleased him. 'You're late.'

'And whose fault is that?'

He grinned, his sulk vanishing as quickly as she suspected it had appeared. He had a kindly face, with large light brown eyes, a beaked nose and leathered skin that spoke of too many long summers spent hunched over an excavation trench. He was dressed in an open-necked shirt and a yellow silk cravat, another hangover from his Oxford days. As ever, he was wearing a moth-eaten grey cardigan for warmth, his refusal to pay the 'extortionate' prices demanded by 'piratical' energy companies condemning his apartment to a Siberian permafrost for at least three months of the year.

'So they did call you?' he crowed.

'I knew it!' she remonstrated angrily. 'Who did you speak to? What did you tell them?'

'The GICO wanted an antiquities expert. They called the university. The university put them on to me. I told them I'd retired and recommended you instead.'

'Did they tell you what they wanted?'

'Of course not. It's the GICO. They never tell you anything.' He paused, suddenly concerned. 'I thought you'd be pleased.'

With a deep breath, Allegra recounted the events of the past twenty-three hours. The inverted crucifixion at the site of Julius Caesar's assassination. The carefully staged beheading in the Pantheon. The apparent link to two Caravaggio masterpieces. Aurelio listened intently, shaking his head at some of the more gruesome details, but otherwise remaining silent until she had finished.

'So the man they found in the Pantheon . . .?'

'Was Annibale Argento's twin brother, Gio.'

'*Merda*,' he swore, for what could well have been the first time since she'd known him. '*They* must be lapping it up.'

They, she knew, referred to the media, an industry he despised, having been tricked a few years ago into authenticating a forged Etruscan vase by an investigative reporter. He gave a contemptuous wave of his hand towards an imagined TV set in the corner of his room, as if trying to further distance himself from an object he had already demonstrably banished from his life.

'I've spent half the day trying to see if there's anything else that links the two sites or any of

Caravaggio's other works. Gallo is trying to get me seconded on to the case full time.'

'I'm sorry, Allegra. I didn't know . . . I didn't mean to get you involved in anything like this.'

She shrugged. It was hard to be angry with him. It was Aurelio after all who, guessing that she would quickly tire of academia, had encouraged her to apply to the art and antiquities unit of the Carabinieri in the first place. He'd only been trying to help.

'I know.'

'Anything to go on?' he asked hopefully.

'Plenty to go on. Just no idea where to start,' she sighed. 'Which reminds me. There's something I wanted to ask you.'

'Anything, of course.'

'Both victims had what looked like an antique coin in their mouths.'

'To pay Charon,' Aurelio guessed immediately.

'That's what I thought. Except it wasn't a coin. It was a lead disc.'

'Lead?' Aurelio frowned. 'That's unusual.'

'That's what I thought. I seem to remember reading that Roman forgers used to fake coins by casting them in lead and covering them in gold leaf, but I wondered if there was some other reference to the Classical world that might.'

'Unusual, but not unprecedented,' he continued, interrupting her. 'Can you reach that red book down for me.'

She extricated the book from between the fifteen or so other academic texts he had written and handed it to him. He held it for a few seconds, his eyes closed, fingers resting lightly on the leather cover as if he was reading braille. Then, opening his eyes, he leafed through it, the brain haemorrhage that he'd suffered some fifteen years before betraying itself in his slow and deliberate movements.

'Here,' he fixed her with a knowing smile, about halfway in.

'Here what?'

'*Threatened by the Persian empire, several Greek states came together in the fifth century BC to form a military alliance under the leadership of the Athenians,*' he read. '*Members had to contribute ships or money, and in return the alliance agreed to protect their territory. Symbolically,*' he paused, Allegra remembering that he used to employ the same theatrical technique in lectures when he was about to make a particularly compelling point. '*Symbolically, upon joining, representatives of the member states had to throw a piece of metal into the sea.*'

'Lead,' Allegra breathed. He nodded.

'*Normally a piece of lead. The alliance was to last until it floated to the surface again.*'

There was a pause, as she reflected on this.

'And you think . . .?'

'You asked about a link between lead and the Classical world.' He smiled. 'Thinking's your job.'

'What was the name of this alliance?'

Aurelio pretended to consult the book, although she could tell it was just an excuse for another of his dramatic pauses.

'They called themselves the Delian League.'

EIGHTEEN

J. Edgar Hoover Building,
FBI headquarters, Washington DC
18th March – 9.37 a.m.
The door buzzed open. Tom didn't bother to look round. He could tell from Ortiz's shuffling steps and Stokes's heavier, wider stride, who it was.

'How long are you going to keep me here?' he demanded angrily.

'A federal agent's been killed, Mr Kirk,' Stokes replied icily, no longer even attempting to mask his instinctive hostility. He dragged a chair out from under the table and extravagantly straddled it. 'So we're going to keep you here pretty much as long as we like.'

'You don't have to tell me she was killed, you pompous bastard,' Tom hissed, holding out a sleeve still flecked with Jennifer's blood. 'I was holding her hand when she died, remember?'

In a way he was glad that Stokes was acting

like this. It gave him a reason to be angry, to give himself over to his rage, to feel its intoxicating opiate course through his veins and his pulse quicken. Better that than allow his sadness to envelop him, feel the paralysing arms of grief tighten around him as he subjected himself to a Sisyphean analysis of what he could and should have done to save her.

Even as this thought occurred to him, he felt Jennifer's image forming in his mind. An image he'd tried to suppress ever since he'd seen the gurney disappear into the bowels of the hospital, and then been escorted back on to Kezman's jet and flown to this windowless interview room. But there she was, bloodied, her face shrouded by an oxygen mask, arms pierced by wires. A martyr? A sacrifice? But if so, for what and by whom?

'If we're going to catch the people who did this, we're going to need your help.' Ortiz, standing to his right, had adopted a more conciliatory tone which Tom sensed was genuine, rather than some clumsy attempt at a good cop, bad cop routine. His cheeks were shadowed by stubble, his eyes tired.

'You're not going to catch anyone, stuck down here,' Tom retorted. 'The longer we talk, the colder the trail. We should be in Vegas.'

'SOP says we pull back and let an IA team step in when an agent falls in the line of duty,' Stokes intoned, sounding as though he was reciting from some sort of manual. 'They're on the ground there already, reporting directly to FBI Director Green.'

'To FBI Director Green?' Tom asked, momentarily encouraged. He knew Jack Green, or at least had met him a few times when working with Jennifer. He had first-hand experience of the help Tom had given the Bureau in the past. 'I want to talk to him. Does he know I'm here?'

Ortiz's eyes flickered questioningly towards the large mirror that took up most of the left-hand wall. Tom's heart sank. Not only did Green know he was here, but, judging from the uncomfortable expression on Ortiz's face, he was probably watching. Jennifer's death had clearly reset the clock. Until they knew exactly what had happened, he wasn't going to qualify for any special treatment.

'You can talk to us instead,' Stokes snapped. 'Tell us what happened.'

'You know what happened. You were there. You saw the whole damn thing.'

'All I know is that twelve hours after Browne brought you into the case, she was dead.'

'You think I had something to do with it?' Tom's anger was momentarily overwhelmed by incredulity.

'Twenty million dollars is a lot of money.' Stokes's eyes narrowed accusingly. 'Even for you.'

'So that's your theory? That this was some sort of botched heist?' Tom wasn't sure whether Stokes was being deliberately provocative, or just plain stupid.

'I think that shooting a federal agent is a pretty good diversion. If one of our agents hadn't secured the suitcases, who's to say –'

'If all they'd wanted was a diversion, they could have shot anyone in that place,' Tom countered. 'They could have shot me.'

'Exactly.' Stokes raised his eyebrows pointedly, as if Tom had somehow proved his point.

'Except they didn't. They chose Jennifer. Maybe you should be asking yourselves why,' Tom insisted.

'What are you talking about?' Stokes said with an impatient shrug.

'Jennifer told me that two weeks ago she'd stumbled across an antiquities smuggling ring,' Tom said, looking to Ortiz who acknowledged this point with a nod. 'Then, out of the blue, a long-lost Caravaggio shows up. One of the few works in the world guaranteed to ensure that Jennifer gets the call. You think that's a coincidence?'

'You don't?' Ortiz asked him with a frown.

'I did until last night.' Tom shrugged. 'But now I'm thinking that there never was any Caravaggio; never was any exchange. That it was all a set-up. That that's why the priest started stalling. Because he was expecting Jennifer. Because he wanted to give the gunman enough time to find her.'

'This was about the money, and you know it,'

Stokes said with a dismissive wave of his hand. 'We just got to it before you or anyone else could.'

'Jennifer told me that the dealer you arrested in Queens had given you a name. Someone in Italy,' Tom said to Ortiz, still ignoring Stokes. 'Who was he? Did he have any ties to the mafia?'

'Why? What do you . . .?'

'That's classified,' Stokes interrupted angrily before Ortiz could answer. 'Browne trusted you with too much, and *you* shouldn't be encouraging him.' He jabbed his finger at Ortiz.

'The mafia control the illegal antiquities business in Italy,' Tom explained. 'They decide who can dig where, and take a cut on everything that comes out of the ground. It's worth millions to them. The same mafia who, if you believe the rumours, have been holding the Caravaggio all these years.'

'What are you saying?' Ortiz breathed, ignoring Stokes's venomous gaze.

'I'm saying it was a professional hit. I'm saying that something she'd stumbled across had made her a threat and that the painting was just a way of flushing her out into the open.'

'If you're right . . .' Ortiz said slowly.

'If I'm right, then we're already too late to catch the killer. You can run a DNA test on the blood traces, but people like that are ghosts. You'll get nothing. But I might still be able to find whoever ordered the hit.'

'*You* might be able to find them?' Stokes gave a hollow laugh. 'We've got a long way to go yet before we'll even let you take a piss without someone holding your dick for you.'

'Let me see her files.' Tom turned to Ortiz. 'I can go places you can't, speak to people you don't know. But I need to move fast. I need to move now.'

Ortiz went to say something, but then hesitated, his eyes again flickering towards the mirror.

'Yeah, sure!' Stokes gave a rasping laugh. 'Get a load of this guy. Our necks are already on the line and now he wants us to bend over and drop our pants too?'

'Then either charge me with something, or let me go,' Tom shouted angrily, rising to his feet. 'Right now you're just wasting my time.'

'Like I said, Kirk, you're going nowhere,' Stokes said coldly, standing up and swiping the door open.

'I'm sorry, man,' Ortiz shrugged, joining him in the doorway. 'But he's right. This is how it's got to be.'

The door sealed shut behind them and the electronic reader flashed from green to red. Saying nothing, Tom reached into his trouser pocket and felt the hard outline of the swipe card Jennifer had pressed into his hand in the helicopter.

Even then, as she lay dying, she'd known how this would play out. Even then, she'd known what he would have to do.

NINETEEN

Ospedale Fatebenefratelli, Isola Tiberina, Rome
18th March – 3.51 p.m.

Allegra had left Aurelio in yet another of his sulks. She had arrived late and was now leaving early, he had complained as she hurriedly saw herself out. She had pointedly reminded him that she was only leaving so she could follow up on a case that he was responsible for her being involved with in the first place. But by then he had turned the radio on and was pretending he couldn't hear her. No matter. All would be forgiven and forgotten by tomorrow, she knew, his moods breaking and clearing as quickly as a summer storm.

Allegra wasn't sure whether the link between the lead discs and the Delian League was meaningful or not, but one thing that she was almost certain about was that Gallo would want to know about it ASAP, so he could make that decision for himself.

Normally she would have called him, but his phone appeared to have been switched off. According to his assistant, this was because there was no reception in the mortuary basement levels, where she would still catch him if she hurried.

Having signed in, she headed down to the cold store in the basement. A young man wearing a white lab coat – a medical student, she guessed, judging by his age – was manning the reception desk and glaring at a monitor.

'Colonel Gallo?' she asked, flicking her wallet open. He jumped up, deftly minimising a game of solitaire.

'You just missed him,' he replied anxiously, leaning over the top of the counter and peering down the corridor behind her as if he still might be able to see him. 'Signor Santos is still here, though.'

'Who?'

'He came in for the formal ID on Argento. Colonel Gallo thought it better that they leave separately.'

She glanced at the door he had indicated and with a curious frown stepped towards it. Peering through the porthole she could see that it opened on to a large and resolutely featureless rect-angular room, the only splash of colour coming from a few moulded blue plastic seats that were huddled for warmth around a water cooler bolted to the right-hand wall. Opposite these were a series of evenly spaced square aluminium doors, perhaps eight across and three high, each with a large levered handle and a name-tag slot. One of the doors was open; the drawer had been pulled out. A man was standing to one side of it, his back to her.

'Signor Santos?'

She pushed the door open and announced herself with a warm smile and an outstretched hand. Santos turned slowly at the sound of her voice. He was in his late forties and looked slim and fit, with a tanned face and teeth the colour of polished ivory. His close-cropped dark hair was sprinkled with silver and started high up his head where his hairline had begun to recede a little. He was immaculately dressed in a Cesare Attolini navy blazer and white flannel trousers that had been cut to crease at just the right place to slightly ride up over a pair of brown Church's. His creamy pink shirt was from Barba in Naples, his striped tie from Marinella, and his belt by Gucci, although given the obvious excellence of the tailoring, this last item was clearly worn for sartorial effect rather than to keep his trousers up.

He gave her a wary, even suspicious look that prompted her into an explanation.

'Lieutenant Allegra Damico,' she introduced herself, holding out her ID. 'I'm working with Colonel Gallo.'

'I see.' He smiled, returning her wallet with a nod. 'Apologies. I thought you might be from the press.'

'They're looking for you?'

'They're looking for an opportunity to snatch a photograph of an elected official grieving over his dead brother's butchered corpse. I'm here to make sure they don't get that chance.'

'Deputy Argento asked you to identify his brother's body instead of him?' she guessed.

'Actually, Colonel Gallo suggested it,' he corrected her. 'He thought it might help . . . simplify matters.'

'How did you know the victim?'

'My apologies –' Santos stepped forward with an apologetic shrug, his hand rising to meet hers – 'I haven't introduced myself. I am Antonio Santos, President of the Banco Rosalia.'

He handed her his business card, the way he held it out with both hands suggesting he had lived, or at least done a lot of business in the Far East. It was stiff and elaborately engraved with a sweeping copperplate script that identified him as:

> *Antonio Santos*
> *President & Director-General*
> *Banco Rosalia*

'Gio used to work for me.'

Allegra moved over to stand on the other side of the open drawer, her ghostly form reflecting indistinctly in the adjacent door's dull aluminium surface.

Giulio Argento was lying in between them, naked and shrouded by a white sheet apart from his uncovered face and where it had fallen away from his left arm, revealing a bar-coded tag fixed to his wrist like a supermarket label. She barely recognised his waxen and hollow features but there was no mistaking, though, the ugly welt of the sword strike where it had opened up his neck like a second smile.

'Liquorice?'

She refused. There seemed something strangely inappropriate about the way Santos was shaking the ornate tin over Argento's body.

'I read that Roman soldiers could go for ten days without eating or drinking with liquorice in their rations,' he said, popping two pieces into his mouth and then slipping the tin back into his pocket. Allegra nodded, deciding against mentioning that she had read somewhere else that too much liquorice could reduce a man's testosterone levels. 'So? Any leads? Any clues as to who did it? Why they did it?'

'I'm sorry, sir, but I can't . . .'

'I understand.' He shrugged. 'Due process, jeopardising a live investigation, respect for the victim's family . . . Gallo spun me a similar line.'

'It's for your own protection,' she insisted.

A pause. Santos looked back down at the body. 'You know, the traffic was terrible the day they found the body,' he said eventually, a strangely vacant expression on his face, as if he couldn't quite see Argento and yet knew he was there. 'Half the streets seemed to have been barricaded off. I remember being angry that it had made me late for a meeting. I never realised that . . .'

'What did Signor Argento do for you?'

'God's work.'

'In a bank?' The words came out sounding more sceptical than she had intended.

'The Vatican Bank is our largest shareholder,' he explained with the weary patience of someone who had had to give this explanation many times before. 'We take deposits in the normal way and then lend money at subsidised rates to worthy projects that might not otherwise get funding. Gio had responsibility for managing the relationships with some of our larger accounts.'

'So no reason to think that anyone would want to –'

'This?' Santos gestured with disgust. 'This is the devil's work.'

'The devil?' she asked, not sure from his expression if he meant it literally or had someone in mind.

'I trained as a priest in Rio before I realised that my true calling lay in financing God's will rather than trying to live by it.' He fiddled with the buckle of his belt, aligning it with his shirt buttons. 'But I still recognise the hand of evil when I see it.'

'Yes.' She nodded. 'Of course.' With the memory of Ricci's staring eyes and Argento's congealed scream still fresh in her mind, it was hard not to agree with him.

'The irony, of course, was that, despite working for us, poor Gio was not a true believer.' Santos glanced up at Allegra with a rueful smile. 'He used to say that life was too short to waste it worrying about what might happen when he was dead. At times like this, when it almost seems that God might have deserted us, I almost understand what he meant.'

Folding the sheet back over Argento's face, Santos made the sign of the cross and then eased the drawer back into the wall and swung the door shut. It closed with a hollow metal clang, the echo reverberating around them as if a stone slab had been dropped over a tomb. Allegra turned to leave, then paused.

'I wonder, did he ever mention an organisation or group called the Delian League?'

'The Delian League? Not as far as I remember.' Santos shook his head, frowning in thought. 'Why, who are they? Do you think they . . .?'

'It's just a name I've come across,' she reassured him with a smile. 'It probably means nothing. Shall I see you out?'

A large Mercedes with diplomatic plates was waiting for Santos on the street outside. The chauffeur jogged round and held the rear door open for him.

'A small perk of the job,' Santos smiled as he shook her hand. 'Saves me a fortune in parking tickets.'

He slipped inside and peered up at her through the open window, an earnest look on his face.

'Gio had many faults, but he was a good man, Lieutenant Damico. He deserved better. I hope you catch whoever did this to him.'

'We'll do our best,' she reassured him with a nod.

The windo hummed shut and Santos settled back into his seat. As the car drew away, he reached for his phone.

'You know who it is. Don't hang up,' Santos said carefully when the number he had dialled was answered. 'I need a favour. And then I'm gone. For good this time, you have my word.'

TWENTY

Hotel Bel-Air, Stone Canyon Road,
Los Angeles
18th March – 7.12 a.m.

Verity always sat at the same table for breakfast. In the far left corner, under the awning, behind a swaying screen of bamboo grass. It was close enough to the entrance to be seen by anyone coming in, sheltered enough not to be bothered by anyone walking past.

'Good morning, Ms Bruce.' Philippe, the maître d', bounded up to her, his French accent so comically thick that she wondered if he worked on it at home. 'Your papers.'

He handed her meticulously folded copies of the *Washington Post* and the *Financial Times*, both still warm from being pressed. Politics and money. The cogs and grease of life's little carousel, even if the deepening global economic downturn had rather slowed things recently

'Your guest is already here.'

She pushed her sunglasses back on to her head with a frown and followed his gaze to where Earl Faulks was sitting waiting for her, absent-mindedly spinning his phone on the tablecloth.

'He tried to sit in your seat,' Philippe continued in an outraged whisper. 'I moved him, of course.'

Faulks had just turned fifty but was still striking in a gaunt, patrician sort of way, his dark hooded eyes that seemed to blink in slow motion looming above a long oval face and aquiline nose, silver hair swept back off a pale face. He was wearing a dark blue linen suit, white Charvet shirt with a cut-away collar, Cartier knot cufflinks and one of his trademark bow-ties. Today's offering was a series of garish salmon pink and cucumber green stripes that she assumed denoted one of his precious London clubs.

'Verity! Looking gorgeous as always.'

He rose with a smile to greet her, leaning heavily on an umbrella, an almost permanent accessory since a riding accident a few years ago. She ignored him and sat down, a waiter pushing her chair in for her, the maître d' snapping her napkin on to her lap.

'Muesli with low-fat yogurt?' he asked, his tone suggesting he already knew what her answer would be.

'Yes please, Philippe.'

'And a mineral water and a pot of fresh tea?'

'With lemon.'

'Of course. And for monsieur?' He turned to Faulks, who had sat back down and was observing this ritualistic exchange with a wry smile.

'Toast. Brown. Coffee. Black.'

'Very well.' The maître d' backed away, clicking his fingers at one of the waiters to send him running to the kitchen.

Verity reached into her handbag and took out an art deco silver cigarette case engraved with flowers. Opening it carefully, she tipped the thirty or so pills it contained into a small pile on her side plate. They lay there like pebbles, an assortment of vitamins and herbal supplements in different shapes and sizes and colours, some of the more translucent ones glinting like amber.

'Verity, darling, if you go on being this healthy, it'll kill you,' Faulks warned as their drinks arrived.

He was American, a shopkeeper's son from Baltimore, if you believed his detractors – of which he had amassed his fair share over the years. Not that you could detect his origins any more; his affected accent, clipped way of speaking and occasional Britishisms reminded her of a character from an Edith Wharton novel. She'd always thought it rather a shame that he didn't smoke – she imagined that a silver Dunhill lighter and a pack of Sobranies would have somehow suited the casual elegance of his slender fingers.

'I mean, what time did your trainer have you

up this morning for a run? Five? Six? Only tradesmen get up that early.'

'I'm still not talking to you, Earl,' she replied, watching carefully as the waiter strained her tea and then delicately squeezed a small piece of lemon into it.

'You were the one who wanted to meet,' he reminded her. 'I was packing for the Caribbean.'

She ignored him again, although she couldn't help but feel a pang of envy. Faulks seemed to ride effortlessly in the slipstream of the super rich as their sumptuous caravan processed around the world: Gstaad in February, the Bahamas in March, the La Prairie clinic in Montreux in April for his annual check-up, London in June, Italy for the summer, New York for the winter sales, and then a well-earned rest before the whole gorgeous procession kicked off again.

She began to sort her pills into the order in which she liked to take them, although she had long since forgotten the logic by which she'd arrived at this particular sequence. Satisfied, she began to take them in silence, washing each one down with a mouthful of water and a sharp jerk of her head.

'Fine, you win,' Faulks said eventually, throwing his hands up in defeat. 'What do you want me to do? Apologise? Wear a hair shirt? Walk up the Via Dolorosa on my knees?'

'Any of those would be a start.' She glared at him.

'Even when I come bearing gifts?' He unfolded his napkin to reveal three vase fragments positioned to show that they fitted cleanly together. 'The final pieces of the Phintias *calyx krater* that you've been collecting for the past few years.' He smiled at her. 'In our profession, patience truly is a necessity, not a virtue.'

'The same fragments I seem to remember you wanted a hundred thousand for last year,' Verity said archly. 'Are you feeling generous or guilty?'

'If I had a conscience I wouldn't be in this business,' he replied with a smile, although there was something in his voice that suggested that he was only half joking. 'Let's call it a peace offering.'

'Have you any idea of the embarrassment you've caused me?'

'You have nothing to be embarrassed about,' he assured her.

'Tell that to Thierry Normand and Sir John Sykes. According to them, I paid you ten million dollars for something that was at best "anomalous", at worst a "pastiche".'

'Pastiche?' Faulks snorted. 'Did you tell them about the test results? Don't they know it's impossible to fake that sort of calcification?'

'By then they weren't listening.'

'You mean they didn't want to hear,' he corrected her. 'Don't you see, Verity, darling, that they're all jealous. Jealous of your success. Jealous that while their donors have pulled back as the recession has begun to bite, the Getty remains blessed with a three-billion-dollar endowment.'

'Sometimes I think it's more a curse than a blessing,' she sniffed. 'Do you know we have to spend four and a quarter per cent of that a year or lose our tax status? Have you any idea how hard it is to get through one hundred and twenty-seven million dollars a year? Of the pressure it puts us under?'

'I can only imagine,' he commiserated, shaking his head. 'That's why the kouros was a smart buy. After all, don't you think the Met would have made a move if they'd been given even half a chance? But you beat them to it.'

'Vivienne Foyle *is* close to the Met.' She nodded grudgingly, remembering how she had twisted the knife right at the end. 'She's never liked me.'

'The problem here isn't the kouros,' Faulks insisted, his full baritone voice taking on the fervent conviction of a TV evangelist. 'The problem is people's unwillingness to accept that their carefully constructed picture of how Greek sculpture developed over the centuries might need to be rewritten. They should be thanking you for opening their eyes, for deepening their understanding, for extending the boundaries of their knowledge. Instead, they're seeking to discredit you, just as the church did with Galileo.'

She nodded, rather liking this image of herself as an academic revolutionary that the establishment was desperate to silence at all costs. The problem was, she didn't have the time or the temperament to become a martyr.

'I agree with you. If I didn't, the kouros would already be on its way back to Geneva. But the damage is done. Even if they're wrong, it'll take years for them to admit it. Meanwhile the director can't look me in the eye, the trustees have asked for a second round of tests, and the *New York Times* is threatening to run a piece at the weekend. I mean, what if something else comes out?'

'Nothing else will come out,' Faulks said slowly, his voice suddenly hard. 'Not unless someone's planning to talk. And nobody's planning to talk, are they, Verity?'

It was phrased as a question, but there was no doubting that he was giving her a very clear instruction. Maybe even a warning.

'Why would I risk everything we've achieved together?' she said quickly.

'You wouldn't,' he said, his eyes locked unblinkingly with hers. 'But others . . . well. I don't like to be disappointed.'

There was an icy edge to his voice and she gulped down a few more pills, wishing that she'd packed some Valium as well. Almost immediately, however, Faulks's face thawed into a warm smile.

'Anyway, let's not worry about that now. I understand that you're upset. And I want to make it up to you. What are you doing tomorrow?'

'Tomorrow?' She frowned. 'Tomorrow I'll be in Madrid. The US ambassador is hosting a two-day cultural exchange. We fly out this afternoon. Why?'

'There's something I want to show you.' He reached inside his jacket and handed her a Polaroid. 'I was hoping you might come to Geneva.'

'Do you really think that, after what happened yesterday, the director is going to let me buy anything from you again?' she asked, taking the photo from him with an indifferent shrug.

'You won't have to. It'll come to you as a donation.'

She glanced down at the photo, then heard herself gasp.

'Is it . . .?' she whispered, her mouth suddenly dry, her hands trembling, her chest tight.

'Genuine? Absolutely,' he reassured her. 'I've seen it myself. There's no question.'

'But no one has ever found . . .'

'I know.' He gave her a schoolboy's wide grin. 'Isn't it wonderful?'

'Who's it by?'

'Come now, Verity – 450 BC? Can't you guess?'

There was a pause, her eyes still not having lifted from the photograph.

'Where is it now?'

'On its way to me.'

'Provenance?'

'Private Lebanese collection since the 1890s. I have all the documentation.'

Another pause as she carefully placed the photograph on the table, sipped some water and then looked up hungrily.

'I have to see it.'

TWENTY-ONE

Headquarters of the Guarda di Finanza,
Viale XXI Aprile, Rome
18th March – 4.25 p.m.

The headquarters of the Guarda di Finanza was located to the north-east of the city centre, just beyond the Porta Pia. It occupied a Spanish-looking building, with shutters at every window and its walls painted a dusty yellow and rich ochre colour. The main entrance was surmounted by the Italian and European Union flags, but these were sagging limply, the light breeze that was chasing the rain clouds away registering only in the rustling fronds of the palm tree that stood to the left of the door.

In a way, Allegra reflected as she stepped out of her taxi, it was perhaps better for her to catch up with Gallo here, rather than at the mortuary. This, after all, was where the physical evidence from the two murders was being kept, giving her the opportunity to have another look at the lead discs in the light of what Aurelio had told her and to get her story straight before seeing him.

Not that the decision to house the evidence here would have been a simple one, given all the different law enforcement agencies with a potential stake in this case. The Guarda di Finanza, for one, was a sprawling empire, covering not only Gallo's organised crime unit but a variety of money-related crimes such as tax evasion, Customs and border checks, money laundering, smuggling, international drugs trafficking and counterfeiting. A military corps, it even had its own naval fleet and air force.

Allegra's art and antiques unit, meanwhile, was part of the Arma dei Carabinieri, a paramilitary force with police duties that also oversaw counter-terrorism operations, the forensic bureau, the military police, undercover investigations and, bizarrely, sanitary enforcement.

Then, of course, there was the state police, a civilian force that, as well as having responsibility for routine patrolling, investigative and law enforcement duties, also oversaw the armed, postal, highway and transport police forces. And this was not to forget the various layers of provincial, municipal and local police, prison officers, park rangers and the coast guard who further crowded the picture.

In fact, Allegra seemed to remember from one of the induction lectures she had had to endure upon first joining up, any one area in Italy could theoretically be under the jurisdiction of up to thirty-one different police or police-type forces. Unsurprisingly, this resulted in a sea-fog of over-lapping responsibilities, unclear accountabilities and red tape that more often than not led to the different agencies competing against each other when they should have been collaborating.

Allegra's temporary secondment from the Carabinieri to their fierce rivals at the Guarda di Finanza was, therefore, a relatively unusual request on Gallo's part, as proved by the raised eyebrows of the duty officer who buzzed her in and directed her towards the basement.

Following the signs, she found the evidence store next to the armoury. It was secured by a steel door with a lock but no handle, suggesting that it could only be opened from the inside. Next to it, a low counter had been chopped out of the reinforced concrete wall. An elderly officer in a neatly pressed grey uniform with gold buttons and a green beret was sitting on the other side behind a screen of bullet-proof glass. Allegra knocked on the window and then placed her ID flat against it.

'You're a long way from home, Lieutenant.' The man gave her a quizzical look over the top of his glasses, his feet up and the newspaper resting across his knee. His badge identified him as Enrico Gambetta.

'I've been seconded on to the Argento case,' she explained.

'You're working with Colonel Gallo!' Gambetta struggled to his feet, anxiously peering out into the corridor as if he half expected Gallo to jump out of the shadows.

'Until he decides he doesn't need me any more,' she said, unable to stop herself wondering what strange gravitational anomaly was securing Gambetta's trousers around his enormous waist.

'So he got my message?' he asked excitedly. 'He sent you to see me.'

'Your message?' She frowned.

'About the other murder.'

'I haven't spoken to him all afternoon,' she said with a shrug. 'I was just hoping to take another look at the lead discs from the Argento and Ricci killings before I see him.'

'The lead disc – exactly!' He beamed, looking like he might break into a lumbering jig. 'Like the ones you found in their mouths, right?'

'How do you know that?' Allegra asked sharply.

'When you've been around as long as I have, you get to hear about most things.' He winked. 'Now, I can't really let you sign it out, but . . .' He paused, clearly trying to decide what to do. 'Wait there.'

A few moments later there was the sound of bolts being thrown back and the steel door opened. Gambetta stuck his head out into the corridor and, having checked that it was empty, ushered her inside.

'Are you sure I'm allowed to . . .?' she began, frowning.

'I won't tell if you won't,' he whispered, as if afraid of being overheard. 'But I need to show somebody. Are you carrying?'

'Yes.' She swept her jacket back to reveal the gun holstered to her waist.

'Pick it up on your way out.' He tapped his desk, the determined look on his face telling her that this was one rule he clearly wasn't prepared to turn a blind-eye to.

'Of course.'

The room was divided into five narrow aisles by a series of floor-to-ceiling metal shelving units. Waddling unsteadily, Gambetta led her down the second aisle. Allegra blinked as she followed him, her eyes adjusting to the anaemic glow of the overhead strip lighting that was competing for ceiling space with a snaking mass of heavily lagged water pipes and colour-coded electrical cabling. Even so, she could see that the shelves were crammed with hundreds, if not thousands, of cardboard boxes and plastic evidence bags, each one sealed and diligently identified by a white tag.

'They think that all we do down here all day is sit on our arses and read the paper,' Gambetta moaned, grabbing hold of a small set of steps and wheeling them ahead of him, one of the wheels juddering noisily on the concrete. 'They forget that we have to check every piece of evidence in, and every piece out.'

'Mmm.' Allegra nodded, wondering how on earth he managed to bend down to tie his shoes every day, until she realised that he was wearing slip-ons. Not that that accounted for his socks.

'Most of the time they barely know what the people in their own teams are doing, let alone the other units,' he called back excitedly over his shoulder. 'That's why they missed it.'

The neon tube above where he had stopped was failing, the light stuttering on and off with a loud buzzing noise, creating a strange strobing effect. Climbing up the steps, he retrieved a box that Allegra could see was marked *Cavalli* and dated the fifteenth of March.

'It's the Ricci and Argento cases I'm interested in,' she reminded him impatiently, but he had already placed the box on the top step and ripped the seal off.

'Three murders in three days. They may have me stuck down here in the dark with the rats and the boiler, but I'm not stupid.' He tapped the side of his head with a grin.

'Three murders?' She frowned.

'I left the details on Gallo's answer machine: Luca Cavalli. A lawyer from Melfi they found hanging from the Ponte Sant'Angelo with this in one of his pockets –'

He reached into the box and handed her a clear evidence bag. It contained a small lead disc, the plastic slippery against its dull surface as if it had been coated with a thin layer of oil. And engraved on one side, just about visible in the flickering light, was the outline of two snakes and a clenched fist.

TWENTY-TWO

J. Edgar Hoover Building,
FBI headquarters, Washington DC
18th March – 10.31 a.m.
Tom had given them half an hour or so before making his move. Long enough for Ortiz, Stokes and whoever else had been lurking on the other side of the two-way mirror to have dispersed, but not so long for them to feel the need to check up on him again.

Stepping quickly to the door he flashed Jennifer's pass through the reader. The device beeped, its light flashing from red to green as the magnetic seal was released. The FBI was good at many things but, as he had suspected, operational efficiency wasn't one of them. News of Jennifer's death would still barely have reached the Bureau's higher grades, let alone filtered down to the foot soldiers who manned the IT and security systems.

That gave him a small window of opportunity that would last until someone joined the dots and triggered whatever protocol disabled her access rights and log-ons.

Tom found himself momentarily clinging to this thought. In a way, it was almost as if she wasn't really dead yet, kept alive instead in a sort of digital limbo. Not that it would last, he realised with a heavy heart. Soon a remorseless and faceless bureaucracy would see to it that the delicate electronic threads to Jennifer's life were severed. One by one, bank accounts, driver's licence, social security number, email addresses would all lapse or be cancelled, each heavy keystroke and deleted file wiping a little more of her from the world, until all that would remain were his fading memories.

Swallowing hard and trying to clear his head, Tom ripped the fire evacuation instructions off the back of the door and stepped out into a white corridor. Not wanting to appear lost amidst the thin trickle of people making their way along it, he immediately turned to his right and followed the arrows on the map at the top of the laminated sheet towards what looked like the main fire escape stairwell.

Just before he reached it, however, he came across an open doorway. Glancing inside, he could see that it appeared to be some sort of storeroom – a photocopier idling in the corner, pens, paper and envelopes carefully sorted by type and size stacked on the shelves. More promising was the blue FBI jacket that someone had left hanging over the back of a chair and the internal phone screwed to the wall. Darting inside he slipped the jacket on as a rudimentary disguise, then dialled the operator.

'I'm trying to find Jennifer Browne's office,' He explained when the call was answered. 'She's normally based in New York with the Art Crime Team, but she's been spending some time here lately. I wanted to swing by and surprise her.'

'Let's see,' the voice came back, her fingernails tap-dancing noisily on her keyboard in the background. 'Browne, Jennifer. Oh yeah, she's got her calls diverting to Phil Tucker's office up on five while he's on leave.'

Memorising the room number, Tom slipped back out into the corridor and headed for the stairwell. He knew that this was a long-shot, that the odds of him getting out of this building undetected and with what he needed were slim. But he'd rather take his chances out here, where he at least had some say in the outcome, than sit in a dark room while Jennifer's killer slipped even further over the horizon. He owed her that at least. He wouldn't allow her to fade away.

Clearing the call, the operator immediately dialled another extension.

'Yes, good morning, sir, it's the switchboard. I'm

sorry to bother you, but you asked that we should let you know if anyone asked for the location of Special Agent Browne's office. Well, someone just did.'

TWENTY-THREE

Headquarters of the Guarda di Finanza,
Viale XXI Aprile, Rome
18th March – 4.36 p.m.

'When was this?' Allegra asked, returning the bag containing the lead disc with a puzzled frown.

'The fifteenth,' Gambetta replied, placing it carefully back in the box.

'The fifteenth?' she shot back incredulously. 'He died on the fifteenth of March? Are you sure?'

'That's what it said in the case file,' he confirmed, looking startled by her reaction. 'Why?'

The fifteenth was the Ides of March, the same day that Caesar had been killed over two thousand years before. Cavalli and Ricci's murders weren't just linked by the lead disc. They were echoes of each other.

'What was he doing in Rome?' she asked, ignoring his question.

'He owned a place over in Travestere. Was probably up and down here on business.'

'Who found him?'

'River police on a routine patrol. He was hanging from one of the statues on the bridge – the Angel with the Cross, from what I can remember. Their first thought was that it was a suicide, until some bright spark pointed out that his wrists were tied behind his back. Not to mention that the rope would have decapitated him if he'd jumped from that height.'

'You mean he was deliberately lowered into the water?' Allegra asked in a sceptical tone.

'The current there is quite strong. Whoever killed him clearly wanted to draw it out. Make sure he suffered.'

She detected the same hint of horrified fascination in Gambetta's voice that she'd noticed in herself when she'd first caught sight of Ricci's body.

'Why's the GDF involved? It sounds more like one for the local Questura.'

'It was, until they impounded his Maserati near the Due Ponti metro and found fifty thousand euro in counterfeit notes lining the spare wheel. Anything to do with currency fraud gets referred here.'

She nodded slowly, her excitement at this unexpected breakthrough tempered by the depressing thought that this was probably going to make an already difficult case even more complicated. Something of her concern must have shown in her face because Gambetta fixed her with a worried look.

'Is everything okay? I hope I haven't . . .'

'You did the right thing,' she reassured him. 'I'm sure Colonel Gallo will want to come down here in person to thank you.'

Gambetta beamed, a vain attempt to pull his stomach in and push his chest out making his face flush.

'Do you mind if I have a quick look through the rest of Cavalli's stuff?'

'Of course not. Here, I'll move it over there where you can see properly.' He scooped the box up and led her a short way further down the aisle to where a battered angle-poise lamp decorated with the small stickers found on imported fruit had been arranged on a folding table. 'That's better.'

'Much,' she smiled. 'You've been incredibly –'

There was a rap against the counter window at the far end of the room. Gambetta placed his fingers against his lips.

'Wait here,' he whispered conspiratorially. 'I'll get rid of them.'

He lumbered back towards the entrance, leaving Allegra to go through the rest of the contents of the box. Much of it was what you'd expect to find in someone's pockets: a mobile phone – no longer working – some loose change, reading glasses, a damp box of matches and an empty pack of Marlboro Lights. His wallet, meanwhile, as loaded with the standard everyman paraphernalia of cash, bank cards, identity card and an assortment of disintegrating restaurant receipts.

There was a nice watch too – round and simple with a white face, elegant black Roman numerals and a scrolling date. Unusually, apart from the Greek letter Gamma engraved on the back of the stainless steel case, it seemed to have no make or logo marked anywhere on it, featuring instead a distinctive bright orange second hand which stood out against the muted background. Finally there was a set of keys – house and car, judging from the Maserati key fob.

An angry shout made her glance up towards the entrance. Gambetta seemed to be having an argument with the person on the other side of the window, his voice echoing towards her. As she watched, he stepped away from the window, unclipped his keys from his belt, and waved at her to get back.

Allegra didn't have to be told what to do. Still clutching Cavalli's keys, she retreated to the far end of the aisle and hid. Gambetta had done her a favour by letting her in here and the last thing she wanted to do was get him in trouble. Even so, she couldn't quite resist peering around the edge of the pier as he unbolted the door.

She never even saw the gun, the rolling echo

of the shot's silenced thump breaking over her like a wave before she'd even realised what was happening. The next thing she knew, Gambetta was staggering back, his arms flailing at his throat, legs buckling like an elephant caught in a poacher's snare. He swayed unsteadily for a few moments longer, desperately trying to stay on his feet. Then, with a bellow, he crashed to the concrete floor.

TWENTY-FOUR

J. Edgar Hoover Building,
FBI headquarters, Washington DC
18th March – 10.37 a.m.

The fifth floor was much busier than the one he had just come from. Even so, Tom wasn't worried about being recognised. Of the eight thousand or so people who worked out of this building, he doubted whether any more than five knew who he was. And rather than hinder him, the floor's bustling, largely open-plan configuration made it easier for him to blend in and move around unchallenged.

What was immediately clear, however, was that here, news of what had happened last night in Vegas had already spread. There was a strained atmosphere, people going about their usual business with a forced normality, judging from their sombre faces and the irritable edge to their voices. Tom, it seemed, wasn't the only one who was finding comfort in anger's rough-hewn arms. And yet, amidst the bitterness, he detected something else in people's eyes, something unsaid but no less powerfully felt. Relief. Relief that it hadn't been them. He wondered how many people had called up their wives or boyfriends or children this morning upon hearing what had happened, just to hear the sound of their voice. Just to let them know that they were okay.

As the operator had suggested, Tom found the room Jennifer had been camping out in the north-eastern quadrant of the building. Like all the other offices that lined the perimeter of the floor, it was essentially a glass box, albeit one with a view of 9th Street and a nameplate denoting the identity of its rightful owner – Phil Tucker. Unlike the rooms which flanked it, however, its door was shut and all the blinds drawn in what Tom assumed was a subtle and yet deliberately symbolic mark of respect. Less clear was whether this was a spontaneous reaction to Jennifer's death or part of some well-defined and yet unwritten mourning ritual that was observed whenever a colleague fell in the line of duty. Either way, it suited him well, concealing him from view once he had satisfied himself that no one was watching him and slipped inside.

Almost immediately, Tom's heart sank. Perhaps without realising it until now, he had secretly been hoping to find a bit more of Jennifer here, even though he knew that this had only ever been a very recent and temporary home for her. Instead it boasted a sterile anonymity that was only partly lifted by Tucker's scattered photographs and random personal trinkets. Then again, he couldn't help but wonder if Jennifer's hand wasn't perhaps present in the clinical symmetry of the pens laid out on the desktop and the ordered stack of files and papers on the bookshelf, that he suspected had probably been littering the floor when she had first taken ownership of the room. And there was no debating who was responsible for the lipstick-smeared rim of the polystyrene cup that was still nestling in the trash. He gave a rueful smile. She had been here, after all. He was a guest, not an intruder.

The safe was in a cupboard under the book-shelf. With a weary sigh, he saw that it was protected by both a password and voice-recognition software, two red lights glowing ominously over the small input screen. Tricky. Very tricky, unless . . . He glanced up at her desk hopefully. The light on her phone was glowing red to indicate that somebody had left her a voice-mail. With any luck, that also meant that she'd recorded a greeting.

He picked the phone up and dialled Jennifer's extension, the second line beeping furiously until it tripped over into the voicemail system.

'You've reached Special Agent Jennifer Browne

in the FBI's Art Crime Team . . .' Tom's stomach flipped over at the sound of her voice, as if he'd just gone over a sharp hump in the road. She sounded so close, so real that for a moment it was almost as if . . . It was no use, he knew. This was an illusion that would dissolve the moment he tried to warp his arms around it. He needed to stay focused. 'Please leave a message . . .'

He replaced the handset. That would do. Now for the password. He bent down and opened each of the desk drawers, guessing that the lipstick on the cup was a sign that Jennifer, for all her refusal to play conventional sexual politics at work, had still occasionally worn make-up. He was right. The third drawer down yielded a small make-up bag and within that, a powder brush.

Kneeling next to the safe, he gently dusted the brush over the keys and then carefully blew away the excess. The result certainly wasn't good enough to lift prints from, but it did allow him to see which keys had been most recently and heavily used, the powder sticking more thickly to the sweat left there.

Reading from left to right, this highlighted the letters A, C, R, V, G, I and O. Tom jotted them down in a circle on a piece of paper, knowing that they formed an anagram of some other word, although there was no way of telling how many times each letter had been used. The key was to try and get inside Jennifer's head. She would have chosen something current, something relevant to what she had been working on. A name, a place, a person . . . Tom smiled, seeing that the last three letters had given him an obvious clue. G, I, O – Caravaggio, perhaps? He typed the word in and one of the two lights flashed green.

Reaching the phone down from the desk, he listened to Jennifer's greeting a few more times to get a feel for the timing of exactly when she said her name. Then, just at the right moment, he placed the handset against the microphone before quickly snatching it away again. The second light flashed green. With a whir, the door sprang open.

He reached inside and pulled out a handful of files and a stack of surveillance DVDs. Returning the discs to the safe, he flicked through the files, discarding them all apart from one that Jennifer had initialled in her characteristically slanting hand.

Sitting at the desk, he unsealed the file and scanned through it, quickly recognising in the typed pages and photographs the details of the case that Jennifer had laid out for him on their way to Vegas. The anonymous Customs tip-off. The discovery of the Eileen Gray furniture hidden in the container. The tracing of the container to a warehouse in Queen's. The raid on the warehouse and the discovery of an Aladdin's cave of illegally exported antiquities. The panic-stricken dealer's stumbling confession. A copy of his doodled sketch of the two snakes wrapped around a clenched fist, the symbol of the so-called Delian League that the forensic lab had reconstituted from strips of yellow paper recovered from his shredding bin. Bank statements. An auction catalogue. And, of course, the name provided by the dealer which Jennifer had passed on to the Italian authorities who had rewarded her with an address in Rome and a promise to follow-up: Luca Cavalli, Vicolo de Panieri, Travestere. It wasn't much, but it was a start.

Closing the file with a satisfied smile he stood up, only to brush against the mouse as he turned to leave. The log-on screen immediately flickered on, the cursor flashing tauntingly at him. He stared at it for a few moments and then, shrugging, sat down again. It was worth a try.

TWENTY-FIVE

**Headquarters of the Guarda di Finanza,
Viale XXI Aprile, Rome
18th March – 4.41 p.m.**

Allegra snatched her head back, heart thudding, fist clenched, the teeth of Cavalli's keys biting into her palm. Gambetta shot. No, executed. Executed here, right in front of her, in the basement of the Guarda di Finanza headquarters. It was ridiculous. It was impossible. And yet she'd seen it. She'd seen it and she only had to close her eyes to see it all over again.

Now wasn't the time to panic, she knew. She needed to stay calm, think through her options. Not that she had many, beyond staying exactly where she was. Not with her gun stranded on the edge of Gambetta's desk and only the length of the room separating her from the killer. Perhaps if she was quiet, she reasoned, he wouldn't even realise . . .

The sudden hiss of polyester on concrete interrupted her skittering thoughts. She frowned, at
first unable to place the noise, until with a sickening lurch of her stomach she realised that it was
the sound of Gambetta's corpse being dragged
towards her.

She knew immediately what she had to do.
Move. Move now while she still could; while the
killer was still far enough away not to see or hear
her. In a way, he'd made things easier for her.
Now all she had to do was figure out which aisle
he was coming down. As soon as she knew that,
she'd be able to creep back to the entrance up one
of the other ones. At least, that was the idea.

She shut her eyes and concentrated on the
noise of the fabric of Gambetta's uniform
catching on the tiny imperfections in the
concrete, fighting her instinct to run as the tick-
tock of the killer's breathing got closer and closer,
knowing that she had to be absolutely sure.
Then, when it seemed that he must be almost
on top of her, she opened them again. The second
aisle. She was sure of it. The one she'd been
standing in a few moments before when looking
through Cavalli's evidence box.

Taking a deep breath, she edged her head
around the pier and peeked along the first aisle.
It was empty. Her eyes briefly fluttered shut with
relief. Then, crouching down, she slipped her shoes
off and began to creep towards the exit, her

stockinged feet sliding silkily across the cold floor. But she'd scarcely gone ten yards before suddenly, almost involuntarily, she paused.

She could see the killer.

Not his face, of course, but his back; through a narrow gap between the shelves as he dragged Gambetta towards her. Maybe if she . . .? No, she dismissed the thought almost as soon as it had occurred to her. It was stupid; she needed to get out of here while she still could. But then again, she couldn't help herself thinking, what if someone here was working with him? It would certainly explain how he had got in. What if they now helped him escape in the confusion once she raised the alarm? She couldn't risk that, not after what he'd done. A glimpse of his face, that was all she needed. Just enough to be able to give a description, if it came to that. If she was careful and stayed out of the light, he wouldn't even know she was there.

Her mind made up, she edged carefully forward, trying to find a place where she could stand up without being seen, occasionally seeing the blur of the killer's leg and his black shoes through cracks in the shelving as he backed towards her. Then, without warning, when he was almost parallel to her, Gambetta's feet fell to the floor with an echoing thud.

Sensing her chance, she slowly straightened up, occasional gaps and openings between the shelves giving her first a glimpse of a belt, then the arrow tip of a tie, followed by the buttons of his jacket and finally the starched whiteness of his collar and the soft pallor of his throat. Through a narrow slit between two boxes.

There. She could see his face, or rather the outline of it, the overhead neon tube having blinked off yet again. Holding her breath, she waited until, with a clinking noise, the light stuttered on again, the image strobing briefly across her retina until it finally settled.

It was Gallo.

She instinctively snatched her head back, but the sudden blur of movement must have caught his eye because he called out angrily.

There was no time to think. No time to do anything. Except run. Run to the door, throw the bolts back, tumble through it, stumble up the steps and stagger out into the street, gasping with shock.

The world on its head.

TWENTY-SIX

**J. Edgar Hoover Building,
FBI headquarters, Washington DC
18th March – 10.47 a.m.**

Tom had found Jennifer's password taped to the underside of the stapler. No great mystery there. It was always the same in these large organisations. Obsessed by security, IT insisted on people using 'strong' passwords that had to be changed every five minutes, and then claimed to be surprised when people chose to write them down. What else did they expect when most people struggled to remember their wedding anniversary, let alone a randomly assigned and ever-changing ten-character alphanumeric code. The government was the worst offender of all.

He typed the password in and hit the enter key. Almost immediately the screen went blue. Then it sounded a long, strident beep. Finally it flashed up an ominously bland error message.

User ID and password not recognised. Please remain at your desk and an IT security representative will be with you shortly.

The phone started to ring. Tom checked the display and saw that it was Stokes, presumably tipped off by some clever piece of software that someone was trying to access Jennifer's account. The Bureau was clearly more nimble and joined up than Tom had given them credit for earlier.

Shoving the file under his jacket, he leapt across to the door and, gingerly lifting the blind, looked outside. To his relief, everything seemed normal, the people working in the open-plan team room on the other side of the corridor still gazing into their screens or talking on the phone. Checking that no one was coming, he slipped out of the office and headed back towards the stairs and swiped the door open.

Almost immediately he jumped back, the stairwell thundering with the sound of heavy footsteps and urgent shouts that he knew instinctively were heading towards him. He glanced around, looking for somewhere to hide and realising that he had only moments to find it. But before he could move, he felt a heavy hand grip his shoulder. He spun round. It was Ortiz, his chest heaving, eyes staring.

'This way,' he wheezed, urging him towards an open office. 'Quickly.'

Tom hesitated for a fraction of a second, but

the lack of a better option quickly made up his mind for him. Following him inside, Tom watched as Ortiz shut the door behind him and let the blinds drop with a fizz of nylon through his fingers.

'Can you really find them?' he panted, peering through a narrow crack as a group of armed men, led by Stokes, charged past them towards Jennifer's office.

'What?' Tom asked, not sure he'd heard right.

'Jennifer's killers? Can you find them?' Ortiz repeated, spinning round to face him, his face glistening, the half-hidden tattoo on his neck pulsing as if it was alive.

'I can find them.' Tom nodded. 'If I can get out of here, I can find them.'

Ortiz stared at him unblinkingly, as if trying to look for the trap that might be lurking behind Tom's eyes.

'Where are you going to go?'

'It's probably better you don't know.'

'What will you do?'

'Whatever I have to,' Tom reassured him in a cold voice. 'What you can't. What Jennifer deserves.'

Ortiz nodded slowly and gave a deep sigh, Tom's words seeming to calm him.

'Good.' He stepped forward and pressed his card into Tom's hand, pulling him closer until their faces were only inches apart. 'Just call me when it's done.'

Releasing his grip, Ortiz reached out and with a jerk of his wrist, flicked the fire alarm switch. The siren's shrill cry split the air.

'Go,' he muttered, his eyes dropping to the floor. 'Get outside with everyone else before I change my mind.'

With a nod, Tom sprinted back towards the stairwell, the siren bouncing deliriously off the walls. Taking the steps two at a time, he raced down towards the ground floor, doors above and below him crashing open as people streamed on to the staircase, their excited voices suggesting that they knew this wasn't a drill.

As he cleared the first-floor landing, however, he was forced to slow to a walk, the crowd backing up ahead of him. Peering over their heads, he saw that a line of security guards was quickly checking everyone's ID before allowing them to leave the building. Had Stokes tipped them off, guessing that he might be using the alarm as cover? Either way, Tom had to do something and do something quickly, before the tide of people behind him swept him into the guards' waiting arms.

Waiting until he was almost at the bottom of the penultimate flight of stairs, Tom deliberately tripped the man ahead of him and, with a sharp shove, sent him crashing into the wall opposite. He smacked into it with a sickening crunch, a deep gash opening up in his forehead, the blood streaming down his face.

'Let me through,' Tom called, hauling the dazed man to his feet and throwing his arm around his shoulder. 'Let me through.'

'Get out the way,' somebody above him called.

'Get back,' someone else echoed. 'Man down.'

Seeing Tom staggering towards them, one of the guards stepped forward and supported the injured man on the other side. Together they lifted him along the narrow path that had miraculously opened through the middle of the crowd, people grimacing in sympathy at the unnatural angle of the man's nose.

'He needs a doctor,' Tom called urgently. 'He's losing a lot of blood.'

'This way, sir.'

The line of guards parted to let them through, another officer escorting them clear as he radioed for a medic. Reaching a safe distance, they sat the still groggy man down on the sidewalk, an ambulance announcing its arrival moments later by unnecessarily laying down three feet of rubber as it stopped. The paramedics jumped out, threw a foil blanket around the man's shoulders and pressed a wet compress against his nose to stem the flow. Tom stepped back, leaving the two guards to crowd round with words of advice and encouragement. Then, seeing that no one was watching, he turned and walked away.

Standing at a seventh-storey window, FBI Director Green watched Tom disappear down D

Street with a smile. Smartly dressed with a crisp parting in his brown hair, plump cheeks and perfectly capped teeth, he was engaged in a running battle with his weight, the various scarred notches on his belt showing the yo-yo fluctuations of his waistline.

He knew Kirk well enough to guess that he'd find a way out of that room and that, when he did, he'd head straight for Browne's safe. That's why he'd ordered her swipe card not to be cancelled. That's why he'd briefed the operator to let him know if anyone called asking for directions to her office.

The truth was that Kirk was her best chance now. While the Bureau was holding its collective dick worrying about who was going to get blamed for one of its most promising young agents getting killed, Kirk would be out there making things happen. Browne had trusted Kirk with her life many times before now. It seemed only right to trust him with her death too.

TWENTY-SEVEN

Viale XXI Aprile, Rome
18th March – 4.51 p.m.

Panting, Allegra sprinted on to the Via Gaetano Moroni and then right on to Via Luigi Pigorini, the cars here parked with typical Roman indifference – some up on the kerb, others end-on to fit into an impossibly narrow gap.

Gallo . . . a killer? It made no sense. It was impossible. But how could she ignore what she'd seen? The shots fired from the doorway; Gambetta staggering backwards and toppling to the floor like a felled tree; Gallo's animal grunt as he had hauled the carcass across the concrete; his stony face and cold eyes.

She found her stride, her ragged breathing slowly falling into a more comfortable rhythm, her thoughts settling.

Had Gallo seen her face? She wasn't sure. Either way, it wouldn't take him long to pull the security footage. The only thing that mattered now was getting as far away from him as she could.

Seeing a taxi, she flagged it down and settled with relief into the back seat as she gave him her home address up on the Aventine Hill.

Whether Gallo had seen her or not, at least his motives seemed pretty clear. He'd killed Gambetta so that he couldn't tell anyone else about his discovery of the links between the murders. Why else would he have paused under the faltering neon light where Gambetta had taken Cavalli's evidence box down from its shelf. He'd been looking for the lead disc, so that no one else would think or know to make the connection. No one apart from her.

'What number?' the driver called back over his shoulder ten minutes later as they drew on to the Via Guerrieri.

'Drive to the end,' she ordered.

With a shrug, he accelerated down the street, tyres drumming on the cobbles as Allegra sank low into her seat and peered cautiously over the edge of the window sill.

There. About fifty yards past the entrance to her apartment. A dark blue Alfa with two men sat in the front, their mirrors set at an unnatural angle so they could see back up the street behind them. She didn't recognise the driver as they flashed past, but the passenger . . . the passenger, she realised with a sinking heart, was Salvatore.

Not only had Gallo clearly seen her, but he had already unleashed his men on to her trail.

'Keep going,' she called, keeping her head down. 'I've changed my mind. Take me to . . . Take me to the Via Galvani,' she ordered, settling on the only other place she could think of. 'It's off the Via Marmorata.'

Making a face, the driver mumbled something about women and directions, only to roll his eyes when they reached the Via Galvani ten minutes later and she again asked him to drive down it without stopping.

'Do you even know where you're going?' he called back tersely over his shoulder.

'Does it even matter as long as you get paid?' she snapped as she warily scanned the street. This time there was no sign of Gallo or any of his men. 'Here, this will do.'

Paying him, she got out and walked back up the street towards Aurelio's apartment.

'*Ego sum principium mundi et finis sæculorum attamen non sum deus,*' came the voice from the speaker.

'Not now, Aurelio,' Allegra snapped. 'Just let me in.'

There was the briefest of pauses. Then the door buzzed open. She made her way to the lift. Aurelio was waiting for her on the landing, a worried look on his face.

'What's happened?' he asked as she stepped out.

'I'm in trouble.'

'I can see that. Come in.'

He led her silently into his office and perched anxiously on one arm of his leather chair rather than settling back into his seat as usual. Pacing from one side of the room to the other and speaking in as dispassionate a tone as she could, she described what she'd seen and heard: the Cavalli murder; the engraved discs; Gambetta's shooting; the flickering shadow of Gallo's pale face. Aurelio listened to all this while turning over a small piece of broken tile in his hands, studying it intently as if looking for something. When she eventually finished, there was a long silence.

'It's my fault.' He spoke with a cold whisper. 'If I'd known . . . I should never have got you involved with any of this.'

'If you want to blame someone blame Gallo,' she insisted with a hollow laugh.

'I know someone. A detective in the police,' Aurelio volunteered. 'I could call him and –'

'No,' she cut him off with a firm shake of her head. 'No police. Not until I understand what's going on. Not until I know who I can trust.'

'Then what do you need?'

'A place to stay. A coffee. Some answers.'

'The first two I can help with. The third . . . well, the third we might have to work on together.'

'Two out of three's a good start.' She bent down and planted a grateful kiss on his forehead.

'I should offer to make the coffee more often.' He grinned. 'Here, sit.' Aurelio stood up and pulled her towards his chair. 'Rest.'

She shut her eyes and tried to clear her mind, finding the familiar smell of Aurelio's aftershave and the merry clatter of pans and clink of crockery as he busied himself in the kitchen strangely comforting. For a few seconds she imagined herself back at home, perched on the worktop, eagerly telling her mother about what had happened that day at school while she prepared dinner. But almost immediately her eyes snapped open.

Rest? How could she rest, after what she'd just seen? How could she rest, that Gallo was out there somewhere, looking for her.

She jumped up and padded cautiously to the window, standing to one side so she could check the street below without being seen. It was empty. Good. As far as she knew, she'd never spoken to Gallo or anyone else on the team about her friendship with Aurelio, so there was no reason to think they would come looking for her here. Not that she was in a position to put up much of a fight if they did, given that she was unarmed.

The realisation made her feel strangely vulnerable, and she patted her hip regretfully, missing her weapon's reassuring solidity and steadying ballast. If only . . . she had a sudden thought and glanced across at Aurelio's desk. Somewhere inside it, she seemed to remember, he had a gun. It was completely illegal, of course – a Soviet Makarov PM that he'd picked up in a souk to protect himself from the local bandits while working on a dig in Anatalya. But right now, she wasn't sure that mattered.

She crossed over to the desk, noticing the closely typed notes for a lecture that according to the cover page Aurelio was giving at the Galleria Doria Pamphilj the following day. Crouching down next to it, she tried each of the overflowing drawers in turn, her fingers eventually closing around the weapon at the back of the third drawer, behind some cassette tapes and a fistful of receipts.

She slid out the eight-round magazine. It was full and she tapped it sharply against the desk in case the spring was stiff and the bullets had slipped away from the front of the casing. The gun itself was well maintained and looked like it had recently been oiled, the slide pulling back easily, the hammer firing with a satisfyingly solid click. It wasn't much, she knew, but it was certainly better than nothing. Satisfied, she slapped the magazine home.

Deriving a renewed confidence from her find, she sat down again in Aurelio's chair and tried to clear her head. But she soon found her thoughts wandering again. To Gambetta and what he'd told her; to Gallo and her escape; to Salvatore and how close she'd come to falling into his grasp; to Aurelio and the sanctuary he was providing. And annoyingly, to the riddle that she had ignored earlier, but which had now popped back into her head.

'I am the beginning of the world and the end of ages, but I am not God.' She repeated the line to herself with a frown.

The beginning of the world – Genesis, dawn, a baby? But then how were any of these the end, she asked herself. And who else but God could claim to be at the beginning and end of time? Maybe she needed to be more literal, she mused – the Latin for world was *mundi* and for ages was *sæculorum*, so the beginning of mundi was . . . her eyes snapped open.

'It's the letter M,' she called out triumphantly. 'The beginning of *mundi* and the end of *sæculorum* is the letter M.'

Grinning, she walked into the kitchen. To her surprise it was empty, the kettle boiling unattended on the stove. Frowning, she turned the hob off and then stepped back into the hall.

'Aurelio?' she called, reaching warily for the gun.

There was no answer, although she thought she heard the faint echo of his voice coming from his bedroom. She stepped over to it, a narrow slit of light bisecting the worn floorboards where the door hadn't quite been pulled to. Not wanting to interrupt, she pressed her ear against the crack and then froze. He was talking about her.

'Yes, she's here now,' she heard him say in an

urgent voice. 'Of course I can keep her here. Why, what do you need her for?'

She backed away, the gun raised towards the door, her face pale, heart pounding, the blood screaming in her ears. First Gallo. Now Aurelio too?

Her eyes stinging, she turned and stumbled out of the apartment, down the stairs and on to the street, not knowing if she was crying from sadness or anger. Not sure if she even cared.

Not sure if she cared about anything any more.

TWENTY-EIGHT

**Villa de Rome apartment building,
Boulevard de Suisse, Monte Carlo, Monaco
18th March – 5.23 p.m.**

It was earlier than usual, but then Ronan D'Arcy figured he'd earned it. After a bloodbath in the first few months of the year, some of his shorts were finally beginning to pay off and the latest round of Middle Eastern sabre rattling had pushed his oil futures back to historic highs. If that didn't warrant a drink, what did?

A helicopter droned overhead, circling low over the palace up on the hill, and then swooping back around to perch gracefully on the deck of one of the larger yachts lying at anchor in the harbour, the sea glittering like gold in the sinking sunlight. D'Arcy gave a rueful smile. It didn't matter how good the market was or how well you thought you were doing, someone else, somewhere, was always doing better. It was a lesson that this place seemed to take a sadistic pleasure in beating into him at every opportunity. Still, he wasn't going to let it spoil his little celebration.

He stepped off the balcony back into his office and quickly scanned the six trading screens that formed a low, incandescent wall on his desk to check that some random market sneeze hadn't wiped out a good month's work. Reassured, he picked up the phone and dialled the internal extension to the kitchen. If it had been a beer he could have fixed it himself, of course – he wasn't that lazy. But celebrations called for cocktails, and cocktails called for mojitos, and Determination was the mojito-master.

Determination. He'd never get used to that name. It was from Botswana, or some other spearchucking African country that he'd never been able to find on a map. He'd heard of names such as Hope and Faith and Temperance. Even a Chastity, if you could believe that. But Determination . . .?

Maybe it wasn't the name but the irony of it that jarred, D'Arcy reflected, his tanned forehead creasing in annoyance as the phone rang unanswered. Indolence. That would have been a more appropriate name. Lethargy. Torpidity. Yes, that was a good one. Where was the shiftless bastard now?

He slammed the phone down and clicked his mouse to bring up the apartment's internal closed circuit TV system. The kitchen, laundry room, gym and billiard room were all empty. So too were the sitting rooms and the dining room. Which only left the . . .

D'Arcy paused, having suddenly noticed that, according to the camera in the entrance hall, the front door was wide open.

'For fuck's sake,' he swore. What was the point of flying in a specialist security company from Israel to fit armoured doors if the stupid fucker was going to leave them wide open?

Muttering angrily under his breath, he turned to leave, and then paused. The lights were on in the corridor outside, the travertine marble floor reflecting a narrow strip of light under his office door. But the pale band was broken by several dark shapes. Someone was standing outside, listening.

He punched the emergency shut-down button on his trading system and then sprang across to the bookcase. In the same instant the door burst open and two men came tumbling through the gap, guns raised. D'Arcy hit the panic-room release button. A section of the bookcase slid back and he leapt inside. The men started firing, the silenced shots searing the air with a fup-fupping noise. He slammed his hand against the 'close' switch, the door crashing shut with a hydraulic thump, leaving him in a strange deadened silence that echoed with the rasping gasps of his adrenaline-charged breathing.

'Fuck, fuck, fuck . . .' Frantically he scrabbled in the sickly light for the phone. It was dead, his clammy fingers sliding on the moulded plastic as he stabbed at the hook switch. There was no dial tone, the line presumably cut at the junction box downstairs.

'Mobile,' he breathed, patting his jacket and trouser pockets excitedly until, his heart sinking, his eyes flicked to the monitor which showed a picture of his office. His phone was still where he'd left it on his desk.

He quickly reassessed his situation. Without a phone, there was no way of letting anyone know he was in here. That meant he'd have to wait until someone came looking for him. The chances were that his brokers in London would raise the alarm when he missed their usual morning call. That would be in – he checked his watch – less than sixteen hours' time. In the meantime he was quite safe. After all, he'd had this place installed by a Brazilian firm who specialised in kidnap prevention. It had five-inch-thick steel walls, forty-eight hours of battery life if they cut the power, access to the CCTV system and a month's worth of supplies. He might as well make himself comfortable and enjoy the show.

He sat back, his pulse slowing, and watched the men with an amused expression. They were arguing, he noticed with a smile. Probably trying to figure out which of them would carry the can for him having got away. At least he only planned to fire Determination, he thought to himself. Judging by their brutal methods, he doubted whether whoever had sent these two would be as forgiving when they learnt of his escape.

Suddenly he sat forward, his face drawn into a puzzled frown. The arguing had stopped, the men now intent on emptying the bookcase on to the floor and arranging its contents into a large uneven mound that pressed up against the panic room's concealed entrance. Seemingly satisfied, they turned their attention to the walls, ripping the paintings down and tossing them on to the pile. They reserved special treatment for his Picasso, one of the men punching his fist through the *Portrait of Jacqueline* that had found its way to D'Arcy after being stolen a few years before from Picasso's granddaughter's apartment in Paris. Then he sent it spinning through the air to join the others.

D'Arcy shook his head, swearing angrily. Did they think he would come charging out to save a few old books and a painting? He valued his life far more dearly than that. Their petty vandalism was as pointless as it was . . .

He lost his train of thought, noticing with a frown that one of the men seemed to be spraying some sort of liquid over the jumble of books and canvases and wooden frames, while the other had lit a match. Glancing up at the camera with a smile, as if to make sure D'Arcy had seen them, the man with the match stepped forward and dropped it on to the pile. The screen flared white, momentarily blinded by a whoosh of fire.

D'Arcy was gripped by a chilling realisation. His eyes rose slowly from the screen to the small metal grille positioned in the right-hand corner of the panic room. To the thin tendrils of acrid smoke that were even now snaking through its narrow openings. To the acid taste at the back of his throat as he felt his lungs begin to clench.

TWENTY-NINE

Vicolo de Panieri, Travestere, Rome
19th March – 7.03 a.m.
Tom had booked himself on to the afternoon flight
out of DC, taking the obvious precaution of using
another name. He never travelled without at least
two changes of identity stitched into his bag's
lining and luckily the FBI had not thought to check
whether he had left anything with the concierge
at the hotel he'd been staying in the previous
night.

There had been a relatively low-key police presence at Reagan International. Understandable, given
that the FBI would probably be focusing all their
efforts on the Vegas area if they were serious about
catching him. After all, he'd dropped a pretty strong
hint to Stokes that that was where he'd head in
the first instance to pick up the killer's trail.

He'd managed to snatch a few hours' sleep,
recouping a little of what he'd lost over the past

two days, and then spent the rest of the flight reading through Jennifer's file in a bit more detail. Most of it was by now familiar to him, although he had paused over the witness statements, bank records and various other documents that the FBI had seized in their raid on the art dealer's warehouse in Queen's which he hadn't seen before. One, in particular, stood out and had triggered the call he was making now as his taxi swept into the city along the A91, accompanied by the dawn traffic and the chirping tones of the driver's sat-nav system.

'Archie?' he said, as soon as he picked up.

'Tom?' Archie rasped, jet lag and what Tom guessed had probably been a heavy night at the hotel bar combining to give his voice a ragged croak. 'What time is it? Where the hell are you?'

'Rome,' Tom answered.

'Rome?' he repeated sleepily, the muffled noise of something being knocked to the floor suggesting that he was groping for his watch or the alarm clock with one hand while digging the sleep out of his eyes with the other. 'What the fuck are you doing in Rome? You're meant to be in Zurich. What number is this?'

'Jennifer's dead,' Tom said sharply. 'It was a set-up. The Caravaggio. The exchange. They were waiting for us.'

'Shit.' Any hint of tiredness had immediately evaporated from Archie's voice. 'You all right?'

'I'm fine.'

'What the fuck happened?'

'Sniper,' Tom said, trying not to think about what he'd seen or heard or felt, concentrating on just sticking to the facts. 'Professional job.'

'You're sure she was the target?'

'Pretty sure. Have you ever heard of an antiquities-smuggling operation called the Delian League?'

'No. Why? Is that who you think did it?'

'That's what I'm in Rome to find out. That's why I need you in Geneva.'

'Of course,' Archie replied instantly. 'Whatever you need, mate.'

'There's a sale at Sotheby's this afternoon,' Tom said, glancing down at the circled entry in the Geneva auction catalogue that had been included in the file. 'One of the lots is a statue of Artemis. It looks like Jennifer thought it was important. I want to know why.'

'No worries,' Archie reassured him. 'What about you? What's in Rome?'

'A name. Luca Cavalli. He was fingered by someone Jennifer arrested in New York. I thought I'd start with him and work my way back up the ladder.'

A pause.

'Tom . . .' Archie spoke haltingly, for once lost for words. 'Listen, mate, I'm sorry. I know you two were . . . I'm really sorry.'

Tom had thought that sharing the news of Jennifer's murder with Archie might help unburden him in some way. But his hesitant awkwardness was so unusual that it was actually having the opposite effect, forcing Tom to reflect yet again on the events that had brought him here, rather than focus on the immediate task at hand.

'Are you going to be all right?'

'I'll be fine,' Tom said. 'Just call me on this number when you get there.'

About fifteen minutes later the taxi pulled up. Tom stepped out.

It was a wide, cobbled street largely populated by neat four-storey buildings with symmetrical balconies and brightly coloured plaster walls. Cavalli's house, by contrast, was a feral, hulking shape. Long and only two storeys high, its stonework was grey and wizened by age, the roof sagging under a red blister of sun-cracked tiles, the flaking green shutters at its upstairs windows betraying years of neglect. An old horse block stood to the right of the front door, while to the left, a large dilapidated arched gate suggested that the building had once served as some sort of workshop or garage.

For a moment, Tom wondered if he'd been misled by the sat-nav's confident tone and been dropped off in the wrong place. But the seals on the door and the laminated notice declaring the premises a court-protected crime scene removed any lingering doubts. He was definitely in the right place. It just looked as though he was too late.

Hitching his bag across his shoulders and checking that the street was empty, Tom clambered quickly up the drainpipe, glad that he had changed out of his suit. Reaching across to the window, he could see that although it had been closed shut, the frame was warped and the latch old and loose. Pushing a knife into a narrow gap, he levered the blade back and forth, shaking the window so that the latch slowly worked itself free, until it popped open and he was able to clamber inside.

He found himself in what he assumed was a bedroom, although it was hard to be sure, the contents of the wardrobe having been swept on to the floor, the bed propped against the wall and the chest flipped on to its back, its emptied drawers lying prostrate at its side. It struck Tom that there was a deliberate violence in the way that the room had been upended. The police, for all their clumsiness, usually searched with a little more restraint. The people who had done this, however, hadn't just been looking for something. They'd been trying to make a point.

He exited the bedroom on to a glass and stainless steel walkway that ran the length of the building and looked down on to a wide, double-

height living space. Here the décor was as modern
as the outside had been neglected, the back wall
made of folding glass panels and looking out on
to a small walled garden, the floor a dull mirror
of polished concrete, the galley kitchen a mass of
stainless steel that looked like it might double as
an operating theatre.

Tom stepped along the walkway past a bathroom and another bedroom that had been
similarly turned upside down. Then he made his
way down a glass staircase to the ground floor,
its icicle-like glass treads protruding unsupported
from the wall. Down here, the brutality of the
assault was, if anything, even more marked – the
large plasma screen lifted off its brackets and
broken almost in two across a chair; the seats and
backs of the leather furniture slashed open, their
innards ripped out in handfuls through the deep
gashes; the coffee table overturned and its metal
legs stamped on so that they were bent into
strange, deviant shapes; the bookcase forced on
to its front, crushing its contents underneath.
There was a distinctive and unpleasant aroma too,
and it was a few moments before Tom was able
to guess at its meaning – not content with
defeating these inanimate foes, the assailants had,
it seemed, chosen to mark their victory by
urinating on them.

A sudden noise from the front door made Tom
look up. Someone was coming in, the bottom lock

clunking open, the key now slipping into the top one. He knew immediately he wouldn't have enough time to make it back upstairs.

That only left him one option.

THIRTY

19th March – 7.22 a.m.

The seal ripped as the door opened. Someone stepped inside and then quickly eased it shut behind them. They paused. Then, with careful, hesitant footsteps, they walked down the small entrance hallway towards him.

Tom, his back pressed to the wall, waited until the intruder was almost level with him and then leapt out, sending their gun spinning across the floor with a chop to the wrist. Rather than press his advantage, however, Tom paused, surprised by the sudden realisation as he caught sight of their dark hair, that it was a woman. But this momentary hesitation was all the invitation she needed to turn and crash her right fist into his jaw, the force of the blow sending him staggering back with a grunt. Spinning round, she stretched towards the gun, but Tom stuck out a leg and tripped her, sending her sprawling headlong into an upturned chair. In a flash he was on top of her, digging his knee into the small of her back, trying to pin her arms to her sides. But with surprising force, she reached behind and, grabbing his arm, flipped him over her head and on to the floor, winding him.

Again she turned and scrambled towards the gun, but Tom, still coughing and trying to get his breath just managed to grab one of her ankles and drag her back, her leg thrashing wildly until she was able to kick herself free. Struggling to her feet, she reached down and grabbed one of the dislocated struts from the coffee table and then lunged at him with it, her face contorted with rage. Tom sidestepped the first downward swipe aimed at his head, but the second wild swing struck him with a painful thump at the top of his right arm, momentarily numbing it. Her attack provided him with an opening, however, because with his other hand he reached out and grabbed the end of the metal rod, and then yanked it sideways. The woman went with it, tripping over a small pile of books and collapsing on to her knees. By the time she was on her feet, the gun was in Tom's hands and aimed at her stomach.

'*Trovisi giù,*' he wheezed. Her chest heaving, she gave him a long, hateful look and then lay face down on the floor as he'd ordered. Tom quickly patted her down, finding her wallet in her jeans pocket.

'*Siedasi là,*' he ordered as he opened it, waving

the gun at a chair. Her eyes burning, she pulled herself to her feet, righted the chair he had indicated, and then sat in it.

'*Siete un poliziotto?*' he asked in surprise, the sight of her ID made him feel a little less embarrassed about his sore chin and throbbing arm. Tall and obviously strong, she was wearing jeans, a tight brown leather jacket and red ballet-style pumps. She was also very striking, with olive skin, a jet-black bob that was cut in a square fringe around her face and mismatched blue and brown eyes embedded within a smoky grey eye shadow. There was something odd about her appearance, though. Something that Tom couldn't quite put his finger on yet, that didn't quite fit.

'Congratulations,' she replied. 'You've managed to assault a police officer and trespass on a crime scene before most people have got out of bed.'

'Where did you learn English?' Tom's Italian was good, but her English, while slightly accented, was almost faultless.

She ignored him. 'Put the gun down.'

'You tell me what you're doing here and I'll think about it,' he offered unsmilingly.

'Who are you working for? Gallo?' she shot back, ignoring his question.

'Who's Gallo?'

'He didn't send you?' There was a hint of hope as well as disbelief in her voice.

'Nobody *sent* me,' he said. 'I work for myself. I'm looking for Cavalli.'

A pause.

'Cavalli's dead.'

'Shit,' Tom swore, pinching the top of his nose and shutting his eyes as he gave a long, weary sigh. Cavalli had been his main hope of working his way back up the Delian League to whoever had ordered the hit. 'How?'

She shook her head, eyeing him blankly, refusing to be drawn.

'What does it matter, if he's dead?' Tom insisted.

Another pause as she considered this, before answering with a shrug.

'He was murdered. Four days ago. Why?'

'I wanted to talk to him.'

'About what?'

'This for a start –' Tom held up the photocopied page showing the sketch of the symbol of the two snakes wrapped around a clenched fist. 'I hoped he might . . .'

'Where did you get that?' she gasped.

'You've seen it before?'

'C-Cavalli,' she stammered. 'They found a lead disc in his pocket, that was engraved on it!'

'Do you know what it means?' Tom pressed, hoping that her obvious surprise might cause her to momentarily lower her guard to his advantage. But she quickly regained her composure, again glaring at him defiantly.

'It means that you've got about five minutes to get out of here before someone comes looking for me.'

Tom studied her face for a few moments. She was bluffing.

'Why wait?' he said, offering her his phone. 'Call it in.'

She gazed at the handset for a few moments, then lifted her eyes to his.

'What are you doing?'

Tom smiled.

'No one even knows you're here, do they?'

She ignored his question, although the momentary flicker of indecision across her otherwise resolute face effectively answered it for him.

'Just let me go,' she repeated. 'You're in enough shit as it is.'

Tom went to reply and then paused, having suddenly realised what it was about her appearance that had been troubling him earlier. It was her hair, or rather the ragged way it had been cut, especially around the back, which seemed at odds with the rest of her. She'd clearly cut it herself. Recently. Probably dyed it too, given its unnaturally deep lustre.

'Where did you put the bottles?' he asked.

'What?' She shook her head, as if she wasn't sure she'd heard him properly.

'The empty dye bottles and the hair you cut off. Did you lose them somewhere safe? Because if you didn't and whoever's looking for you finds them, it won't take them much to figure out what you look like now.'

Allegra gave him a long, curious look.

'Who are you?'

'Someone who can help,' Tom said with a tight smile. 'Because right now, I'm guessing you're in a lot more shit than me.'

Leaning forward, he offered the gun to her, handle first.

THIRTY-ONE

Headquarters of the Guarda di Finanza,
Viale XXI Aprile, Rome
19th March – 7.22 a.m.

'Colonel? We've got her.'

'About time!' Gallo grabbed his jacket off the back of his chair, pausing in front of the mirror to do up the silver buttons and centre his tie. 'Her phone?'

'She switched it on about ten minutes ago,' Salvatore nodded, still standing in the corridor and leaning into the office.

'How long for?'

'Long enough. The signal's been triangulated to a street in Travestere.'

'Cavalli's house?' Gallo snapped, looking up into the mirror to seek out Salvatore's eyes over his left shoulder.

'Could be.'

Salvatore flinched and then relaxed into an

uneasy smile as Gallo turned and raised his hand and gave him a sharp clap on the back.

'Well done.'

Fixing his peaked cap on his head, he strode towards the lift. Twenty seconds later they stepped outside and walked outside towards two waiting cars. They climbed in, but just as Gallo was about to turn the key in the ignition, Salvatore's phone rang. Gallo paused, glancing across questioningly as he took the call.

'We know where she stayed last night,' Salvatore explained, still listening, but with his hand shielding the microphone.

'A hotel?' Gallo guessed.

'Out near the airport. The manager saw her picture this morning and called it in.'

'They ran the story?'

Salvatore reached across to the back seat and handed Gallo a copy of that morning's *La Repubblica*. Allegra's face dominated the front page under a single shouted headline:

Killer cop on the run.

'Apparently she checked in late last night and paid in cash. I guess we got lucky.'

'Funny how much luckier you get when you load the dice,' Gallo growled as he scanned through the article. He wouldn't normally have leaked the details of a case, but he'd seen enough of Allegra to realise that, for all her inexperience, she was smart. And in a city of 2.7 million

people, that was more than enough to hide and
stay hidden. The more people who knew what
she looked like, the better. As long as he found
her first.

Salvatore ended his call. Gallo turned the key.

'Who else is running it?'

'Everyone.'

'What about the old man?'

'Professor Eco?'

'Is that what he calls himself?' Gallo shrugged
as he checked his mirrors and swung out, tyres
shrieking.

'According to him, she took off before telling
him anything.'

'I want him watched anyway,' Gallo insisted.
'Just in case she tries to contact him again.'

'She's probably armed now, by the way. Eco
had a gun. Illegal. Says he can't find it any more.'

'Even better.' Gallo gave a satisfied nod. 'Gives
us an excuse to go in heavy.'

Smiling, he punched the siren on.

THIRTY-TWO

Vicolo de Panieri, Travestere, Rome
19th March – 7.27 a.m.

Allegra wasn't about to take any chances. Snatching the gun from Tom's grasp, she immediately turned it back on him. Unflustered, he settled into his chair.

'Who are you running from?' he asked.

The easy thing, the smart thing, she knew, would be to walk away right there and then. She had enough of her own problems already, without getting swept up into his.

But it wasn't that simple. For a start, it was hard to ignore that, whoever this man was and whatever dark secret had drawn him to this place, it seemed to involve Cavalli and the mysterious symbol that had been linked to three different corpses. What's more, he'd just placed his fate in her hands by handing her the gun. It was, she knew, a rather unsubtle attempt to win her trust.

But it was a powerful gesture all the same, and one that had, if nothing else, earned him the right to be heard.

'How can you help me?' she demanded, answering his question with one of her own.

There was a pause, and she guessed from the slight twitch of his left eye that he was debating how much he should tell her.

'Thirty-six hours ago a friend of mine was murdered,' he said eventually. 'Shot by a sniper in a casino in Vegas. I think they were killed because they were closing in on someone.'

'"Closing in"? What was he, a cop?' Allegra guessed with a surprised frown. This guy didn't look or feel like any policeman she'd ever met.

'*She* was FBI,' he corrected her. 'Special Agent Jennifer Browne. Cavalli was fingered by a man she arrested in New York. A dealer for a tombaroli smuggling ring. She found a drawing of the symbol I showed you in his trash. I've got the case file, if you want to see it,' he offered, leaning forward to reach into his bag.

'Wait,' she said sharply. 'Kick it over here.'

With a shrug, he placed his bag on the floor and slid it towards her with his foot. Keeping her eyes fixed on him, she felt inside it, her fingers eventually closing around a thick file that she pulled on to her lap. Seeing the FBI crest, she shot him a questioning, almost concerned look.

'Don't tell me you're FBI too?'

'No,' he admitted.

'Then where did you get this?'

A pause.

'I borrowed it.'

'You borrowed it?' She gave him a disbelieving smile. 'From the FBI?'

'When one agent gets killed, another one gets blamed,' he said, an impatient edge to his voice for the first time. 'Everyone was too busy covering their own ass to worry about finding Jennifer's killer. I did what I had to do.'

'And came here? Why? What were you hoping to find?'

'I don't know. Something that might tell me why Jennifer was murdered, or what this symbol means, or who the Delian League is.'

'The Delian League?' she shot back. 'What do you know about them?'

'Not as much as you, by the sound of things,' he replied with a curious frown.

'I just know what it used to be,' she said, his story so far and the reassuring weight of the gun in her hand convincing her she wasn't risking much by sharing a little more of what she knew.

'What do you mean, "used to be"?'

'There was an association of city states in Ancient Greece. A military alliance, formed to protect themselves from the Spartans,' she explained. 'The members used to throw lead into the sea when they joined, to symbolise that their friendship would last until it floated back to the surface.'

'Lead. Like the engraved disc you found on Cavalli?'

'Not just on Cavalli,' she admitted, trying not to think of Ricci's sagging skin and Argento's tortured smile. 'There have been two other murders. The discs were found with them too.'

'Did Cavalli know them?'

'I doubt it,' she said, shaking her head. 'Cavalli was an attorney based in Melfi. Adriano Ricci was an enforcer for the De Luca crime family. While Giulio Argento worked for the Banco Rosalia, a subsidiary of the Vatican bank. A priest would have more in common with a prostitute than those three with each other.'

'But the same killer, right?'

Allegra's eyes snapped to the door before she could answer, the sound of approaching sirens lifting her to her feet.

'You must have been followed,' Tom glared at her accusingly.

She ignored him, instead picking up a chair and swinging it hard against one of the sliding glass doors. It fractured on the third blow, the safety glass falling out in a single, crazed sheet. They leapt through the frame as they heard three, maybe four cars roar up the street outside.

'Here –'

Tom cradled his hands and gave Allegra a boost,

then reached up so she could help haul him up on to the garden wall beside her.

'You'll slow me down,' she said with a firm shake of her head.

'You need me,' Tom insisted.

'I've done okay so far.'

'Really? Then how do you explain that?' Tom glanced towards the muffled sound of the police banging on the front door.

'They got lucky,' she said with a shrug, readying herself to jump down.

'You mean they got smart. Let me guess. You turned your phone on just before you got here, right?'

'How did you know . . .?' she breathed, Tom's question pulling her back from the edge. She had briefly switched it on. Just long enough to see if Aurelio had left her a message. Something, anything, that might explain what she had over-heard. But all there had been was a series of increasingly frantic messages from her boss to turn herself in.

'It only takes a few seconds to triangulate a phone signal. You led them straight here.'

She took a deep breath, a small and increasingly insistent voice at the back of her head fighting her instinct to just jump down.

'Who are you?'

'Someone who knows what it's like to be on

the run,' he shot back. 'Someone who knows what it takes, keep running fast enough to stay alive.'

Sighing heavily, she reached down, her hand clutching on to his.

THIRTY-THREE

Verbier, Switzerland
19th March – 7.31 a.m.
It had snowed last week – recently enough for the village's blandly functional concrete heart to still be benefiting from its decorative touch, long enough ago for the briefly pristine white streets to have been turned into a dirty river of slush and mud-stained embankments.

Faulks had never seen the point of skiing, never understood the attraction of clamping his feet into boots that in another age would have likely been in the hands of the Spanish Inquisition, and then hurling himself off a mountain on two narrow planks just to only to get to the bottom so that he could have to queue and pay for the privilege of repeating the whole infernal experience again. And again.

Glancing up from his phone as they drove past, he almost felt sorry for them, a few early starters clomping noisily down the street trying not to break their necks on the ice, skis balancing precariously on their shoulder, their edges sawing down to the bone. It seemed a heavy price to pay to ensure you could hold your own at the school gates with the other parents or be able to join in with the dinner party circuit chit chat.

Still, if there was one thing he'd learnt over the years it was that there was no limit to people's ingenuity when it came to devising irrational ways to spend their money. And the richer they were, the more irrational and ingenious they seemed to become. It was a status symbol. A badge of honour. In fact, compared to some things he'd witnessed over the years, skiing was almost sane.

Chalet Septième Ciel was perched in an isolated spot high above the village, facing westward and with a breathtaking view over the valley below. Converted from an old school, its name meant Seventh Heaven; strangely inappropriate, given that most of its occupants, Faulks was fairly sure, were fated for a far warmer destination when their time came. Maybe that was why they chose here, Faulks mused. The prospect of an eternity roasting in the fires of Hell was perhaps all the incentive they needed to pay the extortionate fees this place charged. Anything to spend their final days somewhere cold.

Faulks's silver 1963 Bentley S3 Continental pulled up and Logan got out to open his door for him. A former paratrooper from the outskirts of Glasgow, he'd done two tours in Afghanistan before realising that he could make more in a year as a private bodyguard than ten being shot at for Queen and country. Wearing a suit and his regimental tie, he had straw-coloured hair and a wide, round face, his nose crooked and part of one earlobe missing. His jaw was permanently clenched, as if he was chewing stones.

A female voice answered the intercom.

'I'm here to see Avner Klein,' Faulks announced in French.

The door buzzed open and he stepped inside, a dark-haired nurse in a white uniform rushing forward to greet him, a stern expression on her face.

'Visiting hours aren't until nine,' she informed him icily.

'I know, but I've just flown in from Los Angeles,' he explained apologetically. 'And I have to be back in Geneva mid morning. I knew that if I didn't at least try to see him now . . .'

'I understand,' she relented, her face softening as she placed a comforting hand on his sleeve. 'In this case . . . well, time is short. I'm sure he'll see you. He's not been sleeping well recently. Follow me.'

She led him downstairs and down a long, dark corridor, Faulks marking every third step with the sharp clip of his umbrella against the wooden floor. Reaching the last door she knocked gently.

From the other side came a faint call that seemed barely human to Faulks, but which the nurse clearly took as permission to enter, nodding at him to go in.

'Mrs Carroll is having breakfast on the terrace,' she called as she retreated back along the corridor before he could stop her. 'I'll let her know you're here.'

The curtains had been partly drawn, throwing a narrow ribbon of light across the otherwise dark room. This had unravelled along the floor and then spooled up and across the bed, revealing the pale hands of the person lying in it, his face wreathed in darkness.

'Avner?' Faulks said, his eyes straining to adjust to the sepulchral half light.

'Earl, is that you?' a thin voice rasped from the bed.

'How are you doing, sport?' Faulks stepped across to the bed with what he hoped was an encouraging smile.

Klein looked barely alive, his cheeks hollowed out, eyes sunk into the back of his head, hair missing, skin wrinkled and sagging. Wires from several machines disappeared under the white bedclothes that shrouded his body, their monitors flashing up a hieroglyphic stream of numbers and graphs and pulsing dots. There was a drip too, Faulks noticed, the line seeming to vanish somewhere in the direction of Klein's groin, the livid purple patches along his wizened forearm suggesting that they couldn't find a vein there any more.

'I'm dying,' Klein replied, the very effort of blinking seeming to make him wince in pain.

'Rubbish,' Faulks assured him breezily. 'You'll be back on your feet in time for the Triple Crown. I've got a killer tip on the Derby this year. A guaranteed winner!'

Klein nodded weakly, although his empty smile told Faulks that they both knew he was lying.

'Thank you for visiting,' Klein wheezed. 'I know you're busy.'

He nodded at the drink next to the bed and Faulks reached across and held it for him, trying not to wrinkle his nose in disgust as Klein's cracked lips sucked at it greedily, a drop escaping from the corner of his mouth and trickling down his chin like a tear.

'Never too busy for an old friend.' A pause. 'And there is something I wanted to show you.'

'Oh?'

Rather than curiosity, there was a resigned sadness in Klein's voice, as if Faulks had somehow confirmed a rumour that he'd been hoping wasn't true.

'I knew you wouldn't want to pass up a chance like this,' Faulks enthused, opening his wallet and extracting a small Polaroid. 'Look –'

Klein lifted himself forward and then almost immediately collapsed back on to his pillow, convulsing under the grip of a sudden hacking cough.

'Verity Bruce wants it,' Faulks continued through the noise, glancing lovingly at the picture. 'I've brought all the paperwork ready for you to sign. All you need to do is authorise the payment and –'

Faulks broke off as Deena Carroll, Klein's second wife, stormed into the room behind him, gold bangles and earrings clanging like a Passing Bell.

'What the hell are you doing here?' she said, roasted coffee bean eyes blazing out of a leathered face crowned by a swooping wave of dyed platinum blonde hair.

'Visiting an old friend,' Faulks shrugged. 'I mean, old friends,' he added with a small bow of his head.

'You're no friend,' she hissed contemptuously, snatching the photograph from him and waving it in his face. 'Friends don't try and hawk their grimy trinkets to a dying man.' She flicked the photograph to the floor. 'You make me sick, Earl.'

'Those grimy trinkets have made the Klein–Carroll collection one of the greatest in the world,' he reminded her tersely as he knelt down stiffly to retrieve the photograph. 'And now that you've donated it to the Met, a permanent monument to your taste and generosity.' He spat these last two words out, as if he'd just bitten into a bar of soap.

'We both know what that collection is and where it came from,' she said with a hollow laugh. 'And if it's a monument to anything, it's to your greed.'

'Be careful, Deena,' Faulks said sharply, still smiling. 'I've buried a lot of bodies for Avner over the years and dug up even more. And I can prove it. You should think about how you want him to be remembered.'

She went to answer but said nothing, glancing instead at Klein. Hands clasped together on the crisp sheets, grinning lovingly at her, he had quite clearly not followed a word of their exchange. She walked over to his side and smiled, tears welling as she stroked the few wisps of hair that clung stubbornly to his scalp.

'Just go, Earl,' she said in a toneless voice. 'Find someone else to dig for.'

THIRTY-FOUR

Lungotevere Gianicolense, Rome
19th March – 7.37 a.m.
They had found a battered old Fiat a few streets from Cavalli's house, Tom preferring it to the Mercedes parked just behind it. It was a suggestion that Allegra was already rather regretting, the rusted suspension jarring with every imperfection in the road as they headed north along the river. And yet she couldn't fault his logic – the Fiat was coated in a thick layer of rain-streaked dirt that suggested that it hadn't been used for weeks, and so was less likely to be missed.

'What are you doing?' he asked as she suddenly cut across the Ponte Principe Amedei di Savoia and pulled in on the Largo dei Fiorentini. 'We can't stop here. We're still too close. If anyone's seen us . . .'

'If you want to get out, now's your chance,'

she snapped, leaning across him and pushing his door open. 'Otherwise, I want some answers.'

'What sort of answers?'

'How about a name?'

He sighed, then slammed the door shut.

'It's Tom. Tom Kirk.' He made a point of holding out his hand so that she had to shake it rather formally. 'Can we do the rest of the Q and A somewhere else?'

'You said you knew what it was like to be on the run. Why? Who are you?' she demanded.

'You really want to do this here?' he asked, his face screwed into a disbelieving frown. She returned his stare, jaw set firm. 'Fine,' he said eventually with a resigned sigh. 'I . . . I used to be a thief.'

'A thief?' She smiled indulgently before realising that he wasn't joking. 'What sort of thief?'

'Art mainly. Jewellery too. Whatever paid.'

She nodded slowly. It was strange, but it was almost as if she'd been expecting him to say something like this. It certainly seemed to fit him better than being police or FBI.

'And now?'

'Now I help recover pieces, advise museums on security, that sort of thing,' he replied.

'What's any of that got to do with Cavalli?'

'I told you. Jennifer had asked me to help her on a case before she was killed. Cavalli was the best lead I had as to who might have ordered the hit.'

'So we both went there looking for answers,' Allegra said with a rueful smile.

'Why – what's Cavalli to you?'

'It's what he is to Gallo that I care about.' She turned back to face the front, her hands clutching the wheel.

'Who's Gallo?' Tom frowned. 'The person you're running from?'

'Colonel Massimo Gallo,' she intoned in a bitter voice. 'Head of the GICO – the organised crime unit of the Ministry of Finance – and the officer in charge of the two Caravaggio killings.'

'What?'

'Ricci and Argento,' she explained impatiently. 'The other murders I told you about. Their deaths had been staged to mirror to two Caravaggio paintings.'

'Jennifer was lured to Las Vegas to help recover a Caravaggio stolen in the 1960s,' Tom explained with the triumphant finality of someone laying down a winning poker hand.

'You think . . .?'

'Don't you?'

There was a pause as she let this sink in. First the symbol. Then the mention of the Delian League. Now Caravaggio. Perhaps he was right. These surely couldn't all be coincidences?

Speaking fast and confidently, she plunged into an account of the past few days – the murders of Ricci and Argento; the choice of locations; the references to Caesar; the Caravaggio staging of the murder scenes; what she knew about Cavalli and his death; Gallo's cold-blooded execution of Gambetta. It was only when she got to describing Aurelio's treachery that her voice faltered. The memory of his betrayal was still too fresh, too raw for her to share anything more than the most basic details. Instead she quickly switched to her tortured flight from his apartment and the restless night that she had spent in the grimy airport hotel until, unable to sleep, she had decided to visit Cavalli's apartment for herself and see what she could find there.

Tom listened to all this without interrupting and she realised when she had finished that it had been strangely calming to talk things through, even if she barely knew him. There had been so much going on, so many thoughts tripping over each other inside her head, that it had been surprisingly cathartic to lay all the different elements together end to end.

'Somehow, it's all linked,' he said slowly when she had finished. 'The murders, Caravaggio, the symbol . . . we just need to find out how.'

'Is that all?' she said with a bitter laugh.

'Sometimes you just need to know who to ask.'

'And you do?' she asked in a sceptical tone.

'I know someone who might be able to help.' He nodded.

'Someone we can trust?'

Tom took a deep breath, then blew out his cheeks.

'More or less.'

'What sort of an answer's that?' she snorted.

'The sort of answer you get when you're out of better ideas.'

There was a pause. Then with a resigned shrug she started the engine.

'Where to?'

THIRTY-FIVE

Fontana di Trevi, Rome
19th March – 8.03 a.m.

Allegra heard the fountain before she saw it, a delirious, ecstatic roar of water that crashed and foamed over gnarled travertine rocks and carved foliage, tumbling in a joyful cascade into the open embrace of the wide basin below. This was no accident, Allegra knew, the Trevi having been deliberately positioned so that, no matter what route was taken, it could only be partially seen as it was approached, the anticipation building as the sound got louder until the monument finally revealed itself.

Despite the relatively early hour, the tourists were already out in force, some seated like an eager audience on the steps that encircled the basin's low stage, others facing the opposite direction and flinging coins over their shoulders in the hope of securing their return to the Eternal City.

Oblivious to their catcalling and the popcorn burst of camera flashes, the statues ranged above them silently acted out an allegorical representation of the taming of the waters. Centre stage loomed Neptune's brooding figure, his chariot frozen in flight, winged horses rearing dramatically out of the water and threatening to take the entire structure with them.

'Was there a Trevi family?' Tom asked as they paused briefly in front of it.

'Trevi comes from Tre Via, the three streets that meet here,' she corrected him in a curt voice. 'Are we here for a history lesson or to actually see someone?'

'That depends,' he said with a shrug.

'On what?'

'On whether you can keep a secret.'

She gave a dismissive laugh.

'How old are you, ten?'

Tom turned to face her, face set firm.

'You can't tell anyone about what you see.'

'Oh come on,' she snorted impatiently.

'Yes or no?' he insisted.

There was a pause. Then she gave a grudging nod.

'Yes, fine, whatever.'

'No crossed fingers?'

'What?' she exploded. 'If this is some sort of . . .'

'I'm only joking.' He grinned. 'Come on. It's this way.'

He led her round to the right to the Vicolo Scavolino where a small doorway had been set into the side wall of the building directly behind the fountain. A flock of pigeons rendered fat and tame by years of overfeeding, barely stirred as they waded through them.

'Here?' she asked with a frown, glancing up at the carved papal escutcheon suspended over the entrance.

'Here.' He nodded, knocking sharply against the door's weather-worn surface.

A few moments later it opened to reveal a young Chinese man dressed in black, his hair standing off his head as if he had been electrocuted. From the way he was awkwardly holding one hand behind his back, Allegra guessed that he was clutching a gun.

'I'm here to see Johnny,' Tom announced. 'Tell him it's Felix.'

The man gave them a cursory look, then shut the door again.

'Felix?' Allegra shot him a questioning look.

'It's a name people used to know me by when I was still in the game,' he explained. 'I try not to use it any more, but it's how a lot of people still know me.'

'The game?' She gave a hollow laugh. 'Is that a word people like you use to make you feel better about breaking the law?'

The door reopened before Tom had a chance

to answer, the man ushering them inside and then marching them along a low passageway, through a second door and then up a shallow flight of steps into a narrow room, with a stone staircase leading both up and down.

'Where are we?' Allegra hissed.

'Listen,' Tom replied.

She nodded, suddenly realising that the dull ringing in her ears was no longer the angry echo of the shot that had killed Gambetta but the muffled roar of water through the thick walls.

'We're behind the fountain,' she breathed.

'The Trevi was pretty much tacked on to the façade of the Palazzo Poli when they built it,' Tom explained as the man ordered them up the stairs with a grunt. 'This space was bricked off as a maintenance shaft, to provide access to the roof and the plumbing in the basement. Johnny cut a deal with the mayor to rent the attic.'

'You're kidding, right?'

'Why? How else do you think he paid for his re-election campaign?'

They climbed to the first floor, then to the next, the fountain's low rumble slowly fading, until it was little more than a distant hum. In its place, however, Allegra was increasingly aware of a whirring, rhythmical clattering noise. She glanced at Tom for an explanation, but he said nothing, his expression suggesting that he was rather enjoying her confusion.

Another man was waiting to greet them on the second-floor landing, a machine gun slung across his oversized Lakers shirt, in place of the rather less threatening Norinco Type 77 handgun that their escort was sporting. The higher they climbed, the more lethal the weaponry, it seemed.

The second man signalled at them to raise their arms and then quickly patted them down, confiscating Tom's bag and Allegra's gun and keys. Then he nodded at them to follow him to the foot of the next flight of stairs, where an armoured steel door and two more guards blocked their way. Unprompted, the door buzzed open.

Swapping a look, they made their way upstairs.

THIRTY-SIX

19th March – 8.12 a.m.
The staircase led to a long, narrow attic room that seemed to run the width of the entire building. A line of squat windows squinted down on to the square below, their view obscured in places by the fountain's massive stone pediment. And running down the centre of the room, hissing and rattling like an old steam engine under the low ceiling, was a huge printing press.

'The sound of the fountain masks the noise of the machine,' Tom called to her over the press's raucous clatter as she approached it. 'It's actually five separate processes, although the machines have been laid out end to end. A simultan machine to print the background colours and patterns. An intaglio machine for the major design elements. A letterpress for the serial numbers. An offset press for the overcoating. And obviously a guillotine right at the end to cut the sheets to size.'

Allegra stepped closer to the press, trying to catch what was coming off the machine's whirling drum, then looked back to Tom in shock.

'Money?'

'Euros.' He nodded. 'Johnny runs one of the world's biggest counterfeiting operations outside of China. He used to print dollars, but no one wants them any more.'

'Johnny who?' she asked, looking back along the room and noticing the small army of people in blue overalls tending silently to the press.

'Johnny Li. His father is Li Kai-Fu. Runs one of the most powerful Triad gangs in Hong Kong,' Tom explained in a low voice. 'A couple of years ago he posted his five sons around the world, via Cambridge, to help grow the family business. Johnny's here, Paul's in San Francisco, Ringo's in Buenos Aires . . .'

'He moved to Rio,' a voice interrupted him. 'Better weather, cheaper women.'

'Johnny!' Tom turned to greet the voice with a warm smile.

Li was young, perhaps only in his late twenties, with long dark hair that he was forever brushing from his eyes, a pierced lip, and a dotted line tattooed around his neck as if to show where to cut. He was also the only person on this floor not in overalls, dressed instead in a white Armani T-shirt, red Ferrari monogrammed jacket, expensively ripped Versace jeans with a stainless steel key chain looping down one leg, and Prada trainers. Flanked by two unsmiling guards and balancing Allegra's gun in his hand as if trying to guess its weight, his face was creased into an unwelcoming scowl.

'What do you want, Felix?' He had an unexpectedly strong English accent.

'Bad time?' Tom frowned, clearly surprised by his tone.

'What do you expect when you turn up at my place with a cop?' Li snapped, stabbing a rolled-up newspaper towards him. 'Even she is bent.'

Tom took the paper off him and scanned the front page, then handed it to Allegra with an awkward, almost apologetic look. She didn't have to read much beyond the headline to understand why. Gallo was pinning Gambetta's death on her. There she was, looking slightly arrogant in her crisp Carabinieri uniform, she had to admit. Beneath it was an article describing her 'murderous rampage', the text scrolling around her, as if the words themselves were worried about getting too close. She felt suddenly dizzy, as if the floor was moving under her, and was only vaguely aware of Tom's voice.

'She's with me, now,' he said.

'Why, what do you want?' Li shot back, flashing Allegra a suspicious glance.

'Your help.'

'I thought you'd retired?' Li's question sounded more like an accusation.

'A friend of mine has been killed. We're both after the people who did it.'

Li paused, glancing at Tom and Allegra in turn. Then he handed Allegra her gun back with a grudging nod.

'What do you want to know?'

Tom handed Li the drawing of the symbol.

'What can you tell me about this?'

Li took it over to an architect's desk on which he had been examining a sheet of freshly printed notes under a microscope and angled it under the light. He glanced up at them with a wary look.

'Is this who you think killed your friend?'

'You know what it means?' Allegra asked excitedly.

'Of course I do,' he snorted. 'It's the symbol of the Delian League.'

Allegra gave Tom a look. As they had both suspected, far from being a footnote in some dusty textbook, the Delian League, or rather some bastardised version of it, was clearly alive and well.

'Who runs it?' Tom pressed.

Li sat back.

'Come on, Tom. You know that's not how things work.' He smiled indulgently as if gently scolding a child. 'I'm running a business here, not a charity. Even for deserving causes like you.'

'How much?' Tom asked wearily.

'Normally twenty-five thousand euro,' Li said, picking at his fingernails. 'But for you and your

friend I'm going to round it up to fifty. A little . . .
five-o surcharge.'

'Fifty thousand!' Allegra exclaimed.

'I can get it.' Tom nodded. 'But it's going to
take some time.'

'I can wait.' Li shrugged.

'Well, we can't,' Tom insisted. 'I'll have to owe
you.'

'No deal.' Li shook his head. 'Not if you're going
up against the League. I want my money before
they kill you.'

'Why don't you just pay yourself?' Allegra
tapped her finger angrily against the sheet of uncut
notes on the desk.

'This stuff is like dope,' Li sniffed. 'You never
want to risk getting addicted to your own
product.'

'Come on, Johnny,' Tom pleaded. 'You know
I'm good for it.'

Li took a deep breath, clicking his front teeth
together slowly as he considered them in turn.

'What about a down-payment?' he asked. 'You
must have something on you?'

'I've told you, we don't . . .'

'That watch, for example.' Li nodded towards
Tom's wrist.

'It's not for sale,' Tom insisted, quickly pulling
his sleeve down.

'Think of it as a deposit,' Li suggested. 'You can
have it back when you bring me the cash.'

'And you'll tell us what we need to know?' Allegra asked in a sceptical tone.

'If I can.'

'Tom?' Allegra fixed Tom with a hopeful look. Unless they wanted to wait, it seemed like a reasonable deal. Tom said nothing, then gave a resigned shrug.

'Fine.' Sighing heavily, he took the watch off. 'But I want it back.'

'I'll look after it,' Li reassured him, fastening it carefully to his wrist.

'Let's start with the Delian League,' Allegra suggested. 'Who are they?'

'The Delian League controls the illegal antiquities trade in Italy,' Li answered simply. 'Has done since the early seventies. Now, nothing leaves the country without going through them.'

'And the tombaroli? Where do they fit in?'

'They control the supply,' Li explained. 'Most of them are freelance. But since all the major antiquities buyers are foreign, the League controls access to the demand. The tombaroli either have to sell to them, or not sell at all.'

'And the mafia?' Tom interrupted. 'Don't they mind the League operating on their turf?'

'The League *is* the mafia,' Li laughed, before tapping his finger on the symbol. 'That's what the two snakes represent – one for the Cosa Nostra. One for the Banda della Magliana.'

'The Banda della Magliana is run by the De

Luca family,' Allegra explained, glancing at Tom. 'They're who Ricci worked for.'

'The story I heard was that the Cosa Nostra was getting squeezed out of the drugs business by the 'Ndrangheta. So when they realised there was money to be made in looting antiquities, they teamed up with the Banda della Magliana who controlled all the valuable Etruscan sites around Rome, on the basis that they would make more money if they operated as a cartel. The League's been so successful that most of the other families have sold them access rights to their territories in return for a share of the profits.'

'Who runs it now?' Tom asked. 'Where can we find them?'

Li went to answer, then paused, crossing one arm across his stomach and tapping his finger slowly against his lips.

'I can't tell you that.'

Tom gave a hollow laugh.

'Can't or won't?'

'It's nothing personal, Felix,' Li said with a shrug. 'I just want my money. And if I give you everything now, I know I'll never see it.'

'We had a deal,' Allegra said angrily. Li had tricked them, first reeling them in to show them how much he knew and then holding out when they'd get to the punchline.

'We still do,' Li insisted. 'Come back tomorrow

with the fifty k and I'll tell you what side of the bed they all sleep on.'

'We need to know now,' Allegra snapped.

Another pause, Li first centring Tom's watch on his wrist and then wiping the glass with his thumb.

'What about the car?' he asked without looking up.

'What car?' Tom frowned.

'Cavalli's Maserati,' Allegra breathed, as she recognized the set of keys that Li had produced from his pocket as the ones that had been confiscated from her on the way in.

'Do you have it?' Li pressed.

'No, but I know where it is,' she replied warily, his forced indifference making her wonder if he hadn't been carefully leading them up to this point all along. 'Why?'

'New deal,' Li offered. 'The car instead of the cash. That way you don't have to wait.'

'Done,' Allegra confirmed eagerly, sliding the keys over to him with a relieved sigh. 'It's in the pound, but it should be easy enough for you to get to.'

Smiling, Li slid the keys back towards her.

'That's not quite what I had in mind.'

THIRTY-SEVEN

Via Principesa Clotilde, Rome
19th March – 8.35 a.m.

Ten minutes later and they were skirting the eastern rim of the Piazza del Popolo, Tom catching a glimpse of the Pincio through a gap in the buildings.

'Who gave it to you?' Allegra asked, finally breaking the silence.

'What?' Tom looked round, distracted.

'The watch? Who gave it to you?'

There was a brief pause, a pained look flickering across his face.

'Jennifer.'

A longer, more awkward silence.

'I'm sorry. I didn't realise . . .'

'We didn't have much choice,' Tom said, sighing. 'Besides, as long as we can get him the car, he'll give it back.'

'It shouldn't be too hard,' she reassured him. 'Three, four guards at most.'

254 THE GENEVA DECEPTION

'It's worth taking a look,' he agreed. 'It's that or wait until I can get him the cash tomorrow.'

'Why does he even want it?' She frowned, checking her mirrors as she turned on to the Lungotevere Arnaldo da Brescia.

'He collects cars,' Tom explained. 'Has about forty of them in a sealed and climate-controlled private underground garage somewhere near Trajan's Column. None of them paid for.'

They followed the river in silence, heading north against the traffic as the road flexed around the riverbank's smooth contours, the sky now bright and clear. Tom caught Allegra glancing at herself in the mirror, her hand drifting unconsciously to her dyed and roughly chopped hair, as if she still couldn't quite recognise herself.

'Tell me more about the Banda della Magliana,' he said eventually.

'There are five major mafia organisations in Italy,' Allegra explained, seeming to welcome the interruption. 'The Cosa Nostra and Stidda in Sicily, the Camorra in Naples, the Sacra Corona Unita in Apulia and the 'Ndrangheta in Calabria. The Banda della Magliana was a smaller outfit based here in Rome and controlled by the De Luca family.'

'Was?'

'You might remember that they were linked to a series of political assassinations and bombings between the seventies and the nineties. But since then they've been pretty quiet.'

She leaned on her horn as she overtook a three-wheeled delivery van that was skittering wildly over the worn tarmac.

'And Ricci worked for them?'

'Gallo said he was an enforcer,' she nodded. 'As far as I know the family's still controlled by Giovanni De Luca, although no one's seen him for years.'

'What about the Cosa Nostra, the Banda della Magliana's partner in the Delian League? Who heads them up?'

'Lorenzo Moretti. Or at least that's the rumour. It's not the sort of thing you put on your business card.'

The car pound occupied a large, anonymously grey multi-storey building at the end of a tree-lined residential street. Two guards were stationed at each of the two sentry posts that flanked the entry and exit ramps. Seeing them walking up to the counter, the officers manning the entrance jumped up and tried to look busy, one of them having been watching TV inside their small office, the other sat outside reading the paper, tipped back on a faded piece of white garden furniture.

'*Buongiorno.*' Allegra flashed a broad smile and her badge in the same instant, snapping it shut before they could get a good look at her name or the picture. 'Sorry to disturb you,' she continued.

'But my friend has had his car stolen.' The two men glanced at Tom accusingly, as if this was somehow his fault.

'It's probably in a container halfway to Morocco by now,' one of them suggested gloomily.

'That's what I told him,' Allegra agreed. 'Only one of his neighbours says they saw it being towed. And this is the closest pound to where he lives.'

'If it's been towed it will be on the database,' one of the officers said to Tom. 'Pay the release fee and you can have it back.'

'He's already looked and it's not there,' she said with a shrug before Tom could answer. 'He thinks that someone might have made a mistake and entered the wrong plates.'

'Really?' The men eyed him like they would a glass of corked wine.

'He's English,' she murmured, giving him the sort of weary look a mother might give a naughty child. The officers nodded in sudden understanding, a sympathetic look crossing their faces. 'Is there any chance we can go up and take a quick look to see if it's here? I'd really appreciate it.'

The two men glanced at each other and then shrugged their agreement.

'As long as you're quick,' one of them said.

'When did it go missing?' the other asked her, ignoring Tom completely now.

'Around the fifteenth of March.'

'We store all the cars in the order they get

brought here,' the first officer explained, pointing at a worn map of the complex that had been crudely taped to the counter. 'Cars for that week should be around here – in the blue quadrant on the third floor.' He pointed at a section of the map. 'The lift's down there on the right.'

A few moments later the doors pinged shut behind them.

'You enjoyed that, didn't you?' Tom said in a reproachful tone.

'It could have been worse,' she said with an amused smile. 'I could have told them you were American.'

The lift opened on to the southern end of the third floor. It was a dark, depressing place, most of the neon tubes missing or broken, the walls encrusted with a moulding green deposit, the ceiling oozing a thick yellow mucus that hung in cancerous clumps. The floor was divided by lines of decaying concrete pillars into three long aisles, with cars parked along both sides and a spiralling up-and-down ramp at one end linking it to the other levels like a calcified umbilical cord.

They made their way over to the area pointed out by the guard, dodging around oily lakes of standing water, until they were about halfway down the left-hand aisle. Jennifer took out the keys and pressed the unlock button. Cavalli's car eagerly identified itself with a double flash of its indicators – a souped-up Maserati Granturismo, worth almost double what Johnny was asking for. No wonder he'd pushed them into this.

'What are you doing?' Tom called in a low voice as Allegra opened the boot and leaned inside. 'It must have been searched already.'

'That doesn't mean they found anything,' she replied, her voice muffled.

'Let's just get out of here before they . . .'

She stood up, triumphantly holding a small piece of pottery that had been nestling in a fold in the muddy grey blanket that covered the boot floor. About the size of her hand, it featured a bearded man's face painted in red against a black background.

'It's a vase fragment. Probably Apullian, which dates it to between 430 and 300 BC.'

'Dionysius?' Tom ventured.

'Yes,' she said, looking impressed. 'I'd guess it was part of a *krater*, a bowl used . . .'

'For mixing wine and water,' Tom said, grinning at her obvious surprise. 'My parents were art dealers. My mother specialised in antiquities. I guess I was a good listener.'

'Notice anything strange?' she asked, handing it to him with a nod.

'The edges are sharp.' He frowned, gingerly drawing his finger over one of them as if it was a blade.

'Sharp and clean,' she agreed. 'Which means the break is recent.'

'You mean it was done after it was dug up?' Tom gave her a puzzled look, still holding the fragment.

'I mean it was done on purpose,' she shot back, Tom detecting a hint of anger in her voice. 'See how they've been careful not to damage the painted area so they can restore it.'

'You mean it's been smashed so it can be stuck back together again?' he asked with a disbelieving smile.

'It makes it easier to smuggle,' she explained with a despairing shake of her head. 'Unfortunately, we see it all the time. The fragments are called orphans. The dealers can sometimes make more money selling them off individually than they would get for an intact piece, because they can raise the price as the collector or museum gets more and more desperate to buy all the pieces. And of course, by the time the vase is fully restored, no one can track where or who they bought each fragment from. Everyone's protected.'

'Then Cavalli must have been working either with or for the League,' Tom said grimly as she dropped the boot lid. 'Perhaps they found out that the FBI had his name and killed him before he could talk?'

The noise of an engine starting echoed up to them from one of the lower floors, and drew a worried glance from Tom towards the exit.

'We should go.' He opened the passenger door

to get in, but then immediately staggered back, coughing as a choking chemical smell clawed at his throat.

'You okay?' Allegra called out in concern.

'It's been sprayed with a fire extinguisher,' he croaked, pointing at the downy white skin which covered most of the car's interior, apart from where it had been disturbed by the police search. 'Old trick. The foam destroys any fingerprint or DNA evidence.'

'Which Cavalli's killers would only have done if they'd been in the car,' Allegra said thoughtfully, opening the driver's side door and standing back to let the fumes clear.

'Where did they find the car keys?' He asked, rubbing his streaming eyes.

'In his pocket, why?'

'I'm just wondering if he was driving. Based on that I'd guess he was.'

'How do you work that out?'

'Because I doubt his killers drove him out to wherever the car was dumped and then planted the keys on him before killing him.' Tom shrugged. "What does it matter either way?'

Taking a deep breath, Tom disappeared inside the car. Leaning over the passenger seat, he plunged his hand down the back of the driver's seat, wisps of foam fluttering like ash caught by the wind. Feeling around with his fingertips, he pulled out first some loose change, then a pack of matches, and finally, pushed right down, a folded Polaroid. He stood up, brushing the sticky white paste from his clothes.

'If Cavalli was driving, that's about the only place he would have been able to hide something once he realised what was going on,' he explained, enjoying the look on Allegra's face. 'Here.' He leant over the roof and handed the photo to her. 'Any ideas?'

'Some sort of statue fragment,' she said slowly. 'Greek, I'd guess, although –'

She was interrupted by a shout.

'*Rimanga dove siete*!' Stay where you are!

THIRTY-EIGHT

19th March – 8.51 a.m.
Spinning round, Allegra immediately recognised the two officers they had talked their way past downstairs. One was hunched over the wheel of the blue Fiat squad car that had ghosted up the ramp behind them, its headlights now blazing through the darkness. The other was standing next to it, his voice echoing off the car park's low ceilings, gun drawn.

'We found the car after all,' Allegra stepped towards him with a smile, switching back into Italian. 'My friend just needs to pay . . .'

'I said stay where you are,' the officer barked again, his trigger finger twitching.

'I don't think he's buying it any more,' Tom whispered out of the corner of his mouth.

'No,' she agreed. 'Get in!'

Diving through the open doors, she jammed the key in the ignition, fired up the engine and selected reverse. Tom jumped in alongside her, the crack of a gun shot whistling overhead. The car leapt backwards and swung out, swiping the rear wing of the car parked next to them and setting off the harsh shriek of its two-tone alarm.

'You're facing the wrong way,' Tom shouted, their windscreen now engulfed by the glare of the squad car's headlights as it accelerated, wheels-spinning, towards them.

'Don't tell me how to drive,' she retorted indignantly, turning to look back over her shoulder. 'If I'd tried to reverse out the other way I'd have wrapped it around the pillar.'

She stamped on the pedal, the car springing backwards and then yawing wildly as she fought to keep it straight, traces of foam making the wheel slick in her hands. Tyres screaming, they rounded the corner and then doubled back on themselves, the engine protesting with an angry whine as they sped down the central aisle, the revs climbing steeply.

Another shot rang out. They both flinched. One of their headlights exploded.

'Head down a floor,' Tom suggested. 'Try and get far enough ahead of them to flip it around.'

She cannoned the wrong way on to the up-ramp, the gloom suddenly lit by a blaze of sparks as she glanced off the concrete and used the ramp's curved walls to guide herself down to the second level.

'Someone's coming up the other way,' Tom warned her as a second squad car, siren pulsing, stormed up the ramp towards them, the sweep of its headlights circling beneath them as it rose, like a shark closing in on a seal.

She steered them off the ramp on to the flat, the floorpan slapping the concrete with a heavy bang. From behind them came the angry squeal of brakes as the squad car chasing them fish-tailed to avoid colliding with the second police car coming up the other way. Allegra sensed her opportunity. Leaning on the clutch, she yanked on the handbrake and jerked the wheel hard to spin them round so that they were facing forward, then shoved the car into gear and accelerated away along the left-hand aisle, tyres smoking.

'You've got one right behind, one to the right,' Tom shouted over the engine noise, pointing to where the second car was now speeding down the central aisle, roughly parallel to them.

'They're going to try and cut us off at the end,' she guessed, before glancing down at her lap. 'What the hell are you doing?'

Tom had leant forward and was feeling under the dashboard between her knees.

'Looking for something,' he said, straining to reach.

'I can see that,' she hissed through gritted teeth, his head almost resting on her lap.

'There –' he sat up, 'the front air-bag switch. They put it down there in case you want to disable them.'

She nodded in immediate understanding.

'Hold on.'

Checking in her mirror to see how close the car behind her was, she stamped on the brake. The ABS kicked in, the car juddering to a halt and forcing their pursuers to run into the back of them, the impact knocking them five or six feet forward and wrenching their boot open, so that it was flapping around like a half-opened tin can. What damage they had sustained was as nothing compared to the Fiat, however, which had, unsurprisingly, come off second best with both front tyres burst, the engine block almost in the front seat, and the bonnet concertinaed back on itself.

Allegra glanced across at Tom with a satisfied grin, but he was pointing at the second police car, which was already at the far end of the second aisle and rounding the corner towards them.

'Here comes the cavalry.'

Dropping the Maserati into gear, she pulled forward and cut through a gap in the parked cars to her right to reach the central aisle and then spun round, so that she was facing back towards the exit ramp.

'What are you doing?' he asked with a frown.

'Enjoying myself,' she breathed.

Gunning the motor hard, she took off, glancing across at the squad car racing down the adjacent aisle to make sure she was far enough ahead, its surging shape strobing across her eyes as she caught glimpses of it through gaps between the cars and the concrete pillars.

'Now!' Tom called, pulling his seat belt tight across himself and hanging on to the grab handle.

She steered away from the line of cars to her right and then carved back in, ramming an Alfa square on. It jumped forward as if it had been fired from a cannon, colliding with the front of the VW parked only a few inches opposite it, which in turn T-boned the squad car as it came past, sending it ploughing into the line of parked cars on the far side of the aisle.

There was an abrupt, empty moment of calm, the squad car's blue light pulsing weakly in the gloom. Then a jarring chorus of car alarms kicked in, each singing in a different key and to a different tempo, roused by the force of the crash.

'Where did you learn to drive like that?' Tom asked with an approving nod.

'Rush hour in Rome.' She smiled, breathing hard.

'Do you think Johnny will notice the damage?'

She glanced in the mirror and saw the boot lid flapping around behind them like a loose sail, then looked along the crumpled bonnet at the cloud of steam rising from the cracked radiator.

'It'll polish out.' She grinned.

Reversing out, the steering pulling heavily to the right, she nursed the car down the exit ramp and then made her way out on to the street.

THIRTY-NINE

Desposito Eroli, Via Erulo Eroli, Rome
19th March – 9.23 a.m.

'I thought you told these idiots to hold off until we got here when they called?' Gallo said in an accusing tone as Salvatore hurried towards him, his notebook clutched to his chest.

Misfortune was snapping at his heels like one of those annoying handbag dogs, it seemed. First the triangulation of Allegra's mobile phone signal, only for her to have vanished by the time they got there. Then a sighting reported by the officers here, only for her to slip through his fingers a second time, it now seemed.

'I did,' Salvatore sighed wearily. 'Apparently they were trying to lock down the area in case they drove off.'

'Lock down the area? The stupid bastards have been watching too much TV,' Gallo glowered at the two men in neck braces being stretchered past him into a waiting ambulance. 'It's just as well she's put them in hospital. She's saved me the trouble.' Cursing under his breath, he lit a cigarette.

'You mean *they* saved you the trouble,' Salvatore corrected him.

'She wasn't alone?' Gallo glanced up, surprised, brushing his long silvery hair back behind each ear.

'There was a man.'

'What man?'

'Not sure yet.'

A pause, as Gallo let this sink in. He'd not banked on her teaming up with someone. Certainly not this soon.

'What were they doing here?'

'They were seen opening up a black Maserati. Registration number . . . JT149VT,' Salvatore read from his notebook.

'Presumably not hers? Not on a lieutenant's salary.'

'Cavalli's.'

Gallo span round to face him.

'Cavalli's?' he spat. 'What the hell was she looking for?' He glared at the building behind him as if it was somehow at fault and owed him an answer. To his surprise, it gave him one.

'There must be a camera up there!' He pointed at the lens fixed above the entrance. 'Get me the disc.'

A few minutes later they were seated around a small monitor in the sentry post, Salvatore forwarding to the time of the last entry in the log. For ten, maybe twenty seconds, the grainy black-and-white footage showed nothing but parked cars and the wet concrete floor, but then, just as Gallo was about to hit the fast forward button again, two people appeared in the shot.

'That's not her,' Salvatore said with a shake of his head.

'Yes it is,' Gallo breathed, reluctantly putting his glasses on so he could see properly. 'She's cut her hair. Dyed it, too. Clever girl.' His face broke into a grudging smile. 'And who are you?' He leaned forward and hit the pause button, squinting to try and make out the face of the man walking next to her.

'Never seen him before,' Salvatore shrugged.

'Get a print of this off to the lab when we've finished,' Gallo ordered, starting the disc again. 'Get them to run it through the system. Interpol too.'

'Where did she get his car keys?' Salvatore asked with a frown as they watched Allegra beep the car open and then step round to the boot.

'Evidence room, they were probably on the same set as . . .' Gallo broke off with a frown as he saw Allegra retrieve something from the boot. He paused the footage again. 'What the hell is that?'

'Christ knows.' Salvatore shrugged. 'The picture's too dark. I'll ask the lab to see what they can do with it.'

'I thought you said that car had been searched?' Gallo barked angrily.

'I . . . I thought it had,' Salvatore stammered. Coughing nervously, he restarted the film only to pause it himself a few moments later.

'He's got something too,' he said, squinting as he tried to make out the image. 'Looks like . . . a piece of paper. Or maybe a photo?'

'I want the names of whoever searched that car,' Gallo said through gritted teeth. 'Their names and their fucking badges.'

A squad car suddenly appeared at the top edge of the screen and one of the guards Gallo had just seen being loaded into the ambulance stepped out. He ejected the disc, lip curled in disgust.

'Put out a revised description of Damico and get something worked up for this guy, whoever he is,' he ordered. 'Then –'

'Colonel, we've found the car!' A young officer had appeared at the door, breathing hard. 'Abandoned in the Borghese Gardens.'

'And Lieutenant Damico?'

'No sign of her, I'm afraid.'

Salvatore stood up, giving Gallo an expectant look.

'Go.' He nodded. 'Take whoever you need. Find her. She can't have got far if she's on foot.'

Gallo waited until the room was empty and then dug his phone out of his pocket and dialled a number.

'It's me.' He lit another cigarette and took a long drag. 'We just missed her again.'

He listened, making a face.

'She came looking for Cavalli's car . . . I don't know why, but she found something he'd hidden in it . . . If I had to guess, a photograph.'

Another pause as he listened, his expression hardening.

'How should I know what was on it?' he said angrily. 'I was rather hoping you could tell me.'

FORTY

**Spagna Metropolitana station, Rome
19th March – 9.27 a.m.**
The train galloped into the station, its metal flanks
elaborately embroidered with graffiti – the angry
poetry of Rome's disenfranchised youth delivered
at the point of an aerosol can. In a few places, the
authorities had scrubbed the carriages clean, no
doubt in the hope of protecting the wider popu-
lation from these dangerously subversive voices.
Their efforts, however, had largely been in vain,
the ghostly outline of the censored thoughts still
clearly visible where the chemicals had bleached
them, like a scar that refused to heal.

The doors hissed open and a muscular human
wave swept Tom and Allegra through the tunnels
and up the escalators, until it broke as it reached
the street above, beaching them in the shadow of
the Spanish Steps.

'Let's head into the centre,' Tom said, shaking

off the street hawkers tugging at his sleeve and pointing himself towards the seductive windows of the Via Condotti. 'Stick with the crowds.'

'I know a good place for a coffee,' Allegra suggested with a nod.

Ten minutes later and they were opposite each other in a small cubicle at the rear of a bar on the Piazza Campo Marzio, tucking into pastries and espressos.

'Too strong for you?' Allegra asked with a smile as Tom took a sip.

'Just right.' He grimaced, licking the grit from his front teeth as he glanced round.

The place didn't look as though it had been touched in thirty years, its floor tiles cracked and lifting, the brick walls stained yellow by smoke and festooned with faded Roma flags, tattered banners and crookedly framed match-day programmes. Pride of place, behind the battle-scarred bar, had been given to a signed photograph of a previous Roma club captain who, in what looked like more prosperous times, had clearly once stopped in for a complimentary Prosecco. Apart from Tom and Allegra, it was more or less deserted, a few construction workers loitering at the bar. One had his foot resting on his hardhat, like a hunter posing for a photo with his kill.

'Did you choose this place on purpose?'

'What do you mean?'

'Caravaggio killed a man near the Campo Marzio.'

'I'd forgotten.' She frowned. 'Some sort of a duel, wasn't it?'

'An argument over the score during a game of tennis,' Tom explained, emptying another sugar into his coffee to smooth its bitter edge. 'Or so the story goes. Swords were drawn, and in the struggle . . .'

'Which is how he ended up in Sicily?'

'Via Naples and Malta,' Tom confirmed. 'He painted the *Nativity* while he was still on the run.' A pause. 'That's the wonderful thing about Caravaggio. That he could be so deeply flawed as a person, and yet capable of such beauty. They say his paintings are like a mirror to the soul.'

'Even yours?' she asked, Tom detecting the hint of a serious question lurking behind her teasing smile.

'Perhaps. If I had one.' He smiled back.

Allegra ordered another round of coffees.

'So what are we going to do about Johnny?' she asked as the waiter shuffled away.

'What can we do?' Tom shrugged. 'Even if we hadn't trashed the car, the cops will be all over it by now. We're just going to have to wait until Archie calls and then pay him the cash instead.'

'Archie?'

'My business partner,' Tom explained. 'He's on his way to Geneva, but he knows people here. The sort of people who can lend us fifty grand without asking too many questions. It might take until tonight, but as soon as we have it we go back to Johnny, hand it over and see what he knows.'

One of the workers made his way past them, returning a few moments later wiping his hands on his trousers and fastening his fly, the toilet flushing lustily behind him.

'Show me that photo again,' Allegra said, when he was out of earshot.

Reaching into his pocket, Tom laid the Polaroid down between them. It showed a sculpted man's face against a black background, a jagged edge marking where part of his chin and left cheek had broken off.

'It looks like marble. A statue fragment,' she said slowly, turning it to face her. 'Beautifully carved . . .' She ran her fingers across the photo's surface, as if trying to stroke its lips. 'Almost certainly looted.'

'How can you tell?'

'Tomb-robbers always use Polaroids. It avoids the risk of sending negatives off to be developed. And they can't be as easily emailed around as digital photos, allowing you to keep track of who has seen what.'

'Are you sure it's marble?' Tom frowned. 'It looks pretty thin. Almost like some sort of mask.'

'You're right,' she said, peering at the image. 'Strange. To be honest, I've never really seen anything like it before.'

'Then we need to find someone who has. The photo was pushed too far down that seat to have fallen there accidentally. Cavalli must have hidden it for a reason.'

'Well the obvious person is . . .' Allegra began, breaking off as she realised what she was saying.

'Your friend, the professor?' Tom guessed.

'I wasn't thinking.' She shook her head. 'There's no way I'm –'

'You won't have to, I'll do the talking,' Tom reassured her. 'Where can I find him?'

'Forget it,' she sighed impatiently. 'Gallo will have someone watching his apartment.'

'He must go out?'

'Not if he can avoid it,' she said with a shake of her head. 'Bad hip and a completely irrational fear of weeds.'

'Weeds?'

'He's old. It's a long story.'

Tom noticed that, for the briefest of moments, she allowed herself to smile. Then, just as quickly, her face clouded over again.

'Then I'll have to find a way in. There must be –'

'What time is it?' she interrupted, gripping Tom's arm.

'What?'

'The time?'

He glanced up at the pizza-inspired clock tethered to the wall over the toilet.

'Just after ten. Why?' Tom asked as she excit-edly stuffed the photograph into her pocket.

'He's giving a lecture this morning,' she exclaimed, sidling along the bench so that she could stand up. 'I saw his notes yesterday. Eleven o'clock at the Galleria Doria Pamphilj.'

Tom jumped up, throwing a handful of change down.

'That doesn't give us much time.'

FORTY-ONE

Hotel Ritz, Madrid, Spain
19th March – 9.48 a.m.

'Oh. It's you.'

Director Bury's face fell, either too jet-lagged or annoyed to conceal his disappointment. It was hard to tell.

'Yes, sir.' Verity Bruce nodded, trying to sound like she hadn't noticed. 'It's me.'

There was a long pause, and he looked at her hopefully, as if she might suddenly remember that she needed to be somewhere else, or that she had accidentally knocked on the wrong door. But she said nothing, playing instead with the silver locket around her neck in the knowledge that it would draw his eyes towards the bronzed curve of her breasts.

'Yes, well,' Bury coughed nervously, his eyes flicking to his feet and then to a point about three inches above her head. 'You'd better come in.'

To say that he had been deliberately avoiding her since the unveiling of the kouros would have been going too far. They'd both had lunch with someone from the mayor's office the previous day, for example, both sat in the first-class cabin together on the flight over and both been guests at that morning's cultural exchange breakfast at the embassy. But to say that he had been avoiding being *alone* with her would have been entirely accurate. He had sought safety in numbers, inventing a reason to leave the lunch early so they wouldn't have to share a taxi back to the museum, arriving at the breakfast late to avoid getting trapped over muffins and orange juice. That's why she'd followed him back to his hotel suite now. She'd known he would be alone and out of excuses.

He walked over to the desk and perched on its edge, indicating that she should sit in one of the low armchairs opposite. She recognised this as one of his usual tricks; a clumsy attempt, no doubt picked up from some assertiveness training course, to gain the psychological advantage by physically dominating the conversation.

'I'll stand, if that's all right,' she said, enjoying his small flicker of anxiety.

'Good idea.' He jumped up, clearly not wanting to get caught out at his own game. 'Too much sitting around in this job.'

'Dominic, I thought it was time we talked. Alone.'

'Yes, yes.' Bury seemed strangely pleased that she'd said this, like someone who was desperate to break up with their partner, but too chicken to bring it up first. He gave a nervous laugh. 'Drink?'

The offer appeared to be directed more at himself than her. She shook her head, her eyebrows raised in surprise.

'It's a little early, isn't it?'

'Not in Europe,' he said quickly. 'When in Rome and all that, hey?'

There was another strained silence as he busied himself over a bottle of scotch and some ice, the neck of the bottle chiming against the glass's rim as his hand trembled while he poured.

'Cheers!' he said, with a rather forced enthusiasm.

'About the other day . . .' she began.

'Very unfortunate,' he immediately agreed, refilling his glass. 'All those people, all those questions . . .' He knocked back another mouthful, swallowing it before it had touched the back of his throat. 'It doesn't look good, you understand.'

'The kouros is genuine,' she insisted. 'You saw the forensic tests.'

'Yes, of course.'

'Only sometimes it's easier for people to attack us than it is for them to accept that their fixed views on the evolution of Greek sculpture might be wrong,' she said, paraphrasing Faulks's rather more eloquent argument from the previous day.

'I know, I know.' Bury sat down wearily, momentarily forgetting his usual mind games, it seemed. 'But the trustees . . .' he said the word as if they were a local street gang who he suspected of vandalising his car. 'They get nervous.'

'Building a collection like ours isn't risk free,' she observed dryly. 'Their canapés and cocktails come with some strings attached.'

'They don't understand the art world,' he agreed. 'They don't understand what it takes to play catch-up with the Europeans and the Met.'

'They're out of their depth,' she nodded. 'And they're dragging us under with them.'

He shrugged and gave a weak smile, not disagreeing with her, she noted.

'They just want to wake up to the right sort of headlines.'

'Then I have just the thing for them,' she jumped in, sensing her moment. 'A unique piece. Impeccable provenance. I'm flying to Geneva tomorrow to see it.'

'Verity –' he stood up again, as if he sensed a negotiation looming and therefore the need to physically reassert himself once more '– I have to tell you that it's going to be a while before the trustees, or me, for that matter . . .'

She thrust the Polaroid Faulks had entrusted

her with towards him. He sat down again heavily, his face pale. 'That's . . .'

'Impossible? Wait until I tell you who I think carved it.'

FORTY-TWO

Piazza del Collegio Romano, Rome
19th March – 10.49 a.m.

This was Aurelio's Eco's favourite art gallery. Quite an accolade, when you considered the competition. Yes, the Capitoline Museum was richer, the Vatican Museum bigger, the Galleria Borghese more beautiful. But their fatal flaw was to have been crudely sewn together from larger collections by different patrons over time, leaving ugly and unnatural scars where they joined and overlapped.

The Doria Pamphilj, on the other hand, had been carefully built over the centuries by a single family. In Aurelio's eyes this gave it a completely unique integrity of vision and purpose that stretched unbroken, like a golden thread, back through time. It was a sacred flame, carefully tended by each passing generation and then handed on to the next custodian to nurture. Even today, the family still lived in the palazzo's private apartments, still owned the fabulous gallery that sheltered within its thick walls. He rather liked this – it appealed to his sense of the past and the present and the future and how they were inexorably wedded through history.

He paused on the entrance steps and snatched a glance over his shoulder, tightening his scarf around his neck. Gallo's men weren't even trying to pretend they weren't following him now, two of them having parked up near where he'd been dropped off by his taxi and following on foot about thirty feet behind. He felt more like a prisoner than protected, despite what they'd told him. With a helpless shrug, he placed his hand on the door and heaved it open.

'*Buongiorno, Professore,*' the guard on reception welcomed him cheerily.

He was early, but then he liked to leave himself enough time to check the room and have a final read through his notes. It was funny, but even at his age, after doing this for all these years, he still got nervous. That was the problem with an academic reputation. It was brittle, like porcelain. All those years of care could be shattered in one clumsy moment. And even if you managed to find all the pieces and reassemble them, the cracks invariably showed.

'Expecting a big turnout today?'

'An interpretation of the archaeological remains of the Etruscan bridge complex at San Giovenale,'

Aurelio recited the title of his lecture in a deliberate monotone. 'I almost didn't come myself.'

'In other words, I'll be turning people away as usual.' The guard's laughter followed him along the entrance hall.

The one thing Aurelio didn't like about this place was the lift. It was ancient and horribly cramped and seemed to rouse a latent claustrophobia that years of archaeological excavations had never previously disturbed. Still, it was only one floor, he thought to himself as the car lurched unsteadily upwards, and with his hip the way it was, it wasn't as if he had much choice.

Stepping out, he limped though the Poussin and Velvets rooms to the ballroom, where two banks of giltwood and red velvet chairs had already been laid out. Enough seating for fifty, he noted with a smile. Perhaps the turnout wouldn't be so bad after all.

'Are you alone?'

He turned to see a man closing the door behind him, the key turning in the lock.

'The lecture doesn't start until eleven,' he replied warily.

'Are you alone, Aurelio?' A woman stood framed in the doorway to the small ballroom, her face stone, her voice like ice.

FORTY-THREE

Galleria Doria Pamphilj, Rome
19th March – 10.57 a.m.

'Allegra?' Aurelio gasped. 'Is that you? What have you done to yourself?'

'How many?' Tom growled in Italian.

'What?' Aurelio's eyes flicked back to him.

'How many men followed you here?'

'Two,' he stuttered. 'Two, I think. Gallo's. They've been watching me ever since . . .'

'Ever since you betrayed me?' Allegra hissed. It was strange. She'd felt many things for Aurelio since yesterday afternoon. Sadness, disbelief, confusion. But now that he was actually standing in front of her, it was her anger, instinctive and uncontained, that had come most naturally.

'We haven't got time for that now,' Tom warned her, bolting shut the door that gave on to the adjacent ballroom. 'Just show it to him.'

'I'm sorry, Allegra. I'm so sorry,' Aurelio

whispered, reaching pleadingly towards her. 'I should have told you. I should have told you everything a long time ago.'

'Save it,' she snapped, stony faced, then pressed the photo into his hands. 'What is it?'

He gazed down at the picture, then looked up, open mouthed.

'Is this real?' he croaked.

'What is it?' Tom repeated.

'It looks Greek,' Allegra prompted. 'I thought the marble could be from Pentelikon.'

'Greek, yes, but that's not marble.' He shook his head excitedly, his eyes locking with hers. 'It's ivory.'

'Ivory?' she repeated breathlessly. It was obvious, now he'd mentioned it. Obvious and yet impossible.

'It's a mask from a chryselephantine statue,' Aurelio confirmed. 'Circa 400 to 500 BC. Probably of the sun god Apollo.' A pause. 'Are you sure this is real?' he asked again.

'Chryselephantine means gold and ivory in Greek,' Allegra quickly explained in English, seeing the confused look on Tom's face. 'They used to fix carved slabs of ivory on to a wooden frame for the head, hands and feet and then beat sheets of gold leaf on to the rest to form the clothes, armour and hair.'

'It's rare?'

'It's a miracle,' Aurelio replied in a hushed tone, almost as if they weren't there. 'There used to be seventy-four of them in Rome, but they all vanished when it was sacked by the Barbarians in 410 AD. Apart from two fire-damaged examples found in Greece and a fragment in the Vatican Museum, not a single piece has survived. Certainly nothing of this size and quality.'

Their eyes all shot to the door as someone tried the handle, rattling it noisily.

'Time to go,' Tom said firmly, snatching the photo from his grasp. 'The private apartments should still be clear. We can go out the same way we came in.'

'Wait,' Aurelio called after them. 'Don't you want to know who it's by?'

'You can tell that from a photo?' Allegra frowned, something in his voice making her pause.

There was a muffled shout and then a heavy drum roll of pounding fists.

'Not definitively. Not without seeing it,' he admitted. 'But if I had to guess . . . there's only one sculptor from that period that we know of who was capable of something of that quality. The same person who carved the statue of Athena in the Parthenon. The same person who carved the statue of Zeus at Olympia, one of the Seven Wonders of the Ancient World.'

'Phidias?' Allegra guessed, her mouth suddenly dry. No wonder Aurelio had turned pale.

'Who else?' He nodded excitedly. 'Don't you see, Allegra? It's a miracle.'

'Let's go,' Tom repeated, grabbing Allegra's arm,

the door now shaking violently. But she wrestled herself free, determined to ask the one question that she most wanted answered.

'Why did you do it, Aurelio?' she snapped. 'Has Gallo got something on you?'

'Gallo? I'd never even heard of him until yesterday,' he protested.

'Then who were you on the phone to?'

There was a long pause, Aurelio's lips quivering as though the words were trapped in his mouth.

'The League.'

'The Delian League?' she breathed, not sure which was worse – Aurelio working with Gallo, as she'd first assumed, or this?

'They said they wouldn't hurt you. That they just wanted to see what you knew,' he pleaded. 'I wanted to tell you everything. Have done for a long time. When you told me about the lead discs and the killings . . . I tried to point you in the right direction. But I was afraid.'

Abruptly, the noise outside stopped.

'They'll be back with a key,' urged Tom. 'Come on!'

'You could have trusted me,' she insisted, ignoring Tom. 'I could have helped you.'

'It was too late for that. It's been twenty, thirty years. They'd kept records of everything I'd ever done for them. The false attributions, the inflated valuations, the invented provenances. I needed the money. You see that, don't you? I needed the money to finance my work. Who else was going to pay? The university? The government? Pah!'

'Who are they?' she pressed. 'Give me a name.'

'Th-there was a dealer who I met a few times,' he muttered. 'An American called Faulks who used to fly in from Geneva. He was with them, I'm sure of it. But everyone else was just a voice on the phone. Believe me, Allegra, I tried to get out so many times. Tried to give it up. But the older I got, the harder it became to throw everything away.'

'Throw what away?'

'Oh, you don't understand. You're too young.' He gave an exasperated sigh, throwing his hands up as if she had somehow let him down. 'You don't know what it means to be old, to be out of breath from tying your shoelaces, to not be able to take a piss without it hurting.'

'What's that got to do . . .?'

'My books, my research – everything I'd ever worked for . . . my whole life. It would all have been for nothing if they'd leaked my involvement.'

'Your books?' she repeated with an empty laugh. 'Your books!'

'Don't you see?' he pleaded, a desperate edge to his voice now. 'I had no choice. My reputation was all I had left.'

'No,' she said, with a broken smile. 'You had me.'

FORTY-FOUR

Quai du Mont Blanc, Geneva
19th March – 11.16 a.m.

There was a definite spring in Earl Faulks's step that morning, despite the slightly bitter taste left by Deena Carroll's sermonising earlier. After everything he'd done for them over the years . . . the ungrateful bitch. The truth was that, having thought about it, he was rather glad she'd turned him down. With Klein as good as dead, he was no use to him any more anyway, so why do her any favours? Better to give someone else a sniff of the action.

Besides, he could afford to take a small risk. Things were going well. Much better, in fact than he had anticipated. His courier had cleared the border at Lake Lugano that morning and was due down at the Free Port any time now. In Rome, meanwhile, events were unfolding far more quickly and dramatically than he had ever dreamt would be possible. That was the beauty of the Italians, he mused. They were an amaretto paper of a race – ready to ignite at the faintest spark.

There had been that unhelpful little episode with the kouros at the Getty, of course, although for the moment at least, tempers seemed to have cooled. Having seen the ivory mask, Verity had understood that there was a far greater prize at stake here than a dry academic debate over a statue's marble type and muscle tone. Barring any last-minute disaster, she was due in from Madrid around lunchtime the following day.

Until then he had an auction to prepare for, lots to examine, commission bids to place . . . On cue, his car drew up outside Sotheby's. He sat back, waiting for his chauffer to jog round and open his door, but then waved him away when his phone began to ring. An American number that he didn't recognise. A call he wanted to take.

'Faulks.'

'This is Kezman,' the voice replied.

'Mr Kezman . . .' Faulks checked his watch in surprise – a classic fluted steel Boucheron. 'Thank you for returning my call. I wasn't expecting to hear from you so late.'

'I'm in the casino business. This is early,' he growled.

'Mr Kezman, I don't know if you know . . .'

'Yeah, I know who you are,' he shot back.

'Avner Klein's a personal friend. He told me about you.'

'And he told me about you,' purred Faulks. 'Said you were a shrewd collector.'

'Don't blow smoke up my ass. I pay people for that and I guarantee they've all got bigger tits than you. If you've got something to sell, sell it.'

'Fair enough. Here's the pitch: seven and a half million and your name in lights.'

'My name's in ten foot neon out on the Strip already.' Kezman gave an impatient laugh. 'Tell me about the money.'

'Seven and a half million dollars,' Faulks repeated slowly. 'Risk free.'

'Why don't you leave the odds to the experts?' Kezman snapped.

'How would you price a federal government guarantee?'

There was a pause.

'Go on.'

Faulks smiled. He had his attention now.

'An . . . item has come into my possession. An item of immense historical and cultural significance. I want you to buy it off me for ten million dollars.'

'Sure. Why not make it twenty?' Kezman gave a hollow laugh. 'The global economy's on its knees, but let's not let small details like that get in the way.'

'Then, you're going to donate it to Verity Bruce

at the Getty,' he continued, ignoring the interruption. 'She will value it at fifty million, its true price. This will lead the IRS . . .'

'To give me a seventeen and a half million tax credit for having made a fifty-million-dollar charitable donation,' Kezman breathed, his flippant tone vanishing.

'Which, subtracting the ten you will have paid me, nets out at a seven and a half million profit, courtesy of Uncle Sam. Not to mention the PR value of the coverage that will be triggered by your generosity,' Faulks added. 'Hell, they'd probably name a wing after you, if you asked.'

'How firm is the valuation?'

'Do you know Verity Bruce?' Faulks asked.

'I had breakfast with her two weeks ago.'

'She's due here tomorrow to authenticate the piece. Something this rare isn't affected by shortterm economic factors. The value will hold.'

Kezman was silent for a few moments. Faulks waited, knowing that his next question would reveal how well he'd played his hand.

'When would you need the money?'

Blackjack.

'A few days. A week at most.'

'If Verity okays it, I'm in,' Kezman confirmed. 'You have my private number now. Just get her to call me when she's seen it.'

'Wait! Don't you even want to know what it is?' Faulks asked with a frown.

A pause.

'Will I make any more if I do?'

'No,' Faulks conceded.

'Then why should I care?'

FORTY-FIVE

Via del Governo Vecchio, Rome
19th March – 11.32 a.m.

The streets were dark and narrow here, the build-ings seeming to arch together over Tom and Allegra's heads like trees kissing over a country lane. It was busy too; people carefully picking their way along the narrow pavements, dodging around the occasional dog turds and an elderly woman who was furiously scrubbing her marble doorstep. The traffic, meanwhile, was backed up behind a florist's van which had stopped to make a delivery. Alerted by the relentless sounding of impatient car horns, a few people were leaning curiously over their balconies, some observing events with a detached familiarity, others hurling insults at the van driver for his selfishness. Glancing up, he made an obscene gesture, and pulled away.

Allegra was silent, her eyes rarely lifting from

her shoes. She was hurting, Tom knew, probably even blaming herself for Aurelio's betrayal, as if his selfishness and pride was somehow her fault. He tried to think of something to say that might comfort her and relieve her imagined guilt. But he couldn't. Not without lying. The truth was that in time the floodwaters of her anger and confusion would recede, leaving behind them the tidemark of their lost friendship. And whatever he said, that would never fade. He, of all people, bore the fears of betrayal.

'What other Phidias pieces are there?' he asked, stepping to one side to let a woman past holding on to five yapping dogs, the leashes stretching from her hands like tentacles.

'There's a torso of Athena in the École des Beaux-Arts in Paris that's been attributed to him,' she replied without looking up. 'And they found a cup inscribed with his name in the ruins of the workshop at Olympia where he assembled the statue of Zeus.'

'But nothing like the mask?'

'Not even close.' She shook her head. 'If Aurelio's right, it's priceless.'

'Everything has a price,' Tom smiled. 'The trick is finding someone willing to pay it.'

'Maybe that's what Cavalli was doing the night he was killed,' she said, grimacing as an ancient Vespa laboured past, its wheezing engine making the windows around them rattle under the strain.

'Meeting a buyer. Or at least someone he thought was a buyer.'

'It would explain why he had the Polaroid on him,' Tom agreed. 'And why he hid it when he realised what they really wanted.'

'But not where he got the mask from in the first place.' She paused, frowning, as the road brought them out on to the Piazza Ponte Sant'Angelo. 'What are we doing here?'

'Isn't this where you said Cavalli was killed?' Tom asked.

'Yes, but . . .'

'I thought we should take a look.'

A steady two-way traffic of pedestrians was streaming over the bridge's polished cobbles, the hands and faces of the statues lining the parapet seeming strangely animated under the sun's flickering caress, as if they were waving them forward. For Tom, at least, the wide-open vista was a welcome relief from the narrow street's dark embrace.

'Where did they find him?' he asked, hands shoved deep into his coat pockets.

'In the river. Hanging from one of the statues.'

'Killed on the anniversary of Caesar's murder, only for Ricci to be murdered on the site of Caesar's assassination,' he said thoughtfully.

'With both Ricci's and Argento's deaths staged as a re-enactment of a Caravaggio painting.' She nodded impatiently. 'We've been through all this.'

'I know.' He shrugged. 'It's just that everything about these murders has been so deliberate. The dates, the locations, the arrangement of the bodies, the careful echoing of some element of the one that had preceded it. It's almost as if . . . they weren't just killings.'

'Then what were they?'

Tom paused before answering. In the distance the glorious dome of St Peter's rose into the sky, massive and immutable. Around it swarmed a flock of pigeons, their solid mass wheeling and circling like a shroud caught in the wind.

'Messages,' he said eventually. 'Maybe someone was trying to have a conversation.'

'If you're right it started with Cavalli,' she said slowly, her eyes narrowing in understanding.

'Exactly. So why kill him here? Why this bridge? They must have chosen it for a reason.'

Allegra paused a few moments before answering, her face creased in thought.

'It was originally built to connect the city to Hadrian's mausoleum. Before becoming a toll road for pilgrims who wanted to reach St Peter's. And in the sixteenth and seventeenth centuries, famously of course, they used to display the bodies of executed prisoners along it as a warning.'

'A warning to who?' Tom frowned, then nodded at the weathered shapes looming over them. 'What about the statues? Do they mean anything?'

'Commissioned from Bernini by Pope Clement IX.

Each angel is holding an object from the Passion. Cavalli's rope was tied to the one holding a cross.'

'Which was then echoed by Ricci's inverted crucifixion and Argento being found in a church.' Tom clicked his fingers as two more small pieces of the puzzle fell into place.

'That's not the only thing,' Allegra added excitedly, a thought having just occurred to her. 'Cavalli's not the first person to have been killed here.'

'What do you mean?'

'A noblewoman called Beatrice Cenci was tortured and put to death on the Piazza Ponte Sant'Angelo in 1599,' she explained. 'It was one of Rome's most notorious public executions.'

'What had she done?'

'Murdered her father.'

Tom nodded slowly, remembering the deliberate violence with which Cavalli's house had been ransacked.

'Patricide. Treason. Maybe that's it. Maybe Cavalli had betrayed the League and this was his punishment?' He gave a deep sigh, then turned to her with a shrug. 'Your guess is as good as mine. Come on, let's try and call Archie. He should have landed by now.'

They turned and walked to the end of the bridge, Tom reaching for his phone as they waited for a break in the traffic. But before they could cross, a large armoured truck gunned down the road towards them. Two men jumped down holding what Tom recognized as what the Sicilian mafia called a Lupara – a traditional break-open design shotgun, sawn off a few inches beyond the stock to make it more effective at close range and easier to manoeuvre and hide. The weapon of choice in old-school vendettas.

A woman behind screamed and Tom could hear the fumbling scramble of panicked feet behind him as people scattered.

'Get in,' one of the men barked.

FORTY-SIX

Lungotevere Vaticano, Rome
19th March – 11.53 a.m.

Looking around him, Tom could see that the truck's interior had been furnished like an expensive office, the floor laid with thick carpet, the sides lined with a cream wallpaper decorated with tropical birds. To his left a red leather sofa abutted what he assumed was a toilet cubicle, its door latched shut. In the far right-hand corner, meanwhile, stood an elegant cherrywood desk on which a brass banker's lamp illuminated a laptop and a police scanner spitting static. Overhead were four flat-panel screens, each tuned to a different news or business channel. Most telling, perhaps, was the gun rack opposite the sofa, which contained four MP5s, half a dozen Glock 17s and a pair of Remington 1100s. Neatly stacked on the shelves below were two dozen grenades and several boxes of ammunition. Enough to start and win a small war.

The gears crunched and the truck swayed forward with a determined snarl. The gunman who had followed them inside waved at them to sit down and then instructed them to handcuff themselves to the hoop bolted to the wall above them so that their arms were held above their heads. Stepping forward, he made sure that the ratchets were tight against their wrists and then emptied their pockets and Tom's bag, pausing over the FBI file and the Polaroid of the ivory mask. In the background, Tom could make out the opening aria of the *Cavalleria Rusticana*.

There was the muffled sound of the toilet flushing. The latch clicked open and a man walked out, placing a folded newspaper down on the desk as he turned to face them. Tall and square faced, he had a thinning head of hair that rose in white waves at the front and then foundered into a black expanse at the rear. He was smartly dressed in a grey Armani suit and gaudy Versace tie with matching pocket hand-kerchief. The collar of his white shirt, however, appeared to be several sizes too small, as if he had gambled on not buying a new one in the belief that he would lose some weight. If so, it was a bet that he appeared destined to lose, his once sharp cheekbones sinking into his face like smudged lines on a charcoal drawing, a fleshy crevice forming in the cleft of his chin.

The guard handed him the file and the Polaroid.

He glanced at each of them, then sat down. Swivelling to face them, he adjusted his cuffs, carefully covering his watch.

'Welcome to Rome, Signor Kirk.' He spoke in a thick accent, his eyes fixing them with a cold, mortuary gaze.

'You know him?' Allegra's voice was both angry and disbelieving.

Tom frowned as he tried to place the face, then gave a small shake of his head.

'Should I?'

'Should he?' the man asked Allegra, his face creased into a question.

'He's Giovanni De Luca,' Allegra replied unsmilingly. 'The head of the Banda della Magliana.'

Tom's eyes flickered in recognition. So much for tracking the Delian League down and the element of surprise. Instead, one half of it had come looking for them and sprung its own trap.

'Felix doesn't know me,' De Luca said, his flickering smile suggesting he was pleased that she had recognised him. 'But I had the pleasure of meeting his mother once.'

'My mother?' Tom breathed, not knowing whether to sound angry or astonished.

'A fundraising dinner many years ago. A beautiful woman, if I may say so. A terrible loss. Of course, it was only many years later that I heard of you.'

'Heard what, exactly?' Allegra asked, eyeing

Tom with the same suspicious look she'd had back in Cavalli's house when she'd first met him.

'It's hard to be good at what Felix does without word getting out. He has a special talent.'

'Had,' Tom corrected him. 'I got out a few years ago.'

'And yet, from what I hear, you're still running.' He nodded towards the scanner.

'Is that what this is about?' Tom asked impatiently. His arms were beginning to ache and every gear change and bump in the road was making the cuffs saw a little deeper into his wrists.

'What's this?' De Luca waved the photo at him.

'We found it in Cavalli's car,' Tom explained. 'We think he was trying to sell it.'

'What do you know about Cavalli?' De Luca shot back, spitting the name out in a way that revealed more than he had probably intended.

Tom nodded slowly, immediately guessing at the truth.

'Why did you kill him?'

De Luca paused, then inclined his head in a small bow, as if acknowledging applause.

'Strictly speaking, the river killed him.'

'Did he work for you?'

'Pfff! He was one of Moretti's.'

Moretti. Tom recognized the name as the person Allegra had identified as supposedly heading up the *other* half of the Delian League. De Luca's supposed business partner.

'What had he done?' Allegra asked.

'I only kill for two reasons. Theft and disloyalty.' De Luca counted them off on his fingers as if he were listing the ingredients for a recipe. 'In Cavalli's case, he was guilty of both.'

'You mean he'd betrayed the League?' Tom asked.

'It seemed fitting to mark his treachery on the spot of an earlier treason,' De Luca nodded, confirming what they'd already guessed on the bridge.

The van turned sharply left. Allegra slid across the seat, pressing up against Tom.

'And Ricci?' Allegra asked.

'I took care of Cavalli to protect the League. But Moretti, the old fool, got it into his head that I was about to make a move on the whole operation.' De Luca's tone hardened, his jaw clenching. 'He had Ricci killed to warn me off. Argento was me evening the score.'

Tom nodded as the realisation dawned that far from being a conversation the careful echoing and symbolism of the various deaths had in fact been the opening shots of a very public, very acrimonious divorce.

'And now it seems my accountant in Monaco has disappeared,' he continued angrily. 'Well, if Moretti wants a war, I'm ready for him.' He struck his chest with his fist, the dull thud revealing that he was wearing a bullet-proof vest under his shirt.

'What did Jennifer Browne have to do with your war?' Tom demanded angrily.

'Who?' De Luca frowned.

'The FBI agent you had killed in Vegas.'

'What FBI agent?'

'Don't lie to me,' Tom shouted, his wrists straining against the handcuffs.

'Cavalli was going to sing, so I clipped his wings,' De Luca said in a low, controlled voice. 'Ricci and Argento – that's just business between Moretti and me. But I had nothing to do with killing any FBI agent. I've never even heard of her.'

'She was closing in on the Delian League, so you had her taken out,' Tom insisted.

'Is that what this is about? Is that why you're here?' De Luca picked up the FBI file and glanced at its monogrammed cover with a puzzled shrug. 'Well, then maybe somebody did us a favour. Either way, I never ordered the hit.'

'Well, somebody in the League did,' Tom insisted. 'And I'll take you all down to find them, if I have to.'

There was a pause. De Luca blew out the sides of his cheeks, clearly mulling something over. Then, with a shrug, he nodded.

'Yes. I expect you probably would.'

Tom felt the needle before he saw it, a sharp stab of pain in his neck where the guard had stepped forward and pulled the trigger on an injection gun. Allegra was next, her head slumping forward as he felt the room begin to spin and darken. The last thing he was aware of was De Luca's voice, deepening and slowing as if being played back at half speed.

'Do give my best to your mother.'

FORTY-SEVEN

Sotheby's auction rooms,
Quai du Mont Blanc, Geneva
19th March – 1.32 p.m.

Short, perhaps only four feet high, she had braided hair that fell across her forehead and down her neck. Dressed in a simple tunic that hung from her body in smooth folds, a hunting strap ran down from her shoulder and across her breasts, pulling the material tight against their firm slope. Gazing straight ahead, she wore a slight smile, lips parted as if she was about to speak. Her arms were cut off at the elbows.

'Statue of the goddess Artemis; fourth century BC,' Archie murmured to himself as he looked down from the marble sculpture to the auction catalogue and scanned through the entry again. 'Believed to be from a settlement near Foggi. Private Syrian collection.'

This last detail made Archie smile. Even if Tom

hadn't asked him to investigate this lot, the fact that it had supposedly come from a Syrian family would have made him suspicious anyway. The simple truth was that, while the contents of most major European and American collections were well documented, little, if anything, was known about the majority of Middle Eastern and Asian private collections. Anyone trying to disguise the fact that an artefact was looted, therefore, was far more likely to tie it back to some obscure family collection where they could convincingly claim it had been languishing for the last eighty years, than to risk the awkward questions that a European provenance might trigger.

He stepped back and pretended to study some of the other lots, ignoring the call on his phone which he guessed, from the New York prefix, was the lawyer they'd met at Senator Duval's funeral still trying to arrange a meeting with Tom. Next time, he'd know better than to hand out his card so readily, he thought to himself with a pained sigh.

Looking up, he caught sight of Dominique de Lecourt standing near the entrance. Seeing her now, blonde hair cascading on to her delicate shoulders, it struck him that her pale, oval face mirrored something of the goddess Artemis's cold, sculpted and remote beauty. There was a parallel too, between the statue's simple tunic and her tailored linen dress, and perhaps even an echo of the carved hunting strap in the rearing stallion that he knew Dominique had had tattooed on her shoulder when younger. But any resemblance was only a fleeting one, the illusion shattered by her Ducati biker jacket and the way her blue eyes glittered with a wild freedom that the marble sculpture would never taste.

She was too young for him, although that hadn't stopped him thinking about what might have been from time to time. Still only twenty-five, in fact. Not that her age had prevented her from successfully running Tom's antiques business, having helped him transfer it from Geneva to London after his father died. This was her first time back here since then, and he could tell she was finding it difficult, however much she was trying to hide it.

She had been close to Tom's father – far closer, in fact, than Tom. The way she told the story, he had saved her from herself, offering her a job rather than calling the cops when he'd caught her trying to steal his wallet. With it had come a chance to break free from the spiralling cycle of casual drugs and petty crime that a childhood spent being tossed between foster homes had been steering her towards; a chance she'd grabbed with both hands. All of which made what they were about to do that much more ironic.

He nodded at her as Earl Faulks turned to leave the room, leaning heavily on his umbrella. Even if the auctioneer hadn't accepted the carefully folded five-hundred-euro note to finger him as the lot's seller, Archie would have guessed it was him. It wasn't just that he had returned four times during the viewing period that had marked him out, but the questioning look he had given anyone who had strayed too close to the statue. It rather reminded Archie of a father weighing up a potential boyfriend's suitability to take their teenage daughter out on a date.

Seeing Archie's signal, Dominique set off, bumping into Faulks heavily as they crossed.

'*Pardon,*' she apologised.

'That's quite all right,' Faulks snapped, a cold smile flickering across his face before, with a curt nod, he limped on.

'Go,' she whispered as she walked past Archie, their hands briefly touching as she handed him Faulks's PDA.

Turning to face the wall, Archie deftly popped off the rear cover, removed the battery and then slipped out the SIM card. Sliding it into a reader connected to an Asus micro laptop, he scanned its contents, the software quickly identifying the IMSI number, before girding itself to decrypt its Ki code.

Archie glanced up at Dominique, who had moved back towards the entrance and was signalling at him to hurry. Archie gave a grim nod, his heart racing, but the programme was still churning as it tried to break the 128-bit encryption, numbers scrolling frantically across the screen.

He looked up again, and cursed when he saw that she was now mouthing that Faulks was leaving. Damn! He'd counted on him staying for the auction itself, although he knew that some dealers preferred not to attend their own sales in case they jinxed them. He looked back down at the computer. Still nothing. Dominique was looking desperate now. Back to the screen again.

Done.

Snatching the SIM card out of the reader, he hurried to the door, fumbling as he slid it back into Faulks's phone and fitted the battery and then the cover. He crossed Dominique, their hands briefly touching again as slipped her the micro-computer, leaving her the final task of programming a new card.

'He's outside,' she breathed.

Archie sprinted into the hall, down the stairs and through the main entrance. Faulks was settling back in the rear seat of a silver Bentley, his chauffeur already at the wheel and turning the ignition key.

'Excuse me, mate,' Archie panted, rapping sharply on the window.

The window sank and Faulks, sitting forward on his seat, fixed him with a suspicious look.

'Can I help you?'

'You dropped this.'

Faulks looked at the phone, patted his breast pockets, then glanced up at Archie.

'Thank you,' he said, his wary look fading into a grateful smile. Taking it with a nod, he sat back, the window smoothly sealing itself shut.

As Faulks's car accelerated away, Dominique appeared at Archie's shoulder.

'All sorted?' he puffed.

'We've got him.' She nodded, handing him the newly cloned phone.

FORTY-EIGHT

Nr Anguillara Sabazia, northwest of Rome
19th March – 8.34 p.m.
Tom's eyes flickered open. The room slowly came into focus. Allegra was lying on the tiled floor next to him. Still breathing.

Gingerly pulling himself upright, he sat with his back against the wall, trying not to vomit. The drugs had left him dizzy and with a bitter taste at the back of his throat. Worse still was the headache centred behind his right eye, the daggered pain ebbing and flowing with the hammer beat of his pulse. Within seconds he'd fainted back to sleep, vaguely aware of a dancing blue light licking the walls, of the whisper of running water, of the deadened echo of his own breathing, and of De Luca's warm breath on his neck. *Do give my best to your mother.*

'Tom?'

Allegra had rolled over on to her side to face

him, her dark hair tumbling forward over her face. She looked worried and he wondered how long she had been calling his name.

He groaned as he sat up, his neck stiff where his head had fallen forward on to his chest.

'What time is it?' she asked.

He checked his watch, then remembered with a rueful grimace that it was still wrapped around Johnny Li's tattooed wrist.

'No idea.'

'*Merda*.' She rubbed her hands wearily across her face, then sat up next to him. 'Where do you think they've taken us?'

Tom looked around with a frown. They were at one end of a windowless room that had been almost entirely swallowed by what appeared to be a large swimming pool. Five feet deep, sixty feet long and thirty feet across, it was lined with white tiles, the water spilling with a gurgling noise over the edges into an overflow trench and washing through skimmers. The underwater lights cast a shimmering flicker on to the white-washed concrete walls.

Standing up, Tom walked unsteadily to the edge. His eyes adjusting, it took him a few moments to realise that the dark shapes lurking under the water's silvered surface were rows of antique vases and jars, each carefully spaced one from the other along the pool floor like vines anchored to a steep slope. Stiff and still, they reminded him of a Roman cohort arranged in a *testudo* formation, their shields held over their heads like a tortoise's shell, bracing themselves for an attack.

'It's a chemical bath,' he said, pointing at the blue drums that explained the slight burning sensation in his eyes.

'I've seen something like this before,' Allegra nodded, joining him. 'But not this big. Not even close.'

'Over there,' Tom pointed hopefully at a door on the far side of the pool.

They passed through into a large room, its tiled walls lined with glass-fronted cabinets that contained a rainbow array of paints and chemicals in differently sized and shaped tins and jars. Beneath these, running along each wall, were polished stainless steel counters loaded with microscopes, centrifuges, test-tube racks, scales, shakers and other pieces of laboratory equipment.

The centre of the room, meanwhile, was taken up by two large stainless steel benches and deep sinks. A trolley laden with knives, saws, picks, tweezers, drills and other implements had been drawn up next to them, as if in preparation for an imminent procedure. In the corner was a coiled hosepipe, the white tiled floor sloping towards a central drain as if to carry away blood.

'Cleaning, touching up, repairs, open-heart surgery . . .' Tom pursed his lips. 'This is a tombaroli restoration outfit.'

'On an industrial scale,' she agreed, Tom detecting the same instinctive anger in her voice as when she'd found the orphan vase fragment in Cavalli's car.

There was another unlocked door which gave, in turn, on to a third room, lit by a single naked bulb whose weak glare didn't quite reach to the corners. Here there was a more rustic feel, the ceiling supported by parallel lines of closely spaced wooden beams, semicircular iron-framed windows set into the stone walls at above head height and welded shut. A flight of stone steps led upstairs to another door. Predictably, this one was locked.

Shrugging dejectedly, Tom made his way back down. Allegra was waiting for him, silently pointing, her outstretched arm quivering with rage.

Looking around, he could see that the paved floor was covered in a foaming sea of dirty newspapers, wooden crates and old fruit and shoe boxes, some stacked into neat piles, others split open or listing dangerously where the cardboard had collapsed under their combined weight. He only had to open a few to guess at the contents of all the others – antique vases still covered in dirt, loose jumbles of glass and Etruscan jewellery, envelopes bulging with Roman coins, gold rings strewn on the floor. In the corner was what had once been an entire fresco, now hacked away from the wall and chain-sawed into laptop-sized chunks. Presumably to make them easier to move and sell.

'How could they do this?' Allegra breathed, her anger tinged by a horrified sadness.

'Because none of this has any value to them other than what they can sell it for. Because they don't care. Look.'

He nodded with disgust towards one of the open shoeboxes. It was stuffed with rings and human bones, the tombaroli having simply snapped off the fingers of the dead to save time.

'You think this is where Cavalli got the ivory mask?' she asked, looking away with a shudder.

'I doubt it,' Tom sighed, sitting down heavily on the bottom step. 'Whoever owns this place must work for De Luca, and he certainly didn't look like he'd ever seen the mask before.'

'He may not have seen it, but he might have found out that Cavalli was ripping him off,' she suggested, sitting down next to him. 'Theft and disloyalty, remember? According to De Luca, Cavalli was guilty of both. Maybe Cavalli was trying to sell the mask behind the League's back.'

'So De Luca killed Cavalli, Moretti evened the score by murdering Ricci, and then De Luca struck back by executing Argento. He was right. We've stumbled into a war.'

'That must be why they both put the lead discs on the bodies.'

'What do you mean?'

'Remember I told you that the original Delian League was to have lasted as long as the lead its members had thrown into the sea didn't rise to the surface? The discs were to signal that this new alliance was fracturing.'

'None of which explains who ordered the hit on Jennifer or why.' He sighed impatiently.

'You don't think De Luca had anything to do with it?'

'I don't know. Maybe . . . No. I think he would have told me if he had.'

'Then who?'

Tom shook his head, still no closer to the truth. There was a long pause.

'She must have meant a lot to you,' Allegra said gently. 'For you to have come all this way. For you to be risking so much.'

'She trusted me to do the right thing,' Tom answered with a half smile. 'That's more than most have ever done.'

There was another, long silence, Tom staring at the floor.

'How did you two meet?'

He was glad that Allegra hadn't picked up on the obvious cue and said that she trusted him too. He wouldn't have believed her if she had. Not yet at least.

'In London,' he began hesitantly. 'She thought I'd broken into Fort Knox.' He smiled at the memory of their first bad-tempered exchange in the Piccadilly Arcade.

'Fort Knox!' She whistled. 'What did she think you'd . . .'

She broke off as the door above them was unbolted and thrown open. A man stood silhouetted in the doorway, his long shadow stretching down the stairs towards them. He was holding a hip flask.

'Let's go for a drive.'

FORTY-NINE

**Banco Rosalia head office, Via
Boncompagni, Rome
19th March – 9.24 p.m.**

'So? How much are we down?' Santos sniffed, helping himself to a half tumbler of Limoncella from the drinks trolley.

Alfredo Geri looked up from his laptop, frowning slightly as he worked through the math. Five feet ten, he was wearing a grey suit, his tie yanked down, jacket trapped under the wheel of his chair where it had fallen on to the floor and he'd run over it. His thin black hair was slicked down against his marbled scalp, his face gaunt and bleached a cadaverous shade of white by lack of sleep and sunlight. To his right, balancing precariously on a slumping battlement of stacked files, was a pizza box that he'd not yet had time to open.

'Now I've had a chance to look properly . . . eight . . . maybe nine?'

'Eight or nine what?' Santos snapped. He sat down heavily at the head of the table, a blanket of scattered paper stretching along its polished surface like an avalanche over a valley floor. 'It's a big number. Show it some respect.'

'Eight or nine hundred million. Euro.'

'Eight or nine hundred million euro.' Santos closed his eyes and sighed heavily, then gave a rueful smile as he kicked back. 'You know, the strange thing is that a few months ago losing just fifty million would have felt like the end of the world. Now, it feels like a rounding error.'

He reached for his tin of liquorice, shook it, then popped the lid.

'It's the CDOs that have killed us,' Geri continued, putting his half-moon glasses back on and hunching over his screen. 'The entire port- folio's been wiped out. The rest is from currency swings and counterparty losses.'

'I thought we were hedged?'

'You can't hedge against this sort of market.'

'And the League's deposits and investments?' Santos asked hopefully.

'Antonio, the bank's entire capital base is gone,' Geri spoke slowly as if trying to spell out complicated directions to a tourist. 'It's all gone. Everything.'

Santos sniffed, then knocked the Limoncella back with a jerk of his wrist.

'Good. It makes things easier. This way I only

need to worry about myself. Where did I come out in the end?'

'I've liquidated what I can,' Geri sounded almost apologetic. 'Most of it at a loss, like I told you when we spoke. But the bulk of your portfolio would take weeks if not months to sell.'

'How much?' Santos snapped.

'Three, maybe four million.'

'That barely gets me a chalet,' Santos said with a hollow laugh. 'What about the money market positions?'

'Already included, minus what you had to sell to fund your fun and games in Las Vegas last week,' Geri reminded him in a reproachful tone.

A long pause.

'Fine,' Santos stood up. 'It is what it is and what it is . . . is not enough. I need the painting.'

'You've found a buyer?'

'The Serbs are lined up to take it off my hands for twenty million,' Santos said with a smile. 'I'm flying out to meet them later tonight.'

'And the watches?'

'I've got one already and another on its way. I'll get the third on the night from De Luca or Moretti. They always wear theirs.'

'They won't let you get away with it,' Geri pointed out, closing his file.

'They won't be able to stop me if they're dead.' Santos shrugged, moving round to stand behind him.

'For every person you kill, the League will send two more. You can't kill them all. Eventually they'll find you.'

'How?' Santos shrugged, stepping even closer until he could see the liver spots and tiny veins nestling under Geri's thin thatch. 'The world's a large place. And you're the only other person who knows where I'm going.'

'Well, you know I'll never tell them,' Geri reassured him, shoulders stiff, staring straight in front of him.

'Oh, I know.' Santos smiled.

In an instant, he had locked his left arm around Geri's throat and pulled him clear of the table. Geri lashed out with his legs, catching the edge of his file and sending it cartwheeling to the floor, paper scattering like feathers. Then with his right hand, Santos reached round and grabbed Geri's chin.

With a sharp jerk, he snapped his neck.

FIFTY

Nr Anguillara Sabazia, northwest of Rome
19th March – 9.56 p.m.

'Drink?'

Fabio Contarelli had turned in the passenger seat to face them, battered hip flask in hand. In his mid forties, short and pot-bellied, he had the warm, jovial manner of someone who prided himself on being on first-name terms with everyone in his village, and who the local butcher had come to favour with the best cuts. Shabbily dressed, his weather-worn face was brown and cracked like a dried river bed, although his fern green eyes shone, as if he was permanently on the verge of playing a practical joke. There was certainly little there to suggest that he had been responsible for the horrors Allegra and Tom had witnessed in the basement of his house.

'*No*,' she refused, then watched as Tom did the same. Contarelli shrugged and took a swig himself, turning back to face the road as the mud-flecked Land Cruiser danced over the pot holes.

'How long have you been a tombarolo?' Tom asked.

'Since I was a boy,' Contarelli said proudly. He spoke fast and mainly in Italian, with a booming voice that was too big for his body. 'It's in the blood, you see. I used to come out to these fields with my father. In those days the earth would be littered with fragments of pottery and broken statues surfaced by the farmers' ploughs. That's when I realised there was another world under there.' He gestured longingly out of the window towards the earthquake-scarred landscape now shrouded by night. 'I sold what I found in the market, used the money to buy some books, got smarter about what pieces were and how much they were worth, climbed through the ranks. Now I'm a *Capo di Zona* and it's the only life I know.'

'And you always go out at night?'

'It depends on the site.' He shrugged, lighting a cigarette from the smouldering stub of the one which had preceded it, his fingernails broken and dirty. He seemed to be enjoying himself. 'For some of the larger ones, we offer the landowner a share in the profits. Then my boys turn up in the day with a bulldozer and some hard hats. If anyone asks, we tell them we're working on a construction project. If they ask again, we pay them off. Or shut them up.'

Allegra felt her anger rising, its delirious scent momentarily blinding her to the danger they were in and to the armed man seated in the back with her and Tom. She'd seen enough already to know that this wasn't just tomb robbing. It was cultural vandalism, Contarelli's brutal methods probably destroying as much as he found. The fact that he was now happily boasting about it only made it worse.

'So you've never been caught?' Tom asked quickly, his worried glance suggesting that he could tell she was about to snap.

'The Carabinieri need to find us before they can catch us,' he explained with a grin. 'They do their best, but there are thousands of tombs and villas buried out here and they can't be everywhere at once. Especially now the politicians are table-thumping about immigration, drugs and terrorism. You know, a few years ago, I even cleared out three graves in a field next to the police station in Viterbo. If they can't stop us there, right under their snouts, what are their chances against us out here?'

He laughed, slapping the knee of the driver next to him in merriment.

'Why do you still do it?' Allegra snapped. 'Haven't you made enough money?'

'I don't do it for the money, my dear. Not for a long time now. Archaeology is my sickness, my addiction,' he explained, his eyes shining, his hands conducting an unheard symphony. 'The thrill of finding a tomb, the smell of a freshly opened chamber, the adrenaline rush as you crawl inside, the fear of being caught . . .'

'What you do is not archaeology,' Allegra snapped. 'It's rape. You take innocence and corrupt it, turning beauty into a bauble for the rich to decorate their mantelpieces with.'

'I bring history back from the dead,' he shot back, his face hardening. 'I restore artefacts from thousands of years of neglect. I provide them with a home. A home where they will go on display and be appreciated, rather than languish in some museum's basement storeroom. Now tell me, is that rape?'

The same tired old excuses, the same self-serving justifications.

'What about *your* basement and the fresco we saw there, hacked into pieces?' she retorted. 'Or the fingers ripped from the dead, or the remains of tombs that have been gouged clean like a back-street abortionist scraping out a womb. Is that archaeology?'

Contarelli, face now like thunder, eyed her coldly, then turned to face the front.

'Stop the car,' he ordered the driver tonelessly. 'We'll walk from here.'

FIFTY-ONE

19th March – 10.31 p.m.

They had parked at the end of a rutted track and then set out across the fields on foot, Contarelli leading the way, his two men at the rear. One of them had a pair of infra-red binoculars that he held to his face every few minutes to scan the horizon, presumably on the lookout for a possible Carabinieri patrol. Tom and Allegra, meanwhile, had been roped together by their wrists; Tom's tied behind his back, Allegra's fixed in front of her so that she could follow behind.

Contarelli was grasping a *spilloni*, a long metal spike that he had explained was used to identify a site's size and entrance. He was still smoking, Tom noted, although he had turned the cigarette around so that the lit end was inside his mouth, to mask its glow when he inhaled. For the same reason no one was using a flashlight, relying instead on the low moon to light their path.

'The most important thing is to be able to read the land,' Contarelli expounded, having decided, it seemed, to focus all his attention on Tom after Allegra's outburst. 'You see how the grass is drier there?' He pointed out a patch of ground that, as far as Tom could see, didn't look any different from the rest of the field. 'The earth above a hollow space has less moisture. And those brambles there –' he gestured to his right – 'when they grow tall and yellowish like that, it means that their roots are leaning on a buried wall.'

Tom nodded, struggling to keep up – Contarelli was proving to be surprisingly nimble over the rough terrain, although unlike Tom he didn't have to cope with his arms being forced up behind his back every time he stumbled.

'Wild fig trees are a give-away too,' he continued. 'And fox and badger tracks can often lead you straight to the entrance.'

'Where are you taking us?' Tom demanded, the hopelessness of their situation growing with every step. Over this rough ground, roped together, they had no chance of escaping.

'Don De Luca told me you were interested in understanding what we do.' Contarelli shrugged, turning to face him.

'I think I've got the general idea, thanks.' Tom gave a tight smile. 'We can make our own way back from here.'

Contarelli gave one of his booming laughs and

strode on, leaving one of his men to prod Tom
forward.

'It takes us two nights to break into a tomb
normally. On the first night we clear away the
entrance and let whatever's inside oxidise and
harden. Then on the second night we come back
and take what we can before dawn. Usually I never
come back a third time. It's too risky. But I've
made an exception for you.'

He stopped and signalled at someone standing
beneath a low hillock covered in trees. The man
was leaning wearily on a shovel and had clearly
been waiting for them. As they approached him
and the dark passage he had uncovered, he waved
back, jumping down to greet them.

'It's an Etruscan burial chamber,' Allegra
breathed.

Contarelli turned, smiling.

'You see,' he said with a pained sigh, as if he
was wearily scolding a small child. 'That's the type
of cleverness that's got you both killed.'

Before Tom could move, a plastic hood was
placed over his head by one of the men standing
behind him and he was forced to his knees.
Working quickly, they deftly passed a length of
duct tape several times around his neck, sealing
the bag against his skin.

He felt himself being lifted and then dragged
along the tomb's short corridor into the Stygian
darkness of the burial chamber. Moments later,

Allegra was thrown down on to the damp earth next to him, struggling furiously.

'Compliments of Don De Luca,' Contarelli intoned from somewhere above them, his disembodied voice echoing off the tomb's domed roof.

For a few moments Tom could hear nothing apart from the rattle of his own breathing and Allegra's muffled shouts as her heels scrabbled in the dirt. But then came the muted sound of steel against stone.

They were filling the entrance in.

FIFTY-TWO

19th March – 11.06 p.m.

They didn't have long, Tom knew. Each breath used a little more of the oxygen sealed within the bag. He could already feel the plastic rubbing against his face, warm and moist; hear it crinkling every time he inhaled, growing and shrinking like a jellyfish's pulsing head. In a few minutes the air would all be gone and then the CO_2 levels in his blood would rise, shutting down first his brain's cerebral cortex and then the medulla.

It was a cruel death – light-headedness, followed by nausea, then unconsciousness. And finally oblivion. But then that was hardly a surprise, given that they were here at the orders of the same man who had, by his own admission, ordered Cavalli to be slowly choked by the Tiber's strong current and Argento to be partially decapitated and left to bleed out like a slaughtered lamb.

Lying next to him, Allegra had stopped struggling

but was still shouting, using up her air far more quickly than she should. He'd have to get to her first. He shuffled back towards her, feeling for her with his hands, which were still tied behind his back. Touching her arm, he bent forward and pulled himself round with his feet until he made contact with the hood's slippery surface. She seemed to guess what he was doing, because she went quiet and bent towards him until he was able to feel the outline of her mouth.

Digging his finger hard into the shallow depression formed between the hard edges of her teeth, he gouged the thick plastic with his nail, weakening its surface until it suddenly gave way. There was a loud whistling noise as Allegra sucked air greedily through the small hole.

But the effort had cost Tom more than he'd expected. He felt light-headed, almost as if he was floating outside of himself. He didn't have long before he went under. Thirty seconds at most. He shuffled down, bending his head towards where he guessed Allegra's hands had been retied behind her back so that she could feel for his mouth. With her longer nails, it took far less time for her to rupture the plastic, the chamber's stale air tasting sweet to Tom's starving lungs.

'You okay?' Tom called through the darkness when his head had cleared, the plastic hood both muffling and amplifying his voice.

'Not really,' she answered, coughing.

'Where are your hands?'

Feeling for her wrists, he carefully picked away at the knot, the rope resisting at first, until little by little he was able to loosen it and then undo it completely. Sitting up, Allegra returned the favour. As soon as he was free they felt for each other in the darkness and hugged with relief – relative strangers brought unexpectedly close by the intimacy of fear.

'Which way's the entrance?' Tom asked as he broke away and ripped the remainder of the plastic hood from his neck.

'We should be able to find it if we feel our way along the walls,' she replied. 'Perhaps if we . . . what's this?'

A light clicked on, forcing Tom to shield his eyes as it was pointed at him. Allegra snatched it away with an apology. Unless it had fallen from Contarelli's pocket, it appeared that he had left them a torch. Perhaps he had anticipated that they might free themselves? Perhaps he was trying to help them escape? The thought filled Tom with hope.

He glanced around excitedly, noting the low domed roof above them and the earthen floor littered with pottery fragments. Lying discarded in the corner was a bundle of rags that Tom suspected marked what was left of the tomb's original occupant.

'That way –' Allegra pointed towards the low tunnel that led to the entrance.

He crawled hopefully down it, but soon found his path blocked. As the shovelling sound earlier had suggested, the entrance had been filled in. And not just with earth, but with a massive stone plug that they must have brought there with this single purpose in mind.

'We should have left the bags on,' Allegra said in a shaky voice. 'I'd rather suffocate quickly than starve down here.'

'I wouldn't worry about starving,' Tom said with a grim smile. 'I'd say we have six hours of air, eight max.'

'That's reassuring.' She gave a short laugh, then frowned as her torch picked out a dull metal object lying near the entrance.

It was a Glock 17. Tom picked it up and checked the magazine. It contained two bullets.

Contarelli, it seemed, was offering them a way out after all.

FIFTY-THREE

Avenue Krieg, Geneva, Switzerland
20th March – 12.02 a.m.

'This can't be it,' Dominique whispered.

Normally Archie would have agreed with her – a half-empty building with a broken lift, shabby communal areas, half the light bulbs blown and the name plate hanging loose, certainly didn't seem to fit with what he'd seen of Faulks. But the porter he'd bribed in the Sotheby's loading bay had been adamant that this was the right address, floor and suite number for the company who'd sold the Artemis. In fact, he'd proved it.

'He showed me the bloody receipt,' Archie grunted as he tried to force the final locking pin out of the way. 'Galleries Dassin is registered here.'

'It just doesn't feel right,' she said, shaking her head. 'We should have spoken to Tom first.'

'I've been trying to get him on the blower all day,' Archie reminded her sharply, his tone reflecting both his irritation at being second-guessed and his concern. It wasn't like Tom to be out of touch this long. Not deliberately. 'Besides . . .' With a final effort, the pin fell into place and the lock clicked open. '. . . We're in now. We might as well have a butcher's.'

Pulling their masks down over their faces, they slipped inside and gently closed the door behind them. The suite consisted of a large open-plan space with perhaps four desks in it, a small kitchen, a meeting room, and what Archie guessed was the owner or manager's personal office.

'Still sure this is the right place?' Dominique whispered as her torch picked out bookcases over-flowing with legal and tax reference books, stacks of paperwork secured by treasury tags, filing cabi-nets, printers and shredders, and a series of insipid paintings of a yacht sailing across the lake. Archie sighed. He hated to admit it, but it looked as though she might be right after all.

'I'll have a quick shifty in there,' Archie suggested, nodding towards the manager's office. 'You have a look through this lot.'

The office was dominated by a vast, monolithic desk whose primary purpose could only have been to intimidate anyone standing on the other side of it. Behind this ran thick-set, mahogany shelves loaded with books, photo frames and various stress-busting executive toys. Archie couldn't help himself but set off the Newton's Cradle, his eyes dancing to the metronomic click-click-click of the balls as they swung back and forth. Glancing up with a smile, he absent-mindedly picked up one of the photo frames, then frowned. Rather than be confronted by Faulks's patrician scowl as he had expected, he instead found himself staring at a heavily overweight man in swimming trunks trying to pour himself into a wetsuit.

Replacing it with a shudder, Archie turned his attention to the two filing cabinets lurking in the corner. Opening the drawers in turn, he walked his fingers along the tabs until he found one marked Galleries Dassin.

'I've got something,' he called in a low voice, carrying it to the entrance. Dominique looked up from where she had been leafing through the papers arranged on one of the desks. '*Galleries Dassin,*' he read, flicking through a few of the pages. '*Registered address, 13 Avenue Krieg.* That's here. *Fiduciary owner, Jérome Carvel.*' He glanced up at the door and saw the same name picked out on it in black letters. 'That's him.'

'What's a fiduciary owner?' Dominique asked.

'Someone who deals with all the administrative bollocks, as opposed to the beneficial owner, who calls the shots and makes the serious wonga and who in this particular instance is . . .' He'd found a shareholder contract and flipped to the signature page, then looked up with a grim smile. 'Earl Faulks. Carvel's a front.'

'Why bother?'

'Fuck knows. But if I had to guess, to hide . . .' Archie paused, struck by a thought. 'Who bought the Artemis again?'

Dominique had approached the auctioneer after the sale and expressed an interest in buying the statue from its new owner. Sensing the opportunity to make another fee, the auctioneer had volunteered their name and offered to broker the deal.

'It was a commission bid for Xenephon Trading.'

Archie vanished back inside the office, returning a few moments later clutching another file.

'*Xenephon Trading,*' he read. '*Fiduciary owner, Jérome Carvel. Beneficial owner . . . Earl Faulks.*' He looked up at her triumphantly.

'He bought it from himself?' Dominique exclaimed. 'That makes no sense. Even if he'd negotiated special rates, he'd still be paying six to ten per cent commission on both sides of the deal.'

'Are those the invoices?' Archie nodded at the sheaf of papers she'd been sorting through.

'Last month's auction.' She nodded.

'Any where Xenephon is the buyer?' Archie went to stand next to her.

Gripping her torch in one hand and flipping the pages over quickly with the other, she quickly counted them up. 'There's one here. Two . . . three . . . four . . . five. And look who's on the other side of the deal here and here: Galleries Dassin.'

'Who's Melfi Export?' Archie tapped his finger on the page with a frown. 'They show up a lot too.'

Without waiting for an answer, he disappeared back into the office, returning a few moments later with a third file and a solemn expression.

'*Melfi Export. Fiduciary owner, Jérome Carvel. Beneficial owner . . . Earl Faulks.* It's the same story – he's selling with one company and buying with another. It makes no sense.'

'He must be getting something out it,' she pointed out.

'Well, I don't see what, apart from a shit-load of paperwork.' He slapped the pile of invoices with a shrug. Dominique turned to him with a smile.

'That's it.'

'What?'

'The paperwork. He's doing it for the paper-work.'

'What the hell are you talking about?'

'It's a laundering scam,' she said excitedly. 'First he puts an item up for auction. Then he buys it back under another name. Finally he sells it on to a real buyer, only this time with a manufactured provenance, courtesy of an official auction house invoice and valuation certificate.'

'Maybe not just about provenance,' Archie said with a slow nod. 'Arms dealers get around embargoes by selling weapons down a network of shell companies and middlemen, so that by the time the shipment gets to the intended customer, no one can tie the final transaction back to the original seller. It's called triangulation. Faulks could be pulling the same stunt here to cover his tracks.'

FIFTY-FOUR

Nr Anguillara Sabazia, northwest of Rome
20th March – 1.13 a.m.
They had both run out of conversation a while
ago. Now they were sitting in silence, locked into
their own thoughts, hugging their knees for
warmth. The torch nestled on the ground between
them in a puddle of light, their bodies huddled
around it as if to shield it from the wind. Tom had
the ominous feeling that once its fragile flame
finally expired, they wouldn't long survive it.

He'd faced death before, of course. But never
with the resigned acceptance and powerlessness
he felt now. The walls were rock solid, the floor
packed firm, the domed roof unyielding, the
entrance sealed. They had no tools, no way of
communicating with the outside world, no
answers. Nothing except for the two bullets that
lay side by side in the torch's pale wash, like bodies
awaiting burial.

'How did you know?' Allegra's voice broke the cloying silence.

'Know what?'

'When we first met at Cavalli's and you handed me the gun,' she reminded him. 'How did you know I wouldn't just shoot you?'

'I didn't.'

'Then why did you trust me?'

'I didn't.' He shrugged.

'Then what . . .?'

'I took the clip out before I gave you the gun.' Tom grinned. 'You couldn't have shot me if you'd wanted to.'

'Why you . . .' Allegra's face broke into a wide smile as she reached across to punch Tom's shoulder.

'Ow.' He winced, his arm still bruised from where she'd hit him that morning.

'Still sore from being beaten up by a girl?' she said, the clear bell of her laughter both unexpected and strangely uplifting in the darkness.

'You landed a couple of lucky shots.' Tom gave a dismissive shake of his head. 'Another few seconds and I . . .'

He paused. Allegra was holding up her hand for him to be quiet, her chin raised like a foxhound who has caught a scent.

'What's that?'

Tom listened, at first not hearing anything, but then making out what seemed to be the faint rattle of an engine.

'They're coming back,' Allegra exclaimed, turning excitedly towards the entrance tunnel.

'Maybe to finish the job,' Tom said grimly, hauling her back and loading the gun.

They sat there, the ground now shaking with a dull throb, the occasional sound of a muffled voice reaching them. Readying himself, Tom took aim at the stone plug that was blocking the entrance, determined to take Contarelli, or whichever of his men he sent ahead of him, down with them.

Ten or so minutes later the massive stone began to move, dirt and moonlight trickling through the crack. The sound of voices was clearer now, someone swearing in Italian, another one groaning under the strain. Then, with a final effort, the stone was rolled free. It fell on to its side with a leaden thump.

A harsh, lightning strike of light flooded down the entrance corridor, washing over them and making them blink. On its heels came the thunder of what Tom realised now was a helicopter, the hammer chop of its rotors echoing off the walls.

For a few moments nothing happened. Then a figure appeared at the tunnel entrance, a black silhouette against the floodlit backdrop.

'Tom Kirk? Allegra Damico? *Andiamo*,' he said, reaching towards them.

They swapped a look, Tom slowly lowered the gun.

'What's going on?' Allegra shouted through the noise.

'I don't know,' Tom called back. 'But it is, it beats being in here.'

Crawling forward, they emerged gratefully into the night, brushing the earth from their clothes and hands as they stood up. But whatever relief they felt at escaping was soon tempered by the realisation that their three liberators were all dressed in black paramilitary clothing – ski masks, fatigues, bullet-proof vests, field boots, guns strapped to their thighs. Two of the men were also equipped with night-vision goggles which they kept trained on the horizon, their Beretta PS12-SDs held across their chests, safety's off.

'Go,' the man who had helped them to their feet ushered them towards the black Augusta Bell 412EP which had landed about thirty feet away, its spotlight trained on the tomb's entrance, the wash of its rotors back-combing the grass. A fourth man was waiting for them in the cockpit.

'Get in,' the first man shouted over the roar of the engine, handing them each a set of headphones. 'Don't worry. We'll put everything back here so they won't know you've gone.'

Slamming the door, he stepped back and gave the pilot the thumbs-up. Throttling up, the helicopter lurched unsteadily off the ground, dipped its rotors, and then climbed at a steep angle into the sky. In a few minutes, the tomb had faded from view, swallowed by the night.

'Military?' Allegra's voice hummed in Tom's ear, worried but with a curious edge.

'I don't know,' he replied, glancing round. 'Their equipment's standard Italian army issue. Could be special forces or some sort of private militia?' He nodded at the back of the pilot's head. 'You could try asking him, but I don't think he'll tell us.'

'Right now, I'm not sure I even care,' she said with a relieved shrug. 'The further we can get . . .' Her voice tailed off into a puzzled frown as she noticed the envelope that had been left on the bench opposite. It was addressed to both of them. Swapping a look with Tom, she ripped it open and glanced inside, then emptied the contents into her lap: about twenty thousand euro secured in a neat bundle, a set of car keys, and five black-and-white photographs of a fire-ravaged apartment attached to an official press release from the Monégasque Police.

'What does it say?' Allegra frowned, handing it to him.

'They're looking for two missing people,' Tom quickly translated. 'An Irish banker, called Ronan D'Arcy and his housekeeper, Determination Smith. It says no one's seen them since D'Arcy's apartment caught fire two days ago. Looks like somebody wants us to take a closer look.' His eyes narrowed as he studied the third photograph again, a small object having caught his eye. Had the police noticed that yet, he wondered?

'De Luca?' she suggested. 'Remember he told us that his accountant in Monaco had disappeared?'

'Why have Contarelli bury us, only to dig us up a few hours later?' Tom asked with a shake of his head.

'But who else would have known where to find us?'

Tom shrugged. She had a point, although right now he was less concerned with who had rescued them than why, and what they wanted.

The pilot's voice broke into their conversation with a crackle.

'What's our heading?'

'What?'

'My orders are to take you anywhere within operational range,' the pilot explained.

'Anywhere?' Tom asked in surprise. He'd assumed that whoever had set them free was planning to have them brought to him.

'Anywhere,' the pilot confirmed. 'As soon as we land, you're free to go.' He reached back and handed them two Swiss passports made out in false names. 'What's the heading?'

Tom paused before answering, flicking through the forged documents. He reckoned a full tank would last them 600 kilometres. More than enough to leave De Luca, Gallo and the murderous madness they seemed to have stumbled into far behind. Allegra seemed to be having the same thought, because she pulled her headset off and yelled into his ear so she couldn't be overheard.

'What do you want to do?'

'If we want out, then this is it,' he called back. 'A chance to walk away while we still can.'

'Walk away to what? Until I can prove what Gallo's up to, I've nothing to walk away to.'

Tom slipped his headset back on.

'Can we make it to Monte Carlo?' he asked.

'Of course,' the pilot confirmed. 'What do you need?'

Tom paused before answering.

'A suit for me. Three buttons and a double vent. A dress for the lady. Black. Size 8.'

PART THREE

'I fear the Greeks, even when they bear gifts'
Virgil, *The Aeneid*, Book II, 48

FIFTY-FIVE

**Over the Ligurian Sea, fifty kilometres
south-east of Monaco
20th March – 2.21 a.m.**

Rigged for black, they had headed west, hitting
the coast just north of Civitavecchia and then
hugging it as far as Livorno, sawing in and out of
the jagged shoreline to stay under the radar. Once
there, they had struck out across the sea, the city's
bright lights fading behind them to a gossamer
twinkle, until there was nothing but them and
the water's empty shadow and the echo of the
rotors as they skimmed low across the waves.

Occasionally the moon would emerge from
behind a cloud, and for a few moments Allegra could
see their spectral reflection in the swell, a ghost ship
carried on neon whitecaps. Then, just as quickly, it
vanished again and the darkness would open
beneath them once more, an endless abyss into
which they seemed to be falling without moving.

Allegra glanced over at Tom, but like her he seemed to be enjoying the flight's noisy stillness, his dirt-smudged face pressed to the window, alone with his thoughts. She wondered if, like her, he could still feel the plastic against his skin, moist and warm, still feel his fingernails lifting as he scrabbled at the chamber's earthen walls.

She hated to admit it, but she had been scared back there. Not danger scared, where adrenaline kicks in and instinct takes over before you even have a chance to think. Dying scared, where there is time for the mind to wander long and lonely corridors of fear and uncertainty. The sort of fear that she imagined lingered in the portentous shadows of a surgeon's forced cheerfulness or a radiologist's brave smile.

Perhaps this explained why she found something strangely comforting about the engine's noise now, its animal roar having settled into a contented purr that was a welcome contrast to the ticking contemplation of death that she had endured in that tomb. A reminder that she was alive. That she had escaped.

Not that she was sure what they had escaped to, exactly, or who had helped them. Clearly somebody had their reasons for wanting them alive and continuing their investigation. Less clear was who that might be. De Luca, perhaps; if she was right about D'Arcy working for him. But then, as Tom had suggested, it seemed unlikely that he would order Contarelli to kill them, only to dispatch a search-and-rescue team a few hours later. But if not him, who? The FBI? Tom had told her that he had worked with them before. Was this them protecting their best chance of finding Jennifer's killer? She shook her head ruefully. The truth was, there was no way of telling.

More certain was her growing trust in Tom. He would never stop, she knew, never rest until he had brought the Delian League down and punished whoever had killed his friend. Part of her almost felt jealous of this fierce loyalty. Did she have anyone who would have done the same for her? Probably not. The realisation strengthened her resolve. If she didn't follow this through to the end, wherever it led her, no one else would. And then Gallo would have won.

Tom suddenly tapped the window.

'Monte Carlo.'

The city had appeared out of the night, a stepped pyramid of lights that clung to the steep mountainside with concrete claws, its jaws open to the sea. The helicopter banked to the left and climbed over the yachts anchored in the harbour before swooping back towards the heliport, a narrow cantilevered shelf that hung over the water. It landed with a bump and then dusted off as soon as their feet had hit the tarmac, climbing steeply until the clatter of its blades was nothing but a warm whisper on the wind.

The heliport was shut for the night, but someone had seen to it that the gate set into the hurricane fence had been left unlocked. The keys left for them in the envelope opened an X5 parked on the street outside the deserted terminal building. Inside, Allegra found a bag of casual clothes and two suit carriers – one containing Tom's shirt and suit, the other a knee-length black dress that they had clearly managed to lay their hands on in the hour or so it had taken them to fly here. Shoes, underwear, cufflinks, comb, make-up – they'd thought of everything, and she knew without even looking that it would all fit. These people, whoever they were, knew what they were doing.

'Ladies first?' Tom offered, closing the door after her and then turning his back.

It was only when she had undressed that she realised how filthy she was; her face, arms and clothes were covered in stains, dirt and small cuts and grazes that she had unconsciously picked up somewhere between Li's oily workshop, Cavalli's foam-filled car, Contarelli's gruesome basement and the empty tomb. Grabbing some wipes, she quickly cleaned herself up as best she could, applied some make-up, and then wriggled into the dress. She checked herself in the mirror before she got out. Not bad, apart from her hair, which would need six months and several very expensive haircuts to get it looking even half decent. But it had served its purpose.

She got out and swapped places with Tom, hoping that his raised eyebrows were a sign of silent appreciation. Five minutes later and he too was ready to go.

'Want to drive?' Tom offered, holding out the keys. 'Only this time you have to promise not to crash into anything.'

She refused with a smile.

'What's the fun in that?'

The casino was only a short drive from the heliport, although, in a country of only 485 acres, everything was, almost by definition, close to everything else. It was still busy, a succession of Ferraris and Lamborghinis processing slowly across the Place du Casino to give the tourists enough time to gawp. Turning in by the central fountain, its bubbling waters glowing like molten glass in the floodlights, they waited in line behind a Bentley Continental for the valet to take their car.

The casino itself was an elaborate, baroque building, its façade dominated by two flamboyant towers either side of the main entrance and encrusted with statues and ornate architectural reliefs. The floodlights had given it a rather gaudy appearance, clothing it in amber in some places and gold in others, while a lush green copper roof was just about visible through the gaps between the towers. A central clock, supported by two bronze angels, indicated it had just gone three.

'You still haven't told me why we're here,' Allegra complained as Tom led her into the marble entrance hall to the ticket office.

He glanced across with an indulgent smile as he paid their entrance fee, as if this was a somehow rather foolish question.

'To play blackjack, of course.'

FIFTY-SIX

Casino de Monte Carlo, Monaco
20th March – 3.02 a.m.
There was a compelling logic to the casino's layout:
the further inside you ventured, the more money
you stood to lose. Although a simple conceit, it
had, over the years, led to the evolution of a
complex and intuitive ecosystem whereby those
at the bottom of the food chain rarely strayed into
the territory of the higher, predatory mammals.

This could be easily observed in the way that
the outer rooms were mainly inhabited by
sunburnt British and German tourists, their
clothes creased from having been kept at the
bottom of a suitcase for the best part of a week
in anticipation of a 'posh' night out, their modest
losses borne with thinly disguised resentment.
The middle rooms, meanwhile, were populated
by immaculately dressed Italian and French
couples – 'locals' who had driven up on a whim

and who seemed to play the tables with an almost effortless familiarity. The inner rooms, finally, had been overrun by Russians; for the most part over-weight men dressed in black and clutching cigars as they would a bayonet, accompanied by dagger-thin blonde women half their age wearing white to better show off their tans. Here they bet with an indifference that verged on boredom, the roulette table lavished with chips, each spin of the wheel a desperate plea to feel something, anything, in a life blunted by having forgotten what it means to want something but not be able to buy it.

As they walked through from the Salle Europe, Tom found his thoughts wandering. He had tried to resist it as long as he could, but it was hard not to be drawn back to the Amalfi, not to let the fairground flash of the slot machines and the piano play of the roulette ball grab him by the throat and catapult him back through time, as if he had stumbled into some strange parallel world.

It was as if he was watching a film. The echo of the shot being fired, Jennifer crumpling to the floor, the smell of blood and cordite, that first, disbelieving scream. A film that he could play, pause, forward and rewind at any time, although it would never allow him to go further back than the crack of the gunshot. That's when everything had started.

'Tom?' The mirrored room slowly came back into focus and he saw Allegra's hand laid in concern on his shoulder. 'Are you okay?'

'I'm fine.' He nodded, the scream still silently ringing in his ears even though now, on closer inspection what struck him most about this place on reflection was less its similarity to the Amalfi than its differences.

Here, they played Chemin de Fer not Punto Banco, for example. The poker tables were marked in French not English. The roulette wheel had one zero, not two. And the air was seared with the bittersweet tang of a century and a half of fortunes being lost and made. Small differences on their own, perhaps, but pieced together and set amidst the jewelled chandeliers, stained-glass windows and ornate sculptures that adorned the casino's soaring rococo interior, they breathed a soul into this place that Kezman could never hope to buy, and revealed the Amalfi in all its silicone-enhanced artifice.

'Deal me in.' Tom sat at an empty blackjack table and placed a five-thousand-euro chip on the box in front of him.

The croupier looked up and smiled. In his early forties, he was a tall precise man, gaunt and with a pianist's long, cantilevered fingers.

'Monsieur Kirk. Very good to see you again.'

He dealt him a king and a five.

'You too, Nico.'

'I was sorry to hear about your loss.' For a moment Tom thought he meant Jennifer, before realising he must be referring to his father. That was almost three years ago now. It showed how long it had been since he was last here.

'Thank you. *Carte.*'

'You don't twist on fifteen,' Allegra whispered next to him. 'Even I know that.'

'Seven,' the croupier intoned. 'Twenty-two.' He scooped the cards and Tom's chip off the baize.

'See?' Allegra exclaimed.

'I've come for my gear,' Tom said in a low voice, placing another five-thousand-euro chip down. 'Is it still here?'

'Of course.' Nico nodded, dealing him an ace and a seven.

'Eighteen. You need to stick again,' Allegra urged. Tom ignored her.

'*Carte.*'

The croupier deftly flicked an eight over to him. 'Twenty-six.'

Allegra tutted angrily.

'You don't like losing, do you?' Tom said, amused by the expression on her face.

'I don't like losing stupidly,' she corrected him.

'Perhaps madame is right,' the croupier ventured. 'Have you tried the Roulette Anglaise?'

'Actually, I was hoping to bump into an old friend here. Ronan D'Arcy. Know him?'

The croupier paused, then nodded.

'He's been in a few times. Good tipper.' A pause. 'Ugly business.'

'Very ugly,' Tom agreed. 'Any idea where I can find him?'

Nico shrugged, then shook his head.

'No one's seen him since the fire.'

'Where did he live?'

'Up on the Boulevard de Suisse. You can't miss it.'

'Can you get me in?'

The croupier checked again that no one was listening, then nodded.

'Meet me in the Café de Paris in ten minutes.'

'I'll need a couple of phones too,' Tom added. 'Here –' He threw another five-thousand-euro chip down. 'For your trouble.'

'*Merci, monsieur*, but four should cover everything.' He slid a one-thousand-euro chip back, then signalled at the floor manager that he needed to be relieved.

'You lost both those hands on purpose, didn't you?' Allegra muttered as they made their way back towards the entrance.

'He charges a ten-thousand-euro fee.'

'Fee for what?'

'For looking after this –' He held up the chip that the croupier had returned to him in change. Two numbers had been scratched on to its reverse. 'Come on.'

Reaching the main entrance lobby, Tom led her

over to the far side of the galleried space, where a mirrored door on the right-hand side of the room gave on to a marble staircase edged by an elaborate cast-iron balustrade. They headed down it, the temperature fading, until they eventually found themselves in a narrow corridor that led to the men's toilets on one side and the women's on the other.

Checking that they hadn't been followed, Tom opened the small cupboard under the stairs and removed two brass stands joined by a velvet rope and an *Hors Service* sign. Pinning the sign to the door, he cordoned the toilet entrance off and then disappeared inside, reappearing a few moments later with a smile.

'It's empty.'

'Is that good?' she asked, an impatient edge to her voice as she followed him inside.

The room was as he remembered it: four wooden stalls painted a pale yellow to his right, six porcelain urinals separated by frosted-glass screens to his left. Unusually, the centre of the room was dominated by a large white marble counter with two sinks set on each set of a double-sided arched mirror. The walls were covered in grey marble tiles.

'Six across, three down.'

He showed her the numbers scratched on to the chip and then turned to face the urinals and began to count, starting in the far left corner and moving six tiles across, then dropping three tiles down.

'I make it this one,' he said, stepping forward and pointing at a tile over the third urinal.

'Me too,' Allegra agreed with a curious frown.

Snatching up the silver fire extinguisher hanging just inside the door, he swung it hard against the tile they had picked out. There was a dull clunk as it caved in.

'It's hollow,' Allegra breathed.

Tom swung the extinguisher against the wall again, the hole widening as the tiles around the opening cracked and fell away until he had revealed a rectangular space. Throwing the extinguisher to the floor, he reached into the space and hauled out a large black holdall.

'How long's that been here?'

'Three or four years?' he guessed. 'Nico paid off the builder the casino hired to re-tile this room. It was Archie's idea. A precaution. Enough to get us operational again if we ever had to cut and run. He chose here and a few other places around the world where we had people we could trust.'

Allegra leaned forward as he unzipped the bag.

'What's inside?'

'Batteries, tools, drill, borescope, magnetic rig, backpack,' he said quickly, sorting through its contents. 'Money, guns,' he continued, taking one of the two Glocks out, checking the magazine was full and placing it in his pocket.

'And this?' Allegra asked, frowning as she

took out a small object the size of a cigarette packet.

'Location transmitter. Three-mile radius,' He pulled out the receiver, slotted a fresh battery in place and then turned it on to show her. 'Stick it on, if you like. At least that way I won't lose you.'

'Don't worry, you won't get rid of me that easily.' She smiled, tossing it back.

'Good. Then you can give me a hand with this up the stairs. Nico will be waiting by now.'

FIFTY-SEVEN

Boulevard de Suisse, Monaco
20th March – 3.35 a.m.

Barely ten minutes later, they pulled in a little way beyond D'Arcy's building. Nico had been right – you couldn't miss it. Not only was a police car parked outside on the narrow one-way street, but the upper stories of the otherwise cream apartment block were scorched and coated with ash, like a half-smoked cigarette that had been stood on its filter and then left to burn down to its tip.

Tom gave her a few minutes to struggle out of her dress and heels and into the casual clothes that had been left for them in the car, and then rapped impatiently on her window. She lowered it and he thrust the second Glock and a couple of spare clips through the gap.

'Ready?'

'Are there actually any bullets in this one?' she asked, eyebrows raised sceptically.

It wasn't that she minded carrying a gun. In fact, she quite liked its firm and familiar presence on her hip, like a dance partner's hand leading her through a rehearsed set of steps. It was just that she preferred to know what she was dealing with.

'Let's not find out.' He winked.

The building was called the Villa de Rome, an appropriate and perhaps not entirely coincidental name if they were right about D'Arcy's involvement with De Luca and the Delian League. Although old, it betrayed all the signs of a recent and rather ill-judged refurbishment, the entrance now resembling that of a two-star hotel with ideas above its station – all rose marble, smoked glass and gold leaf.

'*Bonsoir*,' a junior officer from Monaco's small police force rose from behind the reception desk and greeted them warmly, relieved, it seemed, at the prospect of a break in his vigil's lonely monotony.

'Thierry Landry. Caroline Morel,' Tom snapped in French, each of them flashing the special passes that Nico had produced for them. 'From the palace.'

'Yes, sir, madam,' the officer stuttered, his back straightening and heels sliding almost imperceptibly closer together.

'We'd like to see D'Arcy's apartment.'

'Of course.' He nodded eagerly. 'The elevator's still out, but I can escort you up the stairs to the penthouse.'

'No need,' Tom insisted, stepping deliberately closer. 'We were never here. You never saw us.'

'Saw what, sir?' The officer winked, then froze, as if realising that this was probably against some sort of royal protocol. To his visible relief, Tom smiled back.

'Exactly.'

Leaving the officer saluting to their backs, they climbed the stairs in silence, the fire's charred scent growing stronger and the floor getting wetter as water dripped through from the ceiling like rainwater percolating into an aquifer. There was a certain irony, Allegra reflected, in how the fire brigade had probably caused more damage to the flats below D'Arcy's than the blaze they were meant to be protecting them from. She couldn't help but wonder if there wasn't a warning there for them both: were they causing more harm by trying to fix things than if they had just let matters run their natural course?

On the third floor, Tom stopped and swung his backpack off his shoulder. Reaching inside, he took out a small device that he stuck on to the wall at about knee height, then turned on.

'Motion sensor,' he explained, holding out a

small receiver that she guessed would sound if anyone broke the transmitter's infrared beam.

They continued on, emerging half a minute later on the top landing, the fire's pungent incense now so heavy that she could almost taste the ash sticking to the back of her throat. Tom flicked his torch on, the beam immediately settling on the door to D'Arcy's apartment that had been unscrewed from its hinges and placed against the wall.

'Quarter-inch steel and a four-bar locking mechanism,' Tom observed slowly. 'Either he knew his attackers or someone let them in.'

They stepped inside the apartment on to a sodden carpet of ash and charred debris, weightless black flecks fluttering through their torch beams like flies over a carcass. The walls had been licked black by the cruel flames and the ceiling almost entirely consumed, so that she could see through it to the roof's steel ribs and, beyond them, the sky. The furniture, too, had been skeletonised into dark shapes that were both entirely alien and strangely familiar, although the fire, ever capricious, had inexplicably spared a single chair and a large section of one wall, as if to deliberately emphasise the otherwise overwhelming scale of its devastation.

It was an uncomfortable, dislocating experience, and Allegra had the strange impression of having stepped on to a film set – an imagined vision, rendered with frightening detail, of some future, post-apocalyptic world where the few remaining survivors had been reduced to taking shelter where they could and eking out an existence amidst the ashes.

'This looks like where it started.' She picked her way over the charred wreckage to a room that looked out over the harbour. The fire here seemed to have been particularly intense, the steel beams overhead twisted and tortured, opaque pools of molten glass having formed under the windows, the stonework still radiating a baked-in heat that took the edge off the chilled sea breeze. There was also some evidence of the beginnings of a forensic examination of the scene: equipment set up on a low trestle table, mobile lighting arranged in the room's corners.

'Probably here,' Tom agreed, pointing his torch at a dark mound that was pressed up against what was left of a bookcase. 'As you'd expect.'

'What do you mean?'

Tom reached into his backpack and pulled out one of the photographs that had been left for them in the helicopter.

'What do you see?'

She studied it carefully, then ran her torch over the burnt bookcase with a frown. As far as she could tell they looked the same. There certainly didn't seem . . . She paused, having just noticed a rectangular shape on the photo that the torchlight revealed to be a small metal grille set into the wall at about head height.

'What's that?' she asked with a frown.

'That's what I wondered too,' Tom muttered. 'Probably nothing. But then again . . .' He stepped closer and rubbed gently against a section of the wall. Through the damp layer of soot, a narrow groove slowly revealed itself.

'A hidden door,' Allegra breathed.

'A panic room.' Tom nodded. 'The grille must be for an air intake that would have been concealed by the bookcase. D'Arcy hasn't disappeared. He never even left his apartment.'

'Can you open it?'

'Half-inch steel, at a guess.' Tom rapped his knuckles against the door with a defeated shrug. 'Electro-magnetic locking system. Assuming they've cut the mains power, the locking mechanism will release itself as soon as the batteries run out.'

'Which is when?'

'Typically about forty-eight hours after they kick in.'

'Which is still at least twelve hours away,' she calculated, thinking back to the time of the fire given in the missing persons report. 'We can't hang around here until then.'

'We won't have to,' Tom reassured her. 'Here, give me a hand clearing this away.'

Reaching up, they ripped what was left of the bookcase to the floor, the charred wood crisping as they grabbed it, the dust making them both cough.

'There would have been an external keypad, but that must have melted in the fire,' Tom explained as the panic room's steel shell emerged through the soot. 'But there's usually a failsafe too. A secondary pad that they conceal inside the room's walls in case of an emergency. That should have been insulated from the heat.'

Stepping forward, he carefully ran his hands across the filthy steel walls at about waist height.

'Here.'

He spat into his hand and wiped the dirt away in a series of tarred smears to reveal a rectangular access panel that he quickly unscrewed.

'It's still working,' Allegra said with relief as she shone her torch into the recess and made out the keypad's illuminated buttons and the cursor's inviting blink.

Tom reached into his bag and pulled out a small device that looked like a calculator. Levering the fascia off the panic room's keypad to reveal the circuit board, he knelt down next to it and connected his device. Immediately the screen lit up, numbers scrolling across it in seemingly random patterns until, one by one, it began to lock them down. These then flashed up on the keypad's display, hesitantly at first, and then with increasing speed and confidence, until the full combination flashed up green: 180373.

With a hydraulic sigh, the panic room's door rolled back.

FIFTY-EIGHT

20th March – 3.44 a.m.
Allegra approached the open doorway, then staggered back.

'*Cazzo!*' She swore, her hand over her mouth. Peering through the opening, Tom understood why.

The emergency lighting was on, the room soaked in its blood-red glaze. D'Arcy was lying slumped in the corner and had already begun to bloat in the heat, the sickly sweet stench of rotting meat washing over them. Head lolling against his chest, his eyes were bulging as if someone had tried to pop them out on to his cheek, his stomach ballooning under his white shirt, the marbled skin mottled blue-green through the gaps between the buttons.

Breathing through his mouth, and trying to ignore the way D'Arcy's black and swollen tongue had forced his jaws into a wide, gagging smile, Tom stepped inside the cramped space. Allegra followed close behind.

'The smoke would have killed him,' Tom guessed, pointing out some plastic sheeting hanging loose from the air vent which it looked as though D'Arcy had tried to seal shut with bandages and plasters raided from a first-aid kit. 'Then he must have started to cook in the heat.'

'*Cazzo*,' she breathed to herself again.

Glancing round, it seemed pretty clear that D'Arcy had taken to using the room for storage rather than survival, with filing boxes stacked to the ceiling against the far wall, and a large server array providing some sort of data back-up facility to whatever computers he guessed must have once stood on the desk outside. Clearly, like most people who had these types of rooms installed, D'Arcy had drawn comfort from knowing it was there should he want to use it, without ever really expecting that he would ever need to.

'Help me lift one of these down.'

Mindful of not tripping over D'Arcy's outstretched legs, he lifted down a box and opened it up. Inside were four or five lever-arch files, neatly arranged by year, containing hundreds of invoices.

'Renewal fees for a burial plot in the Cimitero Acattolico in Rome,' Allegra read, opening the most recent file and then turning the pages. 'Private jet hire. Hotel suites. Yacht charter agreements. It's expensive being rich.'

'Anything linking him to De Luca?' Tom asked, hauling a second box down.

'Nothing obvious. Trade confirmations, derivatives contracts, settlement details, account statements . . .' She flicked through a couple of the folders.

'This one's the same,' Tom agreed, having heaved a third box to the floor.

'Look at this, though,' Allegra said slowly, having come across a thick wedge of bank statements. 'Every time his trading account went over ten million, the surplus was transferred back to an account at the Banco Rosalia.'

'The Banco Rosalia?' Tom frowned. 'Wasn't that where Argento worked?'

'Exactly. Which ties D'Arcy back to the other killings.'

'Except there's nothing here that links his death to either Caesar or Caravaggio,' Tom pointed out. 'Why would Moretti have broken the pattern?'

'Maybe he didn't. Maybe D'Arcy locked himself in here before Moretti could get to him,' she suggested.

Tom nodded, although he wasn't entirely convinced. Compared to what he'd heard about the other murders, this one seemed rushed and unplanned. Different.

'What do you know about the Banco Rosalia?' he asked.

'Nothing really.' She shrugged. 'Small bank, majority owned by the Vatican. I met the guy who runs it at the morgue, ID-ing Argento's body.'

'We should take the disks.' Tom pointed at a stack of DVDs that he guessed were server backups. 'If the bank's involved, the money trail might show us how.'

'What about him?' She motioned towards D'Arcy's distended corpse.

'We'll re-seal the door and leave him for the cops to find when it opens tomorrow,' he said with a shrug. 'There's nothing he can tell them that we –' He broke off, having just caught sight of D'Arcy's wrist.

'What's up?'

Tom knelt down and gingerly lifted D'Arcy's arm.

'His watch,' he breathed as he tried to get at the fastening. The cold flesh had risen like dough around the black crocodile-skin strap, his blackened fingers leaving dark bruise-like marks on D'Arcy's pale skin.

'What about it?'

'It's a Ziff.'

'A Ziff?'

'Max Ziff. A watch-maker. A genius. He only makes three, maybe four pieces a year. They sell for hundreds of thousands. Sometimes millions.'

'How can you tell it's one of his?' She crouched down next to him.

'The orange second hand,' he explained, the catch coming free and the strap peeling away, leaving a deep welt in the skin. 'That's his signature.'

'I've seen one of these before,' she frowned, reaching for it.

'Are you sure it was a Ziff?' he asked with a sceptical look. Not only were there so few of them around, but they were so unobtrusive that most people never noticed them when they saw them. In fact that was half the point.

'It wasn't *a* Ziff. It was the *same* Ziff,' she insisted. 'It was in Cavalli's evidence box. White face with no make on it, steel case, roman numerals, orange second hand and . . .' she flipped it over '. . . Yes. Engraved Greek letter on the back. Only this is delta. Cavalli's was gamma.'

'Are you sure it . . .?' he asked again.

'I'm telling you, it was identical.'

Tom shook his head in surprise.

'It must have been a special commission. He normally only makes one of anything.'

'Then we should talk to him,' Allegra suggested. 'If it's unusual, he might remember who ordered it and where we can find them?'

'We'd have to go and see him. He doesn't have a phone.'

'Where?'

'Geneva. We could drive there in a few hours and Archie could –' A sharp electronic tone broke into the conversation. Tom's eyes snapped to the door. 'Someone's coming.'

They leapt towards the exit, Allegra pausing only to hit the close button and snatch her hand out of the way as the door slammed shut. Working quickly, Tom stuffed the keypad back into the recess and screwed the access panel on, rubbing soot over it so that the area blended in with the rest of the wall.

'Outside,' Allegra mouthed, dragging him on to the balcony, the air cool and fresh after the panic room's putrid warmth. Moments later, his back pressed against the stone, he heard the un-mistakeable sound of someone crunching through the ash and debris, entering the room and then stopping. Reaching into his backpack for his gun, Tom flicked the safety off. Allegra, standing on the other side of the doorway, did the same.

'It's Orlando,' a voice rasped in Italian. Tom frowned. He sounded strangely familiar. 'No, it's still shut . . .' A pause as he listened to whatever was being said at the other end, Tom barely daring to breathe in the silence. 'They've cleared away what was left of the bookcase, so they must know it's there . . .' Another pause, Tom still trying to place a voice that he was now convinced he'd heard only recently. If only he could remember when and where. 'I'll make sure we have someone here when it opens. It's the least they can do for us. Otherwise there's someone in the morgue . . . we've got an agreement . . . As soon as they bring the body in . . . Don't worry, everything's already set up. I'll be back before they land.'

The call ended and the footsteps retreated across the room towards the stairs. A few minutes later, the motion sensor beeped again and Allegra let out a relieved sigh. Tom, however, was already halfway across the room, heart thumping.

'Where are you going?' she called after him in a low voice. 'Tom!' She grabbed him by the arm and pulled him back. 'He'll hear you.'

Tom spun round, his eyes blazing, a tremor in his voice that he barely recognised as his own.

'It's him,' he spat angrily. 'I recognised his voice.'

'Who?'

'The priest,' Tom said through gritted teeth, all thoughts of Cavalli and the League and following up on the Ziff watch having suddenly left him. 'The priest from the Amalfi. The one sent to handle the Caravaggio exchange.'

FIFTY-NINE

20th March – 3.52 a.m.
Barrelling through the doorway, Tom took the stairs as quickly as he dared, Allegra on his heels. Nothing made sense any more. Nothing, except that he couldn't let him get away. He connected whatever had happened here to both the killings in Rome and Jennifer's death. He could lead Tom to whoever had ordered the hit.

A few minutes later, they emerged breathlessly into the ground-floor lobby.

'Which way did he go?' Tom barked at the officer, whose smile had quickly faded as he caught sight of the expression on Tom's soot-smudged face.

'Who?' he stuttered.

'The man who just came down ahead of us,' Tom snapped impatiently.

'No one else has been in since you went up,'

the officer replied in an apologetic voice, as if he was somehow at fault.

'He must have come in another way,' Allegra immediately guessed. 'Probably jumped across from a balcony next door.'

They stepped through the sliding glass doors just as the garage entrance on the adjacent building rattled open. A blood-red Alfa Romeo MiTo chased the echo of its own engine up the slope from the underground car park, Tom glimpsing the driver as he quickly checked for traffic before accelerating down the street.

'Is everything okay?' the officer called after them with a worried cry as they sprinted to their car.

'Are you sure it's him?' Allegra asked as she buckled herself in, bracing an arm against the dash as the car leapt away.

'I remember every voice, every glance, every face from that night,' Tom insisted in a cold voice. 'He was as close to me as you are now. It was him. And if he's here, whoever sent him might be too.'

They caught up with the Alfa near the casino, the priest being careful, it seemed, to stay well within the speed limit. Dropping back to a safe distance, Tom followed him down the hill and through the underpass back towards the port, where workmen were busy disassembling a temporary dressage arena and stables under flood-lights. Pulling in, they watched as he parked up and made his way down to the water, where a launch was waiting for him between two top-heavy motor cruisers.

'Drive down to the end,' Allegra suggested. 'We'll be able to see where he's going.'

With a nod Tom headed for the harbour wall and then got out, pausing to grab a set of night-vision goggles out of his bag. Putting them on, he tracked the small craft as it cut across the waves to an enormous yacht moored in the middle of the bay.

'*Il Sogno Blu*,' Tom read the name painted across its bows. 'The Blue Dream. Out of Georgetown.' A pause. 'We need to get out to it.'

Allegra eyed him carefully, as if debating whether she should try and talk him out of it. Then, with a shrug she pointed back over his shoulder.

'What about one of those?'

They ran down the ramp on to a pontoon where three small tenders had been tied up. The keys to the second one were attached to a champagne cork in a watertight storage compartment under the instrument panel. A few minutes later and they were slapping across the waves towards the yacht.

'This will do,' Tom called over the noise of the outboard as they approached. 'If we get any closer they'll hear us. I'll swim the rest.'

She killed the engine, then went and stood over him as he took his soot-stained tie off and loosened his collar.

'You don't know who's onboard or how many of them there are,' she pointed out, the wind whipping her hair.

'I know that someone on that ship helped kill Jennifer.' He kicked his shoes off and stood up, looping the night-vision goggles over one arm. 'That's enough.'

'Then I'm coming with you,' she insisted.

'You need to stay with the boat,' he pointed out, handing her both the phones the croupier had given him and D'Arcy's watch. 'Otherwise it'll drift and neither of us will make it back.'

She eyed him angrily.

'I thought we were in this together.'

'We are. But this is something I have to do alone.'

'I could stop you,' she reminded him in a defiant tone, standing in front of him so that he couldn't get past.

A pause, then a nod.

'You probably could.' A longer pause. 'But I don't think you will. You know I have to do this.'

There was a long silence. Then Allegra stepped unsmilingly to one side. With a nod, Tom squeezed past her to the stern and lowered himself into the water.

'Look, I'm not stupid,' he said, with what he hoped was a reassuring smile. 'I'll be careful. Just give me twenty minutes, thirty max. Enough time to see who's on board and what they're doing here.'

Lips pursed, she gave a grudging nod.

Turning, Tom kicked out for the yacht with a powerful stroke, the waves rolling gently underneath him. He was lucky, he knew. On a rougher day, they might well have tossed him from crest to crest like a dolphin playing with a seal. Even so, it took him five, maybe even ten minutes to cover the hundred and fifty yards he'd left himself, his clothes dragging him back, a slight current throwing him off his bearing.

Up close, the yacht was even larger than it had appeared from the shore – perhaps 400 feet long, with sheer white sides that rose above him like an ice shelf, the sea lapping tentatively around it, as if afraid of being crushed. Even though it was anchored, the yacht's shape made it look as if it was powering through the waves at eighteen knots, its arrowed bow lunging aggressively over the water, its rear chopped off on a steep rake, as if it had been pulled out of shape. Tom counted five decks in all, their square portholes looking as if they must have been dynamited out of the ship's monolithic hull, capped by a mushrooming radar and comms array that wouldn't have been out of place on an aircraft carrier.

The launch had been moored to a landing platform that folded down out of the stern. Swimming round to it, Tom hauled himself on board and then carefully climbed across on to the ship itself. The landing platform was deserted, although he could see now that when lowered it revealed a huge garage and electric hoist, with room to store the launch itself, together with a small flotilla of jet-skis, inflatables and other craft.

Quickly drying himself on one of the neatly folded towels monogrammed with the yacht's name, he buttoned his jacket and turned the collar up to conceal as much of his white shirt as he could. Then he slipped his NV goggles over his head and turned them on. With a low hum, night became day, albeit one with a stark green tint. The outline of the deck's darkest recesses now revealed themselves as if caught in the burst of a permanent firework.

Treading stealthily, Tom made his way up a succession of steep teak-lined staircases to the main deck, which he had noticed on the swim across was the only one with any lights on. Finding the port gangway empty, he made his way forward along it, keeping below the windows and checking over his shoulder that no one was coming up behind him. Two doors had been left open about halfway along, the glow spilling out on to the polished hardwood decking and making his goggles flare. Switching them off, he edged his head round the first opening. It gave on to a walnut-panelled dining room, the table already set with china and crystal for the following morning's breakfast. In the middle of the main wall he recognised Picasso's *Head of a Woman*, taken from a yacht in Antibes a few years ago.

The second open doorway revealed the main sitting room. Hanging over the mantelpiece was a painting that Tom recognised as the *View of the Sea at Scheveningen*, stolen from the Van Gogh Museum in Amsterdam. This room, too, had been set up, although in readiness for what looked like cocktails rather than breakfast: champagne cooling in an ice bucket, an empty bottle of '78 Château Margaux standing next to a full decanter, glasses laid out on a crisp linen cloth.

Turning the goggles back on, he continued along the gangway, wondering if he had chanced his luck long enough up here and whether he should head down below instead. But before he could do anything, a door ahead of him opened. Tom froze in the shadow of a bulkhead. A man stepped out, talking on his phone. Tom's heart jumped. It was the priest, his mouth twisted into a cruel laugh, but recognisably the same man he'd faced in the casino – medium build, white, wavy hair, ruddy cheeks.

Even as Jennifer's image filled his mind, he felt the anger flood through him, sensed his chest tightening and his jaw clenching. Before he knew it, he was clutching his gun, her name on his lips, and death in his heart.

SIXTY

Il Sogno Blu, Monaco
20th March – 4.21 a.m.
It hadn't taken Allegra long to decide to ignore
Tom's instructions and follow him on board.
There'd been something dead in his eyes, something in the way he'd deliberately patted his pocket
to check that his gun was still there, that had
suggested he would need her help – not to deal
with whoever was on board, but to protect him
from himself.

Having approached from behind so that the
wind would carry the engine's breathless echo
away from the yacht, Allegra had pulled alongside the launch and lashed the tender to it. Then
she had paused for a few moments, waiting for
an angry shout and for an armed welcoming party
to materialise. But none came.

Climbing across the launch and on to the
landing platform, she made her way up to the main

deck, pressing herself flat against one of the aluminium staircases when a sentry walked whistling past above her. Unlike Tom, she had no night-vision equipment, so had to feel her way through the darkness, the distant flicker of the steeply banked shore providing only the faintest light by which to navigate. Even so, Tom was proving relatively easy to track, the deck still damp wherever he had paused for more than a few seconds.

Moving as quickly as she dared, she edged forward, ducking under windows and darting across the open doorways until she had almost reached the sundeck area which took up the entire front third of this level. At its centre was a helipad that she realised parted to reveal a swimming pool.

In the same instant she saw Tom ahead of her, crouched in the shadows of the side rail, his gun in his hand. She followed his aim and saw a man standing at the bow, looking out to sea, talking into his phone. Leaping forward, she placed her hand on Tom's shoulder. He spun round to face her, a strange, empty expression on his face as if in some sort of trance.

'Not now,' she whispered. 'Not here.'

For a few moments it was almost as if he didn't recognise her, before his face broke with surprise, and then a flash of anger.

'What . . .?'

She held her finger to her lips, then pointed above them towards the top deck. An armed guard was leaning back casually against the railings above them blowing smoke rings. Tom blinked and then glanced across at her, his eyes betraying a flicker of understanding.

She motioned for him to follow her, the second door she tried opening into a small gymnasium.

'Are you trying to get yourself killed?' she hissed as soon as the door had shut. Their shadows danced off the mirrored walls, the exercise equipment's skeletal frames looming menacingly around them as if they were limbering up for a fight.

'I . . .' he faltered, staring at the gun in his hand as if he wasn't quite sure how it had got there. 'You don't understand.'

'You're right, I don't understand . . .' She broke off at the sound of someone approaching with a squeak of rubber soles, the noise growing and then slowly fading away. 'You said you were just going to see who was here. Not get yourself killed.'

'It's him,' Tom said in a low voice, almost as if he was trying to convince himself. 'He set her up!'

'*He* doesn't matter. What's important is finding out who sent him.'

'I saw him and I . . .' Another long pause, until he finally looked up, his lips pressed together as if he was trying to hold something in. 'You're right. I wasn't . . .'

With a curt nod, she accepted what she assumed was as close as she was going to get to an apology. 'Let's just get off this thing before they find us.'

Checking that the gangway was still empty, Allegra led him back towards the stern. But they were only about halfway along it when the echo of a barked order and the sound of running feet forced them to dive through the open sitting-room door and crouch behind the sofa, guns drawn. Three men tore past the doorway, the approaching thump of rotor blades explaining the sudden commotion.

'Someone's landing,' Allegra breathed.

'Which must be what all this is for,' Tom said, pointing at the carefully prepared drinks and glasses. 'We need to . . . What the hell are you doing?'

'Inviting us to the party,' she said with a wink. Having taken out both the phones Tom had handed her earlier, she used one to dial the other and then slid it out of sight under the coffee table. 'At least until the battery runs out.'

With the phone hidden and still transmitting, they made their way back along the gangway, then down the staircase to the landing platform, the helicopter's low rumble now a fast-closing thunder.

As it landed, they cast off, using the engine noise as cover to throttle up and spin away towards the harbour and the relative sanctuary of their waiting car.

SIXTY-ONE

Santos uncorked the decanter and poured the Margaux into four large glasses. It pained him to share a bottle as good as this at the best of times, but to split it at this time of the night with two former members of the Serbian special forces, whose palates had no doubt been irretrievably blunted by eating too much cabbage and drinking their own piss while out on exercise, seemed positively criminal. Then again, they would recognise the Margaux for what it cost, even if they couldn't taste why it was worth it. And that was half the point in serving it.

'Nice boat,' Asim whistled. 'Yours?'

He was the older of the two and clearly in charge, squat and square headed, with a five-mil buzz-cut and a bayonet scar across one cheek.

'Borrowed from one of my investors,' Santos

replied, sitting down opposite them. 'How was your flight?'

'No problem,' Dejan, the second Serb, replied.

Compared to Asim, he was tall and gaunt, with curly black hair that he had slicked back against his head with some sort of oil. One of his ears was higher than the other, which caused his glasses to rest at a slight angle across his face.

'Good,' Santos replied. 'You're welcome to stay the night, of course.'

'Thank you, but no,' Dejan declined, Santos noting with dismay that he had already knocked back half his glass as if it was tequila. 'Our orders are to agree deal and return.'

'We do have a deal then?'

'Fifteen million dollars,' Asim confirmed.

'You said twenty on the phone,' Santos retorted angrily. 'It's worth at least twenty. I wouldn't have invited you here if I'd known it was only for fifteen.'

'Fifteen is new price,' Asim said stonily. 'Or you find someone else with money so quick.'

There was a pause as Santos stared angrily at each of the Serbs in turn. With Ancelotti's team of forensic accountants due to start on his books any day, he was out of options. And from their obvious confidence, they knew it. He glanced across at Orlando, who shrugged helplessly.

'Fine. Fifteen,' Santos spat. 'In cash.'

'You understand the consequences if you are not able to deliver . . .'

'We'll deliver,' Santos said firmly, standing up.

'Then we look forward to your call,' Dejan shrugged, draining his glass. 'Tomorrow, as agreed.'

Shaking their hands, Santos showed them to the door, waited until their footsteps had melted into towards the engine whine of the waiting helicopter, then swore.

'We could find another buyer,' Orlando suggested.

'Not at this short notice, and the bastards know it,' Santos said angrily. 'It's tomorrow night or never.'

'De Luca and Moretti agreed to the meet?'

'I told them that things had got out of hand,' Santos nodded. 'That business was suffering. Then offered to broker a settlement. They didn't take much convincing. Usual place. No weapons, no men. It'll be our only chance to get the watches and the painting in the same room.'

'As long as we can get to D'Arcy's.'

'We only need three,' Santos reminded him. 'We've got Cavalli's already and Moretti and De Luca should both be wearing theirs. D'Arcy's is back-up.'

'They'll come after you. They'll come after us both.'

'They'll have to find me first.' Santos shrugged. 'Besides, life's too short to waste it worrying about being dead.'

'Amen,' Orlando nodded, topping up their glasses.

SIXTY-TWO

Main harbour, Monte Carlo
20th March – 5.03 a.m.

'Are you sure that was him?'

'I'm telling you, it's Antonio Santos,' she breathed, certain she was right but still not quite able to believe it. 'The Chairman of the Banco Rosalia. He said exactly the same thing about life being too short when he was identifying Argento's body.'

'It wouldn't exactly be the first time a Vatican-funded bank has been a front for the mafia,' Tom conceded with a shrug.

'Do you think he ordered the hit on Jennifer?'

'The priest clearly works for him and, by the sound of it, he had access to the Caravaggio too,' Tom nodded darkly.

'But why would he have done it?'

'My guess is that she found something during that raid on the dealer in New York. A bank statement or an invoice or a receipt. Something that implicated the Banco Rosalia or that tied him back to the League. Something worth killing her for.'

'Even if we could prove that, he's got a Vatican passport,' she reminded him with a shake of her head. 'He can't be prosecuted.'

'Maybe if we can get to the painting before him, he won't have to be.'

'What do you mean?'

'I mean the Serbs will take care of him for us if he doesn't deliver,' Tom explained in a grim voice.

There was a pause as she let the implications of this sink in.

'At least now we know why D'Arcy's murder didn't match any of the other killings,' she said. 'It had nothing to do with the League's vendetta. Santos killed him for his watch.'

'They link everything,' Tom agreed.

'Moretti, De Luca, D'Arcy . . .' She counted the watches off on her fingers.

'Cavalli,' Tom finished the list for her.

'That must have been what Gallo was looking for when he killed Gambetta,' Allegra said with an angry shake of her head. 'He's been working for Santos all along.'

'But why? How can a watch help get to a painting?'

'Even if we knew, we still don't know where the painting is.'

'Ziff's our best hope,' Tom said slowly. 'He'll know why Santos needs them.'

'Will he see us?' Allegra asked.

'Oh, he'll see us,' Tom nodded. 'But that doesn't mean he'll tell us anything.'

SIXTY-THREE

Near Aosta, Italy
20th March – 8.33 a.m.

It was a six-hour drive to Geneva, the road snaking up into the hills behind Monte Carlo and then along the motorway into Italy, before turning north and plunging into the Alps. They'd had no trouble at the border, their Swiss passports earning little more than a cursory once-over from the duty officer and then a dismissive flick of his hand as he waved them through. Even so, Tom was certain that he'd caught him giving them the finger as they'd accelerated away. So much for European harmony.

Allegra had soon drifted off, leaving Tom to take the first shift, although she had at least managed to share what she remembered about Santos's immaculate dress sense, compulsive liquorice habit and cold-eyed charisma before her tiredness had finally caught up with her. Eventually, about three hours in, Tom had turned off at a service station near Aosta on the A5, hungry and needing to stretch his legs before swapping over.

'I need a coffee,' Allegra groaned as he shook her awake.

'We both do.'

'Where are we?'

'Not far from the Mont Blanc tunnel.'

The service station was bright and warm, something indistinct but resolutely cheerful playing in the background. A busload of school children on a ski trip had turned up just before them and they were besieging the small shop. Desperately rooting through their pockets for change, they were noisily pooling funds to finance a hearty breakfast of crisps, coke and chocolate. As soon as the onslaught had cleared, the teachers swooped in behind them to pick over the bones of whatever they hadn't stripped from the shelves and apologise to the staff.

While Allegra queued for the toilet, Tom got them both a coffee from the machine and managed to locate a couple of pastries that had somehow survived the raid. Then he called Archie.

'Where the fuck have you been?' Archie greeted him angrily. 'I've been trying to call since lunchtime yesterday.'

'I had to swap phones. It's a long story.'

'Then make it a good one. Dom was worried. We both were.'

'We think Jennifer was killed because she was investigating a mafia-controlled antiquities smuggling ring called the Delian League,' Tom explained, mouthing Archie's name to Allegra as she returned.

'*We*? Who the bloody hell is "we"?'

Tom sighed. He could see this was going to be a long conversation. But there was no avoiding it. Step by step, he ran through the events of the last day or so – his encounter with Allegra at Cavalli's house, their trip to see Johnny Li, the abortive attempt to steal a car, their interrogation of Aurelio, their capture by De Luca and subsequent escape from the tomb, their trip to the casino and their discovery of D'Arcy's panic room. And finally, the conversation they had just overheard between Santos and the Serbs. Archie was an impatient listener, interrupting every so often with questions or a muttered curse until Tom had finished. Then it was his turn to explain how it seemed that the Artemis Tom had asked them to look into had in fact been bought by a company controlled by the same person who had sold it in the first place.

'Our guess is that it's part of an elaborate laundering scam to manufacture provenance,' Archie added. 'You ever heard of an antiquities dealer called Faulks?'

'Faulks,' Tom exclaimed, recognising the name that Aurelio had mentioned. 'Earl Faulks?'

'You know him?' Archie sounded vaguely disappointed.

'Aurelio mentioned his name,' Tom explained. 'Where he is now?'

'His car had Geneva plates, so I'm guessing he's based here.'

'See if you can find him. When we've finished with Ziff, I'll call you. We can pay him a visit together.'

'Everything okay?' Allegra asked as he ended the call. From her expression, Tom guessed that she'd overhead the tinny echo of Archie's strident tone.

'Don't worry. That's standard Archie,' Tom reassured her with a wink. 'He's only happy when he's got something or someone to complain about.' He held out the car keys. 'Here – it's your turn to drive.'

SIXTY-FOUR

Lake Geneva, Switzerland
20th March – 10.59 a.m.

A couple of hours later, they drew up at the lake's edge. A yacht was skating across the water's glassy surface, its sail snapping in the breeze. In the distance loomed the jagged, snow-covered teeth of the surrounding mountains, their reflection caught so perfectly by the water's blinding mirror that it was hard to know which way was up. It was a strangely disorientating illusion. And one that was broken only when the yacht suddenly tacked left, its trailing wake corrugating the water.

Getting out, they walked up to the gates of a large three-storey red-brick building with steep gabled roofs. Set high up and back from the road behind iron railings, it appeared to be empty; grey shutters drawn across the mullioned windows, walls choking with ivy, the gardens wild and

overgrown. Even so, there were faint signs of life
– tyre tracks in the gravel suggesting a recent visit,
roving security cameras patrolling the property's
perimeter, steam rising from an outlet.

'The Georges d'Ammon Asylum for the
Insane?' Allegra read the polished brass nameplate and then shot Tom a questioning, almost
disbelieving look.

'Used to be,' Tom affirmed, rolling his shoulders to try and ease the stiffness in his back and
neck. 'That's why Ziff bought it. He thought it was
funny.'

'What's the joke?'

'That anyone who spends their life watching
the seconds tick away is bound to go mad eventually. He thought that at least this way, he
wouldn't have far to move.' A pause. 'Swiss
humour. It takes some getting used to.'

Tom pressed the buzzer. No answer. He tried
again, holding it down longer this time. Still
nothing.

'Maybe he's out,' Allegra ventured.

'He never goes out,' Tom said with a shake of
his head. 'Doesn't even have a phone. He's just
being difficult. Show him the watch.'

With a shrug, she held D'Arcy's watch up to
the camera. A few seconds past, and then the gate
buzzed open.

They made their way up the steep drive, the
gravel crunching like fresh snow underfoot, the

building's institutional blandness further revealing itself as it slowly came into view.

'How long has he been here?'

'As long as I've known him,' Tom replied. 'The authorities shut it down after some of the staff were accused of abusing the inmates. They found two bodies under the basement floor, more bricked up inside a chimney.'

Even as he said this, Allegra noticed that the spiked railings girdling the property were angled back inside the garden – to keep people in, not out. She shivered, the sun's warmth momentarily eclipsed by the shadow of a large plane tree.

'How many watches does he make a year?' she asked, changing the subject.

'New? Not many. Maybe three or four.' Tom shrugged. 'His main business is upgrades.'

'What sort of upgrades?'

'It depends. Retrofitting manufactured components with handmade titanium or even ceramic ones, improving the balance wheel and mainspring design, engraving certain parts of the movement, adding new features, modifying the face . . . The only way you'd know it was one of his is from the orange second hand that he fits to everything he touches.'

'So you buy a watch that tells the time perfectly well and then pay him more money to take it apart and rebuild it to do exactly the same thing?' she asked incredulously.

'Pretty much.' Tom grinned. 'People do it with sports cars.'

'But that's to make them go faster. A watch either tells the time or it doesn't. It can't do it better.'

'That's not the point. It's not what it does but the way it does it. The ingenuity of the design. The quality of the materials. The skill with which it's been assembled. It's like people. It's what you can't see that really counts.'

'Some people, maybe.'

The front door was sheltered under an ornate cast-iron canopy at the top of several shallow steps. It was open and they stepped inside, finding themselves in a large entrance hall lit by a flickering emergency exit sign.

Her eyes adjusting to the gloom, Allegra could see that the room rose to the full height of the building, an oak staircase zig-zagging its way up to each floor capped off by a glass cupola far overhead. To their right was what had clearly once been the reception desk, the yellowing visitors' book still open at the last entry, a gnarled claw of desiccated flowers drooping over it as if poised to sign in. Up on the wall was a large carved panel lauding the generosity and wisdom of the asylum's founder and marking its opening in 1896. Next to this, another panel commemorated those who had served as directors over the years, the final name on the list either incomplete or deliberately defaced, it was hard to tell. To the left, a straitjacket had been left slung over the back of a wheelchair at the foot of the staircase, its leather straps cracked, the buckles rusting. Behind it was a grandfather clock, its face shrouded by a white sheet.

Allegra had the strange feeling that she was intruding, that the building was holding its breath, and that as soon as they left the strait-jacket would deftly fasten itself, the doors would swing wildly in their frames, the clock chime and silent screams rise once again from the base-ment's dank shadows.

'Up here,' a voice called, breaking the spell.

She looked up through the darkness and saw a man peering down at them over the second-floor banisters. Swapping a look, they made their way up to him, the wooden staircase groaning under their unexpected weight, their footsteps echoing off the flaking green walls.

'So you've come to visit at last, Felix?' Ziff grinned manically, thrusting his hand towards them as they stepped on to a landing lit by sunshine knifing through the gaps and cracks in the shuttered windows. He spoke quickly and with a thick German accent, his words eliding into each other.

'A promise is a promise.' Tom smiled, shaking his hand. 'Max, this is Allegra Damico.'

'Friend of yours?' Ziff asked without looking at her.

'I wouldn't have brought her here otherwise,' Tom reassured him.

Ziff considered this for a few seconds, then gave a high-pitched, almost nervous laugh, that flitted up and down a scale.

'No, of course not. *Wilkommen*.'

Ziff stepped forward into the light. He was tall, perhaps six foot three, but slight, his reedy frame looking as though it would bend in a strong wind, dyed black hair thinning and cropped short. His features were equally delicate, almost feminine, his face dominated by a neatly trimmed moustache that exactly followed the contours of his top lip and had been dyed to match his hair. He was wearing a white apron over green tweed trousers, gleaming brown brogues and an open-necked check shirt worn with a yellow cravat. His sleeves were rolled up so she could see his thin wrists, the slender fingers of his right hand tapping against his leg as if playing an unheard piece of music, the left gripping an Evian atomiser. Strangely, given his occupation, he wasn't wearing a watch.

She shook his hand, his skin feeling unnaturally slick, until she realised that he was wearing latex gloves.

'I was so sorry to hear about your father.' Ziff turned back to Tom, gripping him firmly by the elbow and leaning in close. 'How have you been?'

'Fine,' Tom nodded his thanks. 'It's been a while now. Almost three years.'

'That long?' Ziff let him go, his head springing from side to side in bemusement. 'You know me: I try not to keep track. I find it too depressing,' He licked the corner of his mouth absent-mindedly, then repeated his shrill laugh.

The sight of a round mark on the wall behind him where the clock that had once hung there had been removed made Allegra wonder if perhaps Ziff hadn't been joking when he had told Tom his reasons for buying this place. Maybe he really did believe that a life spent watching time leak irresistibly away would condemn him to insanity, and that by removing a clock here and covering another there, he might in some way avoid or at least delay his fate.

Ziff seemed to guess what she was thinking, because he glanced up at the ghostly imprint of the missing clock behind him.

'Time is an accident of accidents, signorina.' He gave her a sad nod.

'Epicurus,' she replied, recognising the quote.

'Exactly!' His face broke into a smile. 'Now tell me, Felix. What accident of accidents brings you here?'

SIXTY-FIVE

20th March – 11.14 a.m.
Ziff led them through a set of double doors into
a sombre corridor, its grey linoleum unfurling
towards a fire escape at its far end. Several gurneys
were parked along one wall, while on the other
wall patients' clipboards were still neatly arranged
in a rack with the staff attendance record chalked
up on a blackboard – further confirmation that
the building's former occupants had left in a hurry
and that Ziff had made little effort to clean up
after them.

He stopped at the first door on the left, sprayed
its handle with the atomiser, then opened it to
reveal one of the asylum's former wards. Here,
too, it seemed that nothing had been touched,
until Ziff flicked a power switch and Allegra
suddenly realised that all the beds were missing
and that in their place, lined up between the floral
curtains dangling listlessly from aluminium tracks,

were pinball machines. Sixteen of them in all, eight running down each side of the room, back-boards flashing, lanes pulsing, drop targets blinking and bumpers sparking as they happily flickered into life. Allegra read the names of a few as she walked past – 'Flash Gordon', 'Playboy', 'Close Encounters of the Third Kind', 'The Twilight Zone' – their titles evocative of a distant, almost forgotten childhood. Every so often one of them would call out a catchphrase or play a theme song, and this seemed to set the other machines off, their sympa-thetic chorus building to a discordant crescendo before dying away again.

'They're all vintage,' Ziff explained proudly, stepping slowly past them like a doctor doing his rounds. 'Each one is for a private commission I've completed. A tombstone, if you like. So I don't forget.'

'How many have you got?' Allegra asked, pausing by 'The Addams Family', and then jumping as it blasted out a loud clickety-click noise.

'About eighty,' he said after a few seconds' thought. 'I've almost run out of bed space.'

'Which one's your favourite?'

'Favourite?' He looked horrified. 'Each one is unique, each different. If you were to try and choose one over the others . . .' He tailed off, as if afraid the machines might overhear him.

He stopped by a battered wooden desk marooned in the middle of the ward. Its top was covered in red felt, worn and stained in places with oil. A large magnifying lamp was clamped to one edge and it was on casters, prompting Allegra to wonder if Ziff wheeled it from room to room, moving around the different wards as the mood took him.

He sat down, a steel tray in front of him containing the disembodied guts of a Breguet, a 20x loupe and several jeweller's screwdrivers. Other tools had been carefully laid out in the different drawers of a small wheeled cabinet to his right, as if in preparation for surgery – case openers, tweezers, screwdrivers, watch hammers, pliers, brushes, knives – each sorted by type and then arranged by size.

'Show me,' Ziff said, pushing the tray out of the way and putting on an almost comically large pair of black square-framed glasses that he secured to his head with an elastic strap.

Allegra handed him the watch and he angled the magnifying lamp down over it, peering through the glass.

'Oh yes.' His face broke into a smile. 'Hello, old friend.'

'You recognise it?'

'Wouldn't you recognise one of your own children?' Ziff asked impatiently. 'Especially one as special as this.'

'What do you mean?' Tom shot back eagerly.

'Each of my watches is normally unique,' Ziff

explained. 'A one-off. But in this case, the client ordered six identical pieces. And paid handsomely for the privilege, from what I remember.'

'Six?' Allegra repeated excitedly. They knew of four already. That left two others still un-accounted for.

'They're numbered,' Ziff continued, pointing at the delta symbol delicately engraved on the back of the case. 'Platinum bezel, stainless-steel case, ivory face, self-winding, water resistant to thirty metres, screw-down crown . . .' He balanced it in his hand as if weighing it. 'A good watch.'

'Who was the client?' Tom asked.

Ziff looked at him with an indulgent smile, slip-ping his glasses up on to his forehead where they perched like headlights.

'Felix, you know better than that.'

'It's important,' Tom insisted.

'My clients pay for their confidentiality, the same as yours,' Ziff insisted with a shrug.

'Please, Max,' Tom pleaded. 'I have to know. Give me something.'

Ziff paused before answering, his eyes blinking, then slipped his glasses back on to his nose and stood up.

'Do you like pinball?'

'We're not here to play pinball,' Tom said sharply, although Ziff didn't seem to pick up on his tone. 'We're here to . . .'

'"Straight Flush" is a classic,' he interrupted, crossing over to the door. 'Why don't you have a game while you're waiting?'

'Waiting for what?' Tom called after him, but Ziff was already out of the room, the sprung door easing itself shut behind him.

Allegra turned towards the machine he had pointed out. It appeared to be one of the oldest and most basic in the room, the salmon-coloured back-board illustrated with face-card caricatures, the sloping yellow surface decorated with playing cards that Allegra guessed you had to try and illuminate to create a high-scoring poker hand. She frowned. It wasn't an obvious recommendation, compared to some of the more modern, more exciting games in the room, but then again she had detected an insistent tone in his voice. A tone that had made her wonder if there was something there he wanted them to see. Something other than the machine itself.

'Can you open it?' she asked, pointing at the metal panel on the front of the machine that contained the coin slot.

'Of course,' Tom squatted down next to her with a puzzled frown, reaching into his coat for a small pouch of lock-picking tools.

'He said that each machine was for a job he'd completed. A tombstone so he wouldn't forget,' she reminded him as he deftly released the lock and opened the door, allowing her to reach into

the void under the playing surface. 'I just
wondered . . .'

Her voice broke off as her fingers closed on an
envelope of some sort. Pulling it out, she opened
it, the flap coming away easily where the glue had
dried over the years. It contained several sheets
of paper.

'It's the original invoice,' she exclaimed with
an excited smile. 'Six watches. Three hundred
thousand dollars,' she read from the fading type.
'A lot of money, thirty years ago.'

'A lot of money today.' Tom smiled. 'Who was
the client?'

'See for yourself.'

Allegra handed him the sheet, her eyes blazing
with excitement.

'E. Faulks & Co,' Tom read, his face set with a
grim smile. 'And there's a billing address down at
the Freeport. Good. I'll ask Archie to meet us there.
Even if Faulks has moved we should be able to
find –'

'That's strange,' Allegra interrupted him, having
quickly leafed through the rest of the contents of
the envelope. 'There's another invoice here. Same
address, only twelve years later.'

'But that would make seven watches.' Tom
frowned. 'Ziff only mentioned six.'

Before she could even attempt an explanation,
she heard the whistled strains of the overture from
Carmen echoing along the corridor outside.

Snatching the invoice from Tom's hand, she slipped it back in the envelope, shoved it inside the machine and shut the door.

"Magnets,' Ziff announced as he sauntered in, excitedly waving several sheets of paper over his head. 'I knew they were down there somewhere.'

'What?'

'Magnets,' Ziff repeated with a high-pitched giggle, his glasses hanging around his neck like a swimmer's goggles. 'See.'

Picking D'Arcy's watch up, he held it over the tray containing the watch he was working on. Two small screws leapt through the air and glued themselves to the bezel.

'Each watch has a small electro magnet built into it powered by the self-winding mechanism,' he explained, opening the file and pointing at a set of technical drawings as if they might mean something to either of them. 'They were all set at slightly different resistances.'

'What for?'

'Some sort of a locking mechanism, I think. They never said exactly what.'

Allegra swapped a meaningful glance with Tom. So this was why Santos needed the watches. Together, they formed a key that opened wherever the Caravaggio was being stored.

'Normally I destroy the drawings once a job is completed, but this was the first time I had used silicon-based parts and I thought they might be useful. Turns out it was just as well.'

'What do you mean?'

'The client lost one of the watches and asked for a replacement. The epsilon watch, I think. Without these I might have struggled to replicate it.'

Allegra took a deep breath. That explained the second invoice. More importantly, it meant that there were seven numbered watches out there somewhere. Each the same and yet subtly different. Each presumably entrusted to a different key member of the Delian League.

'By the way, what was your score?' Ziff jerked his head towards the 'Straight Flush' pinball machine he had pointed out earlier.

'Ask us tomorrow,' Tom answered with a smile.

SIXTY-SIX

Free Port Compound, Geneva
20th March – 12.02 p.m.

The Free Port was a sprawling agglomeration of low-slung warehouses lurking in the shadow of the airport's perimeter fence. Built up over the years, it offered a vivid snapshot of changing architectural fashions, the older buildings cinder grey and forbidding in their monolithic functionality, the newer ones iPod white and airy.

For the most part, its business was entirely legitimate, the facilities providing importers and exporters with a tax-free holding area through which goods could be shipped in transit or stored, with duty only being paid when items officially 'entered' the country.

The problem, as Tom was explaining to Allegra on the drive down there, lay in the Free Port's insistence on operating under a similar code of secrecy to the Swiss banking sector. This allowed cargo to be shipped into Switzerland, sold on, and then exported again with only the most cursory official records kept of what was actually being sold or who it was being sold to. Compounding this was Switzerland's repeated refusal to sign up to the 1970 Unesco Convention on the illicit trade in cultural property. Not to mention the fact that, under Swiss law, stolen goods acquired in good faith became the legal property of the new owner after five years on Swiss soil.

Taken together these three factors had, over the years, established Switzerland's free ports as a smuggler's paradise, with disreputable dealers exploiting the system by secretly importing stolen art or looted antiquities, holding them in storage for five years, and then claiming legal ownership.

To their credit, the Swiss government had recently bowed to international pressure and both ratified the Unesco Convention and changed its antiquated ownership laws. But so far the Free Port's entrenched position at the crossroads of the trade in illicit art and antiques seemed to be holding surprisingly firm. As Faulks's continuing presence served to prove.

They turned on to La Voie des Traz, the road choked with lorries and vans making deliveries and collections at the different warehouses, fork lifts shuttling between them as they loaded and unloaded with a high-pitched whine. For a moment, Tom was reminded of his drive into Vegas a few nights before, the vast buildings lining both sides of the street like the casinos studding the Strip.

'There's Archie and Dom –' Tom pointed at the two figures waiting in the car park of the warehouse mentioned on the invoice.

'Everything all right?' Archie bellowed as they got out.

'Tom!' A tearful Dominique tore past him and wrapped her arms around Tom's neck. 'I'm so sorry about what happened to . . . I'm so sorry.'

'Yeah,' Archie coughed awkwardly, lowering his eyes.

Even now, no one could bring themselves to say Jennifer's name, he noticed. Afraid of upsetting him. Afraid of what he might do or say.

'This is Allegra Damico,' Tom said, turning to introduce her.

She nodded hello, Tom realising from their forced handshakes and awkward greetings that they were all probably feeling a bit uncomfortable. Dom and Archie at Allegra stepping inside their tight little circle, Allegra at being so quickly outnumbered, with only Tom providing the delicate thread that bound them all together.

'How was Max?' Archie asked. 'Still bonkers?'

'Getting worse,' Tom sighed. 'Although we did manage to find out why Santos needs the watches.'

'They contain small electro-magnets that open

some sort of lock,' Allegra jumped in. 'Presumably to wherever the painting's being kept.'

'Faulks commissioned seven of them,' Tom continued. 'So as well as the four we know about, there are three more out there somewhere, which might give us a chance to get to the painting before Santos.' He glanced sceptically at the squat, square building behind them, its exterior clad in rusting metal sheeting. 'So, this is it?'

'It's scheduled for demolition later in the year,' Archie nodded. 'Faulks and a few other tenants who are due to move out at the end of the month are the only people left inside.'

'He's got a suite of rooms on the third floor,' Dominique added. 'He's due back at around four for a meeting with Verity Bruce.'

'The curator of antiquities at the Getty?' Allegra frowned in surprise. 'What's she doing here?'

'Having lunch at the Perle du Lac any time now and then doing the usual rounds of the major dealers.'

'How do you . . .' Allegra's question faded away as she saw the phone in Dominique's hand.

'We cloned his SIM. I've got it set up to mirror his calendar entries and record every call he makes.'

'Does that mean you know where they're meeting tonight?' Tom asked hopefully.

'The time's blocked out but there's no details.'

'Well, if they're due back here at four that gives

us . . . just under four hours to get inside, have a look around and get out.'

'I've rented some space on the same floor as Faulks.' Archie held out a key. 'Bloke on the desk thought I was loopy, given they're shutting down, but it's ours for the next two weeks.'

They signed in, the register suggesting that they were the only people there. The guard was all smiles, the momentary flurry of activity clearly a welcome respite from the silent contemplation of empty CCTV screens. To Archie's obvious amusement he seemed to take a particular shine to Dominique.

'You're well in,' he grinned as they made their way to the lift.

'Lucky me.'

'Archie's got a point,' Tom said. 'Why don't you stay down here and keep him busy.'

She gave Tom an injured look.

'Please tell me you're joking.'

'Just until we can get inside.'

She glared at Archie, who was trying not to laugh, then turned wearily back towards the reception as they got into the lift.

'Great,' she sighed as the doors shut.

A few moments later and they stepped out on to a wide cinder-block corridor that led off left and right. The floor had been painted grey, the evenly spaced neon tubes overhead reflecting in its dull surface every fifteen or so feet. A yellow line ran down its centre, presumably to help the fork-lifts navigate safely along it, although the gouges and marks along the greenwashed walls suggested that it had not been that effective. Steel doors were set into the walls at irregular intervals, the relative distance between them giving some indication as to the size of the room behind each one. As was usual in the Free Port, they were identified only by numbers, not company names.

They followed the signs to corridor twelve and then stopped outside room seventeen.

'This is it,' Archie confirmed.

'You know seventeen is an unlucky number in Italy,' Allegra observed thoughtfully.

'Why?'

'In Roman numerals it's XVII, which is an anagram of VIXI – I lived. I'm now dead.'

'She's a right barrel of laughs, isn't she?' Archie gave a flat sigh. 'Do you do bar mitzvahs too?'

'Give her a break, Archie,' Tom warned him sharply. 'She's part of this now.'

The offices were secured by three locks – a central one, common to every door, and two heavy-duty padlocks that Faulks must have fitted himself at the top and bottom. Working quickly, Tom placed a tension wrench in the lower half of the key hole and placed some light clockwise pressure on it. Then he slipped his pick into the top of the lock and, feeling for each pin, pushed them up out of the way one by one, careful to maintain the torque on the tension wrench so that they wouldn't drop back down. In little over a minute, all three locks had been released.

Grabbing the handle, Tom fractionally eased the door open and looked along its frame, then shut it again.

'Alarmed?' Archie guessed.

'Contact switch,' Tom said, glancing up at the camera at the end of the corridor and hoping that Dominique was working her magic.

'Can't you get round it?' Allegra asked.

'The contact at the top of the door is held shut by a magnet,' Tom explained. 'If we open the door, the magnet moves out of range and the switch opens and breaks the circuit. We need another magnet to hold the switch in place while we open the door.'

'I'll go and get your gear out the car,' Archie volunteered.

'Can't we just use this?' Allegra held up D'Arcy's watch, her eyebrows raised into a question. 'It's magnetised, isn't it?'

Tom turned to Archie with a questioning smile.

'Yeah well, I can't think of everything, can I?' Archie sniffed grudgingly.

Taking the watch from her, Tom again eased the door open and then held the back of the watch as close as he could to the small surface-mounted white box he had noticed previously. Then, exchanging a quick, hopeful look with both Archie and Allegra, he pushed the door fully open. For a few moments they stood there, each half-expecting to hear warning tones from the alarm's control panel. But the sound never came.

They were in.

SIXTY-SEVEN

Restaurant Perle du Lac, Geneva
20th March – 12.30 p.m.
'You found it!'

Faulks leant on his umbrella to stand up as the maitre d' escorted Verity along the terrace to the table. She was wearing a black dress and a denim jacket and clutching a red Birkin to match her shoes. Half her face was masked by a pair of dark Chanel sunglasses, a thick knot of semi-precious stones swaying around her neck.

'Earl, darling,' she gushed. They air-kissed noisily. 'Sorry I'm late. Spanish air traffic control was on strike again. *Quelle surprise!* I just got in.'

'Allow me.' He stepped forward and pushed her chair in for her, then handed her a napkin with a flourish. The maitre d', looking put out at having been so publicly supplanted, retreated in stony silence.

'What are we celebrating?' She clapped her

hands excitedly as the waiter stepped forward and poured them both a glass of the Pol Roger Cuvée Sir Winston Churchill that Faulks had specially pre-ordered.

'I always drink champagne for lunch.' He shrugged casually. 'Don't you?'

'Oh, Earl, you're such a tease.' She took a sip. 'You know this is my favourite. And as for the view – ' she gestured beyond the terrace towards the lake, its jewelled surface glittering in the sun – 'you must have sold your soul to get such a perfect day.'

'You're half right.' He winked.

She turned back to him with a suspicious smile, pushing her sunglasses up and shielding her eyes from the sun with a hand.

'Are you trying to soften me up?'

'As if I'd dare!' He grinned. The waiter materialised expectantly at their table. 'I recommend the pigeon breast.'

Their order taken, the waiter backed away. There was a lull, the delicate chime of Verity's long painted nails striking her glass echoing the clink of cutlery from the neighbouring tables, until she fixed him with a casual look.

'Do you have it?'

There. The question he'd been waiting for. Faulks was impressed. It had taken her a full three minutes longer to ask this than he'd thought it would. She'd obviously come here determined to play it cool.

'I have it,' he confirmed. 'It arrived yesterday. I unpacked it myself.'

'Is it . . .?' Her voiced tailed off, as if she didn't trust herself to put what she felt into words, her carefully planned strategy of feigned indifference falling at the first hurdle, it seemed.

'It's everything you dreamt it would be,' he promised her.

'And you have a buyer?' she asked, her voice now betraying a hint of concern. 'Because after the kouros, the trustees have asked for a review of our acquisitions policy. They're even talking about establishing some sort of unofficial black-list. It's madness. The lunatics are taking over the asylum.'

'I have a buyer,' he reassured her. 'And provided you value the mask at the agreed figure, he will happily donate it to the Getty as we discussed.'

'Of course, of course,' she said, seeming relieved.

'What about Director Bury?' It was Faulks's turn to sound concerned. 'Have you spoken to him?'

'That man is a disgrace,' Verity snorted. 'How he ever came to . . .' She broke off, and took a deep breath, trying to compose herself. 'Well, maybe I shouldn't complain. Better a riding school pony on a lead rope than an unbroken Arab who won't take the bit.'

She drained her glass, the waiter swooping in to refill it before Faulks had time to even reach for the bottle.

'So he said yes?'

'If it's in the condition you say it is and I confirm that it's by Phidias, he'll submit the acquisition papers to the trustees himself. Bury may be incompetent, but he's not stupid. He realises that this could make his own reputation as much as mine. And he knows that if we don't take it, someone else will.'

'My buyer has promised me the money by the end of the week if you green-light it. It could be in California by the end of the month.'

'I just wish we hadn't arranged all these meetings today,' she sighed. 'Four o'clock seems like a long way away.'

'Then I've got some good news for you,' Faulks smiled. 'I bumped into Julian Simmons from the Gallerie Orientale on the way in and he wants to cancel. We should be able to head over there by around three.'

'Two and a half hours.' She checked her watch with a smile. 'I suppose that's not too long to wait after two and a half thousand years.'

SIXTY-EIGHT

Free Port Compound, Geneva
20th March – 12.32 p.m.
'What a shithole,' Archie moaned.

Tom had to agree. Withered carpet, wilting curtains, weathered windows, a stern row of steel-fronted cupboards lining the right-hand wall. There was something irredeemably depressing about the room's utilitarian ugliness that even the unusual table at the centre of the room – a circular slab of glass supported by a massive Corinthian capital – couldn't alleviate. Sighing, he opened one of the cupboards and then stepped back, open-mouthed.

'Look at this.'

The shelves were overflowing with antiquities. Overwhelmed by them. Vases, statues, bronzes, frescoes, mosaics, glassware, faience animals, jewellery . . . packed so tightly that in places the objects seemed to be climbing over each other like horses trying to escape a stable fire. The strange thing was that, while there was nothing here of the casual brutality with which Contarelli had treated the objects in his care, Tom couldn't help but wonder if the sheer number and variety of what had been hoarded here, and what it said about the likely scale and sophistication of the Delian League's operation, wasn't actually far more horrific.

'This one's the same,' Allegra said, her voice brimming with anger.

'Here too,' Archie called, opening the one next to her.

There was a gentle knock at the door. Using D'Arcy's watch again, Tom let Dominique in.

'You escaped?' Archie grinned.

'No thanks to you,' she huffed angrily. 'I don't know what you said to him to convince him to rent us some space, but he's been giving me some very strange looks. Luckily he had to go and do his rounds or I'd still be . . .' She broke off, having just caught sight of the open cupboards. 'I guess we're in the right place.'

'You're just in time,' Tom said. 'We were about to have a look next door.'

They stepped through into the adjacent room, the lights flickering on to reveal another Aladdin's cave of antiquities, although here stored with rather less care – a wooden Egyptian sarcophagus sawn into pieces, straw-packed chests with

Sotheby's and Christie's labels still tied to them with string, vases covered in dirt, cylinder seals from Iraq wrapped in newspaper, bronze statues from India propped up against the wall, Peruvian ceramics . . . In the middle of the room, raised off the floor, a quarter-ton Guatemalan jaguar's head glowered at them through the slats of its wooden crate.

'He's got shit here from all over,' Archie noted, taking care to look where he was treading. 'And fakes too.' He pointed at two identical Cycladic statues of a harp player. 'The original's in Athens.'

But Tom wasn't listening, having seen the large safe at the far end of the room. He tried the handle, more in hope than expectation. It was locked.

'Over here.'

Allegra was standing at the threshold of a third room, much smaller than the others, but no less surprising. For where they had been flooded with antiquities, this was drowning in documentation – Polaroids, invoices, valuation certificates, consign-ment notes, shipping manifests, certificates of authenticity, remittance notes. All carefully filed away by year in archive boxes.

The photographs, in particular, told their own grim story. One set picked at random showed an Attic kylix covered in dirt and in pieces in the boot of a car, then the same object cleaned and partially restored, then fully restored with all the cracks painted and polished, and finally on display in some unnamed museum, Faulks standing next to the display case like a proud father showing off a new-born child.

'Like Lazarus raised from the dead,' Allegra murmured, peering over Tom's shoulder.

'Only this time with the evidence to prove it,' Dominique added. She'd found several long rectangular boxes crammed with five-by-eight-inch index cards. Written on each one in Faulks's looping hand was a meticulous record of a particular sale he'd made – the date of the transaction, the object sold, the price paid, the name of the customer. 'The Getty, the Met, the Gill brothers, the Avner Klein and Deena Carroll collection . . .' she said, flicking through the first few cards. 'This goes back fifteen, twenty years . . .'

'Insurance,' Archie guessed. 'In case anyone tried to screw him.'

'Or pride,' Tom suggested. 'So he could remind himself how clever he was. He just never counted on anyone finding it.'

'Does it matter?' Dominique snapped her fingers impatiently. 'It's quarter to one. That means we've only got just over three hours until Faulks gets back.'

'Just about enough time to get his safe open,' Tom said with a smile.

SIXTY-NINE

20th March – 12.46 p.m.

Five feet tall and three feet across, the safe had a brutish, hulking presence, its dense mass of hardened steel and poured concrete exerting a strange gravitational pull that almost threatened to fold the room in on itself. A five-spoke gold-plated handle jutted out of its belly, the Cyclops eye of a combination lock glowering above it, the whole crowned with an elaborate gilded copperplate script that proudly spelt out its manufacturer's name. Under the flickering lights its smooth flanks pulsed with a dull grey glow, like a meteorite that had just fallen to earth.

With Dom having gone to fetch Tom's equipment, Tom, Allegra and Archie stood in a line in front of it, like art critics at an unveiling.

'How do you know the watches are inside?' Allegra asked.

'I don't. But I don't see where else he would keep them.'

'He certainly wasn't wearing one,' Archie agreed.

'Can you open it?' She was trying to sound positive, but she couldn't quite disguise the sceptical edge to her question.

'It's a Champion Crown,' Tom said, rubbing his chin wearily.

'Is that bad?'

'Two-and-one-eighth-inch thick composite concrete walls with ten-gauge steel on the outside and sixteen-gauge on the inside. A five-inch-thick composite concrete door secured by twenty one-and-a-half-inch active bolts. Internal ball-bearing hinges. Sargent & Greenleaf combination dial with a hundred million potential combinations . . .' Tom sighed. 'It's about as bad as it gets.'

'Don't forget the sodding re-lockers,' Archie added with a mournful sigh.

'Re-lockers?' Allegra looked back to Tom with a frown.

'The easiest way to crack a safe is to drill through the door,' Tom explained. 'That way you can use a borescope, a sort of fibre-optic viewer, to watch the lock wheels spin into position while you turn the dial, or even manually retract the main bolt.'

'Only the manufacturers have got smart,' Archie continued. 'Now they fit a cobalt alloy hardplate around the lock mechanisms and sprinkle it with tungsten carbide chips to shatter the drill bits. Sometimes the bastards even add a layer of steel washers or ball bearings too. Not particularly hard, but they spin round when the drill bit touches them, making them a bugger to cut through.'

'The answer used to be to go in at an angle,' Tom picked up again. 'Drill in above or to the side of the hardplate and get at the lock pack that way. So the high-end safes now have a re-locker mechanism. A plate of tempered glass that shatters if you try to drill through it, releasing a set of randomly located bolts which lock the safe out completely. Some of them are even thermal, so that they trigger if you try and use a torch or plasma cutter.'

'So you can't open it?' Given what she'd just heard, it seemed like a fair, if depressing conclusion.

'Everything can be opened, given the right equipment and enough time,' Archie reassured her. 'You just need to know where to drill.'

'Manufacturers build in a drill point to most types of safes,' Tom explained, running his hand across the safe's metal surface as if trying to divine its location. 'A specific place where locksmiths can more easily drill through the door and, for a safe like this, a hole in the glass plate to get at the lock. They vary by make and model, and if you get it wrong . . .'

'You trigger the re-lockers.' Allegra nodded in understanding.

'Drill-point diagrams are the most closely guarded secret in the locksmithing world,' Archie sighed, before turning to face Tom. 'We'll have to get them off Raj.'

'Who's Raj?' She asked.

'Raj Dhutta. A locksmith we know. One of the best.'

'It's too late for that.' Tom shook his head. 'Even if he could get it to us in time, it would still take hours to drill through the hardplate with the kit I've got.'

'Then your only option is a side entry.' Archie dragged three crates out of the way to give them access to the safe's flanks.

'And then in through the change-key hole,' Tom said.

'You what?' Archie gave a disbelieving, almost nervous laugh.

'It'll take too long to drill back through into the lock pack. It's the only way in the time we've got.'

'What's a change-key hole?' Allegra asked with a frown. Hardplate. Re-locker. Change-key. Part of her wondered if they were deliberately tossing in these terms to confuse her.

Dominique interrupted before Tom could answer, breathing heavily as she hauled Tom's equipment bag behind her.

'Did you get lost?' Tom asked, surprised it had taken her so long.

'I got out at two by mistake,' she panted. 'I was

banging on the door like an idiot until I realised that I was on the wrong floor. They all look the same.'

'And there was me thinking your new boyfriend was showing you his torch,' said Archie, grinning.

'I'll bet it's bigger than yours,' she retorted, screwing her face into an exaggerated smile.

'Stop it you two,' Tom said as he knelt down and unzipped the bag, and then carefully lifted out the magnetic drill rig.

'What about all that?' Allegra asked, nodding towards the paperwork in the third room.

'What about it?' Archie frowned.

'It's evidence. Proof of every deal the Delian League has ever done. We can't just leave it.'

'Why not?'

'Because this isn't just about Santos and Faulks. There's enough in there to bring the whole organisation down and implicate everyone who has ever dealt with them.'

'Have you seen how much of that shit there is?' Archie snorted.

'We could photograph some it,' she suggested. 'We've got three hours. That's more than enough . . .'

'Two hours,' Dominique corrected her.

'What?' Tom's head snapped round. 'You said . . .'

'According to his calendar, Faulks just cancelled his last meeting,' she explained, holding up her phone. 'That means he could be here any time after three.'

'Shit,' Archie swore, then shot Tom a questioning glance. 'Can you do it?'

'No way.' Tom shook his head emphatically, running his fingers distractedly through his hair. 'It's a three-hour job. Two and a half if we're lucky.'

'Then we need to buy you some more time,' Archie said. 'Find a way to keep Faulks away from here until we've finished.'

There was a long, painful silence, Tom glaring at the safe door as if it was somehow to blame for the change in Faulks's schedule, Dominique flexing her fingers where they'd gone stiff from dragging the bag.

'Come on,' Archie snorted eventually. 'Nothing? Anyone?'

'Can you get to the surveillance cameras?' Allegra asked.

'The patch panel's probably next to the server room downstairs,' Dominique said with a nod. 'Why?'

'It's just . . . I might have an idea. Well, it was your idea really.'

'My idea?' Dominique looked surprised, the brusque tone she'd reserved for Allegra up until now softening just a fraction.

'Only it'll never work.'

'Perfect!' Archie grinned. 'The best ideas never do.'

SEVENTY

Free Port, Geneva
20th March – 3.22 p.m.

'What did you think?' Verity asked, fixing her lipstick in the mirror.

'Which one?'

The Bentley tacked into the warehouse car park, the chassis leaning gracefully into the bend.

'Sekhmet. The Egyptian lion goddess.'

'Oh, that one,' Faulks sniffed, looking disinterestedly out of the window.

'Don't go all shy on me.' Verity glanced across, wiping the corner of her mouth where she had smudged it slightly. 'What did you think?'

'I don't like to bad-mouth the competition,' Faulks gave a small shake of his head as the car glided to a halt.

'Liar!' Verity laughed. 'You thought it was a fake, didn't you?'

'Well, didn't you?' He threw his hands up in exasperation. 'And not even a very good one. The base was far too short.'

'Are we here?' Verity glanced up at the warehouse's rusted façade with a dubious expression.

'Don't sound so disappointed,' Faulks laughed. 'Most people don't even know I have this place, let alone get to come inside.'

'In that case I'm honoured.' She smiled.

'Anyway, I'm moving. They're knocking it down. It's a shame, really. I've been here almost since I started. Grown quite attached to it over the years.'

'I never took you for a romantic, Earl,' she teased.

'Oh, I'm an incurable romantic,' he protested. 'Just as long as there are no people involved.'

Logan stepped round and opened her door. But as Verity went to get out, Faulks placed his hand on her arm.

'Can you give me five minutes? I just want to make sure everything's set up.'

'Of course.' She sat back with an indulgent smile although there was no disguising the impatience in her voice. 'There are a few calls I need to make anyway.'

Nodding his thanks, he led Logan inside where they both signed in.

'New tenants, Stefan?' Faulks asked, surprised to see four names above his.

The guard checked that no one else was listening then leaned forward with a grin.

'Just until the end of the month,' he whispered excitedly. 'They're making a porno and wanted somewhere . . . discreet. You should see the two girls they've got! The director said I could go and watch them shoot a couple of scenes later this week.'

Faulks mustered a thin smile.

'How nice for you.'

They rode the lift to the third floor and traced a familiar path round to corridor thirteen, stopping outside Faulk's suite. Unlocking the door, he stepped inside and then stopped.

'That's funny,' he muttered.

'What?' Logan followed him inside, immediately alert.

'The alarm's off. I was sure I'd . . .'

Logan drew his gun and stepped protectively in front of him.

'Wait here.'

Treading carefully, he stepped over to the door to the middle room, eased it open and then peered inside. His gun dropped.

'Boss, you'd better come'n see.'

Faulks stepped past him with a frown, the tip of his umbrella striking the floor every second step, then froze.

It was empty. Gutted. Stripped clean. The crates, the boxes, the vases, the statues, the safe – everything had gone.

He felt suddenly faint, the room spinning around him, his heart pounding, the blood roaring in his ears. Turning on his heels, he limped back into the first room and threw one of the cupboards open with a crash. Empty. The next one was the same. And the one after that, the metal doors now clanging noisily against each other like shutters in a storm as he jumped from one cupboard to the next. They were all empty.

'You've been fuckin' turned over,' Logan growled.

Faulks couldn't speak, could barely breathe, felt sick. He staggered to the table, his legs threatening to give away under him at any minute, the open cupboard doors still swaying around him as if they were waving goodbye.

What about the files?

Somehow he found the strength to limp through to the third room, Logan following behind, his warning to be careful echoing unheard off the bare walls. Faulks stopped on the threshold, supporting himself against the door frame, not needing to go inside to see that this room too had also been stripped bare.

He had the strange sensation of drowning, of the air being squeezed from his lungs, the pressure clawing at his eardrums, pressing his eyes back into his head. And then he was falling, legs tumbling away from underneath him, back sliding down the wall as the floor rose up to grab him, umbrella toppling on to his lap. Gone. Gone. Everything gone.

'Earl?' He heard Verity's voice echoing towards him. 'You said five minutes, so I thought I'd come up. Is everything okay?'

SEVENTY-ONE

Free Port, Geneva
20th April – 3.36 p.m.
'He's gone inside.' Archie let himself back into the room with a relieved smile. 'I've left Dom watching the stairs. How are you getting on?'

'Any minute now,' Tom replied, the air thick with the smell of oil, burnt steel and hot machine parts.

Allegra had been right. Her idea had had no reason to work. And yet, like all good ideas, there had been an elegance and simplicity to it that had at least given it a fighting chance of success.

'Dominique said all the floors look the same,' Allegra had reminded them. 'If she's right, then maybe we could try and trick Faulks into getting off on the second floor.'

'It could work,' Tom had said, immediately

catching on. 'We could rig the lift, swap over the wall signs and door numbers, and then use the forklift to move all his furniture downstairs so that when he goes inside his first thought will be that he's been robbed.'

'I'll reroute the camera feed so the guard can't see us,' Dominique had suggested. 'And we could fix the alarm cover panel to the wall so it at least looks the same.'

'What about the cupboards?' Archie had reminded them. 'We haven't got time to unload them all.'

'Check out some of the other empty offices,' Tom had suggested. 'There's bound to be a couple of spares lying around. As long as they look vaguely similar, he'll be too shocked to notice. And by the time he does, we'll be long gone with whatever's inside.'

Tom's safe-cracking kit was surprisingly simple. A 36-volt Bosch power drill, like you would buy at any normal hardware store. A tungsten-carbide-tipped drill bit shaped for steel cutting. A twenty-millimetre diamond-core drill bit, routinely used in the construction industry. And finally a Fein electro-magnetic drill rig to hold the power drill in place and control the pressure.

The method was relatively straightforward too. First fix the rig on to the side of the safe over the chosen breach point with the magnets. Then clamp the power drill into the rig. Then equip the tungsten carbide drill bit, and lower the drill to bore a centring hole in the steel. Finally swap it for the diamond-core drill bit and punch through.

The tricky part was applying the correct combination of drill speed and pressure at the right time. Puncturing the safe's steel casing, for example, required drilling at about 2000 rpm with only medium to low pressure applied by the rig. Getting through the composite material underneath, however, demanded high pressure and low revs, maybe 300 rpm. Even then Tom had to go easy, the diamonds clogging in the angled mild steel plates that had been embedded in the concrete. With only one power drill, that meant he had to be careful not to blow the motor, and he was forced to stop at regular intervals and allow it to cool.

'How are you getting on with the photos?' Tom called, adding some lubricant.

'I've got a system going –' Allegra poked her head into the room – 'I won't get them all, but I'll get enough.'

'Anything that might tell us where the League are meeting tonight?'

'No, but I'll keep looking.'

At last the drill punched through, the motor racing wildly.

'That's it,' Tom called, fumbling for the off

switch and then heaving the rig out of the way.

'Here –' Archie handed him a small monitor that he taped to the side of the safe and then connected to the borescope. The screen flickered with light, indicating it was working.

'Ready?' Tom looked up with a hopeful smile at Allegra, who had run across to join them. She nodded silently as he blew against the hole to cool the scorched metal and then slipped the cable inside.

'Look,' she gasped almost immediately. The outline of a white face was framed on the small screen like a human skull, the grainy image looking like it was being broadcast up through the depths from a long-lost shipwreck. 'It's the ivory mask. Cavalli must have sent it here before he was killed.'

'They must have been working together,' agreed Tom. 'Cavalli supplying the antiquities and Faulks providing the buyers. That way, they didn't have to split the profits with the Delian League.'

'Faulks doesn't have to split anything with anyone now that Cavalli's dead,' Allegra observed wryly.

'Pretty convenient,' Tom agreed. 'It wouldn't surprise me if . . .' He broke off, a sudden thought occurring to him. Of course. It had been so simple. So easy. And once Faulks had realised how much the mask was worth, so necessary.

'Oi, you two,' Archie interrupted. 'Holmes and bloody Watson. Do you mind if we get a move on?'

Tom winked at Allegra, then nodded. He was right.

Looking back to the screen to get his bearings, he bent the cable towards the left and found the back of the safe door. Then he slowly moved it along until he was roughly behind the combination dial.

'There it is,' Archie said sharply.

'There what is?' Allegra leant closer with a frown.

'The key-change hole,' Archie explained. 'Every combination safe comes with a special key that you insert in that hole when the safe's open to change the code.'

'How big is the hole?'

'Not very,' Tom said, jaw clenched in concentration.

'Not big enough,' Archie muttered under his breath. 'That's the problem.'

They watched the image silently, the camera's proximity making the tiny hole look surprisingly large on the screen, the cable catching on its edge as Tom tried to nudge it inside.

'Shit,' he hissed, the cable slipping past yet again. 'It keeps sliding off.'

'Try from the other side,' Archie suggested.

'I've done that,' Tom snapped, smearing oil across his forehead as he wiped the sweat away.

Dominique came in, out of breath from having run up the stairs.

'How much time have we got?' Tom barked without looking up.

'About as much time as it takes them to look out the window and realise they're only two floors up. How are we doing?'

'Shit,' Tom swore as the camera skated past the hole again.

'That well.' She pulled a face.

'Why don't you try coming in from underneath?' Archie suggested. 'You might catch against the upper lip.'

'I don't see why that will . . .' Tom glanced up at Archie with a sheepish smile. It had worked first time.

The screen now showed a fuzzy image of the lock mechanism – four wheels, each with a notch that had to be aligned so that the locking gate could fall into them.

'Someone's going to have to turn the dial for me,' Tom said, carefully holding the cable in place so that it didn't pop out. Allegra immediately stepped forward and crouched down to next to him.

'Which way?'

'Clockwise. You need to pick up all the wheels first.'

Allegra turned the lock, the picture showing the drive cam turning and then gathering up each of the four wheels one by one until they were all going round.

'Slowly,' Tom said, as he saw the notch on the first wheel at the bottom right of the screen moving upwards.

'Stop!' Archie called as the notch reached the twelve o'clock position. Fifteen. 'Now back the other way.'

Allegra turned the dial back, again slowing as the notch appeared on the second wheel and then stopping when Archie called to her. Seventy-one. Then came sixteen.

'The last number's ten,' Tom guessed.

'How do you know?' Dominique asked with a frown.

'Fifteen seventy-one to sixteen ten,' Tom explained with a smile. 'Caravaggio's dates.'

As Tom pulled the borescope out of the hole, Allegra turned the dial to the final number and then tried the gold-plated wheel in the middle of the door. It turned easily, the handle vibrating with a dull clunk as the bolts slid back. Standing up, she tugged on the door, the airtight seal at first resisting her until, with a swooshing noise, it swept open.

The safe had a red velour interior and four shelves containing an eclectic assortment of items that Faulks had presumably felt deserved the extra security – twenty or so antique dinner plates, a set of red figure vases, notebooks, some files, a few maps. And of course, the ivory mask.

Tom's attention, however, was drawn to a rectangular black velvet box, monogrammed with a by now familiar symbol: the clenched fist and entwined snakes of the Delian League. It opened to reveal a cream silk interior moulded to house six watches. Two of the spaces were occupied.

'Epsilon and zeta,' Allegra said, taking them out and turning them over so that they could see the Greek letters engraved into their backs.

'Which gives us the three we need,' Tom said, sliding D'Arcy's watch into place and then snapping the case shut. 'Let's just see if there's anything in here that tells us where they're meeting tonight.'

'What about this?' Archie asked, carefully sliding out the small packing crate containing the ivory mask, its delicate face cushioned by the straw that poked through its eyes and parted lips in a way that reminded Tom of the Napoleonic death mask he and Archie had discovered the previous year.

'Leave it,' Tom said with a shake of his head, glancing up from the handful of notes and maps he had pulled from the safe and was now leafing through.

'Leave it? Are you joking? This thing's worth a bloody fortune.'

'Not to us, it isn't. Besides, the less we take, the more chance that Faulks won't even realise we've been here.'

SEVENTY-TWO

Free Port, Geneva
20th March – 3.46 p.m.
Faulks's initial shock had given way to a bewildered incredulity. It was impossible. The stock. His best stock. The documentation. The safe. Everything gone. Spirited away. Everything. Thousands of items. Tens of millions of dollars. How had they got in? How had they got away without being seen?

'Earl, I don't understand. What's going on? What is this place?' Verity sounded nervous, like someone who'd witnessed a gangland killing and was now worried about being dragged into testifying.

'Did you tell anyone you were coming here?' Faulks spun round to face her, jabbing his umbrella at her accusingly.

'Of course not,' she insisted hotly. 'How could I? I've never been here before.'

He glared at her, his disbelief having slipped into anger, although not with her in particular. With everyone. With everything. She gave a sharp intake of breath, her eyes widening in understanding.

'Oh my God, Earl, have you been robbed?'

He closed his eyes, took a deep breath, exhaled and then opened them again, part of him almost expecting to find that everything was still there after all and that this had just been a terrible dream. Logan reappeared and jerked his head to indicate that they needed to talk. Alone.

'Give me a minute, Verity,' Faulks said, following Logan back out into the first room and closing the door behind him.

'Well?'

'The guard downstairs hasn'a seen nothing,' Logan said in a low voice. 'Nor had th' one on the night shift when we called him.'

'Not unless they're both in on it together,' Faulks pointed out.

'Aye well, I'd know if he was.' Logan gave him a tight smile.

Looking down, Faulks noticed that the Scotsman's knuckles were grazed and that there was a faint spray of blood on his collar. He felt a little better.

'What about the surveillance footage?'

'Backed up remotely. I've asked for a copy. It'll be here in an hour.'

'Anyone else in the building?'

'Just the people who moved in today.'

Faulks snorted.

'Well, there you go then.'

'There's only four o' them and they signed in at twelve thirty,' Logan pointed out with a firm shake of his head. 'Shiftin' all tha' would have tak'n them days.'

'And he didn't hear the alarm go off?'

'No.'

'Bastards must have disabled it,' Faulks hissed, striding over to the control panel next to the main entrance and smacking it angrily, taking some pleasure in the sharp stab of pain as it spread across his palm. 'What's the point in paying for . . .'

He broke off as the keypad fell away from the wall and crashed on to the floor. Frowning, he bent down to pick it up, then noticed the two pieces of black tape that had been securing it to the wall.

'Jesus,' he swore, tossing the panel to Logan. 'It's a dummy. We're in the wrong goddamned room.'

Turning, he limped back out on to the corridor. Ignoring the lift, he made his way to the fire escape and leaned over the banisters, following the staircase as it snaked its way down to the floor below and then . . . to the ground floor.

With Logan at his shoulder, Faulks climbed the staircase as fast as he could, then stepped out on to the empty corridor and turned towards his offices. Here the nature of the deception became abundantly clear – all the signs and door numbers were missing, having presumably been removed and re-attached on the floor below to confuse him.

He flung the door to his offices open. Apart from the cupboards down the right-hand wall, the room was empty and almost unrecognisable without its furniture, carpet or curtains.

And standing at its centre was a woman.

SEVENTY-THREE

Free Port, Geneva
20th March – 3.50 p.m.

'Where's Archie?' Tom asked as he threw his bag into the boot and slammed it shut.

'With Allegra,' Dominique panted, sliding into the passenger seat next to him.

There was a brief lull as they waited, Tom tapping his fingers nervously on the window sill.

'Did you sweep the safe clean?'

'He won't know we've been in there,' she reassured him. 'Not unless he moves the crates and sees where I've taped over the drill hole in the side.'

'Good.'

'So what now?'

'I'm not sure,' Tom admitted. 'We still don't know where they're meeting.'

'What was that piece of paper you took out of the safe, then?'

'Something else that I thought might come in useful.' He craned his neck for a view of the entrance. 'What's taking them so long?'

'Do you want me to go back inside?'

'Let's just give them another –'

'Look, here he comes!' Dominique pointed with relief as Archie exited the building and jogged over to the car.

'Yeah, but why's he on his own?' Tom frowned, his eyes still fixed on the building's entrance.

Archie threw the door open and climbed in.

'Close one.' He sighed with relief. 'Nearly bumped into Faulks coming up the stairs. I think he's finally twigged.'

'Where's Allegra?' Tom asked in an urgent voice.

'Allegra?' Archie looked around, only now, it seemed, noticing that she was not in the car. 'I thought she was with you?'

'Well, she's not,' Tom shot back.

'When did you last see her?'

'Upstairs. She was helping me pack up my kit. I handed her the . . .'

He paused, a sudden thought occurring to him. Flinging the door open, he raced round to the back of the car and popped the boot.

'What are you looking for?' Archie asked as he rooted through his bag.

'This,' Tom said, holding up the receiver for the location beacon.

He turned it on. A faint pulse of light confirmed

what he had already guessed. The transmitter was about fifty yards directly in front of him.

'She's still inside.'

'What the hell's she doing?' Archie's voice was caught somewhere surprise and admiration.

'Playing the only card we have left.'

SEVENTY-FOUR

Free Port, Geneva
20th March – 3.50 p.m.

'Who the hell are you?' Faulks paused on the threshold, wary of another trick.

'Everything's here,' she reassured him. 'I just wanted to make sure I got your attention.'

'Congratulations. You've got it,' he snarled, motioning at Logan to grab her, while he checked the cupboards and stuck his head into the next room.

Unbelievably, everything did indeed seem to be there, the empty desolation of a few minutes ago quickly replaced by a warm wave of relief. And a cold current of anger.

'Who are you?' he repeated.

'Lieutenant Allegra Damico. An officer with the TPA.'

A pause, Faulks giving a thin smile at her

laboured breathing as Logan tightened his grip on her arm which he had bent behind her back.

'What do you want?'

'I have some information for the Delian League.'

'Who?'

'I think we're a little beyond that,' she said, nodding in the direction of the documentation in the small room.

'Earl, are you in here?'

Faulks's head snapped round at the sound of Verity's approaching voice.

'Damn,' he swore, then turned back to Allegra with an impatient shrug. He didn't have time for this. Not today of all days. Not now. But after the lengths she'd gone to . . . there was no telling what she knew or who she'd told. He had to be sure. The League had to be sure. 'You're right. We're way beyond that.'

Stepping forward, he grabbed the end of his umbrella and swung its handle hard against her temple. Groaning, she went limp in Logan's arms.

'Take her to the back and keep her quiet,' he hissed. 'When we're finished here, load her up with the rest of the shipment.'

Turning on his heel, he walked back out on to the corridor. Verity was marching towards him, her face drawn into a thunderous scowl, hands clenched like an eagle swooping to snatch a rabbit out of long grass.

'Earl, I don't know what you're playing at, but . . .'

'Verity, I can't begin to tell you how sorry I am,' he apologised, arms outstretched, palms upturned, his brain working hard. 'There's been a terrible mistake. Terrible. And it's entirely my fault.'

'The only mistake was me agreeing to come here,' she retorted angrily. 'Abused, accused, abandoned . . .'

'We were on the wrong floor!' He laughed lustily, hoping that it didn't sound too forced. 'Can you believe it? It's old age. It must be. I'm losing it.'

'The wrong floor?' she repeated unsmilingly.

'The landlord needed access to my old offices to begin the demolition planning, so they've moved me up here,' he explained, with what he hoped was a convincingly earnest wide-eyed look. 'I'm so used to going to the second floor after all these years, that I didn't even think about it. I'm so sorry.'

'So everything's here?' She glanced past him with a sceptical frown.

'Absolutely.' He gave an emphatic nod. 'Thank God, because for a terrible moment I thought . . .'

'I know. Me too.' She let out a nervous, hesitant laugh. He forced himself to join in.

'Can you ever forgive me?'

'That depends on what's inside.' She flashed him a smile.

Ushering her in, he led her through to the middle room, Verity murmuring with appreciation at some of the items she could see stacked there.

'Good God, Earl, this is wonderful.'

'Even better, it's all for sale,' he reminded her with a smile as he crouched next to the safe, flicked the dial and heaved it open.

'Is that it?' Verity breathed over his shoulder, pulling on a pair of white cotton gloves.

'That's it.' Sliding the shallow box out, he carefully placed it on top of one of the neighbouring packing crates. Removing his jacket, he lay it over another crate so that its scarlet lining covered it. Then he gingerly removed the mask and set it on top of the lining, the pale ivory leaping off the red material. Finally he stepped back and ushered her forward.

'Please.'

Approaching slowly as if she was afraid of waking it, Verity pulled on a pair of white cotton gloves and carefully picked the mask up. She raised it level with her face, eyes unblinking, the colour flushing her throat and cheeks, her breathing quickening, hands trembling. For a moment, it seemed she might kiss it. But instead, she gave a long sigh of pleasure and lowered it unsteadily back into its straw bed, her shoulders shaking.

'So? What do you think?' Faulks asked, after giving her a few moments to compose herself.

Verity made to speak, but no sound came out,

her lips trembling, tears welling in her eyes. She looked up at him, her hand waving in front of her mouth as if she was trying to summon the words out of herself.

'It's so beautiful,' she breathed eventually. 'It's like . . . it's like gazing into the eyes of God.'

'Attribution?'

'Assuming the dating is right . . .'

'Oh, it's right.'

'Then Phidias. Phidias, Phidias, Phidias!' Her voice built to an ecstatic crescendo. 'We would have heard of any other sculptor from that period of this quality.'

'Then I hope you won't mind confirming that to my buyer?' Faulks pulled out his phone and searched for a number. 'Or the valuation you'll put on it once he donates it to you?'

'Of course,' she enthused, snatching the phone from him as soon as it started ringing. 'What's his name?'

SEVENTY-FIVE

Over Milan, Italy
20th March – 6.27 p.m.

Darkness. The smell of straw. A dog barking.

Coming round, Allegra lifted her head and then sank back with a pained cry. There was something above her preventing her from sitting up. Something smooth and flat and . . . wooden. She moved her hands gingerly across it, sensing first its corners and then the constrictive press of the walls at her side. It was a box. She was lying in a wooden box.

The last thing she remembered was Faulks, wild-eyed, raising his umbrella above her like an executioner's axe and then . . . darkness. Darkness, the smell of straw, a dog barking, something hard and uneven underneath her, her head throbbing where he'd struck her. And in the background a low, incessant drone, a rushing whistle of air, a bass shudder.

A plane. She was on a plane. Lying in a wooden box in the hold of a plane.

She nervously patted her inner thigh, and then sighed with relief. The location transmitter was still there – taped to her skin at the top of her leg where they only would have found it if they had stripped her down.

She'd taken a big risk, she knew. A risk that Tom would never have agreed to. But as soon as it had become clear that there was nothing in either Faulks's papers or the safe that was going to give them even the slightest hint as to where the League was meeting that night, she'd known what she had to do. Grab the transmitter and some tape out of the bag. Hold back amid the confusion of their hurried retreat as Faulks pounded along the corridors towards them. And then try to talk or shock him into delivering her to the League himself. It was that or give up on getting to the painting before Santos could hand it over to the Serbs. It was that, or admit that they couldn't stop him.

'Stop' was a euphemism, she knew, for what the Serbs would do to him if he failed to deliver the Caravaggio. The strange thing was that, after the horrors she'd witnessed and endured over the past few days, she felt remarkably sanguine about his likely fate. Especially when the alternative was that, armed with his diplomatic immunity and the proceeds of the Caravaggio's sale, Santos would escape any more conventional form of justice.

Tom had said that the radius of the transmitter was three miles. No use at thirty thousand feet, but if he'd realised what she was doing when she hadn't come back down, and then followed her signal to the airport, he should have been able to work out where she was heading and take another flight to the same destination where he would hopefully be able to pick up her signal again when she landed. At least, that was had been her rough, ill-conceived plan.

For now, all she had was darkness and the sound of her own breathing. Its dull echo, in fact, that seemed to be getting louder and louder as the box's walls closed in, pressed down on her chest, her lungs fighting for air.

Suddenly she was back in the tomb. The entrance blocked, the earth cold and clammy underneath. She called out, her fists pounding against the sides, her feet drumming against the end, twisting her body so that she could lever her back up against the lid.

There. Above her head. Two small, perfectly round holes in the wood that she hadn't been able to see before. She inched forward on her stomach, pressed her face to them, drinking in the narrow rivulets of air and light with relief, her heart rate slowing.

She looked down, struck by a sensation of being watched.

In the dim light, a pair of lifeless eyes stared back up at her, cold lips parted in a hard smile, nose sliced off.

She was lying on top of a statue. A marble statue. But to Allegra the statue might as well have been a corpse, and the box a coffin, and the rumble of the engines the echo of loose earth being shovelled back into her grave.

SEVENTY-SIX

Cimitero Acattolico, Rome
20th March – 10.22 p.m.

'I've lost her,' Tom barked.

'What do you mean, you've lost her?' Archie grabbed the receiver from him and shook it. 'She was just there.'

'Well, she isn't now,' Tom shot back, his anger betraying his concern.

Until now, Allegra had proved surprisingly easy to track, her signal leading them from the Freeport to the cargo terminal at Geneva airport, where they had observed Faulks's driver overseeing several large crates being loaded on to a plane bound for Rome. It hadn't taken much imagination to deduce that she had been placed inside one of them. They had therefore immediately booked themselves on to an earlier flight to ensure that they would already be in position to pick up the signal again by the time her plane landed.

Watching through his binoculars from the airport perimeter fence, Tom had been able to tell that this was a well-established smuggling route for Faulks, the Customs officers welcoming him off the plane on to a remote part of the airfield with a broad smile as a black briefcase had swapped hands.

The cargo had then been split, some heading for the warm glow of the main terminal, the rest to a dark maintenance hangar into which Faulks had driven, the doors quickly rolling shut behind him. Then for two, maybe three hours nothing. Nothing but the steady pulse of her location transmitter on the small screen cradled in his lap. A pulse that had served as a taunting reminder of the fading beat of Jennifer's heart-rate monitor in the helicopter over the desert. A pulse which they had carefully followed here, only to see it flatline.

Sheltered by regimented lines of mourning cypresses and Mediterranean pines, the Cimitero Acattolico nestled on the slope of the Aventine Hill, in the time-worn shadow of the Pyramid of Caius Cestius and the adjacent Aurelian walls. Even by moonlight, Tom had been able to see that it was populated by an eclectic tangle of stone monuments, graves and family vaults, separated by long grass woven with wild flowers. These elaborate constructions were in stark contrast to the trees' dark symmetry: pale urns, broken columns, ornate scrollwork and devotional statuary bursting in pale flashes through the gaps in their evenly spaced trunks, as if deliberately planted there in an attempt to prove the superiority of human creativity over natural design.

If so, it was increasingly obvious to Tom that this was an argument that nature was winning, decades of neglect having left monuments eroded by pollution and tombs cracked open by weeds and the cruel ebb and flow of the seasons. In one place, a pine tree had shed a branch, the diseased limb collapsing on to a grave and smashing its delicately engraved headstone into pieces. In another, the ground had risen up, snapping the spine of the vault that had dared to surmount it. And now it seemed to have swallowed Allegra's signal too.

'Where was the last reading from?' Dominique asked, ever practical.

'Over there –' Tom immediately broke into a loping run, vaulting the smaller graves and navigating his way around the larger tombs. Then, just as he was about to emerge into one of the wide avenues that cut across the cemetery, he felt Archie's hand grab his shoulder and force him to the ground.

'Get down,' he hissed.

Three men had emerged from the trees ahead of them, their machine guns glinting black in the moonlight, torch beams slicing the darkness. Moving quickly, they glided over to a large family vault, their boots lost in the long grass so that they almost appeared to be floating over the ground. As Tom watched, they ghosted up its steps and vanished inside.

'She must be in there,' Tom guessed, standing up.

The vault was a small rectangular building designed to echo a Roman temple, a few shallow steps leading up to the entrance, a Doric frieze carved under the portico, white Travertine walls decorated with columns that gave the illusion of supporting the tiled roof. The entrance was secured by a handsome bronze door that the elements had varnished a mottled green. A single name had been carved over it: *Merisi*. Tom pointed at it with a smile as they crept towards it.

'What?' Dominique whispered.

'Merisi was Caravaggio's real name.'

They paused, straining to hear a voice or a sound from inside. But nothing came apart from the silent echo of darkness.

With a determined nod at the others, Tom carefully eased the door open with one hand, his gun in the other. This and three other 'clean' weapons had been sourced by Archie from Johnny Li while they had been watching the hangar at Rome airport. The price had been steep – the money he claimed Tom still owed him, plus another ten for his trouble. Archie had only just stopped cursing about it, although Johnny had at least held his half of their earlier bargain and returned Tom's watch.

Inside, a thin carpet of dirt and leaves covered the black-and-white mosaic floor and lay pooled in the room's dark corners. At the far end stood a black marble altar with the name *Merisi* again picked out in bronze letters above a date – 1696. In front of this were two high-backed prayer stools, once painted black and upholstered in a rich velvet, but now peeling and rotted by the cold and the damp. Above the altar, suspended from the wall, was a crucifix, one arm of which had broken off so that it hung at an odd angle.

The room was empty.

'Where the hell have they gone?' Archie exclaimed, rapping the walls to make sure they were solid.

Tom examined the floor with a frown.

'How did they expect to bury anyone in here?'

'What do you mean?' Dominique frowned.

'It's a family vault. There should be a slab or something that can be lifted up.'

'No inscriptions either,' Archie chimed in. 'Not even a full set of dates.'

'And the one that's here doesn't fit,' Dominique pointed out. 'This graveyard wasn't used until the 1730s. No one would have been buried here in 1696.'

'It could be a birth year,' Tom suggested, crouching down in front of the altar. 'Maybe the second date has come away and . . .'

The words caught in his throat. As he'd rubbed

the marble, his fingers had brushed against the final number, causing it to move slightly. He glanced up at the others to check that they had seen this too, then reached forward to turn it, the number spinning clockwise and then clicking into place once it was upside down so that it now read as a nine.

Archie frowned. '1699? That doesn't make no sense either?'

'Not 1699 – 1969,' Tom guessed, turning each of the previous three numbers so that they also clicked into place upside down. 'The year the Caravaggio was stolen.'

There was the dull thud of what sounded like a restraining bolt being drawn back from somewhere in front of them. Then, with the suppressed hiss of a hydraulic ram, the massive altar began to lift up and out, pivoting high above their heads, stopping a few inches below the coffered ceiling.

They jumped back, swapping a surprised look. Ahead of them, a flight of steps disappeared into the ground.

SEVENTY-SEVEN

20th March – 10.37 p.m.
The steps led down to a brick-lined corridor set
on a shallow incline. It was dimly lit, the sodium
lighting suspended from the vaulted ceiling at
irregular intervals forming pallid pools of orange
light that barely penetrated the cloying darkness.
In places the water had forced its way in, the
ceiling flowering with calcite rings that dripped on
to the glistening concrete floor.

Treading carefully, their guns aiming towards
the darkness into which the three armed men
who had preceded them down here had presumably disappeared, they crept down the tunnel.
Tom had the vague sense that they were following
the contour of the Aventine as it rose steeply to
their right, although it was hard to be sure, the
passage tracing a bewildering course as it zig-
zagged violently between the graveyard's scattered

crypts and burial chambers. Eventually, after about two hundred yards, it ended, opening up into a subterranean network of interlinking rooms supported by steel props.

'It's Roman,' Dominique whispered, stooping to look at a small section of the frescoed wall which hadn't crumbled away. 'Probably a private villa. Someone rich, because this looks like it might have been part of a bath complex.' She pointed at a small section of the tessellated floor which had given way, revealing a four-foot cavity underneath, supported by columns of terracotta tiles. 'They used to circulate hot air through the *hypercaust* to heat the floors and walls of the *caldarium*,' she explained.

They tiptoed through into the next room, their path now lit by spotlights strung along a black flex and angled up at the ceiling, the amber glow suffusing the stone walls. Dominique identified this as the *balneum*, a semicircular sunken bath dominating the space.

Picking their way through the thicket of metal supports propping the roof up, they arrived at the main part of the buried villa, the tiled floor giving way to intricate mosaics featuring animals, plants, laurel-crowned gods and a dizzying array of boldly coloured geometric patterns. Here, some restoration work appeared to have been done: the delicate frescoes of robed Roman figures and carefully rendered animals showed signs of having been pieced back together from surviving fragments, the missing sections filled in and then plastered white so that the fissures between the pieces resembled cracks in the varnish on an old painting.

An angry shout echoed towards them through the empty rooms.

'You think Santos is already here?' Dominique whispered.

'Allegra first,' Tom insisted. 'We worry about Santos and the painting when she's safe.'

They tiptoed carefully to the doorway of a small vaulted chamber. The walls here had been painted to mimic blood-red and ochre marble panels, while the ceiling had been covered in geometric shapes filled with delicately rendered birds and mischievous-looking satyrs. And crouching on the floor with their backs to them, checking their weapons and speaking in low, urgent voices, were the three men they'd seen earlier.

Tom locked eyes with Archie and Dominique; both of them nodded back. On a silent count of three, they leapt inside and caught the three men completely cold.

'*Tu*?' one of the men hissed as, one by one, Archie taped their hands behind their backs and then gagged them.

It was Orlando – the priest from the Amalfi. Tom returned his hateful glare unblinkingly.

Strangely, the murderous rage that had enveloped him in Monte Carlo had vanished; he felt almost nothing for him now. Not compared to Santos. Not with Allegra's life at stake.

'I'll watch them,' Dominique reassured him, waving the men back into the corner of the room with her gun.

'You sure?'

'Go.'

With a nod, Tom and Archie continued on, a bright light and the low rumble of voices drawing them across an adjacent chamber decorated with yellow columns, to the next room where they crouched on either side of the doorway.

Edging his head inside, Tom could see that they were on the threshold of the most richly decorated space of all, the floor covered in an elaborate series of interlocking mosaic medallions, each one decorated with a different mythological creature. The frescoes, meanwhile, looked almost entirely intact and mimicked the interior of a theatre, the left-hand wall painted to look like a stage complete with narrow side doors that stood ajar as if opening on to the wings. To either side, comic and tragic masks peered through small windows that revealed a painted garden vista.

'Look,' Archie whispered excitedly. Tom followed his gaze and saw that a large recess, perhaps nine feet high, six across and three deep, had been hacked out of the far wall. And, hanging within this, behind three inches of blast-proof glass, was the Caravaggio. It was unframed, although its lack of adornment seemed only to confirm its raw, natural power.

'That's Faulks,' Archie whispered.

At the centre of the room, over a large mosaic of a serpent-headed Medusa, was a circular table inlaid with small squares of multicoloured marble. The man Archie had pointed out was clutching an umbrella and standing in front of three other men who were seated around the table as if they were interviewing him.

'The guy on the left is De Luca,' Tom breathed, recognising the badger streak running through his hair and the garish slash of a Versace tie. 'And the one in the middle who's speaking now . . .' He broke off, his chest tightening as he realised that this was the face of the man he'd overheard on the yacht in Monaco. The same man who'd ordered Jennifer's death. 'That's Santos.'

'Which must make the other bloke Moretti,' Archie guessed, nodding towards a short man wearing glasses who was seated on the other side of Santos. Completely bald across the top, his scalp gleaming under the lights, he had a bristling wire-wool moustache that matched the hair clinging stubbornly to the back and sides of his head. He was wearing a grey cardigan and brown corduroy trousers, looking more like someone's grandfather than the head of one of the mafia's most powerful families.

Tom nodded but looked past him, distracted by the gagged and bound figure he could see slumped in a chair to Faulks's left. It was Allegra. Still alive, thank God, although there was no telling what they might have done to her. Or what they might still be planning.

'She wants to speak to us,' Faulks protested. 'She said she had a message.'

'Of course she does,' Santos shot back in English, his tone at once angry and mocking. 'She's working on the Ricci and Argento cases.' He glanced across at De Luca. 'I thought you said you'd taken care of her?'

De Luca shrugged, gazing at Allegra with a slightly dazed look.

'I thought I had.'

'She managed to locate and break into my warehouse,' Faulks retorted. 'Who knows what else she's found out.'

'She broke in and, from what you've told us, took nothing apart from your pride,' Santos reminded him. 'You should have taken care of her in Geneva. You have no business here.'

'In case you've forgotten, I have two seats on this council.' Faulks spoke in a cold, deliberate tone. 'I have as much right to be here as anyone. If not more.'

'An accident of history that you delight in reminding us of,' De Luca said dryly.

Santos took a deep breath, attempting what Tom assumed was intended to be a more conciliatory tone.

'This meeting was called by the Moretti and De Luca families –' he nodded at the two men either side of him in turn – 'as representatives of the founding members of the Delian League, to resolve their recent . . . disagreements. Disagreements that, as we all know, have led to two former members of this council not being here with us tonight.'

'We had nothing to do with D'Arcy's death,' Moretti insisted angrily.

'Cavalli was a traitor who deserved what he got,' De Luca retorted, both men standing up and squaring off.

'Enough!' Santos called out. Muttering, they both sat down. Santos turned back to face Faulks. 'They asked me here to help mediate a settlement. I let you know we were meeting as a courtesy. But, as I told you when we spoke, there was no need for you to come.'

Faulks looked at them, then nodded sullenly towards Allegra.

'Then what am I meant to do with her?'

'What you should have done already.'

'I dig bodies up, not bury them,' Faulks said through gritted teeth.

'Then I'll finish what you are too weak to begin,' Santos snapped, taking his gun out from under his jacket and aiming it at Allegra's head.

SEVENTY-EIGHT

20th March – 10.54 p.m.

A shot rang out. Santos fell back with a cry, clutching his arm.

'Sit the fuck down. Don't nobody move,' Archie bellowed.

Tom pushed past him to Allegra, pulling the gag out of her mouth, then slicing her wrists free.

'Are you okay?' he breathed as she fell gratefully into his arms.

She nodded, gave him a weak smile. Turning, Tom scooped Santos's weapon off the floor and quickly searched the others.

'I'm bleeding,' Santos shrieked.

'It's a graze. You'll live,' Tom snapped.

'Pity,' Archie intoned behind him. Looking up, Faulks's eyes widened in shocked recognition, although the others didn't seem to notice his expression.

'You have no idea what you've done,' Santos

hissed though clenched teeth, holding his arm to his chest. 'You're both dead men.' He snatched a glance towards the entrance.

'Who are you?' Moretti demanded.

'He's Tom Kirk,' De Luca said slowly, greeting Tom with a half-smile. 'Also risen from the dead, it seems.'

'Kirk?' Moretti gasped.

'Tom Kirk?' Faulks gave a disbelieving smile, his face turning grey.

Tom frowned, confused. Some people, criminals especially, knew who he was, or at least who he had been. But that didn't usually warrant this sort of reaction.

'What do you want?' Santos demanded.

'The same as you,' Tom said simply. 'The Caravaggio.'

'You're robbing us?' De Luca seemed to find this almost amusing.

'I'm borrowing it,' Tom corrected him.

'You'll never get it out of there,' Faulks scoffed. 'Not without destroying it.'

'Even with these?' Tom asked, holding up the monogrammed case he'd taken from Faulks's safe. The dealer went pale, his eyes bulging. 'Here, you might as well collect them all up,' said Tom, tossing Allegra the box. 'Although it is only the three watches I need, isn't it?'

Moretti and De Luca swapped a dumbfounded look.

'How did you know?' De Luca asked as Allegra loosened his watch and then Moretti's, before finding the sixth in Santos's top pocket. 'Did your . . .'

'Santos has struck a deal to sell your painting,' Tom explained. 'We overheard him negotiating the terms yesterday in Monte Carlo. He let slip about the watches.'

Santos rose from his seat.

'*Stronzata*,' he spat, his face stiff with anger.

'Bullshit. Really?' Tom smiled. 'Dom?' he called out.

A few moments later Dominique appeared, ushering Santos's three sullen-faced men ahead of her. Eyes narrowing, Santos slumped back into his seat as she forced them on to the ground and made them sit with their hands on their heads.

'These men work for Santos. We found them next door. You were the only people standing between him and the fifteen million dollars his Serbian buyers have promised him for the painting.'

'He's lying,' Santos seethed, his eyes fixed on Tom. 'It's a trick. We all know to come to this place alone. I would never break our laws.'

'Can you open it?' Tom called across to Allegra, who was crouching in front of the case.

'There are six plates,' she said, pointing at the brass roundels set into the wall under the painting. 'Each one's engraved with a different Greek letter.'

Opening the box, she took out the first watch and carefully matched it to the corresponding plate, the case sinking into the crafted recess with a click. Then she repeated the exercise with another two watches and stood back, glancing across at Tom with a hopeful shrug. For a moment nothing happened. But then, with a low hum, the thick glass slid three feet to the right, leaving an opening that she could step through.

'I'll give her a hand,' Archie volunteered, handing Tom his gun. He followed her through the gap into the narrow space behind the glass, and then helped her lift the unframed painting down. Carrying it back through with small, shuffling steps, they leaned it gently against the wall.

Tom stepped closer. He recognised the scene. It was exactly as he remembered it from the Polaroid Jennifer had shown him in her car. But there was no comparing that flat, lifeless image to the dramatic energy and dynamism of the original. The angel swooping down from heaven like an avenging harpy, the boy's taunting face creased with a cruel laughter, Mary's exhaustion and exultation, the fear and anticipation of the onlooking saints. Light and darkness. Divine perfection and human fallibility. Life and death. It was all there.

'Let's take it off the stretchers so we can roll it up,' Archie suggested.

'Be careful with it,' Moretti warned him.

Tom fixed him with a questioning look, detecting a proprietary tone.

'Is it yours?'

'Not any more,' he admitted. 'We donated it as a gesture of good faith when the League was founded. The De Luca family contributed this villa.'

'I'll return it,' Tom reassured him. 'You have my word.'

'Then why take it?' De Luca demanded.

Tom paused before answering, not wanting to give Santos the pleasure of hearing him stumble over his words.

'You know the FBI officer I asked you about, the one who was shot in Vegas three nights ago?' De Luca nodded with a puzzled frown. 'A few weeks back she got a tip-off about one of your US-based distributors. An antiquities dealer based in New York. Under questioning, he volunteered Luca Cavalli's name.'

'I knew Luca,' Moretti frowned. 'He was careful. He would never have revealed his name to someone that far down the organisation.'

'He didn't,' Tom agreed. 'Faulks did.'

'What?' Faulks gave a disbelieving laugh.

'Remember that photo of the ivory mask we came across in Cavalli's car?' Allegra glanced up at De Luca from where she was helping free the painting from the wooden stretchers. 'We found it in Faulks's safe. It's worth millions. Tens of millions.'

'My guess is that Cavalli had been secretly bringing you pieces for years,' Tom said, turning to stand in front of Faulks, whom he noticed had slid his chair a little way back from the others. 'Pieces his men had dug up and that he had deliberately not declared to the League, so that you could sell them on and share the profits between you. But then one day he unearthed something really valuable, didn't he? Something unique. And you just couldn't help yourself. You got greedy.'

'Cavalli sent me the mask, it's true,' Faulks blustered, looking anxiously at De Luca and Moretti. 'A wonderful piece. But my intention was to split the proceeds with the League in the usual way after the sale. And not just the mask. I have the map showing the location of the site where he found it. Who knows what else might be down there?'

'Can you prove any of this?' De Luca challenged Allegra, fixing her with an unblinking, stony-faced stare.

'Who told you that Cavalli had betrayed you?' Tom shot back.

De Luca paused, then pointed a wavering finger towards Faulks. 'He did.'

'I had no choice,' Faulks protested. 'It's true that Cavalli wanted me to deal with him direct. But when I refused he threatened to go public with everything he knew. What I told you was the truth. He was planning to betray you. He was planning to sell us all out. You know yourself that your informants backed me up.'

'The FBI had Cavalli's name,' De Luca acknowledged, turning his gaze back to Tom. 'They wanted the authorities here to arrest him.'

'Cavalli was ripping you off, but I doubt he was going to go public with anything,' Tom said with a shrug, thinking back to the moment in front of Faulks's open safe when this had all clicked into place. 'The simple truth is that Faulks wanted him out of the way so he could have the mask for himself. So he came up with a plan. First feed Cavalli's name to the New York dealer. Then sell the dealer out to the FBI to make sure he would talk. Finally accuse Cavalli of betraying you, knowing your police informants would confirm that the FBI was investigating him and that you would think he was collaborating.'

'This is crazy,' Faulks spluttered. 'I've never . . .'

'The clever thing was the way he set both sides of the League against each other,' Allegra mused, rising to her feet. 'He knew that Don Moretti would retaliate once you'd killed Cavalli, leaving him free to sell it for himself, while you were busy fighting each other.'

'That was never my intention,' Faulks pleaded angrily. 'Cavalli was a threat. I was simply acting in the best interests of the League. As I have always done.'

'Of course, while all this was going on, Santos was busy taking out a contract on my friend,' Tom continued, turning to face him. 'My guess is . . .'

'How much more of this do we have to listen to?' Santos interrupted, his palms raised disbelievingly to the ceiling. 'I've never –'

'*Basta*,' De Luca cut him off angrily. 'You'll have your chance.'

Santos sat back with a scowl, muttering to himself.

'My guess is that, when she searched the dealer's warehouse, she found something implicating the Banco Rosalia and started kicking the tyres,' Tom continued. 'When Santos realised that she was on to him, he had her taken out, using the prospect of recovering your Caravaggio to lure her to Las Vegas where he had a gunman waiting.'

'She was a threat to us all,' Santos blurted out defiantly.

'You mean this is true? You killed an FBI agent without our permission?' De Luca jumped to his feet, violence in his voice now.

'I did what I had to do to protect the League,' Santos protested. 'I'd do the same again.'

'At first we thought everything was connected,' Allegra admitted. 'It was only later that we realised that the Rome murders and the ivory mask had nothing to do with Jennifer's assassination, or with D'Arcy, who was killed for his watch.'

'The irony is that it was Faulks's tip-off about the dealer in New York that unknowingly led to the FBI looking into the Banco Rosalia in the first place,' Tom said with a rueful smile. 'Without that,

Jennifer would probably still be alive, and Santos wouldn't be preparing to explain to his Serbian friends why he hasn't been able to deliver the painting.'

'No, Kirk,' Santos said with a cruel smile. 'The biggest irony is that –'

A single gunshot cut him off. Tom's head snapped towards the doorway. A uniformed policeman in a bullet-proof vest was standing there, gun pointed towards the roof, five, maybe eight armed police filtering into the room either side of him, machine guns braced against their shoulders.

Tom snatched a look at Allegra. Ashen faced, she mouthed one word.

Gallo.

SEVENTY-NINE

20th March – 11.13 p.m.

'Colonel Gallo, thank God you're here!' Santos rose gratefully from his seat and stepped towards him, switching back to Italian.

'Sit down,' Gallo ordered him back.

'I've been kidnapped. Held against my will. Shot!' He held out his bloodied arm, his voice rising hysterically.

'Sit down, Santos, or I'll shoot you again myself,' Gallo warned him in an icy tone.

'This is an outrage,' Santos insisted. 'In case it's slipped your mind, Gallo, I have diplomatic immunity. You have no legal right to detain me here. I demand to be released immediately.'

'No one is going anywhere,' Gallo fired back. 'Get their weapons.' Two of his men shouldered their machine guns and quickly patted everyone down, tossing whatever they found into the far corner of the room. Santos sank into his chair. Gallo turned to Allegra. 'Lieutenant Damico, are you hurt?'

'N-n-no,' Allegra stammered, bewildered. This was the man she'd been running from; the man she'd seen execute Gambetta and then pin the crime on her; the man who had supposedly supplied Santos with Cavalli's watch. And yet, this same man was now holding Santos at gunpoint and asking if she was okay.

'Good.' Gallo twitched a smile. 'Then maybe you can tell me what the hell is going on down here?'

Again she looked for signs of the person who had been haunting her thoughts for the past few days. But it was almost as if she'd imagined the whole thing.

'There's a secret organisation called the Delian League,' she began haltingly. 'An alliance between the different mafia families to co-ordinate their antiquities smuggling operations and split the profits. Don De Luca and Don Moretti head it up. This man –' she pointed at Faulks – 'was responsible for selling whatever was smuggled out of the country to dealers and collectors around the world. Santos provided the financial backing and laundered the profits for them through the Banco Rosalia.'

'And this?' Gallo kicked the rolled up painting.

'The missing Caravaggio *Nativity*.'

'You're joking!' Placing his gun down next to him, Gallo knelt and unrolled the first few feet of the canvas before glancing up, shaking his head in wonder. 'My God, you're not.'

Without warning, Santos flew forward off his chair, snatched Gallo's gun up and before anyone had time to move, aimed it at his forehead.

'Back off,' he snarled as the armed police belatedly aimed their weapons at him. 'Put your guns on the floor or I'll kill him right here.'

The police ignored him, a few even taking a step closer. Santos immediately took shelter behind Gallo, pressing the gun to his temple.

'You know I'll do it,' he hissed, his lips hovering over Gallo's ear. 'Tell them to back the fuck off.' From the wild look in his eyes, Allegra could tell that he meant it.

'Stand down,' Gallo ordered in a strangled voice, clearly sensing this too. 'Stand down, that's an order.'

One by one, the officers lowered their guns, placing them at their feet, and then backed away. Santos's three men immediately re-armed themselves, Orlando leaping to Santos's side, the other two covering off the rest of the room.

'Now get them out of here.'

Gallo said nothing.

'Now!' Santos roared, striking him on the back of his head with the heel of his gun.

'Fall back the way you came in,' Gallo ordered

grudgingly, clutching his skull. 'Tell them what's happening.'

'Yes, tell them everything,' Santos called after them. 'And tell them that if anyone else comes down here, I'll kill everyone in this room, starting with the colonel.'

There was a pause as Santos waited for the room to empty, a few of the retreating officers glancing nervously behind them in anticipation of perhaps being shot from behind. But the attack never came, and the sound of their leaden footsteps soon faded away. Allegra glanced at Tom, who gave her a grim smile. They were on their own.

'Get the painting,' Santos barked. 'Time to go.'

With Orlando standing guard, the two other men heaved the rolled-up canvas on to their shoulders and staggered towards the entrance. Still holding Gallo's neck in the crook of his arm, the gun pressed to his head, Santos backed across the room.

'I'll be seeing you soon, Antonio,' Moretti called after him. 'Sooner than you think.'.

Santos paused, then shoved Gallo into Orlando's arms and grabbed two grenades from the bag looped around Orlando's neck.

'I doubt it,' he said, smiling as he pulled the pins out and lobbed one, then the other, into the middle of the room.

EIGHTY

20th March – 11.16 p.m.

The first grenade landed at Tom's feet. Without thinking, he snatched it up, and with a deft snap of his wrist, flicked it through the gap in the glass-fronted display case where the painting had been hanging. Hitting the wall, it bounced a short way along the bottom and then exploded.

The room jumped around them, smoke and dust avalanching through the opening, bits of plaster peeling off the walls like the bark on a cork tree, a terrible, angry roar lifting them off their feet and knocking the wind out of them. But, as some primitive, instinctive part of Tom's brain had no doubt intended, the two-inch-thick armoured glass absorbed the brunt of the blast, its surface cracking but holding firm.

There was to be no such reprieve from the second grenade, however. Having struck the marble table it bounced into Moretti's lap. He looked up, his eyes beseeching, mouth gaping as De Luca dived out of the way. Then it went off, cutting Moretti in half and sending a meteor shower of shrapnel across the room.

Tom looked up from where he had thrown himself to the floor, barely able to see through the thick smoke that seemed to have blown in like a sea fog. Ears ringing, he staggered to his feet and made his way unsteadily towards where he had last seen Allegra and the others, tripping over De Luca, who had lost a shoe and whose arm was hanging limply at his side, blood leaking from a deep gash to his head. The two halves of Moretti's body were lying next to him, although the way they had landed made it look as if his legs were growing out of his head. It was a gruesome sight.

Coughing, he knelt by Allegra's side. She seemed okay if a little disorientated, Moretti having clearly absorbed the worst of the explosion. But both Archie and Dominique were injured – Archie clutching the side of his face, the blood soaking through his fingers, while a shard of hot metal had embedded itself in Dominique's thigh.

'Are you okay?' Tom called, knowing that he was shouting but still barely able to hear himself.

'We'll be fine,' Archie said through gritted teeth. 'Just go and shoot the bastard.'

With a nod, Tom jumped across to the pile of guns discarded by Gallo's men, grabbing one for himself and tossing another to Allegra, who was now back on her feet.

'Let's go,' she said, her eyes filled with the same diamond-tipped determination he'd seen when she'd engineered their escape from the car park.

They sprinted back through the various decorated rooms towards the bath complex and the vaulted tunnel that led outside.

'Wait!' Allegra called as he turned towards the entrance. 'Can you feel that?'

He paused, and then realised what she meant. A fresh breeze was tickling his cheek, the air sweet and rich compared to the otherwise brackish atmosphere. Santos must have found another way out.

Turning to her right, she led him down a narrow tunnel that rose in total darkness up a steep incline. Feeling his way along the brick walls, Tom followed closely behind, the breeze getting stronger, until they found themselves in a square chamber. Above them, an iron ladder climbed towards a patch of star-flecked sky. At the foot of the ladder, a body was lying on a bed of rubble. It was Gallo.

'He's alive,' Allegra said, kneeling next to him and pressing her fingers against his neck. Tom wasn't sure if she sounded relieved or disappointed. 'Santos must have thrown him back down the hole.' She pointed at the colonel's arm, which was bent up at an unnatural angle where he had dislocated his shoulder in the fall.

Tom flew up the ladder, emerging under the disapproving glare of an angel that had escaped damage when Santos had smashed through the gravestone she had been guarding. Hauling himself clear, he reached down to help Allegra climb out, the flickering blue lights on the other side of the cemetery indicating where Gallo's man had congregated around the entrance to the Merisi tomb.

'Which way?'

Allegra's question was almost immediately answered by the sound of an engine being started. They ran to the cemetery wall, Allegra giving Tom a leg up, Tom then reaching down and hauling her up behind him. As he jumped down on to the pavement, an ambulance surged out of the darkness, headlights blazing, Santos hunched over the wheel.

Stepping into the road and taking careful aim, Tom unloaded a full clip into the ambulance's onrushing windscreen. Allegra, still perched on the wall, did the same. But they both missed, forcing Tom to leap out of the way at the last minute as the ambulance veered past, followed the road round and then disappeared into the night.

'*Merda*,' Allegra swore.

'I had him,' Tom panted as he clambered back up alongside her. 'I was aiming right at him.'

'Well, you missed. We both did.'

'That's impossible.' Tom shook his head, popping

out the magazine and checking it. 'He was coming straight towards me. He could only have been thirty feet away. Less.'

A sudden thought came to him. An impossible thought. And yet . . . it was the only explanation. Ignoring Allegra's calls, he jumped down and raced back to the stern angel guarding the shattered gravestone. Peering through the opening to check that no one was coming up behind him, he lowered himself inside and then slid down the ladder.

'Don't move!'

Hearing the voice, Tom turned and saw that Gallo was conscious now, propped up against the wall and being attended by a medic. Four armed policemen were eyeing Tom suspiciously, their machine guns raised.

'It's okay,' Gallo rasped. 'He's with us. Her too.'

Tom looked up and saw that Allegra was climbing down towards them. The policemen relaxed, allowing their weapons to swing down across their stomachs.

'What the hell is going on?' Tom demanded angrily.

'What do you mean?' said Gallo, wincing as the medic prodded his shoulder.

'I mean this –' Stepping forward, Tom smashed his forearm into the bridge of a policeman's nose and wrenched the machine gun from the man's grasp as he staggered back, howling in pain.

'Tom, what are you doing?' Allegra gasped as he swung the weapon towards Gallo and flicked the safety off.

'Ask him,' he replied tonelessly, before pulling the trigger.

The gun jerked in his hand, the muzzle flash lighting the narrow tunnel like a strobe light, hot shell casings pinging off the walls, the noise crashing around them with a deafening echo that seemed to feed off itself and last long after the final shot had been fired.

Gallo returned Tom's accusing glare through the smoke. Unharmed.

'Blanks?' Allegra's face turned from horror to understanding, to confusion as she looked from Tom to Gallo.

Pushing the medic roughly out of the way, Gallo heaved himself to his feet.

'We need to talk,' he growled.

'*You* need to talk,' Tom corrected him.

'Fine, but not here.'

EIGHTY-ONE

Ponte Sant' Angelo, Rome
20th March – 11.55 p.m.
With his men forming a cordon at either end of
the bridge, Gallo led them out to the middle, then
turned to face them, his arm strapped across his
chest where the medic had popped his shoulder
back into its socket.

'This will do.'

'Where have you taken Archie and Dom?' Tom
asked angrily.

'To hospital,' Gallo reassured him. 'My men will
take you to them when we've finished.'

'The same men who attempted a rescue armed
with blanks?' Allegra snorted. She didn't believe
a word he said any more.

He gave a heavy sigh.

'It's complicated.'

'Is that your idea of an apology?' she shot back.

'There are forces at work here. Powerful forces.'

'What the hell are you talking about?' Tom's tone was caught between irritation and impatience. 'I want an explanation, not a palm reading.'

Gallo paused, turning to face down the river so that his back was to them.

'Santos is connected. Very well connected,' he began. 'It seems that, over the years, the Banco Rosalia has done a lot of favours for a lot of people.'

'What sort of people?' Allegra pressed.

'People he helped to evade tax and launder money. People who had relied on him to help fund their political campaigns. People who had profited from the sale of tens of millions of dollars in looted antiquities. *Important* people. People who couldn't risk Santos going down and taking them with him.'

'So these . . . people – they're why you helped him get away?' Allegra's voice was heavy with an air of resigned disgust. 'They're why you watched him try to kill us.'

'He wanted it to look as though he'd had to shoot his way out,' said Gallo. 'I didn't know he was going to throw . . . that was . . . wrong.'

'*Wrong?*' Tom repeated with a hollow laugh.

'How long has he had you on a leash?' Allegra asked. 'Since Cavalli was killed? Before?'

'I didn't even know who Cavalli was until I was put on to the Ricci case,' Gallo turned to face them again, pressing his back against the parapet. 'I don't think Santos did either. But when Argento was killed, Santos grew worried that I might somehow connect the murders back to him or the Delian League. So he made some calls.'

'Who to?' Tom asked.

'I've already told you' – Gallo shrugged – 'People. All I know is that, when my orders came, they came from the top. The very top. Protect Santos. Keep a lid on things. Stop the case spiralling out of control.'

'What about Gambetta?' Allegra said sharply. 'Did they tell you to kill him too?'

'I did what I had to do,' Gallo said defiantly. 'Santos had offered us a deal. Cavalli's watch in return for keeping a lid on everything he knew and a promise to leave the country by the end of the week. Gambetta was an old fool who was never going to keep quiet about evidence going missing or how clever he'd been in linking all the murders together. He was a necessary sacrifice.' A pause. 'He's not the first person to have died for his country.'

'A necessary sacrifice?' Allegra shook her head in disgust, a fist of anger clenching her stomach. 'This has nothing to do with patriotism. This is about rich, powerful people doing whatever it takes to protect themselves. This is about murder. You killed Gambetta for doing his job.'

'You don't understand,' Gallo shot back. 'I had my orders. The things Santos knows . . . this was a matter of national security. He was to be protected at all costs. I had no choice.'

'You had a choice,' Allegra insisted. 'You just chose not to make it. You killed a man and framed me for it.'

'I was trying to protect you.'

'From what?'

'Santos found out you were asking questions about the Delian League. He wanted you dealt with. Why else do you think De Luca picked you up? I thought that if I blamed you for the killing and got your face in the papers, I might find you before he did. I was never planning to . . . Look, maybe it was wrong of me. But you'll get a full retraction, an apology, your choice of assignments —'

'You disgust me. You and whoever it is that can decide that an old man should die to stop someone like Santos being caught.'

'I love my country,' Gallo insisted. 'I did what I had to do to protect it, and I'd do the same again. Anyway, I tried to put things right.'

'How? With that little show you and Santos put on tonight?'

'By saving you.'

'What are you talking about?' Tom challenged him. 'Saving us from what?'

'Who do you think dug you out of that tomb?'

'That was you?' Allegra swapped a glance with Tom, almost not wanting to believe him. Anything to avoid feeling that she might in some way owe him something.

'How did you find us?'

'I had a back-up team watching Eco. They picked you up coming out of the gallery and followed you to where De Luca snatched you up and then out to Contarelli's farmhouse. I sent my men in as soon as I could. Luckily, they weren't too late.'

'Luckily,' Allegra repeated in a sarcastic tone, the thought of the plastic bag slick and tight against her lips still making her stomach turn.

'So it was you that fed us the information about D'Arcy?'

'I knew that he worked for De Luca,' Gallo nodded. 'So when I heard about the fire and that he'd gone missing, I realised it was probably connected. The problem was that I didn't have the jurisdiction to investigate. Luckily for me, I'd seen enough of Allegra to know that, if I gave her the option, she'd follow up the lead herself rather than walk away.'

There was a long silence, Gallo glancing at each of them in turn with a look that threatened to veer into an apology, although Allegra knew that he'd never allow himself to actually say anything.

'So what happens to Santos now?' she asked eventually.

'He sells the painting and leaves the country. As long as he never comes back, we forget about him and move on. Let him become someone else's problem.'

'And the Banco Rosalia?'

Gallo laughed.

'The Banco Rosalia is bankrupt. That's why he had to make a move for the painting. It was his last chance to get out with something before the news broke. Not that it ever will. The government and the Vatican have already agreed to jointly underwrite the losses and quietly wind the business down to avoid any bad press. No one will ever know a thing.'

Allegra shook her head angrily, her jaw clenching and throat tightening. The hypocrisy and injustice of a world where a murderer like Santos was allowed to go free to protect a cabal of corrupt politicians and God-knows who else, while Gambetta was . . . it made her feel dirty.

'What about De Luca and Faulks? Aren't you going to charge them?' Tom asked hopefully.

'What with?' Gallo shrugged. 'We know what Faulks does, but we've never had any proof that he's broken an Italian law on Italian soil. And as for De Luca . . .'

'Colonel!' He was interrupted by an officer signalling urgently from the end of the bridge. 'We've found them.'

EIGHTY-TWO

Via Appia Antica, Rome
21 March – 12.29 a.m.

Sirens blaring, they swept through the city, outriders clearing their path, people pointing and staring. Twenty minutes later they reached the Via Appia Antica where curious faces were replaced by the sombre countenance of the Roman funerary monuments that, like foxes pinned down by their headlights, momentarily reared out of the darkness, only to slink away as soon as they had raced past.

'A local patrol unit ran their plates as they came past,' Gallo explained over the noise of the engine as soon as he had finished his call. 'They came up registered to a vehicle stolen last week in Milan. When they tried to stop them, the driver lost control and rolled it into a tree.'

Peering through the seats in front of her, Allegra could see a faint glow on the horizon, a red hue with a blue-edged tint. She looked across to Tom, who gave her an encouraging smile and then reached for her hand. She understood what he was trying to tell her. That this was nearly all over. That they'd almost won.

There were two fire crews on the scene but they were holding back, their flaccid hoses lying uncoiled at their feet.

'The fuel tank could go at any moment and there's no danger of it spreading,' one of the crew explained to Gallo. 'We're just going to let it die down a bit.'

Allegra led Tom to the edge of the semi-circle of policemen and passers-by that had formed around the burning ambulance like kids at a bonfire, the heat from the flames searing her cheeks. Deep ruts in the verge showed where the vehicle had careered off the road and into a ditch, a partially uprooted tree explaining why it hadn't continued on into the field that lay on the other side of the hedge. One of the wheels was on fire and still slowly turning.

Abruptly, the fuel tank exploded, the ambulance jerking spasmodically, the noise of breaking glass and the tortured shriek of expanding metal coming from somewhere inside it. Sparks flitted though the air around them like fireflies.

Allegra glanced at Tom and followed his impassive gaze to the body that must have been thrown clear before the fire had broken out. It was the priest, Orlando. From the way he was lying it didn't look like he would be getting up again. She turned back to the ambulance, straining to see through the swirling flames and smoke, and caught the charred outline of a body in the driver's seat, head slumped forward, hands still gripping the wheel.

'Santos?' she asked Tom.

Tom shrugged and then turned away.

'If you want it to be.'

EIGHTY-THREE

The Getty Villa, Malibu, California
1st May – 11.58 a.m.
One thing was certain – they had all been asked here to witness something special. The clue, as always, had been in the expense lavished on the engraved invitations, the quality of the champagne served at the welcoming reception and the bulging gift bags positioned next to the exit.

When it came to what was going to be announced, however, opinions were more divided. Opinions that, as the minutes passed, grew ever more outlandish and unlikely, until some were confidently predicting that the entire collection of the British Museum was even now being loaded into containers to be shipped to California, and others that it was the Getty itself that was relocating to Beijing. As guesswork was layered on to conjecture, so the noise grew, until what had started as a gentle breeze of curious voices had grown into a deafening storm over which people were struggling to make themselves heard.

Then, without warning, the lights dimmed and three people stepped out on to the stage, one of them wearing sunglasses. The noise dropped as abruptly as if they had passed into the eye of a hurricane, leaving an eerie, pregnant silence.

The shortest person, a man, approached the lectern and gripped its sides, seemingly comforted by its varnished solidity. A large screen behind him showed a close-up of his face – pink, fleshy and sweating.

'Ladies and gentlemen,' Director Bury began nervously, licking the corners of his mouth. 'Ladies and gentlemen, it is my pleasure to welcome you here today. As many of you know, our founder had a simple vision. It was that art has a civilising influence in society, and should therefore be made available to the public for their education and enjoyment.' He paused, his voice growing in confidence as a polite round of applause rippled through the crowd. 'It is a vision that continues to inspire us today as we seek to collect, preserve, exhibit and interpret art of the highest quality. More importantly, it is a vision that continues to inspire others into the most extraordinary acts of generosity. Acts of generosity that have led us today to what I believe is the single most important acquisition in the museum's history. Dr Bruce, please.'

He retreated a few steps, glistening and exultant, and led the clapping as Verity stepped forward. Saying nothing, she waited for the applause to die down, and then nodded. The stage was immediately plunged into darkness. For a few moments nothing happened, people craning their necks to see over or between the rows in front of them, hardly daring to breathe. Then a single spotlight came on, illuminating the jagged outline of a carved face. An ivory face. Behind them the screen was filled with its ghostly, sightless eyes.

Still Verity said nothing, the silence of anticipation giving way to an excited murmur, a few people standing up to get a closer look, one man at the front clapping spontaneously, others turning to each other and muttering words of confusion or shocked understanding. Little by little the noise grew, until the room was once again gripped by a violent, incoherent storm that was only partially muted by the sound of Verity's voice and a second spotlight revealing her face.

'Thanks to the incredible generosity of Myron Kezman, a man of singular vision and exquisite taste whose philanthropy shines through these dark economic times,' she called over the clamour, waving at a beaming Kezman to step forward, 'the Getty is proud to announce the acquisition of the Phidias Apollo, the only surviving work of possibly the greatest sculptor of the classical age.' She paused as the applause came again, unrestrained and exultant. 'As you can see, it is a uniquely well-preserved fragment of a chryselephantine sculpture of the Greek god Apollo. Dated to around 450 BC, it shows –'

'Verity Bruce?' A man in the front row had interrupted her. Standing up, he moved to the stage.

'If you don't mind, sir, I'll take questions at the end,' she said through a forced smile, eyeing him contemptuously.

'My name is Special Agent Carlos Ortiz, FBI,' the man announced, holding out his badge. 'And if you and Mr Kezman don't mind, you'll be taking my questions downtown.'

The audience turned in their seats as the doors at the back of the auditorium flew open. Four dark-suited men entered the room and fanned out.

'What is this?' she called out over the crowd's low, confused muttering, her expression caught somewhere between incredulity and indignation.

'I have a warrant for your arrest, along with Mr Myron Kezman and Earl Faulks,' Ortiz announced, the sight of the piece of paper in his hand raising the audience's muttering to a curious rumble. Kezman said nothing, his indulgent smile having faded behind the blank mask of his sunglasses as two further agents had taken up positions either side of the stage.

'On what charges?' Director Bury challenged him, advancing to Verity's side.

'Federal tax fraud, conspiracy to traffic in illegal antiquities and illegal possession of antiquities,' Ortiz fired back. 'But we're just getting started.'

'This is outrageous,' Verity erupted, shielding her face from the machine-gun flash of press cameras. 'I have done nothing –'

She was interrupted by a commotion at the back of the room as a man tried to make a run for the exit, only to be brought down heavily by the outstretched leg of another member of the audience.

'It seems Mr Faulks is not as confident in his innocence as you appear to be in yours,' Ortiz observed wryly as two of his men pounced on Faulks's prone figure and hauled him to his feet. 'Cuff them.'

Verity and Kezman's shouted protests were drowned out by the hyena howl of the crowd as they leapt from their seats and surged forward to feast.

Amidst the commotion, a man and a woman slipped out, unobserved.

EIGHTY-FOUR

1st May – 12.09 p.m.

'How's your foot?' Allegra laughed as they made their way out into the Outer Peristyle's shaded cloister. A light salt breeze was blowing in from the Pacific and tugging at her hair, which was now its original colour once again.

'He was meant to trip over it, not step on it,' Tom grinned, pretending to limp over the marble floor.

'Do you think they'll let him cut a deal?'

'Unlikely, given what you copied in his warehouse and the tape.'

'What tape?' Allegra asked with a frown.

'Dominique recorded the three of them discussing the mechanics of the whole deal on the phone she and Archie cloned.'

They stepped between two of the fluted columns and made their way down a shallow ramp into a large rectangular courtyard. Running almost its entire length was a shallow reflection pool, its rectangular white stone basin curving at both ends like a Venetian mirror.

'What do you think they'll do with the mask?' Allegra asked as they navigated their way along a labyrinthine arrangement of box hedge-lined gravel paths to the pool's edge.

'Ortiz told me that the Italian government has drawn up a catalogue of forty artefacts acquired by or donated to the Getty over the past twenty years that they want returned. The mask is at the top of the list.'

'That's a start,' she said, sitting down next to him.

'The Greek and Turkish governments are talking about doing the same. And that's just the Getty. There are other museums, galleries, private collections . . . the fall-out from this will take years to clear.'

'But nothing will change,' she sighed. 'When the Delian League finally falls, others will just see it as an opportunity to step in and fill the vacuum.'

'You can't stop the supply,' Tom nodded. 'Contarelli was right about that. The tomb robbers are fighting a guerrilla campaign and the police are still lining up in squares and using muskets. But if the publicity makes museums, collectors and auction houses clean up their act, it might choke the demand. And with less buyers, there'll be less money and less incentive to dig. In time, things might just change.'

There was a silence, Allegra playing with the water and letting it slide through her fingers like mercury.

'They buried Aurelio yesterday,' she said, without looking up.

'I didn't know that . . .?'

'Some kids found his body washed up on the Isola Tiberina.'

'Murdered?'

'They don't think so.'

Tom placed his hand on her shoulder. She glanced up and then quickly looked down again, her eyes glistening.

'I'm sorry.'

'I think he was too.' She shook the water from her fingers and then wiped them on her skirt.

'What's happened to Gallo?'

'Promoted, I expect.' She gave a hollow laugh. 'To be honest, I don't care. Him, the people he was protecting . . . they all disgust me.'

'But he kept his part of the deal?' Tom checked.

She nodded. 'All charges dropped. A formal apology. My pick of assignments. He even had my parking tickets cancelled.'

'So you'll stay?'

'I'll think about it,' she said. 'Not everyone's like him. Besides, I want to see Contarelli's face when I raid his place.' Tom grinned. 'What about you?'

'Me?' He gave a deep sigh. 'Archie's meeting me in New York for Jennifer's funeral. The FBI only released her body last week, After that . . . Who knows? I never like to plan too far ahead. Which way's the sea?'

They stood up and walked through to the other side of the colonnade, following some steps down to a path.

'By the way, did you hear about the Caravaggio?' Allegra asked as they headed up a slope to their right.

'Destroyed?' A hint of surprise in Tom's voice. She shook her head.

'There wasn't any trace of it in the ambulance.'

'And Santos?'

'The DNA from the body at the wheel matched the sample the Vatican provided for him,' she said with a shrug. 'So that's case closed, I guess.'

'Except you think he's still alive,' Tom guessed.

'I think if he's got any sense, he'll stay dead,' she said, the muscles in her jaw flexing with anger. 'Moretti's people are looking for him and the word is that De Luca's put a five-million-dollar ticket on his head.'

They reached a large lawned area and walked to its far wall where there was a view out over the treetops to the sea, white caps rolling in neat parallel lines towards the beach.

'There's one thing I still can't figure out,' Allegra said, hitching herself on to it to face Tom, who was shielding his eyes from the sun. 'Why did Faulks have two watches?'

'What do you mean?'

'De Luca, D'Arcy, Moretti and Cavalli only had one watch each. Why did Faulks have two in his safe?'

'He said he had two seats on the council,' Tom reminded her. 'Presumably to act as a counter-weight between D'Arcy and De Luca on one hand and Cavalli and Moretti on the other. The watches went with the seats, I guess.'

'Except the League was formed by putting De Luca's and Moretti's two organisations together,' she said slowly. 'That must have meant that they would each have had their own dealer at one stage.'

'So what are you saying? That one of the watches used to belong to someone else?' Tom frowned as he considered this.

'De Luca did say that Faulks's two seats were an accident of history,' she said. 'What if the other dealer left? Faulks would have taken over his seat and his watch.'

'Unless the other dealer never handed the watch back. That might explain why Faulks had to go and get a replacement made.' Tom suggested. 'You could be right. Maybe when you see him you can ask him. Which reminds me . . .'

He took a piece of paper from his pocket and deliberately ripped it in half and then half again.

'What's that?' she asked, as he continued to rip it into ever smaller pieces.

'You remember when we went through the papers in Faulks's safe? Well, I found a map. The one showing where Cavalli found the mask.'

'Wait!'

She reached out to grab his hand, but he threw the pieces up into the air before she could get to him.

'Tom!' she shouted angrily. 'Have you any idea what else could be down there?'

He gave her a rueful smile.

'Not everything's ready to be found, Allegra.'

Above him, the scraps of paper fluttered like butterflies in the sunlight, before a gust of wind lifted them soaring into the sky and carried them out to sea, like a flock of birds at the start of a long migration south.

EIGHTY-FIVE

Central Square, Casco Viejo, Panama
1st May – 6.36 p.m.

Antonio Santos, his arm in a sling, stood to one side and pressed the muzzle of his gun against the door at about head height.

'Who is it?'

'DHL,' a muffled voice called back. 'Package for Mr Stefano Romano?'

'Leave it outside.'

'I need a signature,' the voice called back.

Santos paused. He was expecting a couple of deliveries this week under that name, and it would be a shame if they got returned. On the other hand, he needed to be careful until he was certain that he had shaken everyone off the trail.

'Who is it from?' he asked, slowly sliding his face across to the peep hole.

A bored-looking man was standing on the landing dressed in a brown uniform. He appeared to be trying to grow a beard and was chewing gum. Santos's last question had prompted him to roll his eyes and blow a bubble that he popped with his finger.

'It's from Italy,' he replied, glancing at the stamps and then turning it over so that he could read the label on its back. 'Someone called Amarelli?'

Grinning, Santos tucked his gun into the back of his trousers, unbolted the door and threw it open.

'Amarelli liquorice from Calabria,' he explained, signing the form and eagerly ripping the box open. 'The best there is.' He flicked open a tin of Spezzata and crammed two pieces into his mouth, chewing them noisily. 'Want to try some?' he mumbled, thrusting the tin at the courier, who waved them away with a muttered word of thanks. 'I've looked everywhere, but no one seems to stock it here. Lucky for me they do mail order.'

'Lucky for me too, Antonio,' the courier replied. 'Or I'd never have found you.'

His eyes widening as he realised his mistake, Santos immediately kicked the door shut and reached for his gun. But the man was too quick, stamping his foot in the jamb and then shouldering the door open, sending Santos reeling backwards. Swinging his gun out from behind him, Santos lined up a shot, but before he could pull the trigger a painful punch to the soft inside of his arm sent it rattling across the tiled floor, while a forearm smash to his neck sent him crashing to his knees. He made a choking noise, his hands wrapped around his throat, his breathing coming in short, animal gasps.

Quickly checking that no one had heard them, the man eased the front door shut and then dragged Santos by his feet towards the kitchen. Once there he cuffed him, and then attached his wrists to a steel cable that he looped over the security bars covering the window.

'Wait. What's your name?' Santos croaked as he was forced to his feet.

'Foster,' the man replied as he tugged down hard on the cable, the metal fizzing noisily as it passed over the bars until Santos's hands were stretched high above his head, forcing him to stand on the balls of his feet to stop the cuffs biting into his wrists, his injured arm burning.

'Please, Foster, I'll pay you,' he wheezed. 'Whatever they're paying you, I'll double it.'

'You know how this works.' The man eyed him dispassionately. 'Once I've taken a job, there's no backing out. It's why people hire me. It's why you hired me.'

'I don't even know you.'

'Sure you do.' Foster tied the cable to a radiator, twanging it to check that it was under tension. 'Las Vegas? The Amalfi? That *was* you, wasn't it?'

'The Amalfi?' Santos breathed, whatever colour

he had left in his face draining away. 'Please,' he whispered. 'There must be another way. Let me go. I'll disappear. They'll never know.'

'I'll know,' the man replied. 'And I can't have your life on my conscience. Now, open wide.'

'What?'

Santos gave a muffled shout as a grenade was forced into his mouth. The ribbed metal casing smashed two of his teeth as Foster wedged it between his jaws, making sure that the safety handle was at the back so that its sharp edges cut into the corners of Santos's mouth like a horse bit. Santos began to gag on the oily metal, his eyes wide and terrified.

'The person who sent me wanted you to know that he is a reasonable man. A civilised man. So, if you were to feel able to apologise . . .?'

Santos nodded furiously, the pain in his arms now making him feel faint.

'Good!' Foster reached forward, pulled the pin out and placed it on the counter. Then he took out a mobile phone, dialled a number and positioned it next to the pin. 'He's listening now –' Foster nodded at the phone. 'So when you're ready, just spit the grenade out and say your piece. Just remember – you'll need to speak quickly.'

EPILOGUE

'Know thyself'
Inscription on the Temple of Apollo at Delphi

EIGHTY-SIX

Tarrytown, New York
2nd May – 4.03 p.m.
This was how everything had started.

A funeral. Black limos lining the road. A sea of unfamiliar faces. Secret service agents patrolling the grounds. Guests seated in a horseshoe. The coffin draped with the Stars and Stripes. The service droning towards its muted conclusion.

For a moment it seemed to Tom that time had stood still. That he must have imagined everything. That any moment now Jennifer would appear out of the rain and, silhouetted against the headlights of the car behind her, wave at him to run up and see her.

Except today there was no rain, clear blue skies and the crisp spring sunlight conspiring to lift the congregation's sombre mood. Today there was no choreographed ceremony or martial display, the service playing out with a discreet intimacy of its own invention. Today people were there not because of some misplaced sense of duty or to cut a deal, but out of love. And today, rather than be exiled to some sodden, wind swept slope, Tom was sitting amongst them.

Same start. Different ending.

'Thanks for coming,' Tom whispered to Archie as FBI Director Green stepped forward and handed Jennifer's parents the neatly folded flag. Her father took it with a proud nod, clutching it to his chest, his left arm hugging her mother into his collar, her shoulders shaking. Next to them both, Jennifer's sister and her boyfriend were clasping each other's hands.

'You know what? I'll miss her,' Archie sighed, medical gauze still taped to his left cheek. 'Never thought I'd say that about an FBI agent, but I really will.'

'I'm sure she would have said the same about you,' Tom smiled.

'How was Allegra when you saw her?'

'Still angry.'

'Do you think she'll stick with it? With being a copper, I mean?'

'I'm not sure. I don't think she knows herself yet.'

The service ended and the congregation broke up. Some remained seated, alone with their thoughts; others lingered in small groups, swapping memories or phone numbers as old acquaintances were renewed; a few paused at the grave's edge, peering down at the earth-speckled coffin and maybe passing on a final thought.

Tom had a sudden urge to go and introduce himself to Jennifer's parents, to share his memories of her and hear theirs, to let them know the part she'd played in his life and he in hers. But there seemed little point. They had no idea who he was. The truth was, he was as much a stranger here as he had been at his grandfather's funeral.

'Come on then. Let's go.'

He got up and made eye contact with FBI Director Green on the other side of the coffin. He too was preparing to leave, it seemed, but the sight of Tom caused him to mutter some instructions to his security detail and then step towards him. Tom met him halfway.

'Kirk.'

'Mr Director.'

'I thought you might like to know that Santos was killed yesterday. In Panama.'

Tom nodded slowly, a weight that he had scarcely been aware of slowly lifting from his shoulders.

'How?'

'Hard to tell really. There wasn't much left of him. My people tell me a grenade.'

'Dangerous things, grenades.' Tom nodded. 'What about the shooter? This isn't over yet.'

'We're still working on it.' Green shrugged. 'As soon as we get a firm lead, I'll let you know.'

'And the ballistics results? I know someone who . . .'

'We'll find him. And when we do, I promise you that he'll feel the full force of . . .'

'Not if I get him first.'

'Be careful, Kirk. I can't protect you if you do something . . .'

'Excuse me, but are you Tom Kirk?' Jennifer's father had appeared in front of them. A tall man, he was immaculately dressed in a pale grey suit and a black woven silk tie, his eyes sore, a slight tremor in his voice.

'Yes, yes I am,' Tom stammered, feeling both surprised and strangely awkward. 'I'm so sorry . . .'

'I think . . . I think she would have wanted you to have this.'

Biting his lip to hold back his tears, he pressed the triangular shape of the folded flag into Tom's uncertain hands and then, with a tight nod at Green, fell back to his sobbing wife's side.

Tom and Green stood there silently, only a few feet apart, the material strangely warm against Tom's chest. Green glanced around, as if to check that no one was watching, then thrust out his hand.

'Thank you,' he said.

Tom hesitated for a few moments, then shook it. The next instant he was gone, caught up in a flurry of dark suits, Ray-Bans and clear plastic ear-pieces as he was bundled towards his car.

'You think he let you escape from the FBI building on purpose?' Archie murmured.

'I think I did exactly what he'd hoped I would,' said Tom. 'Come on. Let's get out of here.'

'Mr Kirk? Mr Kirk?'

A voice called out as they turned to leave. Tom's eyes narrowed, unable to place the man navigating his way through the crowd, although he recognised his jowly face and the metronomic sway of his gut from somewhere.

'Larry Hewson, from Ogilvy, Myers and Gray,' the man introduced himself enthusiastically.

'I'm sorry, I don't . . .' Tom frowned.

'We met at your grandfather's funeral. I'm the Duval family . . .'

'Attorney, yes,' Tom suddenly remembered. 'How did you . . .?'

'Your associate was kind enough to suggest that I might find you here,' Hewson explained.

Tom fixed Archie with a questioning stare.

'My associate?'

'He kept bloody calling.' Archie shrugged. 'I didn't think he'd actually show up.'

'There's the small matter of your grandfather's will,' Hewson continued. 'As I explained to you when we last met, he specified that I was to pass on to you something that your mother had given him shortly before her death.'

'Yes, I remember.'

'This time I've brought all the paperwork with me. If you wouldn't mind just signing here –' Hewson produced a sheet of paper and a pen and then held up his briefcase so that Tom could lean against it as he signed. 'Excellent,' he exclaimed, popping the briefcase's brass catches and taking out a small wooden box and an envelope that he handed to Tom with a flourish. 'Then I will be on my way.'

With a nod, he filed away the signed sheet of paper and strode off towards his waiting car, a phone snapping to his cheek.

'What is it?' Archie asked in a curious voice.

'A letter from my mother,' Tom replied, the sight of his name written in faded black ink strangely familiar from hoarded postcards.

The envelope opened easily, revealing a white card dated to the year before she'd died, across which she'd scribbled a brief message:

Darling Tom
One day, when you're older, you might want some answers. And if you're reading this, it probably means I'm not there to give them. So what's inside this box might help. Whatever you find, don't think too badly of me. I always loved you. I still do.
Love Mummy

Tom turned away from Archie, his eyes hot and stinging, his throat tightening, and opened the box.

All of a sudden, the events of the past few weeks came flooding back into sharp focus. De Luca's strange familiarity on meeting him, Faulks's open-mouthed surprise at the mention of his name, Santos's veiled questions.

Because inside, nestling on a black velvet background, was a watch.

A watch with an ivory face and an orange second hand.

Note from the Author

The Nativity with St Francis and St Lawrence (also known as *The Adoration*) was painted by the Italian master Michelangelo Merisi da Caravaggio in 1609 during his self-imposed exile from Rome after killing a man in a duel. The six square metre work was stolen from the Oratory of San Lorenzo in Palermo, Sicily on 16th October 1969. Working under the cover of darkness, the thieves cut the work from its frame with razor blades and escaped in a lorry. In 1996, Francesco Marino Mannoia, an informant and former member of the Sicilian mafia, claimed he had stolen the painting as a young man on the orders of a high-ranking mobster. Other sources, however, have pointed the finger at amateurs who acted after seeing a TV programme about the painting the previous week and then sold it on to the local Sicilian mafia when they realised that they couldn't fence it. At one point it is said to have ended up in the

hands of Palermo boss Rosario Riccobono (throttled in 1982 at a barbecue lunch organised for
that purpose by the Corleonesi family) before
passing on to Gerlando 'The Rug' Alberti,
commander of the Porta Nuova district in Palermo.
Other rumours that the work was damaged in
the theft or even destroyed in an earthquake in
1980 have also circulated from time to time, as
have stories of supposed sightings abroad. Today,
however, the *Nativity* remains one of the most
famous unrecovered stolen paintings in the world.
It is listed by the FBI as one of its top ten art
crimes and they have estimated its value at $20
million, although the likely auction value is far,
far greater.

Tomb-robbing has often been called the second
oldest profession. Italy, with over forty UNESCO
World Heritage sites, is a particular target, but it
is a plague that increasingly affects other countries such as Peru, Guatemala, Mexico, China,
Thailand, Turkey, Egypt and Greece, where
poverty, poor security, the buried remains of a
rich civilisation and seemingly insatiable demand
from unscrupulous dealers and collectors have
conspired to rapidly destroy thousands of years
of our shared archaeological and historical
heritage for profit. On 13th September 1995, Swiss
police raided four bonded warehouses in the
Geneva Free Port and seized a large number of
illegally excavated antiquities. The premises were

registered to a Swiss company called Editions
Services, which police later traced to Giacomo
Medici, a man later described as 'the real "master-
mind" of much of [Italy's] illegal traffic in
archaeological objects.' According to the Carabinieri,
the warehouses contained over ten thousand artefacts worth around $35 million at the time, including
hundreds of pieces of ancient Greek, Roman, and
Etruscan art and a set of Etruscan dinner plates
alone worth $2 million. Accompanying these were
files, binders and boxes containing sales records
and correspondence between Medici and dealers
and museums around the world, and thousands
of photographs, some of which illustrated the
journey of single pieces from the ground, to their
restored state, to the display cabinets of some of
the world's largest museums. As a result of these
findings, Medici was sentenced to ten years and
fined ten million euro in 2004 for dealing in stolen
ancient artefacts. Evidence from the Geneva raid
was also used to bring charges against American
antiquities dealer Robert Hecht, Jr. and former J.
Paul Getty Museum curator of antiquities Marion
True for conspiracy to traffic in illegal antiquities,
with True claiming that she was being made to
carry the burden for practices which were known,
approved, and condoned by the Getty's Board of
Directors. Their trial continues. In September
2007, the Getty signed an agreement with the
Italian culture ministry to return forty major

works of ancient art. Similarly in 2006, the New York Metropolitan Museum of Art agreed to give legal ownership of the famous Euphronios krater (sold to it by Robert Hecht in 1972) back to the Italian government. The Museum of Fine Arts in Boston and the Princeton University Art Museum have also returned items. Since the destruction of the Medici smuggling ring and the more stringent acquisition policies put in place by museums and collectors in the light of these events, the latest information suggests that illegal digging is down by half. The Carabinieri art squad also claim that the quality of seized objects has collapsed. Whether this is just a temporary lull, or sign of a more permanent shift, remains to be seen.

The Phidias ivory mask was recovered by Italian police in London in 2003. A unique life-size ivory head of Apollo, the Greek god of the sun, from a fifth century BC chryselephantine statue, it is one of the world's rarest and most important looted antiquities. Many experts believe that it was carved by the classical sculptor Phidias, considered to have perhaps been the greatest of all Ancient Greek sculptors. Responsible for many of the marble reliefs on the Parthenon, Phidias also carved two legendary chryselephantine (Greek for gold and ivory) statues: the Athene Parthenos and the statue of Zeus at Olympia, one of the seven wonders of the ancient world, which was taken to Constantinople and destroyed in a palace fire in AD 475. The Apollo ivory mask was seized from the London antiquities dealer Robin Symes, after he was presented with evidence that the statue had been illegally excavated and smuggled out of Italy. It was originally discovered in 1995 by notorious tombarolo (tomb robber) Pietro Casasanta near the remains of the Baths of Claudius, north of Rome. Chryselephantine statues were built around a wooden frame, with thin carved slabs of ivory attached to it to represent the skin and sheets of gold leaf for the garments, armour, hair, and other details. Such statues were incredibly rare, even in ancient times, and historians believe that all seventy-four of Rome's chryselephantine statues vanished when it was sacked by Alaric, chief of the barbarian Visigoths, in AD 410. Although dozens of fragments are known to have survived, only one other life-size figure has been found in Italy (now in the Apostolic Library in the Vatican). A badly fire-damaged set of statues of Apollo and Artemis can also be seen at the Archaeological Museum at Delphi. The Phidias Apollo is currently the star attraction at an exhibition of looted artefacts that have been returned to Italy at the Quirinale Palace in Rome.

The Getty kouros, supposedly from the sixth century BC, was bought by the Getty from a Swiss dealer in 1983 for a reported $7–9 million. A kouros is a statue of a standing nude youth that did not represent any one individual person, but the ideal of youth itself. Used in Archaic Greece as both a dedication to the gods in sanctuaries and as a grave monument, the standard kouros stood with his left foot forward, arms at his sides, looking straight ahead. The Getty kouros has always attracted controversy, for while scientific tests have shown that the patina on the surface could not have been created artificially, a mixture of earlier and later stylistic features and the use of marble from the island of Thassos at an unexpected date, have caused some to doubt its authenticity. These doubts were compounded when several of the other pieces bought with the kouros were shown to be forgeries, and when a letter accompanying it, supposedly written by German scholar Ernst Langlotz in 1952 indicating that the kouros came from a Swiss collection, was also revealed as a forgery, since it bore a postal code that only came into use in the 1970s. In 1992, the kouros was displayed in Athens, Greece, at an international conference called to determine its authenticity. However, the conference failed to resolve the issue, with most art historians and archaeologists denouncing it, and the scientific community believing it to be authentic. To this day, the statue's authenticity remains unresolved and it is displayed with the inscription: 'Greek, *530 BC, or modern forgery.'*

For more information on the author and on the

fascinating history, people, places and artefacts that feature in *The Geneva Deception* and the other Tom Kirk novels, please visit www.jamestwining.com.